# C. S. Lewis at the Breakfast Table

## and Other Reminiscences

# C. S. Lewis at the Breakfast Table

## and Other Reminiscences

NEW EDITION

EDITED BY

## JAMES T. COMO

A HARVEST/HBJ BOOK

HARCOURT BRACE JOVANOVICH, PUBLISHERS

*San Diego    New York    London*

HBJ

First published 1979 by Macmillan Publishing Company

Some of the pieces in this volume previously appeared in *CSL: The Bulletin
of the New York C. S. Lewis Society, The Brink of Mystery, Anthroposophical
Quarterly, New Blackfriars, Unicorn,* and *Encounter.* Complete citations
may be found in the list of contributors.

Excerpt on page xvii from "The Mystery of
Language" from *The Message in the Bottle*
by Walker Percy. Copyright © 1975 by
Walker Percy. Reprinted by permission of Farrar Straus & Giroux.

Library of Congress Cataloging-in-Publication Data
C. S. Lewis at the breakfast table, and other reminiscences/
edited by James T. Como.
p.    cm.
Reprint. Originally published: New York: Macmillan, c 1979.
Includes bibliographical references and indexes.
ISBN 0-15-623207-3
I. Lewis, C. S. (Clive Staples), 1898–1963. 2. Authors,
English—20th century—Biography. I. Como, James T.
PR6023.E926Z598   1992
828'.91209—dc20    92-28024

Printed in the United States of America
First Harvest/HBJ edition 1992
A B C D E

*To all who would have thanked C. S. Lewis
but could not, and to the rational opposition of goodwill.
And (if an editor may) to my wife, Alejandra.*

# Contents

# *Preface*

WE MAY REASONABLY EXPECT that C. S. Lewis will soon become an established "figure": that is, his literary impact will be recognized by scholars and teachers to such an extent that its importance shall be quite taken for granted, and he will be "typed," so that people who know little will assume much. Given Lewis's stance as a polemicist, this development is noteworthy because chinks in personal armor are often exploited as though they were weaknesses in argument.

Indeed, we may already see the beginnings of such a pattern. I recently read that Lewis, because of his antagonism toward Americans, turned down an invitation to speak in America by writing a nasty refusal on a piece of toilet paper; but the incident never happened, and Lewis is not on record as possessed of an antagonism toward Americans. In a somewhat different vein, a reviewer for *The New York Times* has written that Carlos Castañeda's peyote-cult best-sellers may be derived from

> George MacDonald's pro-Christian fantasies. . . . MacDonald's *Phantastes* and *Lilith* were reprinted in 1964 with an introduction by C. S. Lewis. MacDonald and his student . . . wrote their fantasies in the pregenital stage, disguised in C. S. Lewis's case as Christian morality, a disguise, which Wilhelm Reich would say is transparent. C. S. Lewis is just as afraid of genitality as Castañeda, and toward the end of his life C. S. Lewis's profound hatred of women began to come out in his short stories.

To be sure, this detritus of incantatory devil-terms exemplifies only one extreme branch of the scientism that Lewis and others have made easy work of; and, on the other hand, admirers of Lewis have often indulged a cultism of their own (overlooking, for example, the ambiguities of Lewis's late marriage and even wanting to cover up his brother's alcoholism). So evidently we are witness to the start of that inevitable process that turns public figures into celebrities, "people," according to Daniel Boorstin, "who are famous for being well known."

It would seem, then, that the time has come for the establishing of reliable perceptions, substantive impressions of people directly knowledgeable of, and sensitive to, the shadings of this striking personality. This book is not a biography. The recollections in it are often ruminative, even speculative; rarely do they argue a thesis, and the style throughout is nonscholarly. Most of the essays were written expressly for this volume, and only Professor Wain's has had a prior readership of as many as several hundred. The singular authority of this collection derives from one central fact: all but two contributors (Eugene McGovern and I) were personally acquainted with C. S. Lewis.

On the belief that the sort of response elicited by a person is itself evidence of the sort of person he was, I have kept editorial intrusion to an absolute minimum. It is for the alert reader to note, to ponder, and perhaps to reconcile conflicting impressions among the contributors or between what is said here and prior impressions of Lewis, for the book comprises a great many perspectives. The length of time and the stage of life during which Lewis was known, the degree of intimacy to which he was known, the "angle" of friendship that was shared, and the depth of familiarity with his work—all these vary widely among the contributors.

Thus, the informal Lewis admirer may be startled to read that Lewis did not much indulge in wit, that he evidenced outbursts of hatred, and that he did not talk frequently of his military experience; but that reader should note that *this* Lewis was an abundantly posturing atheist in his early-to-mid-twenties. Did Miss Anscombe "wipe the floor" with Lewis on the occasion of their epic confrontation at the Socratic Club? Opinions differ, and so must answers, depending upon whether one inquires after dramatic impact or soundness of argument. In the realm not of fact but of inference the knowledgeable reader might be tempted to demur, at times, from the opinion of a contributor. Did Lewis "overreact" to the idea of a personal God? Did he maintain that poetry "has nothing to do with the poet's feelings" or, rather, that our judgment of poetry ought to be independent of our knowledge of the poet's personal life?

Most Lewis admirers can wait for the obligatory uniform edition and "Guide to the Works of," and to assure that he does not become merely a "figure" they should welcome such questions—their number and complexity—as those just given. But if Lewis's response to sexuality, for example, is not irrelevant to our interest in him and in his work (though it is, I suspect, far less relevant than our modern temper takes it to be), then impressions of that response ought to be fitted into a comprehensive frame of reference as variegated and as subtle as the person it purports to accommodate. The danger is that we will build into this frame, or impose upon it, assumptions and expectations alien to its subject; that is the sort of partisan or antiintellectual dogmatism that this book—not "systematic" or synoptic—is intended to allay. As with most of Lewis's own books, as with the Green and Hooper *Biography,* as with *Light on C. S. Lewis* (edited by Jocelyn Gibb), this book attempts to allow the reader not so much to study Lewis as to meet him; the appropriate verb, as Lewis might have put it, would be not *savoir* but *connaître.*

There is no strict attempt at chronological order in the arrangement of the essays; instead, the pattern is intended to reflect one existing naturally in the collection. Thus the unity that I hope the reader discerns is not that of, say, an architect's blueprint but that of a plant, unregimented yet whole. Though some contributors make demands on foreign, or nonspecialized, readers, these are few, understandable in context, and interesting per se. The reader is referred to the list of contributors (and, of course, to the essays themselves) for information helpful in defining the authority and uniqueness of each writer's perspective.

I must record the profound personal pleasure that has been mine in collecting these essays. The authors were invariably courteous, often thanking me for having invited their contributions. Of course, the opposite is true: it is I who am deeply appreciative of their grace and generosity. Lewis himself probably would not have liked the idea of this book, and many of the contributors share that reticence; so, on behalf of admirers of C. S. Lewis, I thank them for their efforts, patience, and great goodwill.

For many reasons—not the least of which is the subject of the book—this effort has a special meaning for me, a symbolic meaning, as it were;

so I trust the reader will be understanding of my desire to thank many who have helped both directly and indirectly. Lewis himself, of course, is beyond thanking but not beyond being prayed for, and only the effect of prayer could approximate the magnitude of my debt to him. For help and encouragement, the unrivalled authority Walter Hooper could not be suitably thanked. To the membership of the New York C. S. Lewis Society (especially Hope Kirkpatrick and Eugene McGovern), I owe the opportunity of having been able to think and to write seriously about Lewis among insightful and knowledgeable people. For sparking and for encouraging my earliest interest in Lewis, I am grateful to Professor Jeffrey Hart of Dartmouth and to Professor Dorothy Jones, of Queens College of the City University of New York. And I always remember Margaret O'Dea for first allowing me to think well of myself scholastically.

JAMES T. COMO
*August 1978*

# Preface to the New Edition

NEARLY FOURTEEN YEARS after the preface to the first edition of this book, there hardly seems much within the scope of a second preface that wants saying. It is tempting to reflect upon the works by and about Lewis that have been published in that time: They do point to a thicker, richer, more interesting Lewis—but hardly to a new one. Reviewers of the original edition of this book were generally kind, and those who were not vented themselves much more against Lewis than against this collection. Writers and researchers apparently have found its contents useful; many readers have written to me with praise or thanks.

These latter are misplaced, of course. The appeal and authority of this book reside now, as then, with the contributors, who (with but two exceptions) knew Lewis personally. Whether writing as scholars, as journalists, or as memoirists; enthusiastically, with reserve, or even adversarially, they evoke a vital Lewis, more interesting than his public persona ever suggested. The list of these contributors cannot do justice to any of them—not to their distinction, their achievements, or their diversity. It is in their generosity of spirit that they remain of a kind, and in the intrinsic interest each holds.

All of us belong to several different groups, but not to all that many real (as opposed to politically created) communities. I think these contributors—even though many do not know each other—form a Community. They may be variously disinterested, loyal, zealous, aloof, affectionate, or sometimes even cranky, but they are never merely nostalgic or sentimental. And none—ever—approximates "cultism" or remotely occasions it in the reader. They are a collective "fifth business," but in the exalted, providential sense explored so appreciatively by Robertson Davies.

I emphasize the contributors because what C. S. Lewis said of judging books in *An Experiment in Criticism* is largely true of human beings: The way attentive and receptive people speak of one is a reliable guide to one's worth. Lewis does not differ from any famous literary personality. His prominence has occasioned a fair amount of professional jealousy, personal resentment, academic self-aggrandizement, and plain old literary politics. Yet it is preponderantly the case that, among those who knew Lewis or who know and understand his work well, these are rare. (Those same people generally esteem George Sayer's biography above a recent pretender's, for both its scholarship and its balance.)

Lewis is certainly on his way to becoming a "well-established figure," though not quite (as I had suggested) "famous for being well known." There was a London and Broadway hit *(Shadowlands)* about his love for, and marriage to, Joy Davidman; and it does remain a puzzlement that the general body of professional critics, scholars, and theorists have not afforded his varied work the attention it merits. But the reasons for the latter are, I believe, largely adventitious, and the problem of popular simplification is more than offset by the great amount we have learned about his life—especially through the publication of his diary *(All My Road Before Me)*, the second edition of the *Letters of C. S. Lewis*, his letters to Arthur Greeves *(They Stand Together)*, Warren Lewis's diary *(Brothers and Friends)*, short memoirs by such people as Kenneth Tynan, Ruth Pitter, and Jill Freud (in Stephen Schofield's *In Search of C. S. Lewis*), and the various biographies.

Readers of Lewis (scholars, fans, admirers, and cultists alike) often ponder his prospective reputation, the regnant theory being that the children's writer and, to a lesser degree, some aspects of the Christian apologist will endure. Perhaps the magnitude of Lewis's popular appeal along these lines and the avowedly Christian substance of the lines themselves account for the academic disregard mentioned above. Indeed, as an apologist who always defended—but was never sorry for—his Faith, Lewis was in many ways the prototypical *homo rhetoricus* and the archetypal Knight of Faith. Walker Percy's words are apt:

Existentialists have taught us that what man is cannot be grasped by the science of man. The case is rather that man's science is one of the things that man does, a mode of existence. Another mode is speech. Man is not merely a higher organism responding to and controlling his environment. He is . . . that being in the world whose calling it is to find a name for Being, to give testimony to it, and to provide for it a clearing.

—*The Message in the Bottle*

It is gratifying to play any role, even as *sixth* business, in that effort, and especially gratifying to note that this book, even as Lewis's contemporaries and their successors depart, will continue to advance it.

This new edition adds to the first in two substantive ways that should prove of interest to readers. The first addition is a brief (and somewhat unconventional) chronology of Lewis's life; the second, and fundamentally important one, is Walter Hooper's Supplement to his Bibliography of the writings of C. S. Lewis (and the concomitant revision of his Alphabetical Index of the writings of C. S. Lewis). Those works first appeared in *Light on C. S. Lewis* (edited by Jocelyn Gibb over twenty-five years ago, and as valuable now as then) and were initially brought up-to-date for the first edition of this book. The Supplement to the Bibliography and the revision of the Index once again make them current: The expansions are considerable. When consulting the Supplement the reader should remember that the taxonomy is the same as in the Bibliography proper, with the numbering of the items within each category picking up here where it left off there. All of the new items are, of course, included in the Index and are there marked *, thus directing the reader to the Supplement for their full entries.

To those I thanked in the first preface I must add James Dundas-Grant. From 1978 through the middle of 1985 I exchanged several letters with "D.G." If these letters to me are typical of his letters in general, then they should certainly be collected and published, as much for the good they would do and the pleasure they would give as to commemorate this extraordinary gentleman. And for their help and good counsel I thank Ernest Zocchi (who helped sell the old edition of this book), Tim Corkery, and John Ferrone (formerly of Harcourt Brace Jovanovich). I am delighted to follow Walter Hooper's instruction to thank, and thus to acknowledge the indefatigable bibliographic contribution of, Jerry Daniel and Steven Thorson, who over the years have kept us current in *CSL: The Bulletin of the New York C. S. Lewis Society.*

JAMES COMO
*March 1, 1992*
*York College*
*City University of New York*

# Acknowledgments

The following graciously allowed whole essays to be reprinted (complete citations may be found in the list of contributors): *Anthroposophical Quarterly*; *CSL: The Bulletin of the New York C. S. Lewis Society*; *The Chronicle* (the bulletin of the Portland, Oregon, C. S. Lewis Society); *Encounter*; *New Blackfriars*; SPCK (Society for the Propagation of Christian Knowledge); and *Unicorn*.

Short quotations by Lewis and others are gratefully acknowledged as from: *American Scholar*; *Selected Literary Essays*, Cambridge University Press; *Cambridge Review*; *Cherwell*; *Private Faces/Public Faces*, Doubleday; *God in the Dock* and *The Weight of Glory*, Wm. B. Eerdmans Publishing Company; *Fern-seed and Elephants* and *Screwtape Proposes a Toast and Other Pieces*, Fontana Books; *Zen and the Art of Motorcycle Maintenance*, Bantam Books; *Letters of C. S. Lewis*, *Letters to Malcolm: Chiefly on Prayer*, *Light on C. S. Lewis*, *Reflections on the Psalms*, and *The World's Last Night and Other Essays*, Harcourt Brace Jovanovich; *The Great Divorce*, *Mere Christianity*, *Miracles*, and *The Ring of Truth*, The Macmillan Publishing Company, Inc.; *Sprightly Running: Part of an Autobiography*, The Macmillan Company (London); *Poems*, Harcourt Brace Jovanovich; *An Experiment in Criticism*, Cambridge University Press; *C. S. Lewis: The Shape of His Faith and Thought*, Harper & Row; *The Allegory of Love*, Oxford University Press; the New York *Times*; *Baker's Dictionary of Theology* (and J. L. Daniel for suggesting the comparison of Lewis to *Baker*); and *The Socratic Digest*.

Part of a previously unpublished letter quoted by Leo Baker copyright © 1979 by A. O. Barfield.

# INTRODUCTION
## *Within the Realm of Plenitude*
### JAMES T. COMO

"The Church militant has no son more full of hope than he."—
Beatrice of Dante, *Paradise, XXV.*

For one stretch during World War II, his was the second most recognized voice (after Churchill's) on the BBC. Since his death in November 1963, sales of his books have increased sixfold (with several titles selling more than one million copies per year in some twenty languages). One of the few people in this century to win a triple first at Oxford, he achieved fame as the foremost scholar of medieval and renaissance English Literature; yet, he is known to the lay reader as the author of science fiction, fairy tales, parables, poetry, one novel, and (especially) Christian apologetics. He was old-fashioned, claimed to like monotony, traveled abroad only twice, and saw himself as one of the last "dinosaurs," whose sensibilities did not go beyond the eighteenth century; but he has been praised nevertheless (by such diverse personalities as Eldridge Cleaver, Charles Colson, and Eugene McCarthy) for his keen insight into contemporary psychology, his worldly sophistication, and his devastating wit. Very many people have attributed their religious conversions, reawakenings, and even vocations to Lewis's influence, which could be as pervasive as it was dramatic. Nearly fifteen years ago, for example, I came upon Jeffrey Hart's "The Rebirth of Christ" in the *National Review,* a piece that completely fulfilled the promise of its title.

Before reading the article, I had never heard of C. S. Lewis; while reading it, there rose within me a mounting, incredulous excitement mingled with a sort of personal rebirth of optimism. Could it be? Could a man who so unashamedly expressed his Christian beliefs not be laughed at as a fool, scorned as a zealot, or patronized as an eccentric? Could he not only be taken seriously but also, without apology, put the enemy to flight from the very center of its own strength, the university? (At that time, I was an undergraduate at a large city university and felt put upon, the abject but unwilling victim of those intellectual bullies who, while screaming the loudest for academic freedom, do nothing but propagandize their pupils.) Such enthusiasms, we come to learn, wear themselves out or (at the very least) ought to swing to and fro, like the pendulum of a clock; and so it seems to the stricken, until they attain a longer perspective than the original one and see that the whole clock has been getting ever bigger. Then I learned that there was a multitude just like me.

Now several societies exist for the purpose of studying Lewis's thoughts; film rights to several of his books have been purchased, and filmed documentaries of his life have been produced; both popular and scholarly books on Lewis are being published with increasing frequency (so that the Modern Language Association cites Lewis as one of the most rapidly increasing objects of literary study in the world); and Lewis's own work continues to be issued and regularly reissued. Through it all, though, C. S. Lewis remains that which Quintilian, the Roman rhetor, has taught us so greatly to cherish, "the good man speaking well." Thus, since I read Hart's article, my incredulity may have subsided, but the excitement not at all. For the variety of Lewis's appeal is endlessly engaging; and his reasoning, analysis, and style (in any given work) are thoroughly arresting. But most challenging, even frightening, are the constancy and consistency of his premises, intellectual and emotional. He and his work are whole and organic, and an attempt to apprehend this compelling integrity ought to be made.

I

In 1924 C. S. Lewis received a temporary appointment at Oxford as a philosophy tutor; thirty years later he was elected Professor of Medieval and Renaissance English Literature at Cambridge University. The chair had been created especially for him. At both universities students regularly stood in auditoriums filled to capacity—a rarity at both institutions—in order to hear his lectures. Nevill Coghill, Lewis's old friend and colleague, has lamented the

loss of his living force in the kind of study in which [he was] engaged, the study of English, of which he was easily the greatest teacher of our time in his chosen fields.

To William Empson, he was the best-read man of his generation, one who read everything and remembered everything he read.

On both his parents' sides, articulacy was a prominent feature of professional and of family life. By the age of eight Lewis had created and (with his older brother, Warren) written up the world of Boxen, a land populated by dressed and talking animals. His argumentative and, according to Lewis, garrulous and overbearing father quite naturally turned to William T. Kirkpatrick—"The Great Knock"—to tutor the adolescent Lewis, for the man (an atheist and former tutor of the elder Lewis) was the very soul of dialectical ruthlessness. The young man, though stunned at first, bloomed, and a pattern was set for the rest of his life. Owen Barfield, one of his oldest friends and his adversary in "The Great War" (mostly by letter) over Anthroposophy, imagination, "chronological snobbery," and Christianity, has attested to the delight that Lewis took in argument; John Lawlor, pupil and friend, has said that argument was the *only* form of conversation ever employed by Lewis in Lawlor's presence. Friends often marveled at Lewis's ability to expostulate, analytically, upon a point unto the smallest divisible unit of thought, just as though he were the first to come upon it (even though it might be a cultural commonplace). In short, he seemed constitutionally incapable of allowing an assumption, or premise, to pass undissected.

After training with The Great Knock, at Oxford he would have read (for honors in classics) the histories, moral and political philosophy, metaphysics, and psychology; additionally, he would have studied Bacon's logic and Fowler's *Modern Logic*. With the exception of Book Ten of Quintilian's *Institutes* and of Cicero's *Oratore*, no classical rhetorical or poetic theory was required; in fact, given Lewis's choice to be tested in the history of Roman poetry and in Latin prose style, and to go on to read modern philosophy and philology, he would not even have read (necessarily) the orators themselves, whom he did not have in his library. (Of course, much of this reading he would have down at school or with Kirkpatrick; and the younger Lewis lacked the money to own every book he read.) His logic books (e.g., H. W. B. Joseph's *Introduction to Logic*) are very heavily annotated, his (Aristotle's) *Rhetoric* not at all. Lest we think this a small point, we must note the manner in which Lewis annotated almost all his books: if one lacked an index, he would provide it; each chapter would be summarized to the length of several hundred words; and his marginalia would inevitably be argumentative, usually covering the four blank borders surrounding the printed page. Here is an example from his Joseph:

It is true that what we seem to be thinking in hypothetical judgment often is, "if I could solve A, I could solve B"=solution of B depends upon solution of A. But (1) if anyone asked why, we should have to reply (speaking of the *things* and not of the *problems*) "because if A, then B"—as we often do when explaining a problem to a dunce. Which leaves us where we were. (2) The judgment "solution of B depends upon solution of A" is hypothetical. E.g., "if I knew you leaf and all/I should know what God and as Man is" asserts that the solution of B depends on solution of A, which *we can't find.* I.e. that one nonexistent depends on another—which is the whole trouble.

How telling it is that within a single year of his conversion to Christianity he would write *The Pilgrim's Regress*: tautly structured, compulsively thorough (and autobiographical), dogmatic, and belligerent beyond any other Christian work he was ever to write. The quickness of mind, the toughness of will, the sheer analytical power, and—*most* of all—the need to undertake publicly the dialectical enterprise are all there. Lewis himself characterized its tone as being of "an uncharitable temper," but from this point on (temper notwithstanding) he "never looked back." He spent the remainder of his life moderating all the unattractive qualities of this book, giving a meaning to the word *popularizer* only rarely achieved in the history of Christian writing. Fully ten of his books are either argumentative defenses of Christian doctrine or explanations of it for the purpose of persuading in its favor or manifestly didactic fictions with Christian intent; others, though, fulfill these same functions, however the intention may be veiled or the Christian content submerged; and exactly the same could be said of the primarily mimetic fiction and of much of the poetry.

Lewis often took explicit note of his posture as a Christian apologist.

About his planetary novels, he wrote, in 1939, that "any amount of theology can now be smuggled into people's minds under cover of romance without their knowing it." He called himself a "translator" and very much perceived himself as "a converted pagan living among apostate Puritans." He was, therefore, particularly sensitive to the danger inherent in discharging his burden; in a poem not published during his lifetime, Lewis wrote:

> From all my lame defeats and oh! much more
> From all the victories that I seemed to score;
> From cleverness shot forth on thy behalf
> At which, while angels weep, the audience laugh;
> From all my proofs of Thy divinity,
> Thou, who wouldst give no sign, deliver me.
>
> . . . . . . . . . . . . . .
> Lord of the narrow gate and the needle's eye,
> Take from me all my trumpery lest I die.

The print and broadcast apologist, the novelist, children's fantasist, and poet (his first and abiding aspiration), the teacher, and the critic—these were never comfortable with international fame; and it is likely that the fame cost Lewis professionally: the animosity of many of his secular-humanist colleagues prevented his being elected Professor of Poetry and made him receptive to the Cambridge invitation.

Among a local audience, however, Lewis enjoyed the respect he gained as a brilliant conversationalist, a match for Dr. Johnson himself (with whom Lewis shared some striking similarities but, as well, some telling dissimilarities); as a public speaker and debater; and as an indefatigable, thoroughly selfless, epistolist who steadily corresponded with literally thousands of strangers seeking advice and comfort. Perhaps he did, as some have claimed, crave an audience; certainly he craved live, rational opposition. John Wain, in his autobiography *Sprightly Running*, insightfully depicts his former tutor:

All these people I admired. . . . were all dramatic personalities, making a strong impact. None of them bore any resemblance to the ordinary, commonplace, faceless citizen. Each had a characteristic style, not merely writing or thinking but a style of presenting himself to the outside world. . . . They attracted me because in their different ways they all treated life *as if it were an art*. I do not mean that they posed. They simply recognized, intuitively, that the presence of other people, even the humblest and fewest, constitutes an audience, and toward an audience one has certain duties. . . . They are always giving a performance in the *role for which they have cast themselves,* making up the play as they go along, and tacitly inviting others to collaborate. . . . It is no mere matter of posing, of permitting oneself to trifle or be insincere. Rather it is the recognition of a duty toward life *and toward one's fellow-man*: not a duty that is binding on everyone, but one that is instinctively accepted by those who fall into this type. . . . Such people are in fact fulfilling a moral duty. The Creator . . . has equipped them with a certain identity, and they are all the time delightfully aware of this identity and out to get, and to give, as much fun as possible with it. (Italics mine.)

By now the events, influences, and preferences that shaped Lewis's life are well established and easily accessible in such places as *C. S. Lewis: A Biography,* W. H. Lewis's "Memoir" in the *Letters of C. S. Lewis,* the superb *C. S. Lewis: Images of His World* (by Clyde S. Kilby and Douglas Gilbert), and in Lewis's own *Surprised by Joy.* He derived a staggering amount of meaning from thought and from experience, and he was fearless. His lessons were hard fought, relentlessly so, but the battle makes possible this statement: There must have been very little about himself that he did not know. With regard to much more than his literary judgment can we understand the famous self-characterization offered in his inaugural address upon assuming the chair at Cambridge:

And yet, is that the whole story? If a live dinosaur dragged its slow length into the laboratory, would we not all look back as we fled? What a chance to know at last how it really moved and looked and smelled and what noises it made! . . . One thing I know: I would give a great deal to hear any ancient Athenian, even a stupid one, talking about Greek tragedy. He would know in his bones so much that we seek in vain. . . . Ladies and gentlemen, I stand before you somewhat as that Athenian might stand. I read as a native texts which you must read as foreigners. . . . And because this is the judgment of a native, I claim that, even if the defense of my conviction is weak, the *fact* of my conviction is a historical *datum.* . . . That way, where I fail as critic, I yet may be useful as specimen. . . . Speaking not only for myself but for all other Old Western men whom you may meet, I would say, use your specimens while you can. There are not going to be many more dinosaurs.

## II

The experience most ubiquitous and compelling and central to Lewis's work is that which he called by the German word *Sehnsucht* and the English word *joy*: a painful longing, a nostalgia, a romantic memory of an episode or event that seemed charged by some unearthly flavor. It explains his glorious love of nature and his deep fondness for Wordsworth; it was the story of his life. But he was not happy merely to describe the feeling and to roll it about his palate, for he believed the feeling had meaning, that it was a message, and that if "the dialectic of desire" were pursued, the source of the message would be discovered. He insisted that if we were not happy in this world it was because we were made for another; so it was this dialectic, in all its manifestations, through which Lewis worked most of his public life. Like almost every other capacity and resource possessed by the man, joy, too, was mined for its "apologetic" utility. From his first postconversion book, *The Pilgrim's Regress*, to the last he prepared for publication during his life. *Letters to Malcolm: Chiefly on Prayer*, he followed the trail single-mindedly, for it is (he believed) central to conversion, to becoming persons worthy of entering into the Person; and as Walter Hooper has observed, "Lewis struck me as the most thoroughly converted man I had ever met."

The end he sought to effect, more by his manner of defense than by particular defenses, was a reinvigorated intellectual respectability for Christianity; his, we must remember, was a militant intellect, and though he saw Imagination as the organ of meaning he never deviated from his belief in Reason as the organ of truth. But Lewis was a tactician as well as a strategist; given the terrain, he could adapt with the adroitness of a field commander, and there was almost no terrain for which he was not somehow suited. Thus was he "militant" in the universal sense: He would argue or reconcile or sympathize or browbeat or confess or (ostensibly) withdraw, as the particular circumstances seemed to demand; but he seemed never to make a choice that was not in pursuit of his ultimate goal.

It is, therefore, a curious irony that such a *rhetorical* man—for adaptation to the "particular case" is the essence of rhetoric, which is itself an instrument of reason—should have so little trust in the art. In his volume of the *Oxford History of English Literature*, for example, he adequately summarizes the prevalent rhetorical theory but admits to being profoundly unsympathetic to it; in fact, *rhetorical* was often used by him (in private notes) as a term of derogation, as when he refers to the *Anticlaudianus* of Alanus de Insulis as "abominably rhetorical." In *Perelandra*, when the protagonist Ransom begins to lose the debate with the Un-man; in *The Silver Chair*, when the Witch's word-enchantment has nearly brought success; when all the Voluble Selves of *The Great Divorce* are about to rhetorize their way back to hell—in each of these cases, Lewis abandons argument for action, remonstration for demonstration. In a self-effacing effort to call a correspondent's attention to her own besetting vice, he wrote, "talking too much is one of my vices, by the way." He knew what he was doing; in searching for "the available means of persuasion" (to use Aristotle's words from his *Rhetoric*) he found *himself*. So those, for example, who would find *Mere Christianity* mere logic-chopping would find *Surprised by Joy* quite affecting, and those who might be repelled by *The Problem of Pain* would be stirred to their roots by *A Grief Observed*, his record of the pain brought on by the death of his wife.

From an examination of his essays, addresses, sermons, broadcasts, and books, we can say that Lewis (a) never left a doctrine undefended simply because it was unpopular or "outdated," (b) made those defenses as vigorously and as aggressively as was appropriate to the circumstances, (c) sought opportunities to make the defenses, and (d) chose for defense those doctrines that, collectively, were necessary and sufficient for upholding the Christian faith in the twentieth century. We live, he believed, in a post-Christian age, where we are to pagans what a divorcee is to a virgin; or, to alter the analogy, we are like a population living in enemy-occupied territory. The hopeful news is that good forces, like commandoes, have dropped behind the lines, and it is for each of us to somehow join in the effort. In this respect Lewis was, as he admitted, always ready to rush to the weakest point of the foremost trench. As Austin Farrer put it:

There are frontiersmen and frontiersmen, of course. There is what one might call the Munich school, who will always sell the pass in the belief that their position can be more happily defended from foothills to the rear. Such people are not commonly seen as apologists. . . . They are too busy learning from their enemies to do much in defense of their friends. The typical apologist is a man whose every dyke is his last ditch. He will carry the war into the enemy's country; he will not yield an inch of his own.

The burden of his assault was borne, of course, by his pellucid style: simple, precise, conversationally rhythmic (Lewis always wrote for the ear), as intimate as the occasion would tolerate, and strikingly vivid. (Sir Arthur Quiller-Couch praised *Spirits in Bondage*, Lewis's lyric cycle of 1919, for its rich metaphor, and the use of metaphor, according to Aristotle, is the heart of poetry and cannot be taught.) Being guided by faith, for example, is like walking confidently through a momentarily darkened but thoroughly familiar room; our relationship to Christ must be that of a novice mountain climber to an experienced companion: abandoning what appears to be safety—when we reach a chasm and cannot go back—by leaping to him trustingly, according to instruction. Perhaps a simple comparison can best illustrate the attractions of Lewis's style. The first passage is from *Baker's Dictionary of Theology* and purports to describe "time":

The interconnected redemptive *kairoi* supply the threadline of salvation history. Yet the divine *kairoi* at the same time secretly enfold the entire secular movement of time . . . for the fulfillment, often unwittingly, of God's ultimate purposes.

As the *kairos* is a decisive momentary unveiling of the eternal, so the *aion* discloses the Lord of ages who divides the long sweep of time according to his own purposes. The *kairoi* are decisive turning points within the larger *aiona*.

Now Lewis, from *Mere Christianity*:

Our life comes to us moment by moment. One moment disappears before the next comes along; and there is room for very little in each. That is what time is like. And of course you and I tend to take it for granted that this Time series—this arrangement of past, present, and future—is not simply the way life comes to us but the way all things really exist. We tend to assume that the whole universe and God himself are always moving on from past to future just as we do. . . .

Almost certainly God is not in Time. His life does not consist of moments following one another. If a million people are praying to Him at ten-thirty tonight, He need not listen to them all in that one little snippet which we call ten-thirty.

If you picture Time as a straight line along which we have to travel, then

you must picture God as the whole page on which the line is drawn. . . .
God, from above or outside or all around, contains the whole line, and sees
it all.

A single passage inevitably belies the fact that it is the whole of Lewis's
work that displays to us a man possessed of that happiest combination of
communicative gifts: a bountiful imagination, a refined and far-reaching
sensibility, and a decisive command of the language. These uncannily
tensile and glittering instruments retrieve, in Lewis's hands, the muscle,
bone, and sinew of belief, its reasonableness, without which the returns
of exhortation constantly diminish and with which exhortation becomes
effectively unnecessary. In its place, he gives us something far better, for
by way of the commonplace and ordinary he addresses each of us, as it
were, in *our* own terms. In his brilliant *C. S. Lewis: The Shape of His
Faith and Thought,* Paul Holmer has best described this phenomenon:

And he does not offer a theory of the good. He shows us repeatedly in his
novels how a kind of moral certitude is finally achieved. He sends us back to
our fathers, mothers, nurses, poets, sages, and lawgivers. The dignity he
ascribes to all of us is exceedingly flattering. . . . The tissue of life around
us, when taken with seriousness, is already a moral order. We have to become
its qualified readers. Every reading is qualified. The world has no single
character, and it must be understood in a variety of ways. To read it with
everything moral and esthetic abstracted out is to make it a caricature of
itself. . . . This is why, too, his own paragraphs are a sort of splendid conversation. . . . His books create, almost as Kierkegaard did, the living variety
of paradigms. . . . Here the requirements are new capabilities, new capacities
altogether. . . . For his works, especially the novels, have a way of creating a
kind of longing for innocence, for purity, for humility, candor, and content-
ment. . . . It is not as if Lewis invades our privacy with his alien moral
authority. . . . Only its occasion can be created by another, and that is what
Lewis's literature becomes. Wisdom has to be read off the whole shape of his
thought and is not one trick within it.

The features that constitute his life, faith, thought, and literature—
there is barely a telling of them apart—provide a sort of arsenal, for they
possess a polemical utility perfectly suited to the *Zeitgeist.* Though wary
of the danger of an absurd reductionism, nevertheless I offer them in summary fashion. (1) *Joy* has already been mentioned; as a rationale for a
belief in Heaven, it serves as the perfect antidote to the otiosity of modern

life. (2) The *validity of reason* and the *objectivity of the natural moral order* are argued, above all, in Lewis's most important work, *The Abolition of Man*. (3) *Quiddity*, the "thingness" of things, expressed as attention to the concrete, is the reason why (for example) Lewis eschewed all theories and methodologies. (In responding to the charge, in his most mature work, *Letters to Malcolm: Chiefly on Prayer*, that he lacked a theory of the Eucharist, Lewis reminded us that "our Lord said, 'take and eat,' not, 'take and understand.'") (4) *Imagination is epistemologically reliable* and is most effectively embodied in (5) *myth*, which (as an extension of metaphor and symbolism) is best suited to arousing Joy, "spilled religion." After radical subjectivism, the besetting ailment of our century is (6) *chronological snobbery*, whereby we indulge the great modern myth of progress (an offshoot of Darwinism, or Emergent Evolutionism) and treat past achievements as though they were museum pieces. (7) The *Law of Inattention* urges us especially to disregard the Self, to look along the sunbeam instead of at it, to not be like "The Man Born Blind," who wanted to *see light*; "I believe in Christianity," said Lewis, "as I believe the sun has risen not only because I see it but because by it I see everything else." (8) *The supernatural is solid and impinges upon us imminently.*

Doubtless each reader of Lewis could add to this list, which is important not for its thoroughness but for the diffusion of its members throughout his work; as premises—like features of a varied landscape—they are absolutely trustworthy. But Lewis cannot be taken for granted; rather like Aslan, he was not completely tame, as (to their surprise) his admirers often learn. A conservative, he reasoned that a truly Christian society most likely would be a socialist one; himself chaste, he records the diabolical Screwtape as being frustrated that Hell can find no way to eliminate the physical pleasure attendant upon illicit sexual intercourse; and he could recommend that lovers who take vows lightly would do better to live together without marrying rather than cynically to swear, then abuse, the vows.

### III

C. S. Lewis's influence is widespread and growing steadily. If his letters can no longer bring comfort and instruction to private correspondents, then the letters and the other works can continue to exert a profound and enduring personal influence—as was the case with a young lawyer in 1952. According to Abigail McCarthy (*Private Faces/Public Places*), her husband, Senator Eugene McCarthy, and she were offended by a colleague who had used the McCarthy name in a misleading manner. To have exposed the impropriety would have meant great jeopardy to the honest young staff lawyer who brought the abuse to McCarthy's attention, but he nevertheless decided upon a denunciation. It meant

he was leaving an inner circle for a world uncharted, unknown and, for him, not at all rewarding. But Gene sometimes quoted C. S. Lewis on the inner circle. . . . It had made a powerful impact on us because of its very clear articulation of a fact on which our society rests. . . . The most subtle and most compelling of all temptations, Lewis had said, is the temptation to the inner circle. Men will lie, betray their wives and friends for admission to that circle.

With regard to the larger arena of social thought, it is not too much to claim that Lewis's holding action may be on the brink of being relieved, for there are signs that the (highly diversified) troops have regrouped and are launching a counterattack. Michael Walzer (author of *Just and Unjust Wars*) reports and welcomes, in the pages of *The New Republic,* the decline of relativist ethics and the "rediscovery" (in the academy!) of objectively based ethical analyses. Lawrence Kohlberg, of Harvard, rises to prominence by promoting a method of moral education that asserts that relativism is philosophically and scientifically false and that reasserts the "Platonic faith in the power of the rational good." (In *his* turn, Kohlberg is criticized, in *The Public Interest,* because friendship, love, regard for work, care for home and family, and other values common in Lewis's work are trivialized.) In his startling and highly regarded *Zen and the Art of Motorcycle Maintenance,* Robert Pirsig writes that "value, the leading edge of reality, is no longer an irrelevant offshoot of structure" but its predecessor; "to understand structured reality requires an understanding of the value source from which it's derived." And on another front we are told (by Robert Jastrow, a leading astronomer writing in *The New York Times Magazine*) that the big-bang theory of the origin of the universe is very nearly confirmed, and with it the creation story in Genesis; the scientists—the *real* scientists, as Lewis would say—have caught up with the theologians, "who have been sitting there for centuries."

Psychiatrists—or, at least, the real scientists among them—are expressing concern over the New Narcissism, as evidenced, say, by those who would subscribe to *Self* magazine (*"Vogue, Glamour, Mademoiselle, House & Garden* . . . and now *Self"*) or who, having failed (as most of us do) to live a good life, deny its intrinsic value. *Psychology as Religion: The Cult of Self-Worship* has been praised by Karl Menninger (Gervase Fen, the indomitable Oxford professor-detective created by Edmund Crispin, pricks the balloon once and for all when he observes, "I always think that psychology is wrong in imagining that when it has analyzed evil it has somehow disposed of it"); and Christopher Lasch has rent to pieces the Culture of Narcissism. Lewis, too, was concerned—one might almost say solely concerned—with human personality, but always (as in *The World's Last Night and Letters to Malcolm*) within the context of what each personality is *meant* to become. *Till We Have Faces*, a stirring psychological novel in the modern mode and perhaps Lewis's greatest work of fiction, embodies the pathology of this "pestilent notion" of Personality, inviting us never to forget the Law of Inattention. "At a certain stage in his life," writes Owen Barfield, "he deliberately ceased to take any interest in himself. . . . I suggest that what began as deliberate choice became at length (as he had no doubt always intended it should) an ingrained and effortless habit of soul."

This getting-out-of-the-self and its use as a resource in the battle over this enemy-occupied territory must lead to a new self, very nearly a demigod, a coming-into the Personhood of Christ. Lewis has expressed this principle beautifully, not only in overtly Christian works but in *An Experiment in Criticism*, not about the religious experience but about the literary one:

My own eyes are not enough for me; I will see through those of others. Reality, even seen through the eyes of many, is not enough. I will see what others have invented. Even the eyes of all humanity are not enough. I regret that the brutes cannot write books. Very gladly would I learn what face thing. present to a mouse or a bee; more gladly still would I perceive the olfactory world charged with all the information it carries for a dog.

Literary experience heals the wound, without undermining the privilege, of individuality. There are mass emotions which heal the wound; but they destroy the privilege. In them our separate selves are pooled and we sink back into subindividuality. But in reading great literature I become a thou-

sand men and yet remain myself. Like the night sky in the Greek poem, I
see with a myriad eyes, but it is still I who see. Here, as in worship, in love,
in moral action, and in knowing, I transcend myself; and am never more
myself than when I do. Lewis's great achievement is that he allowed us the
same opportunity, engaging us with a re-established grammar of "regression"
and enabling us (the process no longer stigmatized) to "become as little
children."

I have often thought that the best explanation of his appeal is expressed
by these lines from Pope in *An Essay in Criticism.*

> Something, whose truth convinced at sight we find,
> That gives us back the image of our mind.

Yet, as appropriate as they are in so many ways, I have thought again. In
writing about his beloved Spenser, Lewis has provided by far the most
telling insight into the meaning of his own life and writing:

His work is one, like a growing thing, a tree . . . with branches reaching to
heaven and roots to hell. . . . And between these two extremes comes all the
multiplicity of human life. . . . To read him is to grow in mental health.

# Chronology of C. S. Lewis's Life

This much-abbreviated list is intended merely to suggest the shape of events in and around C. S. Lewis's life. With few exceptions it omits the publication of his works, and other events and people mentioned in this book. Its sources are various, the most thorough being Green and Hooper, *C. S. Lewis: A Biography*. An indispensable adjunct to any Lewis chronology is that on Warren Lewis found in Kilby and Mead, *Brothers and Friends: The Diaries of Major Warren Hamilton Lewis* (Harper and Row, 1982).

*1862 Florence ("Flora") Augusta Hamilton,* C. S. Lewis's mother and one of four children, born to Thomas Hamilton and Mary Warren. She will win Honors in algebra and geometry, in *1880,* then in logic and mathematics in *1885,* from Queen's College, Belfast.

*1863 Albert James Lewis* (solicitor), C. S. Lewis's father and one of six children, born to Richard Lewis and Martha Gee in Cork, Ireland.

*1872 Janie King Moore (Askins),* Lewis's companion, "adopted mother," and mother of Maureen and Paddy Moore, born.

*1895 Warren Hamilton Lewis,* C. S. Lewis's brother and dearest friend; soldier, historian (of seventeenth-century France), editor, and diarist, born. *(Joseph) Arthur Greeves,* Lewis's Belfast neighbor and lifelong friend, born.

*1898 Edward Francis Courtenay ("Paddy") Moore,* Lewis's bunkmate and army buddy, born.

*1898 CLIVE STAPLES LEWIS BORN, NOVEMBER 29.*

*1905* The prospering Lewis family moves to a new house, "Little Lea," in County Down.

*1906* *Maureen Daisy Helen Moore,* Lewis's "adopted sister" (now Lady Dunbar of Hempriggs), born.

*1908* *Flora Lewis dies, August 23.*

*1911* *AT SCHOOL IN ENGLAND, LEWIS CEASES TO BE A CHRISTIAN.*

*1914* Lewis begins private tutoring with W. T. *Kirkpatrick (1848–1921),* a severe dialectician and atheist, for whom Lewis will develop great affection.

*1915* *(Helen) Joy Davidman,* later Mrs. C. S. Lewis, born, Bronx, New York.

*1917–19* Though accepted to Oxford, Lewis enlists in the army and spends his nineteenth birthday in the trenches. After suffering trench fever he returns to action, takes prisoners, and is wounded in battle. *1918: Paddy Moore killed* in action. *1919:* Lewis returns to University College and establishes a household with Maureen and Mrs. Moore, with whom he visited before his departure to France.

*1925* After winning three firsts (philosophy, *1920;* classics, *1922;* English literature, *1923*) and substituting for E. F. Carrit as a philosophy tutor for one year at University College, Lewis is elected to a fellowship in English language and literature at Magdalen College.

*1929* *Albert Lewis dies, September 24.* Shortly thereafter Lewis returns to a belief in God (though not yet in Christ).

*1930* The Lewis brothers (Warren now retired from the army) and the Moores purchase and move into the Kilns, in Headington Quarry, just outside Oxford. Maureen will leave the household in *1941,* when she marries Leonard Blake.

*1931* *C. S. LEWIS BECOMES A CHRISTIAN* and learns that Warren has, quite independently, also converted to the Faith.

*1933–50* *Lewis most active as author and speaker. Friendships flourish with the Inklings and on walking tours, and he achieves great fame and earns several honors.* The following items suggest the varied richness of this period: BBC broadcasts (Aug. *1941,* Jan.–Feb. *1942,* Sept.–Nov. *1942,* Feb.–Apr. *1944*); Socratic Club presidency *(1941–54);* publication of some fifteen books of apologetics, fiction, and scholarship. Of particular interest are his meeting with *Charles Williams (b. 1886)* in *1936,* Williams's death in *1945,* and the publication of *The Screwtape Letters* in *1942.* The latter (along with his BBC talks) bring Lewis his greatest fame, an enormous correspondence, and his picture on the cover of *Time* magazine (September 8, *1947*). In the summer of *1948* Mrs. Moore retires permanently to a nursing home, and by March of *1949* Lewis has completed the manuscript of *The Lion, the Witch and the Wardrobe,* which will be published in *1950.* The remaining six books of *The Chronicles of Narnia* will be published annually through *1956,* the same year in which *Till We Have Faces,* surely his greatest fiction, is published as well.

*1951* *Janie King Moore dies, January 12.* Lewis declines the honor of being named commander of the Order of the British Empire.

*1952–53 Lewis and Joy Davidman (Gresham) meet* in September, after having corresponded at length. In January of *1953* Joy returns to the United States; then again, in December, she comes to England, this time with her two young sons.

*1954* Lewis is elected professor of Medieval and Renaissance English Literature at Magdalene College, Cambridge. He will assume the chair in *1955.*

*1956–58 Lewis and Joy Davidman are married at the Oxford registry office (April 23, 1956);* by November she is near death from a recurrence of cancer; in response to her request, *Lewis marries Joy in a bedside ecclesiastical ceremony (March 21, 1957).* By December Joy is walking again. In June of *1958* Joy's cancer is arrested, and in July the couple honeymoon in Ireland.

*1960 Three months after a physically painful trip to Greece with Lewis, Joy Davidman Lewis dies, July 13.*

*1963 C. S. LEWIS DIES, NOVEMBER 22.*

*1966 Arthur Greeves dies, August 29.*

*1973 Warren Lewis dies, April 9.*

# The Contributors

*Leo Baker.* An exact contemporary of C. S. Lewis, Mr. Baker was among his first friends at Oxford and a close companion for some time thereafter. In his youth an actor with the Old Vic Company, Mr. Baker retired with his wife to Surrey, where he died in 1987.

*Peter Bayley.* Mr. Bayley was formerly a fellow of University College, Oxford, and a University Lecturer in English. In 1946 he returned from World War II and took a first in English in 1947. He has written extensively on Spenser and Milton and has been a visiting professor at the University of the South and at Yale University. Formerly Master of Collingwood College, Durham University, and Berry Professor of English at the University of St. Andrews, Mr. Bayley is now Emeritus Professor at the latter and Emeritus Fellow of University College, Oxford.

*Derek Brewer.* Master of Emmanuel College, Cambridge University, Mr. Brewer returned from World War II a captain in the British Infantry, obtained a degree in English from Magdalen College, Oxford, in 1947, and later earned a doctorate from the University of Birmingham, where he also taught. He has been published widely on medieval English literature. Dr. Brewer's latest book is *Chaucer and His World*. He is now living in retirement in Cambridge.

*Jane Douglass.* A former actress and playwright, Miss Douglass belonged to Walter Prichard Eaton's "Listener's Theater," and her *Play on Your Harp, Little David* is a Clemence Dane Award–winning play. She was born in Nashville, Tennessee, and educated privately in Boston, New York, and London. Her essay first appeared in *CSL: The Bulletin of the New York C. S. Lewis Society*, May 1970.

*James Dundas-Grant.* After finishing at Eton, Mr. Dundas-Grant entered the Royal Navy, volunteering for the Air Branch and seeing much action in World War I. As a member of the Royal Naval Volunteer Reserve, he was given command (in 1939) of the Oxford University Naval Division. Commander Grant was a choirmaster and a member of Lloyd's. He and his wife lived in Surrey before his death in 1985.

*Austin Farrer.* One of the most famous theologians in England and a lifelong friend to C. S. Lewis, the Reverend Dr. Farrer was, until his death in 1968, Warden of Keble College, Oxford. He was chaplain, tutor, and lecturer, member of the Church of England liturgical commission, and prolific author (*Finite and Infinite, A Science of God?*, among many others). "In His Image" first appeared in *The Brink of Mystery* (ed. Conti).

*Adam Fox.* Author, preacher, and poet, the Reverend Canon Fox, late of Westminster, was born in 1883 and went on to win the Sacred Poem prize, to be a Fellow of Magdalen College, Oxford, and to be Professor of Poetry at Oxford University. His many publications include *Old King Coel, Plato for Pleasure, Meet the Greek Testament, Plato and the Christians,* and *God Is an Artist.* "At the Breakfast Table" first appeared in *CSL: The Bulletin of the New York C. S. Lewis Society,* May 1972. Canon Fox died in 1977.

*Charles Gilmore.* Formerly Commandant of the Chaplain's School (Royal Air Force), Mr. Gilmore was born in 1908 and now lives in retirement in Norfolk, England.

*Roger Lancelyn Green.* A prolific author, Lewis co-biographer, expert on Andrew Lang, Lewis Carroll, and Arthur Conan Doyle, Mr. Green was deputy librarian at Merton College, Oxford, a Visiting Lecturer at the University of St. Andrews, and editor of the *Kipling Journal.* His more than fifty published books include *From the World's End* and *Into Other Worlds.* His assistance on the Narnian books has been acknowledged by Lewis. Mr. Green died in 1987.

*Alan Bede Griffiths.* A Benedictine monk living in India, Dom Bede earned a B.A. at Magdalen College, Oxford, in 1929. He has won the gold medal of the Catholic Art Association for his ecumenical work and is the author of several books, including *The Golden String* (an autobiography) and *Christian Ashram.* He is conversant in Sanskrit and in Syriac and is deeply knowledgeable of Hindu tradition.

*Arthur Cecil Harwood.* A lifelong friend of C. S. Lewis, whose exact contemporary he was, A. C. Harwood was known as "a wholly imperturbable man." His influence upon his intimate companion is acknowledged in Lewis's *Surprised by Joy.* "About Anthroposophy" first appeared in *Anthro-*

*posophical Quarterly*, winter 1973; "A Toast to His Memory," in *CSL*, September 1975. Mr. Harwood died in 1975.

*Robert E. Havard.* The Lewis brothers' personal physician, Dr. Havard was born in 1901 and died in 1985 on the Isle of Wight. He was an Inkling, a speaker at the Socratic Club, and he came to be one of Lewis's closest companions. His paper was originally written at the request of Professor Clyde S. Kilby for the Marion C. Wade Collection at Wheaton College.

*Walter Hooper.* Lewis's personal secretary and now an Estate adviser, Hooper (born in North Carolina, and educated at Chapel Hill and at Oxford) has edited several collections of Lewis's writings (including *They Stand Together: The Letters of C. S. Lewis to Arthur Greeves*), coauthored Lewis's biography, and written several essays on Lewis and his work. An earlier version of his bibliography appeared in *Light on C. S. Lewis*.

*Richard W. Ladborough.* The late Dr. Ladborough, born in 1908, was Lewis's closest friend at Cambridge. His essay first appeared in *CSL*, July 1975.

*Gervase Mathew.* A close companion of Lewis's and an Inkling, the late Father Mathew was born in 1905, entered the Order of Preachers in 1928, and went on to establish his reputation as a scholar in patristics and Byzantine art, Medieval English literature and social theory, and the archaeology of East Africa, where he conducted many archaeological surveys. Some of his many books are *Byzantine Painting*, *The Reformation and the Contemplative Life* (with his brother David), and *The Court of Richard II*. "Orator" appeared in *New Blackfriars* (1974) as a review of the Green and Hooper biography.

*Eugene McGovern.* Mr. McGovern works in the field of casualty insurance on actuarial matters. He is a founding member of the New York C. S. Lewis Society and for ten years edited its *Bulletin*. He is married and is the father of three sons.

*Clifford Morris.* Mr. Morris was born in 1914. In addition to practicing in the ministry and serving in World War II, he has written two books of verse and an appreciation of his father, who was a prominent Methodist. He is married, has two daughters, and now resides in Headington, Oxford.

*Luke Rigby.* A member of the Order of St. Benedict, Father Rigby is Abbot of the Saint Louis Priory in Missouri. "A Solid Man" first appeared in *CSL*, January 1974.

*Erik Routley.* Dr. Routley was born in 1917 and has been Professor of Church Music, Princeton, since 1975. He obtained his degree at Magdalen College, Oxford, in 1940 and his D.Phil. in 1952. Ordained in 1943, he served as a Tutor, a Chaplain, and as President of the Congregational Church in England and Wales. His books include *Church Music and Theology* and *Hymns Today and Tomorrow.* "A Prophet" first appeared in *CSL,* January 1973.

*George Sayer.* A student of Lewis's who later became a good friend, Mr. Sayer (born in 1914) became Chairman of the English Department at Malvern College, a school that figured briefly but dramatically in the life of C. S. Lewis. He is the author of *Jack: C. S. Lewis and His Times,* widely regarded as the best biography of Lewis, and now lives in retirement in Malvern.

*Nathan C. Starr.* The late Dr. Starr was born in 1896. His distinguished career took him from Oxford (M.A.) to Harvard (Ph.D.) and many points in-between. During World War II he worked for the United States State Department, and from 1963 he was Professor Emeritus at the University of Florida. His books include *The Pursuit of Learning* and *The Humanistic Tradition.* "Good Cheer and Sustenance" was first published in *Unicorn,* 1972.

*John Wain.* Novelist, essayist, biographer, scholar, and Professor of Poetry at Oxford University, Mr. Wain has taught throughout England and in Paris. His books include *Hurry on Down* (fiction), *Weep Before God* (poetry), *A House for the Truth* (criticism), and *Samuel Johnson* (a biography for which he won the James Tate Black Memorial Prize and the Heinemann Award). "A Great Clerke" first appeared in *Encounter,* May 1964.

*Charles Wrong.* For some time a professor of history at the University of South Florida, Professor Wrong was educated in England. His essay first appeared in *CSL,* February 1973. Mr. Wrong now lives in retirement in Canada.

# PART ONE
## *Earliest Perspectives*

# I

## *Near the Beginning*

### LEO BAKER

Eᴀʀʟʏ ɪɴ ᴍʏ ꜰɪʀꜱᴛ ᴛᴇʀᴍ at Oxford in October 1919 (can you dive back nearly sixty years?), I had a caller from another college. He had heard of me "as a poet," from a school friend I had run across in the hospital. This caller was R. M. S. Pasley, himself ambitious to reach the slopes of Helicon and eagerly seeking the company of fellow travelers. He told me there was one such in his own college, a strange fellow who seemed to live an almost secret life and took no part in the social life of the college. "He has been noticed coming into college and going out," joked Pasley, "and opinion varies as to whether he is a college messenger or a don in some obscure subject. You must meet him. He is in fact a scholar of the college and a bit of a brain. He has shown me a few formal lyrics. Right up our tree. I'll try and get hold of him." A few days later in Pasley's rooms I met C. S. Lewis.

Memory is weak, illusive, and often a lying jade. Fortunately there are two objective props to memory, first the letters in my possession written to me by Lewis, and second a snapshot for which he posed on one of our walks, for soon after that first introduction we met again and planned some afternoon walks together and the exchange of our poems for mutual comment. Such walks were possible because it was a convention at Oxford that afternoons were consecrated to active sports, which held no interest for Lewis and from which I was invalidated by war disabilities.

We were both just twenty-one, eager for what we could pick up from

Oxford and "The World," yet by no means fresh from school, for we had both seen active service as commissioned officers in France, been wounded, and had the subsequent experience of operations and months in a hospital. Eager for "The World"? Not quite true. "The World" meant very different things to each of us. I was interested in contemporary events, social conditions, the arts, marriage, and even politics. Lewis was not. He crossed them all out, except insofar as they bumped into him. He lived in an enclosed world with rigid walls built by his logic and intelligence, and trespassers would be prosecuted. Within these walls were his ambition and single-minded determination to get the highest class in the examinations, which in his case meant the classics and philosophy (to which he added, by artistic impulse, poetry, and by deductive logic, atheism).

For me fundamental atheism was a new experience. One day over the tea cups in my room, Lewis cried out in an angry crescendo, "You take too many things for granted. You can't start with God. *I don't accept God!*" I was surprised into silence. As a subject, religion was out. So was German philosophy, a necessary subject for him, a blank of ignorance for me. He was impatient with my lack of logic and of rationalism. He profoundly distrusted my interest in mysticism. Under the circumstances one can well be amazed that our friendship matured so quickly and was as of such importance to Lewis as his letters show.

Our initial link was, without question, poetry. From this our friendship grew, and for a considerable time I was his closest friend and the first (and for long the only one) admitted to the hideout at Headington. He had made friends with one man in the war, but this man was killed. His friend's mother, Mrs. Moore, had a house in Headington, a suburb of Oxford, and invited Lewis to move out of college and to take his lodging there. This became a home for Lewis, far preferable to the one in Belfast. Mrs. Moore was an Irish lady with an ebullient temperament. I was often invited up there, for meals even, and greatly enjoyed her exceptional rice puddings, of which she was justly proud.

Why was Lewis so remote from normal university life, so secretive, one who literally shied away from friendship? Lewis was essentially kind, to me often very kind, yet on two occasions he burst out with deep and uncontrollable hatred for which in the first instance I could find no explanation. At the time, he was staying with me at my home in London. So far as I knew there was not a cloud in the sky. On the second occasion he sent me a most violent letter in which he said he did not wish to see or hear from me again. This led, alas, to a breach of several years. It ended when, in a letter of 28 April 1935, he made a full and most sweet apology, asking forgiveness and hoping "to pick up some of the old links." No doubt I was at fault, but could it also be that such unexpected outbursts, not unlike volcanic eruptions, were a sign of his fear of any close human relationship? Before he was twenty-one he had known three major wretched experiences. The lesson was that to escape from personal suffering he must hedge himself round, keep apart from emotional contacts, and live the life of a very private man.

He lost his mother early, and as he told me repeatedly he had no sympathetic relationship with his father, a Belfast lawyer. The house at Stradtown was not a happy home for him. He opens a letter of 12 January 1920, "The fact of being at home, which to me is a synonym for busy triviality, continual interruptions, and a complete lack of privacy. . . ." Two stories he told me more than once, and they may seem to us now almost humorous, but they were not to him, for he told them with bitter emotion. One concerned the "Sunday afternoon walk" (you must imagine the sneer) with his father, who would always ask, "Where shall we go?" To which Lewis always gave the same, easiest answer, "Where you like." "And always we went the same way, the ugliest way, by the gasworks." When his first book of poems came out, of course he gave a copy to his father, who returned it with the heartening words, "I shouldn't leave this about. The servants might see it!" In 1935 he wrote to me, "my father is dead. I have deep regrets about all my relations with my father (but thank God they were best at the end.")

From this rather cold house he was sent to a boarding school in England, and there, he said, he was miserable. He was thrown into a mode of life with which this unsociable boy could not cope. He was driven inward and became his own society. Then, with a scholarship, he had a very brief glimpse of the wonderful freedom of Oxford, but was soon plunged into the army and war. I know nothing of his army life. It is difficult to imagine him in charge of a platoon in the trenches. We hardly ever mentioned the war from which we had both so recently and so miraculously escaped with our lives. It was as though that hiatus in growing up was put firmly behind us; we took a deep and thankful breath and started a new life—or almost new. I once asked him how on earth he had managed in the army. "I

loathed it." "Were you much frightened in France?" He replied with
great emphasis, "All the time, but I never sank so low as to pray."

So to Oxford. He was determined not to suffer there as he had done in
those previous societies. Hence the secrecy and privacy. Mixing was not
for him. He was ambitious for scholarship and poetry; therefore he must
concentrate. But of course some companionship was inevitable. Pasley was
a great mixer, and meeting with Pasley one made other contacts, but brief
ones. The more lasting companions came through me. I introduced him
to my closest friends in Wadham, Owen Barfield, in later years a very close
friend to Lewis, and W. E. Beckett. Both had brilliant university careers
and went on to achieve fame in the wider world. They were certainly the
intellectual equals of Lewis. Barfield brought into our group A. C. Harwood and W. O. Field.

With Lewis, an important addition, we met informally but with some
constancy in each other's rooms and discussed almost anything and everything except the two subjects that one understands are favourites with the
young today, revolution and sex. We continued our companionship after
Oxford and planned an annual walk together through favourite countryside. Walking, but above all talking, with Lewis in full voice. This does
not mean that he monopolized the talk, but he played a full part and was
always central.

.As a talker Lewis was completely impressive, even if one disagreed with
his thesis. He very seldom asked questions, except in a Socratic manner.
He gave answers, made statements, and developed his points with delib-
eration and logical form. His voice, with the slight remains of a Belfast
accent, flowed forth in measured periods, with little variety of tempo, often
decorated with quotations supplied by his prodigious memory. It seemed
as though not only had he thought the subject out thoroughly but also
that the expression had been previously chiseled, so well framed that what
he said could be printed with hardly any revision; yet it was often a completely spontaneous fountain, unprepared. This facility was one of his
many gifts.

Some years later my wife and I visited Oxford and sat down with Lewis
in Wadham gardens. I told him that we contemplated work in the craft
movement that still continued after the fresh inspiration given to it by
William Morris. What did he think? Lewis then gave his advice with
unhesitating and uninterrupted fluency for, according to our memory,

some twenty minutes. (The heart of his argument was that one cannot put the clock back.) My wife found this performance astonishing and has often referred to it since.

From the beginning one probably realized that one was not his intellectual equal, but there were the natural resilience and upsurge of youthful confidence to protect one from too much humility. For two or three years perhaps, I was not overawed by his Johnsonian intelligence. Then his authority and depth became more and more marked. One day I said to him, "You know I begin to feel like an ignoramus talking with you." "Well, you aren't," rejoined Lewis. "If you divided all the men for intelligence into A, B, or C, you would be an A." Congratulations, Baker.

Does he sound somewhat heavy and humourless? He was certainly not so in the early days. When I dined with him at the high table in Magdalen around 1940, I met a Lewis used to authority and showing a marked trace of confident eccentricity. He was heavier, redder in the face, and his voice was louder. When he marched into the senior common room with me in tow, he introduced me to two youngish dons standing silently together. "Introduce Dr.—— and Dr.——, scientists. Quite uneducated, of course," boomed Lewis, and we marched on.

If we return to 1920 and look at the snapshot, we see a slight young man of average height, well built. He is smiling somewhat shyly at the camera, no doubt at my request. Short hair of course. What is a bit surprising is the neat bow tie. The dark college blazer is by no means straight, and the grey flannel trousers are very near disaster. And what is that? He wears boots. That must be a touch of the Irish.

What did we talk about on those walks? Naturally, of first importance were the poems we had most recently written. These were carefully studied before comment, for the event of creation was a matter of real importance. *Whence did inspiration come?* It was not ratiocination that made Wordsworth write,

> The Rainbow comes and goes,
> And lovely is the Rose.

or Coleridge,

> A savage place! as holy and enchanted
> As e'er beneath a waning moon was haunted
> By woman wailing for her demon-lover.

Neither will nor wish would bring inspiration. The muse, we decided, descended whenever she judged the time to be ripe. Then the poet felt a sudden warmth within himself, followed by a bright luminosity focusing on "the subject." There was much talk of the importance of the subject, especially as Lewis insisted that one's mind should be tuned to ancient myth. We rejected Greek and Roman as already well used in the past, and the Arthurian legends belonged to Tennyson and the Pre-Raphaelites, so our choice therefore must be the *Mabinogion*. In March 1921 Barfield wrote (enclosing a sonnet sequence for comment), "It is at such times as these that we wretched personal poets envy the austere people like yourself and Lewis, who write about Llewellyn and how he brought the good news from Pwhlli to Gwlch." A just joke. We were adamant that expression must be formal with rhythm and rhyme. Lewis urged me, so rightly, to pay more attention to technical expertise; we regarded with arrogant scorn the free versifiers, and especially we disliked the far too clever Sitwell trio and their publication *Wheels*. Lewis called them the vorticists.

Before the Christmas vacation Pasley proposed that five of us should contribute to an anthology to be a counter to *Wheels* and to show that there were new poets who could sing of contemporary life within classical forms. Lewis was enthusiastic and proposed the title "The Way's the Way," a quotation from Bunyan. He and I were asked each to write a preface to proclaim our beliefs. When I sent him my effort (April 1920), he replied that he had given up the attempt: "I am become more and more convinced of the futility of any theorists about poetry. It is not by theories that we shall stand or fall. If our work is good, it will live; if the Vorticists are bad, 'without doubt they shall perish everlastingly.' It was not the Preface to the *Lyrical Ballads* but the *Lyrical Ballads* themselves that moved mountains."

The novelist Alec Waugh introduced me to Harold Munro, as he thought him to be the best bet for a publisher. Munro approved the idea but after a few weeks returned the manuscript with a refusal. Lewis and Pasley then approached Basil Blackwell in Oxford. Blackwell kept it, returned it, then asked for it back again. Lewis wrote me, "Of this sacred anthology of ours I am heartily sick. The chief motive for sticking to such a waterlogged craft is the disappointment which I think Pasley would feel if he were marooned." Later came a note from Lewis starting with half a dozen lines in rhyme (perhaps as a mock dirge). Then, "The blow has fallen. Basil refuses to publish the damn thing unless we raise some money. I forget how much. Please find enclosed your own babes from the ruined creche."

In the two preceding paragraphs are compressed many anxious hours. Hours spent in choosing the material, in debates over principles, in those interviews with publishers, in the trepidation of waiting and waiting—fraught hours. Lewis grew to hate them and at the end wrote, "My own feeling of relief is something wonderful and has inspired me to write several immortal poems in the last few days."

Meanwhile, during term time, Lewis and I spent many hours together. Apart from poetry we shared two lighter literary interests. The one of lesser importance was the novels of H. Rider Haggard. The other, most important, indeed almost an obsession, was the book by that leprechaun James Stephens, *The Crock of Gold*. Here we found a food we both needed: an amalgam of humor, poetry, myth, philosophy and, above all, imagination. I have no doubt that Lewis was quite deeply influenced by this book. We knew chunks of it by heart and quoted from it delightedly when words or events presented an opportunity. Even now the thought of "the thin woman of Inis Magarth," or even more the so-often repeated negative, "I will not, said the Philosopher," conjures up Lewis's young face grinning.

He was not a laughing man and did not often indulge in wit. On the whole one might say, "he carried a load of mischief." He did not inflict his unhappiness on others, but in almost every letter in my collection he complained of unspecified difficulties and worries, often with the hint of a wry smile. A typical example is, "I have lived this many a day in a world of incredible problems that offer me the alternative, 'Heads I win, tails you lose,' of things once deemed impossible yet undertaken from dire necessity at the last moment." Later in the same letter we get a couple of more clues to melancholy. (He is writing in Somerset.) "I have been recuperating in most divine scenery . . . perfect beauty and solitude; indeed I have seldom found anywhere quite so alone. Up there the emptiness, if it says anything, seems to say, 'Admire if you will, but you have no lot nor part in me.' I am constitutionally incapable of the harmony you feel. The more beautiful and desolate it is, the more I feel myself a trespasser: there is always someone waiting over the crest to warn me off."

Naturally he changed with the years, as we all do. His literary tactics changed, although he said he remained principally a medievalist. In 1920–21 he wrote at length about his two literary foundation stones, Spenser and Milton. In 1936 he is taken up (in both senses) by Icelandic prosody, and in the same letter discovers Charles Williams: "He has the power (absolutely unknown in our generation) of painting *virtue*." In September 1920 he could write, "You will be interested to hear that in the course of my philosophy on the existence of matter I have had to postulate some sort of God as the least objectionable theory; but of course we know nothing." Ten years later he could write, "I am a Christian."

That should really be the finis to these early memories. But I would like one more quotation from 1935. Lewis could not foretell the future. He wrote, "I suppose we have all lived to discover that we are not great men, and not to mind; there are better things than that in the world, and out of it. We have so spoiled language that I cannot even say God bless you without pausing to try and explain that I mean the words in their literal sense."

# 2

# *The Adventure of Faith*

## ALAN BEDE GRIFFITHS, o.s.b.

I ENTERED MAGDALEN COLLEGE, OXFORD, as an undergraduate in October 1925 just after C. S. Lewis entered as a fellow and tutor in English literature. For the first two years I had no contact with him, as I was reading classics, but in my third year I decided to read English literature, and found that I was to have Lewis as my tutor. From that time I had to present an essay on some subject in English literature every week, which he would then criticize, and we would remain talking for some time after. These talks were gradually extended, as acquaintanceship ripened into friendship. I remember how on one occasion we continued talking almost till midnight, and I had to run to be out of college before the clock finished striking twelve, as no one was allowed in or out of college after midnight.

After I left Oxford we continued to correspond, and I visited him from time to time, and in 1932 I went on a walking tour with him and his friend Owen Barfield. By this time our interests had gone beyond English literature, and we were both engaged on the venture of faith that was to lead to our becoming convinced Christians. During this period, from 1929 when I left Oxford till 1932, when we were both undergoing a conversion to Christian faith, I was probably nearer to Lewis than anyone else. He has described in *Surprised by Joy* how he "kept up a copious correspondence" with me at this time, and for these three years we were both following the same path. When in December 1932 I became a Catholic, our ways parted and, though we remained friends, we never again shared the thrill of that adventure, when we were both discovering the truth together and almost every day brought some new insight into the goal we were seeking.

It may be imagined that, as a result of this close association at the time of our conversion, I would have something of value to add to what Lewis has written of the stages of his own conversion. But, in fact, I am afraid that I can add very little. Lewis himself once said that friends, unlike lovers, are looking not at each other, but at something they hold in common. It was so in our friendship. I was not looking at Lewis as a person different from myself but as one who shared my own interests and enthusiasms. I was scarcely conscious of any difference between us, though, of course, I was aware of his vastly greater knowledge. But Oxford is not a place which encourages humility, and an undergraduate normally has very little respect for a don. I was thus quite unaware that there was anything exceptional in this friendship, and it was only years afterward that I began to discover other aspects of his mind and character, which were then completely hidden from me. In fact, it was only after his death that I came across the Narnia stories and recognized in them a power of imaginative invention and insight of which I had no conception before. It must be remembered that Lewis always affected (I think that it was deliberate) to be a plain, honest man, with no nonsense about him, usually wearing when out on a walk an old tweed hat and coat, and accompanied with a pipe, a stick, and a dog. It was, no doubt, the expression of a determination to avoid all pretentiousness, which later developed into a real and profound humility, but it prevented anyone from taking him for a "great man" and often concealed his real greatness.

It was characteristic that when quite early on he gave me to read his poem *Dymer*, which he had written under the name of Clive Hamilton, he did not reveal that he was the author, and I would never have credited him with the capacity to write a poem of such unashamed romanticism. In fact, Lewis was just then growing out of his earlier romanticism, as I myself was beginning to do, and adopted a saner and more rational philosophy. I remember at our first meeting, when I explained to him my reasons for reading English literature, he protested strongly against my view. After reading for Honor Mods (the first part in a classical degree), I had come to the conclusion that mere intellectual knowledge was of little value, and that it was through poetry and imagination, not through reason and intellect, that one could find fulfillment.

Lewis himself was just then reacting against this view and saw its one-sidedness, but he realized also, I think, that I was prepared to study English literature seriously. He lent me, perhaps as a kind of answer to my need, a little work he had just written called *Summa Metaphysica contra Anthroposophos*. This was the first writing of his that I ever saw. I don't know what became of it; probably it was destroyed. It was his reaction to his friend Owen Barfield, who together with other friends had become a disciple of Rudolf Steiner. I don't remember this little essay in any detail, but I do remember that he outlined in it his conception of the Spirit—the Universal Spirit behind all phenomena. This was exactly what I needed, and from that time I became a confirmed idealist.

I think that Lewis later reacted rather too strongly against this "universal Spirit" in favour of a personal God on the ground that one could not enter into personal relations with it. But the impersonal, or rather transpersonal, aspect of the Godhead is surely as important as its personal aspect. Lewis saw the danger of substituting abstract terms for concrete and personal terms, when speaking about God, but he seems to have reacted too much against this danger. In his *Letters to Malcolm* he wrote: "What soul ever perished for believing that God the Father really had a beard?" It may be that no soul ever perished for this reason, but the impoverishment of religious faith due to this, and the scandal caused to unbelievers by such childish religious beliefs, are surely just as harmful as any liberal theology that takes refuge in abstractions.

Another book that Lewis lent me at an early stage was Owen Barfield's *Poetic Diction*, which had a permanent effect on my life. Barfield was a philologist, which did not naturally endear him to me, but he had discovered by the study of words what I felt, and still feel, to be one of the most profound secrets not only of the growth of language, but also of the evolution of man and the universe. He showed how a word such as *spiritus* in Latin or *pneuma* in Greek could mean several different things, namely, wind or air or breath or life or soul or spirit. The common understanding of this phenomenon is that man began by using words to signify material things such as wind and air and breath and then went on by gradual stages to discover more abstract concepts such as life and soul and spirit.

But Barfield showed, on the contrary, that the original words contained all these meanings together. This is why early languages are immensely rich and suggestive. Then in the course of time the different meanings are distinguished and separate words assigned to them. Thus language progresses from symbols that are deep and rich and manifold in meaning to words that are precise and clear and prosaic but lacking the poetic quality of early speech. This threw a flood of light for me on human evolution. We do not progress from a simple materialistic view of life to a mere spiritual understanding, but from a rich, complex, global experience of life to a more rational, analytical understanding, in other words from poetry to prose.

Thus my view of life was shaped by some basic insights that Lewis gave me, and his influence must have been felt in innumerable ways that I cannot now recall. But there was one point on which we disagreed, and I cannot help feeling that in this he was wrong. This was on the question of what he called the "personal heresy." I had written an essay on Sir Philip Sidney, in which I said that his poetry was so much better than much Elizabethan love poetry because he wrote from his own personal experience. Lewis immediately attacked this view, maintaining that poetry had nothing to do with the poet's personal feelings, a theory he afterward developed in his book *The Personal Heresy* from a debate with Dr. Tillyard. I was unable to answer Lewis at the time, but it appears to me now that Dr. Tillyard had much the better of the argument, and that this was really a blind spot with Lewis. Lewis seems to have concentrated his attention on the aspect of poetry as an art or skill and to have underestimated the unconscious. But, as Dr. Tillyard pointed out, that is on the conscious aspect of poetry. But the imagination, as Coleridge and Wordsworth understood it, is the meeting place of conscious and unconscious, and it is through the unconscious that the poet is linked not only with his own personal feelings but also with the experience of the race, the collective unconscious of mankind. This is why the poet has been called a seer, or *rishi* in Hindu tradition, and is said to have been inspired by the Muses.

Another problem is that Lewis defined personality as "that which distinguishes one man from another," but this is to take a very limited view of the human person. It would be better to keep the word *individuality* for that which distinguishes one man from another, and to say that the person is that by which a man exists in himself and is related to other persons. Person implies relation, as is seen in the doctrine of the Trinity, and it is in his person that a man is open to humanity and to the universe. This may seem to be labouring a small point, but I believe that it marks a difference in Lewis's outlook, which affected his whole understanding of the relation between the life of the intellect and the life of the imagination. This was a perennial source of debate between us, and for Lewis himself it was one of the principal problems of his life, how to reconcile his extraordinarily powerful intellect, which made him one of the greatest critics of English literature, with his no less-powerful imagination, which was to flower in the planetary novels and the Narnia stories. It is a measure of the gap between them that in all my acquaintance with him he never revealed his imaginative side. I knew him only as a master mind, not as an imaginative genius. This was the image he projected.

I remember once when I spoke disparagingly of Dr. Johnson how vehement was his reaction. Dr. Johnson was a hero to him, and he himself has often been compared to Johnson (though he would have repudiated the suggestion), and this is surely revealing. Dr. Johnson also had a powerful intellect with a kind of gap between it and his imagination. Was there the same kind of gap in Lewis's mind that made him, on the one hand, a great critic and a great moralist and later a great writer of children's stories but never, as he had once hoped, a great poet?

This had its effect also on Lewis's understanding of religion. Both he and I came to religion by way of literature. Even before I left Oxford in the summer of 1929, we were beginning to discover together the religious values in literature, and it will be remembered that it was in the autumn of 1929 that he underwent his first conversion to theism. When I left Oxford I undertook a course of reading in philosophy at Lewis's recommendation, and soon afterward I entered on that experiment in common living with two Oxford friends in a small cottage in the country, which was to lead to my own conversion. During all this time Lewis and I kept up copious correspondence, and our reading followed much the same lines. In particular, I began to read the Bible seriously for the first time. But in doing so, I was reading it as literature. I approached it just as I had approached Chaucer and Spenser, Shakespeare and Milton, Wordsworth and Keats. I was looking for a way of life. That which I was leading in a small village in the country, where the daily life of the farm and the cottage reflected the background of many of the Bible stories and the poetry of Wordsworth, gave all this experience a setting in real life. And so my whole life came together in a coherent whole, and I found it after a time as natural to pray as to read poetry or to walk among the hills.

I am not sure how far Lewis's experience differed from mine in this respect. I unfortunately never thought of keeping the many letters he wrote to me at this time, though I kept most of his later ones. There was no thought of fame on his side at this time. We were simply two friends finding our way to what was believed to be the truth, and I don't think that either of us thought that anyone else would be interested in what we had to say to each other. The only letter of mine I can remember was one I wrote commenting on the text, "For as in Adam all die, even so in Christ shall all be made alive." I think that I had then grasped clearly the fact of the solidarity of mankind, that all men together make one man and that Adam, whom St. Paul describes as the "type (or figure) of him who was to come" was representative of all mankind and was a kind of "myth" or symbolic figure of whom Christ was the fulfillment.

It will be remembered that the turning point in Lewis's conversion to theism had been when his friends Dyson and Tolkien had convinced him that in Christ the myth had become history. I think that this understanding of the relation between myth and history was the key to Lewis's conversion to Christianity and in a sense to his whole life. He has described how his first awakening took place when he discovered Siegfried and the Twilight of the Gods, and the world of Norse mythology took possession of his imagination. Later he has described how the "joy," which he experienced in all this romantic literature, began to fade, and he came to think that all he had loved in this world of myth was imaginary, while all that he believed to be real was "grim and meaningless." This was the period when he became an atheist. His mind and his imagination were completely divided. But then the change took place. He read *Phantastes* by George MacDonald (a book I have never been able to read, but in these cases it is not so much the book in itself that is important as the point in one's own development, when a book suddenly sets fire to the imagination), and the world of imagination began to become real for him again.

When I first came into contact with him, Lewis had passed beyond his atheism and reached the stage of belief in a Universal Spirit, such as he described in the *Summa Metaphysica contra Anthroposophos*, though he still would not call this Spirit God, nor was there any thought of prayer to this or any other Spirit. We were both therefore very close to each other at this stage. As we read English literature together, we both began to discover more and more of the religious background of what we were reading. He has described in *Surprised by Joy* how "The Dream of the Rood" and the poetry of Langland, whose Piers Plowman is a figure of Christ, had moved him.

Gradually this Christian mythology, as we both would have called it, began to impress us more and more, and the idea that it might after all be true began to dawn on us. For me the turning point came when I was reading the Bible in my retreat in the Cotswolds with my two friends and I began for the first time since my childhood to pray. For Lewis it had come a little before in the Trinity term of 1929 when he "gave in and admitted that God was God." But for both of us the passage from theism to Christianity had to be made, and it was here that Lewis's sense of the meaning and value of myth helped him so much. He was able to reconcile his imagination and his reason in Christian faith. It will be remembered that he gave as a subtitle to his *Pilgrim's Regress, an Allegorical Apology for Christianity, Reason and Romanticism,* and this expresses exactly how we both came to accept the Christian faith.

It is needless to say that in all this, though the place of imagination was crucial, reason was hard at work all the time. The most obvious fact about Lewis in my first encounter with him was his sheer intellectual power. He could be as witty and amusing as anyone in Oxford and was ready to discuss anything, but he never abated his rigorous criticism of any argument, as he had learned to do in the school of his master Kirkpatrick. It was this union of rigorous critical intellect with rich poetic imagination that, it seems to me, gave Lewis's Christian apologetics such an extraordinary force. But there was another element in it, which I would not have expected. In my first acquaintance with him, Lewis never gave the impression of being a moralist or of having any great psychological insight. No doubt, his intellect was just as active in the moral sphere, and he was learning at this time to relate his life to the demands of morality, but I would never have imagined that he would have developed such astonishing psychological insight, as he showed in *The Screwtape Letters* and in his *Broadcast Talks.* This capacity to speak to the common man and see into the hidden motives in the heart of everyman was something that perhaps came to him together with his Christian faith. In other words, not only his extraordinary imaginative gifts but also his psychological insight were aspects of his personality that escaped me.

During all this time until December 1932, when I became a Benedictine monk, Lewis and I had been moving in the same direction. When I became a Catholic I went on writing, as I had done before, but from then on I came across an impenetrable barrier. Lewis had no desire to follow me in that direction. This was a great disappointment to me. I had felt that I was simply following the path we had both been following to its logical conclusion, and I expected the debate to continue on the same lines.

But obviously the change in my life involved more than I realized. Lewis felt that I was trying to convert him. "You in your charity," he wrote in a letter to me, "are anxious to convert me; but I am not in the least anxious to convert you." I doubt whether I was really anxious to convert him to Catholicism any more than I had wanted to convert him to Christianity. I wanted simply to continue the debate between us, and I was not aware of any change in my attitude. But he complained in another letter: "If you are going to argue with me, you must argue *to* the truth of your position, not *from* it. The opposite procedure only wastes your time and leaves me to reply moved solely by embarrassment, *tu sei santo ma tu non sei filosofo.*" No doubt, I was carried away with enthusiasm for my new faith, and I did not realize how far it was from his. But the problem for me was that this new understanding of the Christian faith was all-important for me, whereas for him it had very little significance.

As he wrote in another letter: "One of the most important differences between us is our estimate of the importance of the differences. . . . You think my specifically Protestant beliefs a tissue of damnable errors; I think your specifically Catholic beliefs a mass of comparatively harmless human traditions that may be fatal to certain souls, but which I think suitable for you." I doubt whether I ever felt that Protestant beliefs were a "tissue of damnable errors." When I passed from Anglicanism to Catholicism, it was not so much with the sense of rejecting anything as it was with a sense of total fulfillment, and it was this that I wanted to share with him.

Lewis went on to say: "I therefore feel no *duty* to attack you; and I certainly feel no *inclination* to add to my other works an epistolary correspondence with one of the toughest dialecticians of my acquaintance, to which he can devote as much time and reading as he likes, and I can devote very little." As my stand with Lewis from the beginning of our acquaintance had been that of an "anti-intellectual" and was to continue so in many ways to the end, I was surprised and rather pleased to be described as a "tough dialectician," but Lewis went on to say: "As well, who wants to debate with a man who begins by saying that no argument can possibly move him?" I think that what I had meant was that my faith would not be influenced by anything he said, but I was only too anxious to share my understanding of the faith, and in this I would have hoped to learn from him as I had done in the past.

The result was that we agreed not to discuss our differences any more, and this was perfectly satisfactory to Lewis; for me it was a great embarrassment. It meant that I could never really touch on much that meant more to me than anything else, and there was always a certain reserve therefore afterward in our relationship. I think that Lewis himself felt this, and he remarked once on this difference between us, which was one not only of faith but also of character and temperament. But in all this it is remarkable how Lewis never gave the faintest sign that he recognized any difference in knowledge or intelligence between us. He always treated me as an equal in every respect, as I believe that he treated all his other friends. In going through his correspondence with me, which covered more than thirty years, I have been touched to see how unvarying was his friendship, how totally he accepted me, appreciating what I said, disagreeing when necessary, but always with complete sincerity, giving his time and attention to answering my letters, as though he had nothing else to do. Only once did he complain when I wrote at Christmas, saying that he had so many letters to answer at Christmas that it had become more of a penitential season for him and begging me to write at other times. I think that it was through him that I really discovered the meaning of friendship.

But apart from personal differences between us, I think that there was one thing that prevented Lewis from ever taking the question of Catholicism *versus* Protestantism very seriously. This was his almost total lack of concern about the Church as an institution. "To me," he wrote in *Surprised by Joy*, "religion ought to have been a matter of good men praying alone, and meeting by twos and threes to talk of spiritual matters." This is surely a very revealing remark. It would be difficult to imagine a more Protestant, a more totally unecclesiastical conception of Christianity than this. And this was what Lewis's character and temperament inclined him to. "The idea of churchmanship," as he wrote in *Surprised by Joy*, "was to me wholly unattractive." It was the externals of church worship that he found so unattractive, " a kind of wearisome, get-together affair." Hymns and organ music were also especially unattractive. "Hymns were (and are) extremely disagreeable to me. Of all musical instruments I liked (and like) the organ least."

To a large extent this feeling remained with him to the end of his life. When I wrote to him a year before he died about Syriac and the liturgy of the Syrian Church in Kerala, he wrote back complimenting me on learning yet another language (though, in fact, I have not been at all successful with Indian languages) but added, "I hardly share one of the purposes for which you use it. I cannot take an interest in liturgiology. I see very well that someone ought to feel it. If religion includes cult and cult requires order, it is somebody's business to be concerned with it. But not, I feel, mine. Indeed, for the laity I sometimes wonder if an interest in liturgiology is not rather a snare. Some people talk as if it were itself the Christian faith."

It can easily be understood why, having this feeling for the Church and her liturgical worship, Lewis felt very little attraction toward Catholicism, even if there were not other factors, such as his Northern-Irish background, which naturally prejudiced him against it. For myself I had probably as little interest in liturgy, originally, as he had, but the concept of the Church as the Mystical Body of Christ (which I had discovered first in Hooker, for whom we both shared a great admiration) had been the leading motive in my becoming a Catholic. From this I went on to see the liturgy of the Church as the worship of the Mystical Body of Christ or Christ himself, as St. Augustine said, praying in his members. Lewis was later to acquire a deep reverence for and understanding of the mystery of the Eucharist, but this aspect of the Church as a worshipping community and of cult as something "sacred," a reflection on earth of a heavenly reality, remained hidden from him.

It is perhaps strange that he, with his passionate interest in pagan mythology, should have missed this aspect of religion, but as far as I recall, though he was interested in myth, he never showed any interest in ritual as the dramatization of the myth. This, again, may have been partly due to the fact that he was personally extremely clumsy with his hands and found any kind of ceremony awkward. He wrote rather amusingly of his admission ceremony at Magdalen: "English people have not the talent for graceful ceremonial. They go through it lumpishly and with a certain mixture of defiance and embarrassment, as if everyone felt that he was being rather silly and was at the same time ready to shoot anyone who said so."

It is remarkable also that Lewis showed very little interest in the Fathers of the Church. With his wide classical culture one would have expected him to be naturally attracted to the Greek and Latin Fathers, but apart from mention of St. Augustine's *Confessions,* I don't remember his ever referring to one of the Fathers. This again would suggest that he had very little sense of the Church as a living organism, growing by stages through the centuries, as Newman portrayed it in his *Development of Christian Doctrine.* In fact, I remember his saying to me once that he thought that Charles Kingsley had the better of the argument with Newman, which produced the *Apologia.* This is surely a surprising judgment and shows how fundamentally unsympathetic he was to the Catholic outlook.

Finally, it must be said that he was most unsympathetic to the revival of Thomism, which was taking place during the thirties and forties. I don't think that he found St. Thomas himself very attractive (though, of course, he appreciated the Thomist elements in the poetry of Dante), and neo-Thomism he objected to most strongly. He wrote to me once: "A man who was an atheist two terms ago and admitted into your Church last term and who had never read a word of philosophy came to me urging me to reread the *Summa* and offering to lend me a copy." One can understand his irritation at this sort of thing, and though it was not due to a rejection of Scholasticism as such, he showed little sympathy with it by continuing: "By the way, I hope that the great revival of religion now going on will not get mixed up with Scholasticism, for I am sure that the renewal of the latter, however salutary, must be as temporary as any other movement in philosophy." This sums up very well his attitude toward Scholasticism. He was not attracted to it himself, and with considerable prescience he regarded it as a movement in philosophy that was destined to pass along with others.

In this connection, it may be worth remarking that Lewis's own defense of the Christian faith at the Socratic Club in Oxford, of which he was president for many years, suffered a similar fate. His arguments for the existence of God were challenged by Elizabeth Anscombe, a Catholic, who was a logical positivist. I remember Lewis saying to me that she had completely demolished his argument and remarking that he thought that, as she was a Catholic, she might at least have provided an alternative argument. Later, he was to write to me: "At the Socratic the enemy often wipe the floor with us." Lewis was certainly disturbed by this but, of course, it did not affect his faith. He had no illusions about the relation of philosophy to faith. As he wrote in the letter, which I have quoted on Scholasticism: "We have no abiding city even in philosophy: all passes except the Word." This is a very profound statement and could be of crucial importance, but I am not sure in what exact sense Lewis intended it. That theology, like philosophy, was also "passing" I think he would have agreed, at least in some sense. The object of Christian faith is the Word of God himself, as Lewis himself had said, and that Word is a "mystery" that can never be fathomed.

Yet, of course, there are some statements like those of the New Testament and some of the Creeds, which are nearer to the truth and therefore more adequate than others. Yet one wonders how far—when in *Miracles*, for instance, Lewis says the "Original Thing must be not a principle or a generality, much less an 'ideal' or a 'value,' but an utterly concrete fact," and again that "no thinking person would in so many words deny that God is concrete and individual"—how far did he take such statements to be necessarily true, and how far he would have allowed that they are analogical statements, which always stand in need of correction. Lewis felt very strongly the danger of abstract and impersonal terms in reference to the Godhead, but perhaps he did not realize sufficiently the equal danger of concrete and personal terms.

This raises the question of his attitude toward mysticism. In the *Letters to Malcolm* Lewis has spoken very clearly on the subject of mysticism. He describes himself as belonging to the "foothills" of prayer. "I do not attempt the precipices of mysticism," he said. Yet when one thinks of the experience of "joy," which he described in *Surprised by Joy*, it would be difficult to deny that this was a mystical experience. He speaks of it as an experience of "unsatisfied desire," which was itself "more desirable than any other satisfaction," and he has no hesitation in calling it the "central" experience of his life. Now the specific character of mystical experience is its ineffability. He himself remarked in *Letters to Malcolm* that "one thing common to all mysticism is the temporary shattering of our ordinary spatial and temporal consciousness and our discursive intellect." But as he shrewdly observes, this negative aspect of mystical experience is not everything. "The value of this negative experience," as he says, "must depend on the nature of the positive experience for which it makes room." This is something that is often forgotten when speaking of mystical experience. For

Lewis it was the search for the origin of this joy, which he had experienced, which was the "central story of [his] life."

It was to lead him, of course, to the discovery first of God in the traditional sense and then of Christianity. The question is whether in becoming a Christian Lewis reached the fulfillment of mystical experience. I think that he would have replied in the negative. There is no doubt that he had a profound kind of mystical intuition, which gave him such an extraordinary insight into the mysteries of Christian faith, and there are times, especially in the *Letters to Malcolm,* when he comes near to a genuine mystical insight. But on the whole, he was so much on his guard against any kind of pantheism and so much inclined, as he confessed, to go as near to dualism as possible that he generally stops short of mysticism. Perhaps his very emphasis on the Person of God and the Incarnation made it difficult for him to go "beyond personality" and experience the presence of God beyond all images and concepts, which is characteristic of mystical experience. I had some correspondence with him on this subject, and I remember that he did not seem to understand the point I was making. I think that he regarded mystical experience as a rare event to which the ordinary Christian (with whom he would have classed himself) need not aspire.

I think that Lewis's understanding of the place of mystical experience in religious life and the whole problem of the relation of the Personal God to the absolute Godhead would have grown if he had been able to make a deeper study of Hinduism. In *Surprised by Joy* he had written that there were really only two possible answers to the question, Where was the fullness of religion to be found?—namely, either in Hinduism or in Christianity. Long before, he had written to me: "You will remember that long ago you and I had agreed, being still unbelievers, that Hinduism and Christianity were the only two things worth serious consideration. I still think that it was a sound decision." But Lewis was never able to study Hinduism in depth, and the objections he raised to it in *Surprised by Joy* were not altogether relevant. But he did touch on what I would consider the essential difference—the question of myth and history. Yet I think that he was inclined to think that myth was an expression of the childhood of humanity, which modern man had outgrown.

The meeting of myth and history in the Incarnation was the turning point in the history of religion, as he had realized. But it was not simply that myth had been fulfilled in history and was now outgrown, but rather that myth was revealed as a dimension of history and history as a dimension of myth. History is not simply a record of events abstracted from the context of the total reality, but the record of events realized in the total context of reality, human and divine, as is seen in the biblical revelation. And myth is not simply an ideal, symbolic expression of ultimate reality, but an expression of the ultimate meaning of life in the context of actual history. To speak of the "myth of the God incarnate" can therefore be a perfectly accurate expression, provided that it is properly understood. This raises the question of how far, if he had lived, Lewis would have been influenced by the new currents in theology and biblical criticism that have developed since the Second Vatican Council. It is impossible to answer the question, but it would have been of great interest to have been able to follow his thoughts in this direction.

This whole question of myth is relevant because Lewis himself had the myth-making faculty so highly developed. It is remarkable how, in his later years, he was driven to express himself more and more in terms of myth, in the planetary novels and above all in the Narnia stories, which I am sometimes inclined to regard as his greatest work. It is perhaps significant that the book to which he attached the greatest value, *Till We Have Faces,* is at once the most profoundly mythical of all his writings and one of the least popular. Perhaps there was something in him that was striving for expression and could not find a completely adequate form. My suggestion is that the mythmaker and the poet in him were never quite reconciled with the philosopher and the moralist, or rather that they did not reach the supreme fulfillment in the poetry of prophecy, as one might have hoped. But this is a very delicate question, which cannot really be answered.

In making these criticisms I would be understood as putting forward an argument, just as I would have done if Lewis were alive, and there is nothing I would wish more than that he were alive to answer such questions. When I look over the years of our friendship, I realize how much I owed to the constant stimulus of his critical mind and to the inspiration of his kindness. When we last met, a month before his death, he reminded me that we had been friends for nearly forty years. There are not many things in my life more precious to me than that friendship.

# 3
## *About Anthroposophy*
### A. C. HARWOOD

During the lifetime of C. S. Lewis not a few people found in his various works—perhaps especially in his imaginative works—ideas, descriptions, allusions that seemed so close to anthroposophy that they wrote to ask him if he got them from Steiner. They *accuse* me, he once said, of being an anthroposophist. This of course he was not. He had a natural horror of the occult, to which he gave no favourable image in his imaginative works. He knew of course—and he was shocked to know—that some of his old friends had found Christianity through Steiner's work, but in the first published work in which he alludes to it, *The Pilgrim's Regress*, he places the shire *Anthroposophia* abutting on *Occultica* and bounded by the *Palus Theosophica*.

But even if his dislike and distrust of the occult were instinctive rather than discriminative, he was always prepared to argue the case—and no one could argue with greater force and clarity. In those letters of his that I have preserved (alas, not all) he advances in succession three main objections to anthroposophy. One he withdrew, one he modified, but the third remained an insuperable obstacle.

The first objection appears in a letter bearing the postmark 28 October 1926. It was just after the publication, under a pseudonym, of his long poem *Dymer*. The letter first touches on some criticism of this work, and continues:

About powers other than reason—I would be sorry if you mistook my position. No one is more convinced than I that reason is utterly inadequate to the richness and spirituality of real things; indeed this is itself a deliverance of reason. Nor do I doubt the presence, even in us, of faculties embryonic or atrophied that lie in an indefinite margin around the little finite bit of focus that is intelligence—faculties anticipating or remembering the possession of huge tracts of reality that slip through the meshes of the intellect. And, to be sure, I believe that the symbols presented by imagination at its height are the working of that fringe and present to us as much of the superintelligible reality as we can get while we retain our present form of consciousness. My skepticism begins when people offer me explicit accounts of the superintelligible and in so doing use all the categories of the intellect. If the higher worlds have to be represented in terms of number, subject and attribute, time, space, causation, etc. (and thus they nearly always are represented by occultists and illuminati), the fact that knowledge of them had to come through the fringe remains inexplicable. It is more rational to suppose in such cases that the illuminati have done what all of us are tempted to do: allowed their intellect to fasten on those hints that come from the fringe, and squeezing them has (? *have*) made a hint (that was full of truth) into a mere false hard statement. Seeking to know (in the only way we can know) more, we know less. I, at any rate, am at present inclined to believe that we must be content to feel the highest truths "in our bones": if we try to make them explicit, we really make them untruths. At all events, if more knowledge is to come it must be the wordless and thoughtless knowledge of the mystic; not the celestial statistics of Swedenborg, the Lemurian history of Steiner, or the demonology of the Platonists. All this seems to me merely an attempt to know the superintelligible *as if it were a new slice of the intelligible*: as though a man with a bad cold tried to get back smells with a microscope. Unless I greatly misunderstand you, you are (in a way) more rationalist than I, for you would reject as mere ideology my "truth felt in the bones." All this, by the bye, is meant for exposition not arguement [*sic*].

I cannot resist adding part of the conclusion of this letter that is so characteristic of the sheer humanity of Lewis that shines through all his letters.

I should dearly like a visit. . . . But seriously, are you certain that I shall not be a bother? I know that even an intimate friend cannot come to a house without disturbing to some extent the even tenor of its way—and there is the *parvus puer*.[1] Please make quite sure about this; and above all don't let

---

[1] Our first child then five months old.

Daphne persuade herself that it won't be a bother, because she thinks you'd enjoy having me. The fact that you have inflicted the whole of *Dymer* on her—

> ("Unhappy fate the poet's wife attends—
> He reads his own stuff, and he reads his friends.")

has given me such large ideas of her altruism that I am afraid.

I have no copy of any reply I sent to this letter. I should of course have told him that Steiner is always lamenting the difficulty of conveying spiritual perceptions in the language of the senses and of reason, and that the ultimate grasp of spiritual things comes through the raising into consciousness (through Intuition) of the "truth felt in the bones" to which he refers. If he had already written his essay called "Bluspels and Flalansferes" (which he had not), I could have pointed to his own conception of "magistral metaphors"—metaphors in which one who knows some truth directly clothes his knowledge in a picture in order to make it intelligible —or partly intelligible—to a less-advanced mind.

In comparing Steiner to Swedenborg, Lewis is here applying to the former Dr. Johnson's criticism of the latter, which I once heard him quote: "Sir, if he had seen *unspeakable* things he would have been more *reticent* about them."

It was about this time also that Lewis wrote a *Summa Metaphysica contra Anthroposophos*. But in a letter, not to me but to my first wife Daphne, dated March 28, 1933, he withdrew from this position, while at the same time advancing a second criticism of anthroposophy. He wrote:

> I am glad you never read my *Summa,* for all that is dead as mutton to me now: and the points chiefly at issue between the anthroposophists and me then were *precisely* the points on which anthroposophy is certainly right— i.e., the claim that it is possible for man, here and now, in the phenomenal world, to have commerce with the world beyond—which is what I was denying. The present difference between us is quite other. The only thing that I now would object eagerly to anthroposophy is that I don't think it can say, "I believe in one God the Father Almighty." My feeling is that even if there are a thousand orders of beneficent beings above us, still the universe is a cheat unless at the back of them all there is the one God of Christianity. But I did not mean to raise controversial points: there is certainly quite a lot

for us to agree on as against nearly the whole contemporary world! I would quite agree, for instance, with your discovery that it is the *Will* wh. lets the cat out of the bag—and also with your refusal to read Croce. His is the kind of idealism that for all practical purposes is indistinguishable from materialism. What a ghastly pun that his name should mean "Blessed Cross." I don't understand the point about the eternal feminine (and masculine) in your letter, and look forward to hearing more about it when next we meet. . . .

I suppose a suitable reply was sent to this letter. The Trinity of Father, Son, and Holy Spirit is as vital to anthroposophy as it is to the Athanasian Creed. But it would seem that the immense importance attached to the "Mystery of Golgotha" in anthroposophy, not only for the individual human soul but also for the whole evolution of the world—an importance of which he certainly received some knowledge from his anthroposophical friends—seemed to him to obliterate rather than enhance the importance of the Father. For as late as 1946 in a letter to a minister of religion, who had written to him asking his opinion of anthroposophy and who was kind enough to show me this letter, Lewis wrote that anthroposophy, while possessing many points of agreement with orthodox religion, was a kind of "inverted Arianism," giving a higher place to the Son than to the Father. Naturally I expostulated with him over this view, but I never felt that I convinced him, even though he withdrew the letter in question.

There was a third matter, however, that he felt divided him most deeply from anthroposophy. In the letters I have preserved, it grows out of a correspondence he had (again with my wife) in March 1942 on the subject of "being in love." The first of these letters is an excellent example of his vigour of style and lucidity of argument.

My view of being in love [he writes] is that (like everything except God and the Devil) it is better than some things and worse than others. Thus it comes in my scale of values higher than lust, selfishness, or frigidity, but lower than charity or constancy—in fact about on a level with friendship. Like everything (except God and the Devil) it therefore is sometimes opposed to things lower than itself and is—in that situation—good: sometimes to things higher than itself and is—in that situation—bad. . . . The trouble arises when poets and others set up this thing (good in certain conditions with its own proper degree of goodness) as an absolute. Which many do. . . . Treat "Love" as a god and you in fact make it a fiend. . . . As to Fate, which

I call Providence—I believe that the coming together of a man and woman, like everything else (e.g., the fall of a sparrow) is in the hand of God. In our society this (word illegible) is usually displayed in the form of mutual "falling in love." In the society to which our Lord spoke about "one flesh" this was not so: marriages were usually arranged by parents—and so in the vast majority of times and places.

The answer to this letter—evidently suggesting an evolution in the basis of matrimony—received a reply as follows:

I doubt if we differ as fundamentally as appears. I don't "pooh-pooh any evolution in morals" but neither do I know the future, and so I cannot say that the recent N. W. European development has come to stay, nor do I know whether it is an improvement. . . . But my main feeling is, as I said in my last letter, that what we specially need to emphasise is the "Neither is this Thou" aspect. If one is taught to treat even religious emotion as a mere servant wh. must never be allowed to rule, how much more must we think this of erotic emotion! All these things, in my view, are capable of *receiving* spiritual value, but can't *give* it. And the moment they forget their *creaturely* status they become demons. I think the real difference between us is on a more general topic wh. I can't well go into now—I don't think the conception of *creatureliness* is part of your philosophy at all, and your system is anthropocentric. That's the real "great divide."

I think that Lewis could never have accepted the idea that man is on the way to becoming a tenth hierarchy—a unique hierarchy of freedom and love. Once, when we were talking about freedom, he made a statement I have never forgotten: "I was not born to be free—I was born to adore and obey." I think he was right in describing this as the "great divide."

On a more human level I fear his anthroposophical friends must sometimes have irritated him. In one of the letters to my wife, already quoted, he takes her up for accusing him of bowing to authority.

As for "increasing Authoritarianism" [he wrote], well! If that doesn't take the bun. When you have heard half as many sentences beginning "Christianity teaches" from me as I have heard ones beginning "Steiner says" from you and Cecil (Harwood) and Owen (Barfield) and Wof (Captain Field)— why then we'll start talking about authoritarianism! I humbly put out a few platitudes about marriage that could be paralleled in several moralists; you reply with an exact account of which species of angels are concerned in human love affairs! You may be right and I wrong. But which is the more authoritarian?

I think I should really leave Lewis with the last word, which he was very capable of having. But as his letter mentions Captain Field, I may be allowed to add a sentence he wrote about him on hearing of his death: "Wof was the most completely lovable man, almost, I have known. I am so glad to have known him that it almost obliterates the loss."

# PART TWO
## *Master*

# 4

## *A Prophet*

### ERIK ROUTLEY

I CAN'T SAY THAT I MET LEWIS PERSONALLY more than two or three
times; but I gladly set down a few memories that will remain with me as
long as I live. Oxford during 1939–45 was a sombre place. I took my first
graduation examinations in June 1940, and I shan't soon forget the way
the invigilator said before the first session, "You will be advised, if our
postal services are still in operation, whether you are required to attend
an oral examination." We thought we might well be all required to speak
German by September (those were the pre-Eisenhower days). As I look
back on those student days of mine the one thing I am profoundly thankful for was that they were the years when C. S. Lewis and Charles Williams were doing their astounding double act in Oxford. One can't think
of one without the other (Lewis would have been the first to insist on that).
Lewis regarded his Christian lay ministry as his "war work," and did his
best to give it up (except for his writings) as soon as the war ended. But
what days those were!

Actually I was from 1936 to 1940 an undergraduate at Magdalen,
Lewis's college, and until 1939 I didn't know who he was (Magdalen was
an uncomfortable and fragmented society in those years). But on the second Sunday of the first term of the war, in October 1939, I saw that he was
billed to preach in the University Church. It was odd enough in those days
to have a preacher there who wasn't a clergyman of the Church of England, and I thought I would go along. The service was held at 8:00 P.M.

on Sunday, and I suppose I arrived about ten minutes before eight. There
was hardly a seat to be had. The one I got was right under the pulpit. I
could see the preacher only when he was going up the steps—and I said
to myself, "So *that's* Lewis!" The church was dim; only minimal lighting
was allowed, and most of us had to sing the hymns from memory. But
Lewis gave us the sermon called "Learning in Wartime," which was, I
suppose, his debut as a preacher. "A Syrian ready to perish was my father,"
from Deuteronomy, chapter 26, was his text.

I think the next time he preached was in June 1941, and this one was
"The Weight of Glory." This time it was a summer evening, so lighting
was no problem; but the place was packed solid long before the service
began. The last hymn was "Bright the Vision that Delighted." The sermon
took three quarters of an hour to deliver; its stunning effect is something
one can hardly communicate. Just to read it now is to be captivated by its
uncanny combination of sheer beauty and severe doctrine. Here, you feel
even when reading, and you felt ten times more so when listening, was a
man who had been laid hold of by Christ and who enjoyed it.

Lewis had a superbly unaffected delivery—a deep voice that went well
with his cheerful and bucolic appearance (all pictures of him that I know
are good ones). It was a voice that really did vindicate the saying that the
medium is the message. No rhetorical tricks; he read every word. Yet the
way he used words as precision tools, the effortless rhythm of the sentences,
the scholarship made friendly, the sternness made beautiful—these things
all made it impossible for the listener to notice the passing of time. I call
this passage a "vintage" example of his style—it comes from this very
sermon:

At present we are on the outside of the world, the wrong side of the door.
We discern the freshness and purity of morning, but they do not make us
fresh and pure. We cannot mingle with the splendours we see. But all the
leaves of the New Testament are rustling with the rumour that it will not
always be so. Some day, God willing, we shall get *in*.

I would counsel any preacher, or any public speaker, to study every
letter of that short passage; to notice how many of its words are of one syl-
lable; and what contrasting effect the two-syllable words have. Who else
would have spoken of the leaves of the New Testament "rustling"? That's

poetry in the service of the Gospel. Well—imagine what it was like to *hear* that.

But Lewis's main work was not preaching—he would do it when asked, but what he probably did more comfortably was more informal. In those days when the university term was on, you never knew where you'd find him next. John Wain gives a very good picture of the Socratic Club in his autobiographical book, *Sprightly Running*; that was a weekly meeting for good-humored and high-level Christian debate, where students crowded into a room and sat on the floor or under the piano, and Lewis took the chair. Somebody, I remember, who'd been drinking deep of positivist philosophy, asked in the course of discussion, "Well, how can you prove anything? I mean, how can you prove there isn't a blue cow sitting on that piano?" To which Lewis replied, "Well, in what sense *blue?*"

Sometimes some learned men would produce a defense of agnosticism or an assault on Christianity. That was the signal for Lewis to reply. I heard him deliver *extempore* a satisfying devastation of such an attempt by A. L. Rowse, a distinguished man of letters. "Mr. Rowse," I recall Lewis saying, "reminds me of a friend of mine called Bulver, whose wife has perfected what I call the technique of Bulverism. When Mr. Bulver remarked to his wife that the three angles of a triangle together add up to 180 degrees, Mrs. Bulver replied, 'You say that because you're a man.' " (There's a section on this in *The Pilgrim's Regress*, you will remember.) The point was, of course, that attributing an argument to a temperament didn't invalidate the argument. Then there was the hilarious occasion when Lewis and Charles Williams were in a double bill in Magdalen College dining hall— I don't know how many hundred crammed themselves in—to talk about "Free Love." (That was when the permissive society was still underground.) With terrifying conviviality they demolished "free love" and expounded the Christian teaching on sex. How solemn and boring it would be nowadays if anybody tried to do it!

Lewis always said he owed everything to Charles Williams. In a sense he mediated Charles Williams to ordinary people. Williams was a genius, of course; him, I think, you absolutely had to hear in the flesh. As a writer he is brilliant but tough. As a speaker he was electrifying—that spluttering London accent, those streaks of energy that sparked out of him, that faculty for recreating a whole scene of Shakespeare by dancing from one side of the rostrum to the other and taking each part as it came. Williams talked at about two hundred and fifty words to the minute, Lewis about half that speed. Williams was a tenor, Lewis a bass. Williams was thin and intense, Lewis comfortable and placid. Williams smoked cigarettes, Lewis a pipe. On Williams's sudden death in 1945, Lewis wrote unforgettably, "When he died it was our idea of death that changed."

I am conscious that much of what I write will be known. But I do want to express the hope that you people know and value one of Lewis's earliest Christian works, *The Pilgrim's Regress,* which I mentioned previously. My final memory of those otherwise dim Oxford days is sitting up unto the small hours night after night with the first edition of that book—the one without the preface and the running headline—working out what it was all about: getting inside his "north-south" pattern and understanding all the allegorical references on every page. I did this with my friend who shared my lodging and is now my brother-in-law. We took some satisfaction, when the explained edition came out, in finding that we had pretty well got it right. That, I remember, and the *Summa Theologica* of St. Thomas Aquinas, more or less kept us sane.

I know myself what others know far better—how unfailingly courteous Lewis was in answering letters. I think I corresponded with him on three or four occasions. If I said I was on the outer fringe of his acquaintance, I'd probably be doing myself more than justice. I can't ever have been more to him than just one more confounded writer of letters. But there was a reply every time—it might be quite brief (Lewis had a habit of writing all his letters continuously on a sheet of typing paper and snipping them off in strips, but it was always written for you and for nobody else.

I think this was his great secret. He hated casual contacts; human contact must, for him, be serious and concentrated and attentive, or it was better avoided. It might be for a moment only, but that was its invariable quality.

That is not only why so many people have precious memories of him; it is also why he couldn't write three words without the reader's feeling that they were written for him and him alone. It's why his massive books of scholarship read as delightfully as his children's stories, and why he's one of the few preachers who can be read without losing their message.

True courtesy has its roots in precision, not in casualness. That's true of personalities and of writers. If ever there were a man who exploded the slander that "academic" means remote, dull, and inhuman, that man was Lewis.

If this is true it explains why he is at present, in his own country, so scandalously undervalued, especially among theologians. His courtesy was formidable. His skill was never unkind. Qualities such as those are quoted pretty low on our stock exchange just now. So thank goodness there are people in the United States who seek to keep his memory alive. But then we know what J. B. Phillips said about him in *The Ring of Truth*: how shortly after death, Lewis came into his room and was present with him for a moment, "a *red* vision, glowing with health." Having met both Lewis and Phillips I entirely believe in the veracity of that vision. My best wish would be that he would from time to time haunt me just like that.

# 5
## *A Solid Man*

### LUKE RIGBY, O.S.B.

After almost thirty years, my recollections of C. S. Lewis will be hazy, to say the least. Since Mr. Lewis's renown has spread way beyond expectation, I must beware of fantasy, of gathering into my recollections impressions I have gained from subsequent hearsay and reading.

I went up to Oxford in October 1944 to read English. I was at Saint Benet's Hall, a private hall where the young monks of Ampleforth Abbey, as well as those of other English monasteries, lived and attended the university. It was an Oxford decimated by war but steadfastly maintaining an academic program. Mr. Lewis agreed to be my tutor, since his college, Magdalen, lacked students to fill his schedule.

The relationship of tutor and undergraduate in the English school in those days was a simple one: they met each week for an hour; the under-graduate read to the tutor an essay assigned the previous week; the tutor would comment on the essay and would add his own reflections upon the subject at hand; finally a subject would be assigned for the following week, together with a reading list. I suppose it was the ultimate in self-study. Mr. Lewis tutored me in English literature, covering mainly the Eliza-bethan and Restoration Dramatists and John Milton.

I will divide my recollection into three: of the man, the tutor, the lecturer.

Mr. Lewis was no academician in the narrow sense. In appearance and manner, he was hale and hearty—a big man, ruddy of complexion, rarely separated from his pipe in tutorials and often with a mug of beer. He dressed in tweeds and flannels (jacket and trousers, respectively) verging on the shabby, and I have a strangely detailed memory of a tattered pair of carpet slippers. His appearance both reflected and belied the man within. It reflected the warmth and geniality of the man—a true kindness that soon put a green and overawed freshman at his ease; it reflected a straightforward and down-to-earth condemnation of the pseudo—the shoddy and the insincere.

On the other hand, it belied the depth of his learning that I was early to witness; it belied, too, the poetic and personal sensitivity that was evident in his perceptive enthusiasm and appreciation of beauty in words; in particular I think it belied what I was but dimly aware of at the time, the sensitive and lonesome man of vision. What stands out in my memory is the warmth of the man. He was always welcoming and showed total interest and concern. The startling contrast between his achievement in the world of literature and my mediocre promise did not open a gulf; he was the true master, the true teacher. He shared his appreciation and enthusiasm and thereby instilled confidence and demanded effort; to some extent he was a hard taskmaster but that seemed good. I cannot say I was close to Mr. Lewis on a personal level as was one of my undergraduate friends in Magdalen. I was his pupil for a year only and finding my feet in college. I did not know him as counselor and friend, a role he had for not a few undergraduates.

Before I went up to Oxford, a warm and wise counselor with perhaps a sombre cast of mind said to me: "The university will be for you a lesson in humility. What you may learn of your subject will not compare in value with what you learn from being in contact with minds immeasurably more gifted than your own; you will marvel at the potential of the human mind." Mr. Lewis provided me with my first and most abiding lesson in this sphere. Again, the recollection I have is superficial, but I hope it conveys something of the quality of Mr. Lewis's learning. He would call upon me to read my essay, as often as not busying himself with the selection of a pipe and then filling and lighting it; it didn't take long to realize that such extraneous activity didn't impair his listening. He would sit there and comment in detail on the essay, correcting this or that, elaborating on a theme, proposing an entirely different theory or simply pouring out his own reflections on the particular author or work. To note it all down without shorthand was a feat. He never referred to a text, all the while illustrating his points with hearty declamations of some minor Elizabethan tragedy or a remarkably sensitive rendering of the verse forms, say, in *Samson Agonistes*. I clearly recollect coming away without depression and yet so aware of how little I had perceived (and not infrequently how facile had been my perception) after Mr. Lewis had shared something of his vision with me.

My recollections of Mr. Lewis as a lecturer who invariably filled his lecture hall are not so vivid. I heard him lecture mostly on the medieval background to English literature; this was very much the same material that he used in *The Allegory of Love*. I recollect struggling to absorb the closely reasoned, profusely illustrated material. Invariably I would have to go back to *Allegory* to try and sort it out or would have to seek elucidation from him at my next tutorial. I was under no illusions about where the limitations lay; however I believe Mr. Lewis was more adept with a pen in his hand or on a one-to-one basis round the fire in his rooms at Magdalen.

Rarely did the question of theology or churchmanship blossom into prolonged discussion. I had not started my theological studies and found my energies well absorbed in literature. It is hearsay to talk of his absorbing interest in and concern for the Christian faith. I do recall indirect references that showed a deep knowledge of the works of medieval theologians, notably St. Thomas Aquinas and Duns Scotus. Of course, his circle of friends included several medievalists, among them the Dominican theologian, historian, and lecturer, Father Gervase Mathews. It is one of those quirks of memory that I recall a clerihew said to have been Mr. Lewis's on Father Gervase:

> Father Gervase
> Makes inaudible surveys
> On little-known sages
> Of the Middle Ages.

Perhaps I can end with that. He was a man with friends—this is well known. Though I was in a different league, I know why he had friends. The kindness, sensitivity, the zest for life, the fun, the deep sense of humor, the seriousness, the depths, the unexpectedness: they combined to make a man who was exhilarating to be with.

# 6

## *The Tutor: A Portrait*

### DEREK BREWER

THE MOST INTENSE PARTS OF MY EXPERIENCES in Magdalen as an undergraduate, 1941–42 and 1945–47, were mainly from reading literature and from the tutorials that were so closely connected with them. One very good reason for this was my good fortune in having C. S. Lewis as a tutor. This meant a weekly meeting of an hour with him in his room for seven eight-week terms in order to read him an essay and discuss the subject with him. Within this range I got to know Lewis reasonably well because of the generous richness of his mind and temperament.

On my return from the war I also met him at dinner with friends once a term, and I saw him on a few other occasions, but deep as was my respect and liking for him, I cannot claim to have known him well. I was never one of his inner circle and knew nothing directly of his private and family life. I was much too shy to call him Jack, as many did, and this must have corresponded to some inner reserve in himself, for even I, like everyone else, managed to call his friend and contemporary, the uproarious and witty Hugo Dyson, by his Christian name. So I saw Lewis from a very specific point of view, on the basis of our common interest and, as it were, professional relationship. I never consulted him (or any one else) about my personal affairs.

An Oxford tutor is very different from a Cambridge tutor, and perhaps from that of any other university. By no means have all Oxford tutors been as conscientious and efficient, let alone as brilliant, as Lewis. He was an unusually good example of the ideal. The ideal itself was very much of its own time and place, and perhaps even in Oxford modern life makes it increasingly hard to achieve. It conceived of learning as a way of life, exemplified by the bachelor fellows who normally lived in the college. They read books in their own rooms, where they lived, not in "offices"; they had no secretaries. Their reading, thinking, and writing were part of a unified life, neither "job," nor "recreation," because they were both. And the fellows included, *mutatis mutandis*, scientists as well as arts-men. They did not, strictly speaking, "teach." In the mornings and evenings of term they were visited in their rooms by arrangement by their pupils, who "read the subject with them." It was not exactly an egalitarian society, but there was a sense of fundamental equality and unity, divided into ranks and stages. I had no doubt, at the age of eighteen, that for all the differences of temperament, intelligence, ability, learning, repute, and age between me and this distinguished, jolly man, we were nevertheless of the same kind, engaged in the same pursuit. And the reason I felt this was no doubt because that was how Lewis treated me. I was not a schoolboy to be taught and disciplined, not a "student," but a "man" in his college, who came to "read with him," and he treated me more or less as an equal without thinking about it. On the whole, this attitude, derived from the nineteenth century (of which Lewis and I were natural inhabitants) managed to last in many English universities until the disturbances of the late sixties and early seventies.

Lewis, like the ideal he exemplified, and like the whole school of English at Oxford, was empirical and pragmatical, with an unself-conscious innocence about his underlying literary assumptions, unaware that there could be other valid assumptions, but he felt, and even, I suspect, took a pride, in being old-fashioned—typical again in this respect. In his Inaugural Lecture as first Professor of Medieval and Renaissance Literature at Cambridge, he referred to himself as one of the last examples of Old Western Man, almost as antiquated as a dinosaur. There is in this self-dramatisation an apocalyptic touch not uncommon in his generation, but he was right. Changes in university, society, and in the Western world and the developing professionalisation and fragmentation of literary studies on the model of science have eroded the old ideal. But it was strong in Lewis. Being a tutor was for thirty years his bread and butter, very much his central workaday preoccupation.

Before he went to Cambridge his writing, apart from his two, big, learned books, was done mostly in the evenings, when he was too tired (as he once said to me) for serious work. He wrote because he could hardly stop himself, running off a few pages on return to his room late at night, just for the fun of it, writing at his table with his steel-nibbed dip-pen. He threw a lot away. "It's easy enough to get published," he once said to me. "The difficulty is to get people to *read* your stuff." Even his religious books were in this sense by-products. His primary energy went into tutorial teaching.

He did not particularly enjoy it. How pleased one would be, he remarked at the end of a tutorial with me, if, while staying at a hotel, one met a man with whom one could pass an hour talking about literature; yet what a bore tutorials are, doing the same thing! One of the many reasons why he loved having the chair at Cambridge was that it relieved him, as it was clear Oxford never would, from the heavy labour of constant daily tutorials.

Those who knew him slightly but were not given tutorials by him tended to assume that in a tutorial he would be hectoring. That was far from the truth. There was perhaps something sharp and schoolmasterly about his lectures, deriving from his conviction, energy, and clarity of mind, not from any desire to dominate. He despised teaching. What worse, he once said, than to teach those who are going to teach others, to teach others, to teach, etc. Yet I suppose that many of his pupils became teachers of one sort or another, and all, or most of them, became his friends. He said to me after his Cambridge move that a life of teaching had been a great good fortune to him because it had given him so many friends so much younger than himself.

Since he "taught" (though that is not exactly the right word for his conduct of tutorials) the whole of the Oxford syllabus, extending from Old English to 1830, including a history of the language paper and a would-be theoretical paper, a pupil could know him better than one knows a tutor in the nowadays more usual systems whereby students tend to have several tutors or supervisors, more or less specialized.

I first met Lewis when I was being viva'd (examined orally) for a demyship (i.e., scholarship) at Magdalen in March 1941 when I was seventeen. Waiting on my own in a little book-filled study in St. John's Quad, I panted with nervousness. The interview was conducted in a large, pleasant sitting room, in the presence of three or four dons sitting about in armchairs. They did everything they could to put a nervous, provincial grammar-school boy as much at ease as one can be at the crisis of one's life, when all that one desires is at stake. The plump cheerful man, with a large, red countryman's face and a loud voice, who rolled his r's, and who asked most of the questions, was Lewis, though I did not know it. One or two bits of the discussion are burned into my memory. Lewis asked me some general question about Johnson. "Which Johnson do you mean?" I asked, cautiously. "Ben or Sam?" "Oh, either!" So I replied, "I know nothing about either!" He agreed that my misquotation from Milton's *Samson Agonistes*, "All weakness is wickedness," might well represent Milton's own view.

Later Lewis wrote me in his own hand in response to a query about what books I should read. I imagine that it was the first time I had ever been addressed as Mr.

> Magdalen College
> Oxford,
> April 8th, 1941
>
> Dear Mr. Brewer,
>
> Congratulations on your Demyship. The answer to your question depends a little on whether, as is most likely, you are liable to Military Service and what the calling-up age is likely to be by October. In the meantime, however, as a basis for any English studies, the following cd. hardly be wrong.
>
> 1. Greek is largely irrelevant, but if you know any Latin *keep it up*. I shd. make large use of the Loeb Library (you know—with Lat. & Eng. on opposite pages) getting the hang of things from the Eng. & turning to the Latin for the important bits. The most *relevant* books are the *Aeneid,* Ovid's *Metamorphoses,* Boethius *De Consolatione Philosophiae,* & Cicero *De Republica* (the part at the end about Scipio's Dream). If you can't scan hexameters, learn how to.
>
> 2. A fairly sound biblical background is assumed by most of the older Eng. writers: if you lack this, acquire it. The most relevant books are the historical books of the O. T., the Psalms, & the Gospel of (say) St. Luke. (The Vulgate is very easy Lat. & reading it is a good way of keeping up the language & getting scriptural knowledge at the same time.)
>
> 3. Chaucer, Shakespeare, Milton are certainties whatever shortened course or ordinary course you take. Next to these in importance come

Malory, Spenser, Donne, Browne, Dryden, Pope, Swift, Johnson, Wordsworth. After that it becomes more a matter of taste. The great thing is to be always reading but not to get bored—treat it not like work, more as a vice! Your book bill ought to be your biggest extravagance.

Write freely again if I can help.

Yours sincerely,
C. S. Lewis.

In the following October (1941) I came up for a year. One visited Lewis on the Saturday morning at the beginning of the eight-week term when one "came up," and one "went down" on the last Saturday. He suggested lectures that one might (and, alas, usually did not) attend, and arranged a time for the weekly tutorial. At each of these he also gave one the reading for the following week, sometimes pointing out the most important texts. Rarely did he suggest any critical books, and in those days there were indeed few that were much good. Neither he nor anyone else ever mentioned to me such names as I. A. Richards or F. R. Leavis. Nor did Lewis ever mention his own work. When in a discussion of Addison I quoted some published opinion of his own at him, he said, "Ah, if you ever become a tutor, never publish anything!"—advice that a number of Oxford dons must have taken and given.

Lewis's method was not unfamiliar to me. I had been taught by brilliant men at my grammar school, the Crypt School, Gloucester, on my own, and in the Oxford way of concentrating on actual texts and their historical meaning, rather than on modern critical books. Lewis's education had been similar. In 1959 he said to me that he had read few critics and been little influenced by them; though some very bad literary historians had influenced him greatly when young. I wish I had asked him for their names.

He wrote me another equally characteristic and Oxonian letter of advice when I was returning from the army just after the war. This time it was typed, a little unevenly, by his brother the major, signed by Lewis, and given a reference number that emphasizes, though I doubt if it were meant to, the hugeness of his correspondence. It is on a strip of typing paper three-inches deep, just big enough to hold the text.

REF. 337/1/45                                              Magdalen College,
                                                           Oxford.
                                                           19th September, 1945.

Dear Brewer,

I think, in view of the book famine, most of your spare time had better be spent in secondhand bookshops picking up all the major English writers you can lay your hands on. If you've sold or lost your original O. E. books, try to replace them at once (Wardale's *Grammar*, Sweet's *Primer*, and *Reader*, Klaeber's *Beowulf* or, failing that, Chambers'). For the rest, just read as much as you can. I'm delighted to hear that you are coming back.

Yours,
C. S. Lewis

Tutorials were held once a week, lasted an hour, and in 1941 I was on my own. Even when I returned, 1945–47, though there was some pairing, for several terms I had a tutorial to myself; and in my first year it seemed, and still seems, an amazing privilege for an earnest boy of eighteen; no wonder Lewis felt them a bit of a labour. I used to knock on his door as the hour struck from Magdalen Tower, and usually my successor was equally prompt. In the crowded days just after the war, he gave tutorials from 10:00 A.M. to 1:00 P.M. and 5:00 P.M. to 7:00 P.M., (apart from one or two lectures) from Monday to Friday. A heavy load.

He had a set in the middle of the handsome eighteenth-century New Building at Magdalen. The high-ceilinged principal room faced north over the deer park, and we met there in groups for Old and Middle English translation and occasionally for individual tutorials. A door led off to a bedroom, and another to a small inner room, with windows looking south to the rest of the college, where Lewis kept his books and where we often had tutorials. All the furniture was very shabby. A large table filled the middle of the main room, where he wrote, with wooden chairs around, and there were a couple of battered armchairs by the marble fireplace in which we sat opposite each other for tutorials. There was a smell of pipe tobacco. My most vivid memory of Lewis in this room is during the great freeze-up in the winter of early 1947, when there was no heating, and he sat in his armchair fully clothed, with a dressing gown on top, and on top of that a blanket that came up over his head like a cowl. It was rather like medieval castles, he said, where you put on *extra* clothes when you came inside, as Sir Gawain did in the poem.

His lack of interest in material possessions extended to books. Notwithstanding his admirable advice about my book bill, his own library was small and consisted mostly of books inherited from his father. He once showed me the edition of the twelfth-century poet Chrétien de Troyes that he had used for that remarkable and splendid, though misleading, book *The Allegory of Love*. It was the old Everyman's Library translation and had his own manuscript index at the back. But apart from such practical and logical annotation, I suspect he did not mark books, especially as he must have used library and friends' copies for his vast reading.

The general form of the tutorial was simple. First, after two or three minutes of general conversation, one read one's essay. The reading for this and the effort of composition were, if done seriously, the major part of a hard week's work that included preparation of translation of Old and Middle English texts and attendance at lectures, which could only rarely be on the subject at hand.

Reading my essay usually took me about ten minutes, though I have heard of men who occupied almost the whole hour. Lewis listened with extreme intentness, not, I am all too sure, because of the fascination of my words, but because it was his duty. Once, in the middle of my essay, his phone rang. I stopped, and he answered it in the other room. When he returned after a five-minute interruption, he repeated *verbatim* my last sentence as far as it had got. He had an astonishing verbatim memory and could repeat whole passages of prose to illustrate a point arising in discussion. Given any line in *Paradise Lost*, he could continue with the following lines.

As I read my essay he made notes. Many of these were minute points of verbal structure, rhythm, clarity, precision, which he raised when I finished reading. In general Lewis had a Johnsonian literalism. He always claimed to be baffled by the phrase, too often applied to Chaucer, "with tongue in cheek," and would put it to absurd visual effect. Such literalism, both on this small scale, and more generally, was a very important part of his criticism, his religion, and of the Socratic *faux-naiveté* that he often used in argument: both a strength and a weakness. As a trivial example, of which he was humorously aware, he once said that he could not for many years properly enjoy the poetic phrase "the chambers of the sun" because of the all-too-literal image evoked for him by the word *chamber*, i.e., the old-fashioned euphemism for chamber pot. In compensation he was able to appreciate the description by one of his pupils (not me) of the institution of "courtly love" as "a vast medieval erection." I myself cannot use the word *aspect* in a general sense even today without feeling guilty. Lewis wished to preserve the word's original astronomical meaning. (He was much interested in astronomy. Once, when letting a friend and me out of college late at night, he pointed out to us the extremely rare conjunction of five planets all brilliantly visible in a circle in the sky at once.)

To return to the essay, if he started to doodle I knew I was being boring, because he once said, of a dull patch, "You were a bit dull there, and so we [i.e., he and my fellow pupil] started to doodle." When the essay was finished he first gave a general word or two of judgment. One week I surpassed myself on Shakespeare's tragedies and rejoiced in high praise. Next week I thought I had produced something equally stunning, a typically modern and undergraduate condemnation of Shakespeare's late romances. "Well," he began, "I couldn't disagree more." He was a "romance critic" not (as most modern critics are) a "tragedy critic." His love of romance, with its inherent optimism and acceptance of the wonderful, was the opposite side of his literalism, a part of his warmth and generosity, and equally important for his criticism and religion. His now-famous, but then very early and unfashionable, interest in science fiction was also part of his love of romance. After the general comment on the essay he usually pointed out the small-scale deficiencies, not at all in a captious way. Then we discussed the principal points made and any other things to be said about the texts. This was almost always delightfully interesting. He had a vivid response to the most various literature, expressed in ready penetrating comment and wit. One of his most notable characteristics as a man as well as a tutor was his magnanimity, his generous acceptance of variety and difference, sure of his own standards but tolerant of others, and of others' failings. Add to this an almost inexhaustible interest in literature and ideas.

I noted in my diary, or remember, some characteristic remarks. Oddly enough he was least stimulating (at least to me) on medieval literature. I noted on 1 March 1946, that he had little to say on medieval drama, and that we had a dull tutorial. This was most unusual, and the only occasion ever on which the tutorial fell a little shorter than the full hour. It must be added that Lewis also had a dreadful cold, and a tutor less conscientious, or a pupil less ruthless, would have given up much earlier.

Years later he told me that he had little to say about Chaucer, although he greatly enjoyed him, and especially *Troilus and Criseyde,* which he had first discovered while convalescing from his war wound, astonished to find so great a poem almost entirely unknown. Langland, with his serious struggle with the problem and sorrows of life, engaged Lewis's interest perhaps more naturally, but he did not know Langland's *Piers Plowman* so well. Once when we had a revision group of about six of us before schools (i.e., the final examination for the B.A.), we all had a long argument about the meaning of the poem, during which it became clear that he had confused one part of the poem with another: entirely forgivable, especially with that poem, but we were amused; such a slip was so very unusual for him.

He was vivid on Elizabethan poetic drama. "*The Spanish Tragedy* is the first competent commercial art." "Marlowe, next to Carlyle, was the most thoroughly depraved of English writers." This latter remark was evoked particularly by the portrayal of Tamburlaine, whom he described as Giant the Jack-killer, and who evoked all his intense feeling against authoritarianism and brutality. In my essay I had referred to "Tamerlane," and Lewis pointed out how Marlowe had transformed a phonetically insignificant name into a splendid one by the addition of that *b*. He liked *Hero and Leander.* "It may be vice, but at least it's natural vice!"

When I remarked on the inappropriateness, in one of Lady Winchelsea's poems, of comparing the corncockle with the sea, he riposted by admiring the insight that saw the same blue, the same common quality, in the tiny humble flower and the ocean's immensity. He enormously enjoyed Swift's humour and thought his work fuller of real laughs than almost any other, but thought Swift's antiwar pamphlet, *The Conduct of the Allies,* was disastrous, since it forced the government into making an ill-advised peace when it was on the brink of success. He had no touch of that *entre guerre* pacifism that we agreed distorts, for example, Tillyard's criticism of Milton. Of Wordsworth's *Excursion* and Byron's *Don Juan* he made the same joke, that each poem grows steadily less good, so that however much you read, you've always read the best of it. He naturally enjoyed Hazlitt, who was brilliant and stimulating, but found him, he said, a little tiring sometimes, like the experience of talking to a man much more intelligent than oneself. (A tutorial often had the same effect on me.)

At the end of our discussion Lewis would suggest the reading for next week. He had no intention of driving a pupil, but he did mention a lot of books. One week I was set to work on Elyot's *The Governour*; Ascham's *Schoolmaster* and *Toxophilus*; Hoby's translation of Castiglione's *The Courtier*; Sidney's *Apology*; with no instruction as to what to look for. At other times necessary paths were traced through the wilderness. When we read Addison and Steele he gave a long list of specific *Tatler* and *Spectator* essays to be read, illustrating various lines of interest; and he did the same with *The Rambler* and *Idler* in one of the weeks we spent on Johnson. When we came to the Romantics the chief topic was "Revolutionary Romanticism," and he suggested a rather unusual mixture of Wordsworth and Shelley. (He loved Shelley particularly, but we also shared an even more unfashionable pleasure in Scott and Lamb.) Jane Austen of course we both loved. Blake seemed to have little appeal for him.

At the last tutorial of the term, Lewis suggested some vacation reading. He never prepared any lists; the titles just tumbled out of his memory. He once rattled off a list of twenty or thirty Elizabethan and Jacobean plays we might read, among other things, during one shortish Christmas vacation. The man I was with that term met my eye in an expressive glance, which Lewis caught. He roared with laughter (I doubt if he could have laughed softly)—and agreed that these were only suggestions from which we would select.

Since the English course then finished at 1830, we had no formal tutorials on later authors, but on other occasions we talked, for example, about Morris's prose romances, then very unfashionable, which we both greatly enjoyed, especially *The Well at the World's End*; Meredith's *The Egoist*, which I had just read, and which he said he reread every year, and a number of other authors, up to and including W. H. Auden. T. S. Eliot's work he greatly admired. He was once on a committee with Eliot to revise the translation of the Psalms and referred to himself, in comparison with Eliot, as a "whippersnapper"—pronounced very Irish, with aspirated initial *hw* and strongly rolled *r*'s.

It is only later in life that one realizes how much a course of tutorials represents a specific approach to the subject and how much it formulates one's own attitudes. I know very well that few other Oxford tutors were as thorough, conscientious, learned, or perceptive as Lewis. Rumour told of the don who would keep his pupils waiting in silence for a long period in the tutorial hour while he wrote at his desk. Others then, as now, forgot, or were ill, or had other business. Some gladly sought relief by spending the tutorial in a walk round the meadows and bright persiflage. And no doubt many pupils welcomed such easements.

Nevertheless, the generous breadth of interest, the concern with the English language, the lack of moralizing exclusiveness, the empiricism, the historical sense and sympathy, the jokes, seem to me to be genuinely representative of an Oxford tradition, at least as it was then. It had weaknesses: a lack of theory; an unawareness of its own presuppositions, which might lead, though not in Lewis, to an arrogant narrowness; a lack of analytical concepts. It could be not only unintellectual but also antiintellectual, genteel, and conceited. To sum up, it was amateur in both good and bad senses. In consequence, at its best, it was, and still, with some tutors, is, profoundly humane, individualistic, generous, varied, open, undoctrinaire, unmoralistic; with a real desire to understand and enjoy; attentive to words, to the differences of meaning, to the historic values of English traditional culture.

Concomitant with the literature tutorials, and an essential element in the power of the Oxford school, as in Lewis's own mind, was the study of the language of earlier English literature, known often as "language work." Apart from the literature tutorials, we had one class a week of about eight of us studying Old and Middle English. These began with learning the grammar from scratch, which Lewis conducted with genial vigour and schoolmasterly conscientiousness. He tested our paradigms each week and dictated simplified versions of sound-change laws, which he also tested our memory for. We simultaneously started reading genuine Old English texts, which was interesting.

After a term we left the grammar and did only translation. Each week we prepared a hundred or two lines (which meant doing the principal work during vacation and revising for the tutorial). Then we each round the class translated fifteen to twenty lines or so aloud at sight from the text. Lewis paid much attention to accuracy and style and a little to annotation, mainly on matters of textual criticism. We were expected to know, and he would occasionally give a brief note on, the *pros* and *cons* of a textual crux, with possible solutions. In none of this did he claim to be an expert, always referring to Professor Tolkien (Tollers) as the great authority. Essentially the method, like Tolkien's own lectures, was to translate and, for "criticism," to hop from crux to crux. Lewis's own appreciation and insight were evident, but to indulge them was not the prime aim of the class. Some of my less enthusiastic fellow pupils became adept at drawing interesting red herrings across the trail, especially when they had not prepared very much.

At the beginning and end of the term, we had collections. At the end of the term every man in college appeared on his own for a minute or two before the tutorial committee, five dons with the president at the head, sitting at the end of the high table in Hall. The man's tutor then made a brief verbal report. On one occasion soon after the war, one man, now a respectable don in another college, whose name it would be mere flattery to reveal, already drunk, though it was still morning, marched up to the august body with considerable bravura, swinging in his hand, for what reason I cannot imagine, a lavatory chain. No one took any notice. In his reports Lewis made no attempt to flatter. "Lacks pep," he once said of me.

At the beginning of the term we had a different kind of collections, more serious. On the first Monday of the term Lewis set all the men reading English two three-hour papers, one before lunch and one after, one on Old or Middle English, and one on the later literature, covering the work of the previous term and vacation. This must have been a general college practice, I suppose, for one understood in those days that the college actually sent down men whose work was unsatisfactory for a term or two and who did poorly in collections. Lewis carried out this exercise with his usual conscientious efficiency and must have marked some thirty or forty papers in the course of the first week of term. He read them carefully. I made, in one, some mistaken remark about Wyatt as opposed to Surrey. He wrote on my paper, "I've read them both again, and the opposite is true." He had little notion of sparing one's feelings, and he would not have imagined one could feel hurt, though I often did. At the foot of one of my essays on Milton he wrote, "Arise, arise, or be for ever fall'n!" The wit mollified the sting a little, but it was the reading again to find out if what I had said was true that struck me, just as I was struck to find him once reading the text we were about to discuss when I came in just before a 10:00 o'clock tutorial.

Though he took collections at the beginning of term seriously, he was not solemn. The pantry was on the landing opposite the entrance to Hall, where we sat on our fifteenth-century benches, writing at the long dining tables. Once, after the war, halfway through a three-hour paper in the morning, he stood me a pint of beer at the pantry counter, with a pleasant chat. As he once said, after the war, it was like teaching his own generation again. One term I had tutorials from 6:00 to 7:00 on Friday evenings, and toward the end of term, at the end of a tutorial, I invited him to have a drink before dinner in the steward's room, then called Bond's Room. Being a small room, its use was restricted to second- and third-year men and old members. As a don and old University College man, he came into none of these categories. I suppose we had sherry. As we drank, he looked around and said, "Just fancy. In twenty years in this college I have never been in this room and wouldn't be now but for the modern labefaction of manners!"

The tutor was responsible for an undergraduate's general welfare. Lewis was no disciplinarian and especially in the days after the war, when most undergraduates ranged in age from about twenty-three (like me) to thirty and many had had years of responsibility for their own and other people's lives and deaths, there were a clear understanding of conventions and an acceptance or calm disregard of restrictions, the very existence of which boys of nineteen nowadays consider an intolerable affront to their dignity. So I do not recall any problems of discipline, though undergraduates naturally know very little about what goes on in a college beyond their own immediate acquaintance. There were however acts of help. In my first year, I was short of money, with not quite enough money from my scholarships (it was about £200) and my parents unable to help, so I told Lewis and he persuaded the college to make me a grant of twenty pounds, for which I was and still am very grateful. During that year, for my sins I was made college representative of the Student Christian Movement and on one occasion, to my unutterable embarrassment, I had to go around asking for funds for some charity. Lewis was one of the few people I nerved myself to ask, and to my hesitant words he immediately replied with a pound note and a Chaucerian quotation, "Myn ere is aken of thy drasty speche!"

After the war a friend of mine, one of his pupils, with Quixotic generosity lent a foreigner his last hundred pounds, remains of a gratuity for much wartime suffering. When he couldn't get it back, he asked Lewis for advice. Firstly, said Lewis, if a man asks you for a loan of a hundred pounds, do not lend it to him, but say, "I will *give* you five pounds if that is any help." Secondly, Lewis said that he belonged to a group of people who tried to help deserving cases, and he arranged for this group to reimburse his pupil's hundred pounds. But I have always suspected that that "group" was Lewis himself. Such known charities were only the tip of a huge iceberg, I am sure, of generous giving.

Apart from giving tutorials, Lewis also gave lectures. These were sometimes held in the college hall, but this was uncomfortably crowded. In the end they were given in the Examination Schools, where they were hugely attended by about four hundred undergraduates. (The same lectures in Cambridge attracted a mere handful.) The famous lectures were the "Prolegomena to Medieval Literature" and "Prolegomena to Renaissance Literature," which finally appeared, condensed, enriched, and turned into book form, as *The Discarded Image*, 1964. The lectures were schematic, beautifully organised in a clear intellectual scheme, very precise, rich with quotations familiar and unfamiliar, which both illustrated and were illustrated by the points made. I heard them twice, once in 1941–42 and then about 1946 on my return from the war. They were remarkably fresh, and extremely well designed for note-taking. They did not change much, but he kept a notebook for further illustration of these and other works, which he called "thickening."

On my second hearing I could remember a good deal from my first hearing, and what I particularly noticed was that the jokes were so successful because they were so well planned. The fuse might be lit several minutes before the actual, yet unexpected, explosion. His voice rang loud and clear, his address to the audience direct, without a detailed script, though I also heard him read a more formal learned lecture on Tasso in English literature, in some special course at the Taylorian, which, by contrast with the energy of the undergraduate lectures, was dull.

His voice in lectures or otherwise was rich and strong, laced with some characteristic Ulster touches, particularly with his *r*'s, and in the way he pronounced *Lat'n*. Rather comically, he told me that he never knew what an Oxford accent was until he heard his own voice on a recorded program on the BBC. He didn't like it.

Although not a big man, of medium height or slightly less, and tubby, he had a good presence. When walking he was round-shouldered but he stood up vigorously when lecturing. He usually walked with a knobbed walking stick, or with both hands behind his back. He always wore a gown but never carried his "square," or mortarboard. He normally wore a sports coat, and one noticed the rare occasion when he had a new one. He always wore a hat out-of-doors, with the brim pulled down all round in a rather rustic manner. It went well with the red, moonlike face, itself so much at variance, except in good-humour, with the penetrating, eager, witty mind and delicate sensibility.

I find from my diary that he was lecturing at 12:00 M on Saturday, 16 February 1946, and that he indulged in several of his more pointed antifeminist witticisms and remarks. Unfortunately I made no note of these and have entirely forgotten them. I noted also that, "I am told that many women are revolted by his whole personality—though this is probably an exaggeration." Late one evening I once, while still an undergraduate, hinted at this antifeminism, and he rather warmly told me that in fact he received a large fan mail (though I am sure he didn't call it that) from women and even offers of marriage. I am rather appalled now at my cheek in mentioning such a subject, but he was not annoyed. Any antifeminism must have been superficial, as his idyllically happy late marriage showed.

I also heard him give the sermon in Mansfield College entitled "Transposition." This was splendid. It was like his university lectures, only more personal, though with no confessional element. It was well ordered, full of interesting ideas, devotional without piety, instructive without moralization, and with that generous warmth, zest, and touch of self-mocking humour that were so characteristic of him.

Lewis led a busy and well-organized life, so it was rare to meet him, at least for an undergraduate, in a casual, accidental way. Although I went occasionally to Evensong at the college chapel it was rare to see him there. I noted for Friday, 1 February 1946, that, "I meet Lewis occasionally in the mornings, he going toward Addison's [Walk, a mile circuit around part of Magdalen grounds], I returning. So we rush past each other, hastily calling out our respective informations about primroses and snowdrops." When I was on leave during the war, I occasionally called on him, always to be received with kindness, though such calls must have been a nuisance. On one such occasion he talked of the uselessness of pity unless it could lead to practical action; how we came to be discussing St. Augustine's theories of sexual love on that or a similar occasion I cannot now imagine.

He was a man of wide culture, and it is probably my fault that I can recall few remarks made about subjects other than English literature. He liked Mozart, and it was rumoured that he and Tolkien went annually to London to see Wagner's *Ring*. This must be an exaggeration, but it suggests a liking for certain aspects of Wagner. I never saw him at a concert. Toward the end of his life he helped a young sculptor, I believe, by buying or commissioning some works from him. I think he liked the art of the Italian Renaissance, and he had a big, rather dull, reproduction of Bronzino's luscious *Allegory of Venus and Cupid* above his mantlepiece, as Peter Bayley reminds me. But when I mentioned going to Italy he said, "Ah, good. You'll be able to drink Chianti." He loved wine, though he was not in the least bibulous and was probably never drunk in his life. I am told by his friend Mr. R. M. Dias, one of the fellows of Magdalene College, Cambridge, when Lewis was there, that it is the custom after dinner for the Junior Fellow to take around the port and pour it for each Fellow. Lewis always genially insisted that the glass should be filled to the brim. Then he carried it to his lips with an utterly steady hand.

He had nothing of the modern Puritan's ascetism, schematicism, and rejection of history. Yet he had simple tastes, or no taste at all, in clothes and furnishings. So in food. In the war years butter was strictly rationed, and he remarked to me with pleasure on his discovery that margarine did quite as well as butter because all you wanted was a layer of something impermeable to keep the jam from making the bread soggy.

His chief indulgence was in smoking, whose dangers none of us in those days realised. He smoked cigarettes and a pipe, and I forget if it were he or I or who recalled Stevenson's remarks about the pleasure of smoking a cigarette while you were filling your pipe. Lewis once commented on the fragrance of the first cigarette of the day, and apologized in tutorials for being no longer able to afford handing around cigarettes as he had used to do in the thirties. In tutorials he used to smoke a pipe, and I can still see the rich brown shreds of the weed dangling over the burned, uneven edge of the bowl, pressed down by a stubby finger, constantly relit with matches, and I smell the thick puffs he produced. He had a number of pipes on the big table in his main room, sometimes ready-loaded for a class.

Most of the time that I was an undergraduate, he went home to his own house at Headington in the evenings, though I think he spent all day in college. He once said how irritating it was that one seemed to get one's best ideas with both hands in hot water doing the washing up, unable to make notes. One of my friends after the war expressed his regret at his own lack of domesticity. "Ah" said Lewis, "You have too little of it and I have too much."

But he held a few evening gatherings for undergraduates, where he shone with his most characteristic light. The first of these was sometime early in 1942 when Charles Williams came to Magdalen to give a lecture on "Free Love" after dinner to some university society. The hall was well filled, though Williams came to the then-expected conclusion. Lewis took the chair and, after one rather irrelevant observation from the floor during the discussion, he said that the meeting must now make up its mind whether it wished to discuss the habits of bees or those of human beings. Seeing the issue of relevance to the subject, he nevertheless had no intention of forcibly steering or even managing the discussion toward that subject, let alone to any preconceived conclusion.

After the lecture and discussion, which managed to drop bees, Lewis asked me and two or three others up to his room to meet Williams and have a drink. Williams was wearing an old blue suit, scattering cigarette ashes all down his waistcoat, talking vigorously—the only time I ever knew Lewis positively to encourage anyone else to talk, though he never attempted to dominate. In the talk Lewis and Williams evolved the proposition that you could no more avoid pleasure in this life than pain—this a propos the situation of being invited home by a loose woman; whether you accepted or refused. Lewis encouraged Williams to read from his poem *Taliessin Through Logres,* which he did in a rather mushy voice, with great gusto. It was a wonderful evening.

On 21 May 1946, according to my diary, Lewis invited a group of undergraduates to drink beer in his room, and I am sorry to say we kept him up till 1:30 with a long and complicated argument on a hypothetical legal question. There was no impatience on his part that I noticed or can remember, though my own experience of such evenings with undergraduates leads me to suppose that even if there had been, short of starting to take off his tie and his shoes, we would not have noticed. On a few other occasions he would come, if free, to drink beer with me and a friend; one evening we had a splendid long session on Donne's poem "Aire and Angells"; but all subjects were of interest to him. He also gave all his pupils what seemed to us a splendid dinner with wine in college at the end of our first year, and again when we had taken schools. It was at this latter that I expressed the view that it was quite pointless to think about Heaven. In his most Johnsonian manner Lewis replied, "On the contrary, we don't think about Heaven nearly enough."

On such an evening, sitting in his room, he would arrange a reading round of Amanda McKittrick Ross's *Irene Iddesleigh,* in an original edition. This was long before her ridiculous style made her a minor cult. Each person was to read aloud for as long as he could before laughing, changing the reader as soon as he laughed. The readers changed rapidly. Lewis's father, it seemed, had been Mrs. Ross's solicitor at some time, and he quoted from a letter from her, containing gross solecisms in that celebrated style.

The best of such evenings were the meetings to dine and talk that I had with Lewis; his old friend Hugo Dyson (the English don at Merton); Philip Stibbe, an undergraduate at Merton; Tom Stock of Magdalen; and Peter Bayley of University College. The first was 30 June 1946. The entry in my diary, jejune and sketchy as alas it is, with an embarrassing emphasis on the drink, nevertheless perhaps conveys better than any remarks made over thirty years later some of the quality of the evening.

We drank some sherry. Lewis came in cursing from a meeting of the tutorial board and its decision to expand the College. A few amusing stories of the shaggy-dog variety were told.

The dinner was magnificent, and so were the hock and conversation.

Upstairs again after dinner into Tom's room, where we drank excellent port and graduated on to beer. It was an excellent evening, conversation amusing and intelligent and monopolised by no one.

Although the amusing anecdote is very much the staple of Oxford conversation, Lewis himself relied simply on intelligence, knowledge, learning, zest, wit, and witty quotation. He had only one formal joke, which I heard only once, though I remember it perfectly well, and he told it on that same evening. It went on rather a long time, was told with an excruciating attempt at an uneducated English accent, turned on a verbal point connected with suppositories, and was not really very funny.

It was at one of these evenings that he said that when he first became a tutor he had thought it a great triumph if he taught a second-class man so well that he got a first-class degree, but now he thought it a disaster. The other way round didn't matter.

We met once a term at these meetings, and I suppose it was Lewis who named them an *eranos* "a communal meal," but only one other of these meetings is significant for this essay. We met on Wednesday, 4th February

1948, first in Philip Stibbe's room, then at the Roebuck, where we ate. Once again my diary:

None of us at first very cheerful—one has to work hard to keep up with Lewis. He was obviously deeply disturbed by his encounter last Monday with Miss Anscombe [the distinguished philosopher and Roman Catholic, then at Oxford, now Professor of Philosophy at Cambridge], who had disproved some of the central theory of his philosophy about Christianity. I felt quite painfully for him. Dyson said—very well—that now he had lost everything and was come to the foot of the Cross—spoken with great sympathy.

Lewis described the club meeting, where Miss Anscombe had delivered, at her own request, such an onslaught against his views, with real horror. His imagery was all of the fog of war, the retreat of infantry thrown back under heavy attack (five of us had been infantry officers at the age of nineteen and had seen action; a curious commentary on English scholarly life in the twentieth century).

Much of the evening was spent in cheerful ribaldry, but Lewis was really still miserable and went early. I finally noted, with a young man's cheerful egotism: "a good evening, and a little less boisterous and exhausting than others."

The encounter with Miss Anscombe had been at the Socratic Club. Just after the war the Socratic was a very popular university society for the investigation of general religious questions in an uncommitted spirit. Lewis came regularly—he was not chairman but was probably honorary president—and various people read papers, to which it usually fell to Lewis to make the first reply in discussion. I went sometimes, though I missed Miss Anscombe's evening, and occasionally we exchanged a word or two about the previous evening's meeting at the beginning of a tutorial. Lewis attended, I formed the impression, entirely as a sacrificial duty, and loathed it, though I suppose there must at bottom have been some satisfaction in it for him.

Toward the end of my time as an undergraduate, I decided I should like to do research and become a scholar. Lewis, though kind, was here not much help. He had the then usual Oxford contempt and indeed incomprehension for that kind of activity. He was as ever tolerant and did what he could, soon beginning a long series of letters supporting me in my many unsuccessful applications for jobs. I took schools in December 1947, along with a small number of other especially keen ex-servicemen who wished to do particularly well. We had been granted an extension of six months to the course because of the interruption of war service to our studies. In my case, being earnest and hardworking rather than clever, I certainly "overprepared the event" and, as might perhaps have been expected, the examiners made hay of us. Most of the candidates are now university professors, etc.

Dec. 21/47

Dear Brewer,

Oh Lor!—I never but once saw anything like this year's class list . . . but that way madness lies. It has not in the least altered my opinion either of you or of ———, nor I think will it affect your chances in the Fellowship.

There *may* be something still to do on Gower tho' I'm not quite sure what. But go on nosing a bit. I enclose the formal testimonial wh. is all that is needed. All the best.

Yours
C. S. Lewis

The reference to the fellowship is to the fellowship by examination that the college held every year and for which I then entered. Needless to say, I did not win a fellowship.

At one stage I applied for an assistant lectureship in New Zealand. Yet once more did I have to ask him to write a reference for me. He was decidedly encouraging about going out there. It was a country where the Victorian age was still strong, he said, and I would avoid the third and final World War. (His political views were somewhat simple, partly because he never read the newspapers. "Someone will always tell you if anything has happened," he said.)

As usual I failed to get the New Zealand job, but when at last I was appointed an Assistant Lecturer I had one of the typewritten notes.

Ref. 284/49

Magdalen College
13th June 1949

Dear Brewer,

Hurray! I'm so glad. Yes, I have had a very heavy cold.

Yours,
W. H. Lewis
(for C. S. Lewis, ill).

The 284th letter and only June! In April 1950 I had one numbered 206.

Lewis's tutorial functions were not quite over. A year or two later I asked him to act as general editor for a series of Medieval and Renaissance English texts being edited by two colleagues at Birmingham and myself. I introduced the subject on a visit to Oxford, after he had been made Professor of Medieval and Renaissance English Literature in Cambridge. He kept his house at Headington Quarry, Oxford, which I never saw, and lived in Oxford on weekends and during vacations. We had a long talk in the Eastgate Hotel over beer, and I explained what our aims and hopes were. He was innocently sympathetic, and when I asked him to be general editor, much surprised. With his usual generosity he agreed. With equally usual and typical generosity he refused even the token fee that the editors received.

Though he never initiated a project and never understood our intentions, for he knew by long training and second nature the kind of things that we thought needed to be spelled out to post-Christian, new-Western man, and he thought we were rather pedantic, he was always most helpful. He suggested that we should publish a Latin work, by the seventeenth-century astronomer Kepler, which he considered to be the first genuine piece of science fiction. He pulled our legs occasionally, but I have a long list of several pages in his own hand commenting on points in my draft Introduction to my edition of *The Parliament of Fowlys* that consists of remarks not unlike the points he made about essays in tutorials, which testifies to the sharpness and care with which he performed this valuable but tedious chore. Accompanying the list and also in his own hand was the following letter.

> The Kilns
> Headington Quarry
> Oxford

August 30th 1958

Dear Brewer,

—"Trusteth wel I am not textual" [a quotation from Chaucer], so I won't meddle with your text at all. I enclose some comments on your introduction and notes. They are mostly merely stylistic, but not all. When I ask to be reassured about matters of fact, this does not mean that I know your statements to be false but only that I don't know them to be true (the only *howler* I confidently detect is where you make the *De Planctu* a poem). Such discomforts are chiefly bunched between pp.

19 and 32, where I rather get the impression—let's mix our metaphors well—that you are skating on thin ice over various hornets' nests that might at any moment burst into flame. You have authority for all these statements have you? If the authority is at all doubtful—and all secondary authorities are—the next question is, do you need to make them at all. . . . By the way, I have known you write better than you do in this introduction.

That was a delightful reunion at Jack B's. I wish you and I met more often.

I'll return the text when I've got a large enough envelope. (If only you scholards wd. use ordinary quarto sheets and *not* enclose your MSS in great flapping containers . . .)

Yours
Jack Lewis

One or two of his comments:

(P. 21) Does this imply in C's mind the same clear distinction between the plant and the goddess [Venus] that there is in ours? If so, I wonder are you right?

(P. 24) Very well put.

(P. 26) The two more's, comparison within comparison, a bit awkward. This whole page—forgive me—is hardly a favorable specimen of your style. Para 3 line 4 is v. uncomfortable!

(P. 31) *necessarily existing*. Are you right? Was not Creation itself unnecessary? And wasn't the sublunary world anyway the home of contingence?

(P. 46) *religio*—Great Snakes, you can't do that with a noun whose nominative is already in *-io*! *Theologico*—if you must do it (at) all. But I'd prefer "religious and scientific concepts."

(P. 47) (Rum chaps, those mediaevals . . . they actually thought temptations ought to be tempting).

One of several letters of advice:

Magdalene College
Cambridge
16 Nov 1959

Dear Brewer,

1. Yes. A Jonsonian masque with a good introd., packing tight all we now know about masques, wd. be an excellent choice.

2. No. Haven't you discovered yet that I'm not a Scholar but only a Learned Man[1]?

Lor' bless you, I can't *edit* any more than I can audit. I'm not accurate. Sorry.

It was lovely to see you and I hope you'll come again, some night when I'm fully free.

Yours,<br>C. S. Lewis

(1) A Cambridge don asked me the other day whether the last syllables of *polymath* and *aftermath* were derived from the same word!

He was able to take so much trouble partly because Cambridge relieved him, at the age of fifty-five or thereabouts, of the burden of tutorials. When he moved to Cambridge he told me he could for the first time in his life, when he woke up in the morning, ask himself what he would like to do. He loved Cambridge, finding it much more gentle and less wordly than Oxford. He also enjoyed being at Magdalene College, Cambridge, and greatly appreciated the opportunity to refer to his two colleges separately as the Penitents and the Impenitents.

This was a characteristically allusive joke. His conversation sparkled with quotations and references that poured out as inadvertently as the jewels from the mouth of the good girl in the fairy tale. His conversation was rapid and changing. He would stop and look hard and seriously into space as he evolved a new thought, then change rapidly into beaming good humour. His literalism could be disconcerting. If I felt embarrassed by a pause or felt I was not keeping my end up properly in a conversation, and so filled in with an empty remark, or simply said something silly, he was quite capable of remorselessly dissecting the feeble worm. The quality of his mind was naturally critical. He could make cheerfully disparaging remarks about other people with a snort. I can imagine him being sharp, and he enjoyed argument. He seemed not particularly sensitive to blows himself and did not imagine others were (the debate with Miss Anscombe went deeper, in matters much more important). There was also a difference in what he said and what he wrote. In writing he was careful not to hurt—his letter to me about my introduction to *The Parlement,* quoted previously, expresses criticism honestly but very gently.

He had a public written controversy on literature with Dr. Tillyard of Jesus College, Cambridge, which like all his arguments was entirely without personal animus. I asked him after he went to Cambridge how he got on with Dr. Leavis, a famous literary controversialist. He replied that they were always on opposing sides of the question in any committee on which they met, but that Leavis "was all right," he was 'saved.' He did not mean religiously, but that ultimately his values were the right ones. Lewis was, I am sure, a poor committeeman, who, as in the case of the postwar expansion of Magdalen, which did not involve the vast amount of new buildings that he envisaged, did not really grasp practical issues.

But as I reflect on him, and learn more from recent books about his group, I am more and more impressed by his magnanimity. He had no malice. He spoke to everyone on the same terms of equality, and this led occasionally to inadvertent rudeness, as he said what he thought to those not always as robust and so totally without *amour propre* as himself. In this respect he had a vein of robust insensibility. And there was also something explosive inside him, part of his great powers of mind and spirit, strongly controlled, but also potentially alarming. A very eminent Cambridge scientist, who had practically nothing in common with Lewis, once remarked to me—and it is one of the finest tributes to Lewis I have heard—that he met Lewis only once, at some evening occasion, and felt that he was a very good man, *to whom goodness did not come easily.*

One has always to remember that the bit of our worlds that I am discussing, formed by the overlapping segments of our personal lives, was at that time, long before his marriage and mine, in college and university, by modern standards a very old-fashioned, English, masculine world. Each of us was different, with varying experiences and attitudes, but this was our common ground. It had "clubbability." Different as we were, we had in common that we were university and college men; ex-soldiers, who loved English literature, walking in the English countryside, and talking in pubs about literature and life but not about ourselves. We had deep reserves, and it would not have occurred to me to tell Lewis of my private joys and miseries, any more than I should have expected him to tell me of his.

I suspect that such groups exist more widely spread nowadays than it is usual to think, but they are not now taken for granted as typical. They depend on a profound sense of masculine comradeship, engendered in worlds in which women could not by definition in those days enter: the fighting services, Oxford and Cambridge colleges, Rugby teams, pubs with "gentlemen only" snugs, and so forth. They had their own rituals and conventions, which had something either irritatingly or charmingly boyish about them to women, depending upon the women. Sex, love, and religion were discussed frequently, especially since so much of literature is based on such subjects, but in a nonpersonal, largely analytical way. Religion was discussed without either piety or blasphemy. Sexual love was usually assumed to be the ultimate secular experience. Chastity, even for men, was accepted as the normal ideal, even if so many of one's acquaintance broke it (never Lewis, of course). Sexuality was often the subject of ribald humour, though there was very little of our conversation that an educated lady even of those days might not have heard without blushing, and I suspect that our vocabulary was less coarse than that of some modern university mixed company nowadays.

Homosexuality was of no interest and was in itself as self-excluding as femininity. Lewis told with satiric amusement how a fresh-faced infantry officer in the World War I gave a lecture to officer-cadets on the subject, "Being Keen on the Platoon," which found its way into everybody's notebook as, "Being Keen on the Platoon Commander."

Lewis was not touchy about sex. A friend of mine, also a pupil of Lewis's and a devout Christian, as cheerful and sane a man as they come, wrote an article pointing out what he felt (correctly in my view) is an element of morbid sexuality in the novels of Charles Williams. Lewis could not see this at all and thought that on such matters our friend must be unduly (in the Elizabethan phrase) "tickle o' the sere," that is, too easily set off.

This kind of masculine world, with its now-antiquated idealisms and repressions, is well portrayed by Kipling, as Lewis points out somewhere, but it is of an ancient heritage. Hugo Dyson, who had been very severely wounded in the World War I, and had had the strange experience of seemingly looking from above at his own shattered body lying face-downwards, with a shell-wound in his back, once expressed this sense of traditional comradeship and continuity by saying, with splendid hyperbole, "I too fought at Thermopylae"—and he was not talking about reincarnation! I labour to define this world of masculine comradeship because it seems nowadays less easily understood, not to express nostalgia for it. Its limitations were as marked as its now less-valued virtues.

Of course, being the people we were, our particular version of the masculine world depended much less on experience and much more on literature, thought, and imagination than might have been the case with other groups. Lewis claimed neither extensive worldly material experience nor the capacity to respond to it. Thus he said once, apropos of experience and immediate enjoyment, that for him "nothing was any good" until "it had been down in the cellar for a while." He was referring, I took it, not to the way memory falsely gilds the past, but to the way, as he saw it, that mental, emotional, and thus imaginative possession of experience in memory led to a truer understanding and enjoyment of it. I hope I gloss him correctly.

It will easily be recognized that though the bit of the world I discuss was not especially anomalous at that time, it was quite out of touch with the socially glamorous, the morally advanced, or the political Oxford of the modern reminiscences of now-famous men.

Because I am describing only a fragment of Lewis's world as it overlapped with a fragment of mine, my account must be partial and in a sense superficial. I do not describe Lewis's considered thoughts about literature, his literary achievements or his religious convictions, aware of them as I was, because they are more fully adequately expressed in his books. Much of our conversation was serious, much not—cheerfulness would keep breaking in! He and I shared, if that is the right word, some common values. We also differed. He had a profound skepticism about the world. He believed, he once said to me in a characteristic phrase, "as I think the New Testament allows me to," that the world is almost entirely under the dominion of evil. This led to a certain fruitful dichotomy of attitudes. All his public expectations, for the country, for the nature of society, were pessimistic; yet he seems to me to have had a personal resolute hopefulness, even cheerfulness (granted that no one is cheerful all the time). I have described his criticism, which was personal, as "romance" criticism, as optimistic. And in his personal life, as I have already said, his deeds of generosity to increase the goodness of the world were both practical and far reaching.

There was a similar dichotomy in his attitude toward authority. By nature he was the least authoritarian of men. As a college officer (vice-president, etc.) he always seemed to give undergraduates what they wanted at the first request. As a tutor, if one asked to be excused a tutorial he usually gave permission before it occurred to him to ask the reason why it was sought. (Of course he lived in a society of young and old that, unlike ours, recognised and accepted its own conventions, so it was easy for him to be so liberal.)

On the other hand, he would have venerated authority if he could. Once in a tutorial, though I fully shared Lewis's love of Milton, I commented adversely in a modern young man's way on Milton's concept of God as expressed in the line, "As ever in my great Taskmaster's eye." An unduly schoolmasterly and demanding notion of God, I thought. Not at all, said Lewis; how marvelous to think of everything you do as being watched and weighed. This reveals in him a higher level of conscious and unconscious virtue than I can reach, but chiefly it is a fine perception of the need for, and availability of, real objective significance in our lives, as based on religious obligation, duty, and achievement. A strenuous Protestant ethic! He could have quoted sympathetically (though I do not recollect his ever having done so) the centurion's words, "For I also am one under authority." Lewis had no need to be told the evils of dictatorship, but his approval of democracy was based mainly, and rationally, on his recognition of the evil in men.

Rational convictions were what he sought. He was always "thinking for his life," to use the phrase he once used approvingly of Professor Gilbert Ryle, the great Oxford atheist philosopher of his day, who was also a fellow of Magdalen. This explains the attraction for him of the medieval scholastic philosophers and that passionate disapproval of the Humanists, whom he thought trivial, concerned with "mere" literature, which he develops in his great book on sixteenth-century literature. Yet paradoxically, he got this wrong. The Scholastics no doubt deserved his praise, as more recent scholarship has shown; but the Humanists sought truth in literary and imaginative experience just as Lewis did, and it was they who developed historically that vein of literalism that so characterized him. In every good sense of the word, Lewis was a Christian Humanist.

I did not know about his serious illness, though I had heard that he was not well, and wrote to him in 1963 about some matter I have now forgotten. He replied in his own hand on a postal card:

8 Oct.                              The Kilns, Headington Quarry, Oxford.
Yes, certainly. All good wishes. I had to retire (they thought I was dying last July) but I'm quite comfortable and cheery.

C. S. L.

The next I heard was that he had died.

# 7
## A Great Clerke
### JOHN WAIN

Most dons, like most schoolmasters, are more or less conscious "characters." Their lives are lived in the gaze of numerous watchful young eyes, and their ordinary human traits are discussed and commented on by eager young tongues until they become magnified into lovable or laughable idiosyncrasies. Student generations succeed each other so rapidly that by the time a don has been in his post for a mere fifteen years or so, his pupils are being asked by people who seem to them middle-aged, "Is old So-and-so still as such-and-such as ever?" In time, even the most retiring don becomes a legend; his face and voice, walk and gestures, are studied far more intimately than those of a mere public figure such as a politician. For the don is semiprivate. He "belongs to" the university at which he works. His activities are watched and criticized by an audience who feel themselves personally insulted if he does something they don't like, personally complimented if they approve.

For this reason every don is equipped with a persona, a set of public characteristics that in time he finds hard to lay aside even in private. After all, the politician who sets up an image simple enough to be adopted by cartoonists, or the "maverick" man of letters who aims to capture the attention of journalists and TV interviewers needs only to construct a scarecrow with some faint resemblance to himself. But the don's image is tested and scrutinized by alert twenty-year-old eyes, half-a-dozen times a day, in the privacy of his study fireside. It has to be lifelike. It must be very nearly approximate to his real character: the mask must have almost the same play of expression as the face beneath it. So that the don who makes an impact on the wider scene (Gilbert Murray, F. R. Leavis) or becomes a star performer in a mass medium (C. M. Joad, A. J. P. Taylor) starts with a big advantage over the cruder performer from Westminster or Fleet Street. Such men are like Dickensian characters. We know they are not real, that no human being was ever quite like that; but we cannot deny that they are true to a certain kind of "nature."

C. S. Lewis was a rare case of the don who is forced into the limelight by the demands of his own conscience. He had a secure academic reputation before beginning that series of popular theological works that made him world famous; I believe he would never have bothered to court the mass public at all had he not seen it as his duty to defend the Christian faith, to which he became a convert in early adult life, against the hostility or indifference that surrounded it. Many of his Oxford acquaintances never forgave him for *The Screwtape Letters*, with its knockdown arguments, its obvious ironies, its journalistic facility. But Lewis used to quote with approval General Booth's remark to Kipling: "Young man, if I could win one soul for God by—by playing the tambourine with my toes, I'd do it." Lewis did plenty of playing the tambourine with his toes, to the distress of some of the refined souls by whom he was surrounded at Oxford. He had a naturally rhetorical streak in him that made it a pleasure to cultivate the arts of winning people's attention and assent.

Lewis's father was a lawyer, and the first thing that strikes one on opening any of Lewis's books is that he is always persuading, always arguing a case. If he wrote a book or an essay about an author, the assumption was that he had accepted a brief to defend that author. It was his duty to bring the jury around to his point of view by advancing whatever argument would be likely to carry weight with them. It is this, more than anything else, that gives his literary criticism its curious impersonality. We feel that Lewis is simply not interested in telling us what it was that first made him, Lewis, a devotee of Spenser or Milton or William Morris. He consistently attacked what he called "the personal heresy," and despised the *argumentum ad hominem*. To him, every important issue lay in the domain of public debate. Whether it was the choice of a book to read or the choice of a God to believe in, Lewis argued the matter like a counsel. His personal motives were kept well back from the reach of curious eyes. All was foren-sic; the jury were to be won over and that was all.

For this reason the parts of Lewis's work that are most disappointing are those that ought to be personal and aren't. He wrote a great deal about Christian belief and liked to begin his discourse with, "When I was an atheist. . . ." But the personal revelation was entirely mechanical; the former Lewis had taken a generalized atheistic position, the present-day Lewis took a generalized Christian position. So that when his autobiog-raphy *Surprised by Joy* appeared in 1955, many people turned eagerly to the account of his own conversion, hoping at last to have a glimpse of the personal reasons behind it, the reasons that counted for something in the silence of his own heart. The result was disappointment. The account is as lame and unconvincing as it could possibly be. All one brings away from it is the fact that it occurred at Whipsnade.

This inability to share his inner life is of course no disgrace to Lewis. We have suffered too much in this century from men and women who rush in, proffering their souls on a tin plate, eager to buttonhole us and "tell all"; and then, in most cases, making up a pack of lies. Lewis would have been too honest to follow their example. And on the rare occasions when some kind of personal element was needed—in his work or in his relationships with people—what held him back was not lack of honesty but simply a deep-seated inhibition that he could not break.

Everyone who knew Lewis was aware of this strange dichotomy. The outer self—brisk, challenging, argumentative, full of an overwhelming physical energy and confidence—covered an inner self as tender and as well hidden as a crab's. One simply never got near him. It was an easy matter to become an acquaintance, for he was gregarious and enjoyed matching his mind against all comers. And if he liked what he saw of you, it was easy to go further and become a friend—invited to visit him at Mag-dalen and enjoy many hours of wide-ranging conversation. But the terri-tory was clearly marked. You were made free of a certain area—the schol-arly, debating, skirmishing area that the whole world knew. Beyond that, there was a heavily protected inner self that no one ever saw. No one? Doubtless there were a few, here and there; two or three friends of forty-years' standing, who were of his own generation and shared his Christi-anity; the wife he married late in life; possibly a few blood relations. But if anyone ever really knew his inner mind, the secret was well kept.

If anyone doubts this, let him take a look at the book Lewis wrote about
the experience of having to endure his wife's death and the subsequent
religious and philosophical turmoil of his thoughts. It was published by
Faber & Faber in 1961 as *A Grief Observed*, by "N. W. Clerk." ("N. W."
was Lewis's signature for the clever pieces of light verse he was at one time
in the habit of contributing to *Punch*; it stands for "nat whilc"—more correctly, I think, "hwilc"—which is Anglo-Saxon for "I know not whom.")
This book, evidently composed with a great deal of care as a refuge from
grief and a monument to love, is just as impersonal, as nonintimate, as
anything signed by Lewis. One gets no impression of the living presence
of a real woman. I don't mean only that we are not told whether she was
tall or short, fat or thin. (Though even *that* would have helped.) The
want is subtler. A palpable human presence is there, but it is the presence
of a mind; it has no heartbeat or smell or weight. Characteristically, we are
given a description of her mind; it was "lithe and quick and muscular as a
leopard. Passion, tenderness, and pain were all unable to disarm it." Beyond that, nothing. Not that the book fails to take us into a human situation. Its notes on the psychology of grief are interesting and valuable. But
what we see is generalized grief, not one particular man's. It is what Johnson desiderated for literature, a "just representation of general nature."

What caused this withdrawal, this inner timidity, I do not know. I
could make a clumsy, amateur effort to psychoanalyze Lewis, but my findings would not be of any clinical value, and in any case I shrink from any
such probings; I liked and admired the man, and if he wanted his inner
self let alone I think we should let it alone. I mention the matter only
because it is one of the keys to the work he has left us. In his writings Lewis
adopts a strongly marked role, for the reasons I gave at the beginning. But
this role is a wooden dummy. It bears the individual features of no living
man.

Lewis grew up in the Edwardian age, and his chief allegiances were to
that age. He become a fellow of Magdalen in 1925, and from then on it
was easy for him to ignore the modern world; the interior of an Oxford
college has probably changed less since Edwardian days than anywhere,
always excepting the House of Commons. And even before he got his
fellowship, he had noticed the 1920s only to draw away from them in hos-
tile dissent. From about 1914 onward, he disliked modern literature because
it reflected modern life.

This withdrawal from the age he lived in went easily hand in hand with Lewis's impersonality in human contacts, his construction of a vast system of intellectual outworks to protect the deeply hidden core of his personality. As time went on, and younger people he met began to seem more and more Martian (as they do to all of us, goodness knows), Lewis deliberately adopted the role of a survival. He was Old Western man, his attitudes dating from before Freud, before modern art or poetry, before the machine even. When, in 1954, he left Oxford for Cambridge, he introduced himself to his new audience in this role.

You don't want to be lectured on Neanderthal Man by a Neanderthaler, still less on dinosaurs by a dinosaur. And yet, is that the whole story? If a live dinosaur dragged its slow length into the laboratory, would we not all look back as we fled? What a chance to know at last how it really moved and looked and smelled and what noises it made! And if the Neanderthaler could talk, then, though his lecturing technique might leave much to be desired, should we not almost certainly learn from him some things about him that the best modern anthropologist could never have told us? He would tell us without knowing he was telling.

Hence:

Speaking not only for myself but for all other Old Western men whom you may meet, I would say, use your specimens while you can. There are not going to be many more dinosaurs.

Such a public application of the grease paint did him, I believe, no good among the stern, no-nonsense men of Cambridge, who have no time for playacting. And it must be admitted that there is an element of disabling unreality about the striking of such an attitude. A man born in 1850 might naturally inhabit an older "order"; a man born, as Lewis was, in 1898 could only reconstruct it from boyhood memories and adult reading. Lewis, who was twenty-four in the year that saw the publication of *The Waste Land*, couldn't claim to belong to a generation whose taste in poetry, for instance, was formed before Eliot "came alone." His true role was not that of either Old Western Man or a dinosaur, but the humbler and more commonplace role of *laudator temporis acti*.

Once this has been grasped, the all-pervading contentiousness of Lewis's writing becomes more explicable. He was fighting a perpetual rear-guard action in defense of an army that had long since marched away. In some respects this may be a valuable thing to do; to be "modern" and up-to-date is not necessarily a good quality—many of the most appalling people have it. On the other hand, Lewis's parallel about the dinosaur creeping into the laboratory is an unhelpful oversimplification. Lectures given by an Elizabethan critic on Shakespeare would be very illuminating, but only to scholars who already understood the main points of sixteenth-century thought and wanted clarification on the finer shades. To interpret the masterpieces of one age to the young of another, we need such understanding as we can muster of both ages. As Allen Tate has remarked, "The scholar who tells us that he understands Dryden but makes nothing of Yeats or Hopkins is telling us that he does not understand Dryden." What Lewis was actually doing, most of the time, was interpreting the past in terms of the Chesterton-Belloc era as he reconstructed that era in his own mind.

Thus we find him, in an after-dinner speech on Scott (*They Asked for a Paper*, pp. 98–99), admitting the charge that Scott often turned out work that he knew to be inferior and was quite happy so long as it sold. "There is little sign, even in his best days, of a serious and costly determination to make each novel as good in its own kind as he could make it. And at the end, when he is writing to pay off his debts, his attitude to his work is, by some standards, scandalous and cynical." And Lewis goes on:

Here we come to an irreducible opposition between Scott's view of the world and that of our more influential modern men of letters. These would blame him for disobeying his artistic conscience; Scott would have said he was obeying his conscience. He knew only one kind of conscience. It told him that a man must pay his debts if he possibly could. The idea that some supposed obligation to write good novels could override this plain, universal demand of honesty would have seemed to him the most pitiful subterfuge of vanity and idleness. . . .

Two different worlds here clash. And who am I to judge between them? It may be, as Curtius has said, that "the modern world immeasurably overvalues art." Or it may be that the modern world is right and that all previous ages have greatly erred in making art, as they did, subordinate to life, so that artists worked to teach virtue, to adorn a city, to solemnise feasts and marriages, to please a patron, or to amuse the people.

The point is gracefully made; but that list of the possible motives for art in the traditional society simply breaks down when we try to apply it to Shakespeare or Michelangelo or Beethoven. (Or is Beethoven already corrupted to modernity?) And whatever Curtius may have meant by his remark, do we in the twentieth century actually *feel* that we live in an age that "overvalues" art, or values it at all, for that matter? But how characteristically skillful of Lewis to bring up a big gun in defense of a weak point!

It is early days yet for a final estimate of Lewis's work, but I think the general view, ultimately, will be that his writing improves as it gets further from the popular and demagogic. Thus, in a miscellany such as *They Asked for a Paper,* the weaker pieces are those in which he could assume an audience less intelligent than himself (e.g., the English Association lecture on Kipling or the banquet speech about Scott) and the best those in which he addressed himself to some problem before fully qualified people (e.g., the very original and acute "Is Theology Poetry?"). Setting aside his novels, which I take it are simply bad—he developed in later years a telltale interest in science fiction, which is usually a reliable sign of imaginative bankruptcy—I think I would put his *Reflections on the Psalms* at the bottom of the scale, and at the top his contribution to the *Oxford History of English Literature, English Literature in the Sixteenth Century.* The psalms volume is frankly popular, addressed to the average Christian who would like to use the psalms as an aid to piety but is put off by certain features that baffle or repel. Lewis goes at these great poems like a hard-worked Church of England parson making Sunday morning sermons out of them; making hardly any attempt to deal with their quality as poetry, he draws simple moral and devotional lessons from them and often falls into that detestably hard, almost menacing tone that dogs his weaker writings, I mean, for example, the chapter on "Connivance," where he argues that the Christian ought not to associate with people who behave in an un-Christian fashion, ought not to give them the benefit of his company and conversation. And Lewis goes on to regret the good old days when people who didn't toe the line of Christian morality were made to feel their guilt by various bits of bullying:

It may be asked whether that state of society in which rascality undergoes no social penalty is a healthy one; whether we should not be a happier country if certain important people were pariahs as the hangman once was—blackballed at every club, dropped by every acquaintance, and liable to the print of riding crop or fingers across the face if they were ever bold enough to speak to a respectable woman.

When Lewis got into his silly-truculent mood, his historical sense always failed him; surely it is obvious that the adulterer or horse doper in 1850 was in a better position than his modern counterpart, since the hideous weapons of the gutter press and the flashlight camera did not exist to be used on him.

It is true that Lewis immediately adds, "To this question I do not know the answer." But there is in this passage, as in some of the diatribes of Screwtape—so unfortunately licensed by the presiding "irony"—a flavour of eagerness, something suspiciously like relish.

At the other extreme, his *Oxford History* volume is a model. Here, where too intrusive a personality would be fatal, Lewis has just the right amount of idiosyncrasy, combined with that wonderful intellectual vitality and zest. Time after time he performs the feat of writing about some deservedly forgotten book, or some crabbed controversy among the theologians of the Reformation, in a way that makes one follow him with a real eagerness. Not by gimmicks or Chestertonian antics: simply by that keen—almost fierce—pleasure in debate and exposition that made him such a great teacher.

It would be a pity if this fine book were never to be read by any but literary students, for it is many things in one. There are passages of pure exposition, examples of how to set out a complex question with economy and lucidity, which ought to be studied by everyone who has to use his mind for a living; e.g., the brilliant and rapid sketch of Renaissance poetics at the beginning of the chapter "Sidney and Spenser." Or thumbnail portraits of key characters in the story, such as the beautiful miniature of King James IV of Scotland (on pp. 66–67). There is, likewise, a fine humility in the book. Lewis, unlike so many dazzling stars of the business, is not too proud to get down and do some of the dull, slogging work involved in the academic study of the subject—making a bibliography, looking up endless dates, all the long vistas of headaches and inky fingers.

That humility is crystallized for me in a personal reminiscence. As he worked on the book—and it took nine years—Lewis showed various chapters in typescript to friends who might advise him. I got, for some reason,

"The Close of the Middle Ages in Scotland." I read it with nothing but admiration; I knew nothing of most of the writers mentioned in it, but his account made them seem attractive. I laid it on his desk on one of my visits to him, without comment; and a year or two later, when the book came out, he complained half-comically, "I never got any criticism of that chapter I gave you." It was like his humility to bring work of that quality, so deeply pondered and so brilliantly written, to an insignificant young man in his twenties, completely unknown then in the world of letters, and ask quite genuinely for "criticism." God rest him; "gladly wolde he lerne and gladly teche."

# 8

## *From Master to Colleague*

### PETER BAYLEY

SURELY THE CHOICE OF PICTURE was significant? Was it perhaps even deeply significant? It was a reproduction of the National Gallery picture *The Origin of the Milky Way* by Tintoretto. I think it was the only picture in Lewis's rooms in the eighteenth-century New Buildings at Magdalen, but memory may play me false and indeed is now suggesting to me that there was at least one other Tintoretto reproduction. It doesn't matter greatly. The point is that in a dull, soulless, unaesthetic college room, which was of noble proportions and could have been beautiful, the only cheering or beautiful object, except for a coal fire, was this alluringly erotic picture.

Sitting engulfed in the large, deep sofa before the fire as a freshman undergraduate pupil in 1940 (Lewis invariably sat on the left of the fireplace with the light behind him), I could not ignore the picture and indeed gazed entranced at it in the brief periods I dared to give myself from complete attention to my tutor's criticisms of my essay and further leadings-on into the subject we were discussing. I did once comment on it at the end of a tutorial. (If your tutorial were just before lunch, and if he were pleased with what you had done, Lewis would sometimes place a couple of bottles of beer in the hearth to unchill and we would drink.) On this occasion I made some comment on the picture and he responded briefly: "Yes. Jolly, isn't it?" but he did not open out a conversation on it. At the time I think I assumed that he chose the picture because of his interest in the Renaissance and in mythology. I was disappointed he did not talk about it. I was always disappointed that he never showed a trace of any aesthetic sense except about literature.

His room was bare and dully and sparsely furnished. Apart from the large sofa and two armchairs I recall a poor dining table and some cheap dining chairs, just like those you would find in a not very well-off undergraduate's room. I never went or saw into the inner room, which Lewis would often emerge from when you arrived or retreat to as you left. Perhaps that was nicer and held books—for I do not recall any books in the tutorial room. His clothes were no more elegant or tasteful than his room. He usually wore a slightly too small Harris tweed jacket, of a rather hot brown, with all three buttons done up over his, at this time, rather stout figure. His grey flannel trousers were baggy and unpressed. He was large, but rather narrow shouldered and shapeless.

As I was a freshman at University College, which then had no fellow in English, I was sent with the few other freshmen to Lewis, who kindly taught us because we were members of his old college and he had been a lecturer there. Lewis was forty-two. He seemed older. He was already a well-known figure and beginning to be famous. He gave us a heartily friendly welcome, and my dominating recollection of him is of forced geniality, which I think he adopted partly because he wanted to seem friendly and partly to preserve impersonality. It was not false or insincere, and I think it had become an inseparable part of his public persona. It gave one an impression of a more toughly masculine and aggressive character than perhaps he was.

The young never assume or realize that older people can be shy. Lewis refers to his own shyness several times in *Surprised by Joy*, but it never occurred to me at that time, so celebrated was he in his profession and seemingly so overwhelmingly confident. His voice had rather harsh tones and was a little overloud, and so was his laughter, which was frequent and hearty. Thinking back, I believe the almost boisterous bluffness and geniality covered uncertainty or even timidity in social relations. There is a paradox, for while there was something almost schoolboyish in his heartiness, he was also Jove-like, imperious, certain, absolute. I found the mixture alarming. Even more alarming was his ceaselessly active, almost aggressive conduct of the tutorial.

Most tutors have off days, and most have little spells of seeming inattentiveness or even boredom. I have since heard that Lewis grew to dislike tutorial work and was often bored, but I don't remember him ever showing any signs of it. He would listen to your essay intently, while smoking his pipe, or rather constantly relighting it. I have never seen a man keep a pipe going for so short a while or use so many matches in relighting it. He would occasionally interrupt, turning his face toward you, arresting you with his eyes, which were very dark brown and liquid. In themselves the eyes were rather expressionless, yet the total impression of his face was one of great liveliness and humor much of the time. In a tutorial, if he was amused by something in your essay he would laugh delightedly. That was a very pleasing sensation, and I used deliberately to try to occasion it. If he were pleased with the essay and praised it, you felt tremendous elation, and as if you had been temporarily admitted to a new area or era of cameraderie.

I am not sure that he was an outstandingly good tutor, although it was wonderful to go to him, and incredibly inspiriting. But he wanted to convert you to his point of view, and he did this by posing a series of apparently simple questions and exposing the folly or untenableness of your answers. I was always suspicious of being trapped, especially as there was something a little cut and dried about his teaching (as indeed there is likely to be after a few years with any don in the excellent but remorseless Oxford tutorial system, as I found when I became a don myself).

I was up for three terms in 1940–41 and then went into the army. When I returned in 1946 Lewis was no longer able to teach University College men because he had too many Magdalen pupils, and so we went to Hugo Dyson of Merton, a contemporary and an old intimate of Lewis's (who lauded his "untiring intellect and the selfless use he makes of it" in the preface to *The Allegory of Love*). I do not remember how it came about, but there began a small dining club in 1946 or 1947 consisting of "Jack" Lewis and Hugo Dyson, myself, and three other undergraduates: two of them old school friends of mine and, as Demies of Magdalen, pupils of Lewis's, Tom Stock and Derek Brewer, and the other, Philip Stibbe, a Merton friend and a pupil of Hugo Dyson's. We had in common, the six of us, the study of English and the fact of all having been wartime soldiers, although of course Lewis and Dyson had been in a different war.

We dined once a term for three or four terms, sometimes in the upper room of the Roebuck in Market Street, sometimes in Magdalen, and sometimes in Merton. Both Lewis and Dyson were reliving memories of a war and the experience of going up or back to the university after that war. At this time, both would have been in their late forties. We were all twenty years and more younger. They threw themselves wholeheartedly into merriment, and we had glorious evenings of anecdote, literary talk, and laughter, and even, sometimes, sang soldier songs. Lewis's gleaming good fellowship on these occasions and his serious but light-in-hand intelligence were set off by Dyson's incredible energies of wit, wordplay, and conversational fantastication, but I think none of us felt we ever got on to any more intimate terms with Lewis. I now think it surprising—and virtuous—of him to have wasted his time with us undergraduates, and I am regretful that we still did not know him any better.

I always remained a little frightened of him, and so did Hugo Dyson, although they had been close friends for many years. There was something unintentionally rebuffing about Lewis's intellectual supremacy. He never exerted it unkindly, but he liked to win or to score, and that he could do easily. I confess that he turned me sometimes into a stammering fool who would occasionally, halfway through a sentence, forget what the end of it was meant to be, even at these informal dinners. But once, years later, I was at a private dinner party at the Mitre, given by Roger and June Lancelyn Green, and I suddenly overheard Lewis saying to his neighbor, over port, while I was on the edge of another conversation: "Yes, oh, yes; he turned me into a stammering idiot. I couldn't at all do myself justice in his company." I wish I had seized the moment and asked him who *his* overcomer was, but the moment passed.

I ought to have realized from this little episode that he was a shy and vulnerable man, but the assumed persona was too strong. It is probable that he had early assumed it as a defense from victimization or mockery at school, and enlarged it as a young officer in the last year of the Great War, and that it gradually took over in the third of the men's worlds he inhabited —the male preserve of an Oxford college and common room, of which the majority of residents were confirmed and older bachelors.

Everyone knows that he lost his mother before he was ten. No one knows what his relationship with his "adopted mother" Mrs. Moore was. He lived a solidly male existence and, with the exception of Mrs. Moore and her daughter, there was hardly a woman in his life until his middle fifties, when he met and later married Joy Davidman. I think he was a man shy of intimacy, pretty self-reliant, deeply absorbed in his profession. He avoided merely social occasions and might seem rude or impatient when forced into one. He was happy and triumphant in intellectual discussion, which was always deeply serious as well as playful and amusing. Possibly he was happiest in his rooms reading and writing. At the peak of his renown, in the 1930s and 1940s, when he was full of certainty and power, he seemed confident and dominating, but his friendliness I found somehow bludgeoning.

Here is an example. When I was first about to lecture on Spenser I wanted to dispute some important points Lewis had made in his writing about the Bower of Bliss in Book II of *The Faerie Queene*. Partly out of courtesy, but partly also to provoke a response in case I had actually misunderstood him, I wrote to him about it, outlining what I intended to say. I addressed the letter "Dear Mr. Lewis." Very soon I received a long reply, in which he refuted my argument (I think unconvincingly) in a rather dismissive way, so that I felt completely daunted. I don't mean that it was bullying, but it was overforceful and, as quite often I think also in speech, the tone seemed wrong. Yet he was at bottom a sensitive man, because he obviously realized this, and he ended the letter with what I am sure were meant to be expressions of friendliness: the P.S. was, "And don't Mister me," to which he added, "Hoots!" I should of course in the way of those days have addressed him "Dear Lewis," but this would have seemed to me to be claiming too much intimacy and equality with him. The matter is trivial, yet not without significance.

The point on which I had taken issue with him was about sexuality in the Bower of Bliss. To go back over our disagreement will suggest a great strength and a great weakness of Lewis as teacher and critic. His greatness lay in extraordinary powers of clarification and illumination. His weakness lay in this very strength: he could not resist oversimplification and beautifully neat conclusions. He loved to be able to clap his hands and cry "Quod erat demonstrandum." *The Allegory of Love* not only provides several examples of this but also is itself an example of it. He oversimplified the idea of courtly love in a way that long baffled and bedeviled criticism of medieval literature, presenting it as if it were a cut-and-dried, established, codified, and neatly recorded single phenomenon found over several centuries in many literary works in several languages. Further, his investigation of the rise, apotheosis, and decline of the ideal of courtly love he made too immaculately to run parallel with demonstration of the rise, apotheosis, and decline of the form allegory. *Quod erat demonstrandum.*

Of course the enterprise was immense. I doubt if any other scholar of this century could have brought a survey of such magnitude to such triumphant fruition or have written with such transcendent and illuminating power—and yet so engagingly—about so much almost lost or unknown medieval literature. The sweep and the economy of his writing on both Chaucer and Spenser are as remarkable as the sensitive and usually accurate perception. Lewis was obviously at the top of his form as he wrote this magisterial and brilliant book. It is full of imperishable Lewisisms and certainties. "The best preparation for a study of Guillaume de Lorris is to read a curious little dialogue in which Mr. Aldous Huxley, whether consciously or not, has revived its method." (*The Allegory of Love,* 1936 and later, p. 117.) "In the unlikely event of finding a beginner in philosophy who read [sic] Old French I should confidently direct him to the *Romance of the Rose* for an introduction to this particular part of the subject" (p. 143). "Whatever claims reverence risks ridicule. As long as there is any religion we shall laugh at parsons; and if we still . . . make fun of women, that is because the last traces of *Frauendienst* are not yet wholly lost" (p. 144). (Something uncomfortably lordly and masculine here.) "Where the turf was so smooth a gallop of thousands of couplets proved irresistible" (p. 145). "Humanity does not pass through phases as a train passes through stations: being alive, it has the privilege of always moving yet never leaving anything behind. Whatever we have been, in some sort we still are" (p. 1).

This is all glorious—Lewis as a sort of Drydenesque Chesterton, even more confident, blustering, mischievous, and amusing, and dismissive in his apothegms and certitudes. But he is a remarkable scholar and a much more perceptive, widely read, and enriching critic. Yet the demonstration of an overwhelming proof or the clinching of a long argument occasionally makes one feel that a great crack has appeared that he has not noticed or will ignore.

One of Lewis's great achievements, and all within the compass of one chapter, sixty pages or so, of *The Allegory of Love,* was to reveal the firm structure of organized and developing meaning in *The Faerie Queene,* seemingly so wandering and loose. A good example is the exploration of

Spenserian contrasts between nature and art. Lewis compares the Garden of Adonis, with its natural beauty and spontaneity, with the Bower of Bliss, first seen in Book II canto 5, when Cymochles is found asleep under an "Arber greene" that "art, striving to compare with nature" had "dispred." Then he turns to the imitation ivy in metal that adorns Acrasia's "bathing-pool." This pool is soon to provide an example of Lewis's occasional lapses in taste and tone (the forced jocular vulgarity—seeking unhappily to make contemporaneous a contempt he felt Spenser felt, when he named the naked damsels: "Their names are obviously Cissie and Flossie . . . ducking and giggling in a bathing-pool for the benefit of a passer-by: a man does not need to go to fairie land to meet them"). In an important "digression" he turns to "pictures" in Malecasta's house (luxurious corruption), contrasted with the Temple of Venus that has no depiction of lovers, but the living lovers themselves, and then contrasts the pictured Cupid in Busirane's house with the "flocks of little loves," all alive and fluttering about the neck and shoulders of Venus. Then the naked damsels in the pool are contrasted with the naked ladies dancing with the Graces before Colin Clout in Book VI. He returns again to love pictured and actual: Venus and Adonis in Malecasta's tapestries and the real Venus and Adonis in the Garden, the latter presenting a picture of actual fruition, for Venus

> . . . whenever that she will,
> Possesseth him and of his sweetnesse take her fill,

the former a presentation "not of 'lust in action' but of lust suspended—lust turning into what would now be called *skeptophilia*," for Venus is "merely looking at him,

> And whilst he bath'd, with her two crafty spyes
> She secretly would search each daintie lim.

The contrasts between virtuous "natural" love and meretricious or reprobate carnality or crude sexuality, and between nature and art, are all the clearer to readers of Spenser for Lewis's explorations of them, but a dubious thread in the exposition is picked up and made too much of. The secret gazing of Venus at the sleeping Adonis in the tapestry at Malecasta's house is related to Cymochles's pretending to be asleep but actually peeping "with his wanton eies" at the half-naked damsels playing dissolutely about him (II. 12.32ff), and then both are related to the presentation of Acrasia in the Bower of Bliss. "Acrasia herself *does* nothing: she is merely 'discovered', posed on a sofa beside a sleeping young man in suitably semi-transparent raiment." (Notice again the near-jocular, knowing tone and also the—not uncommon—inaccuracy of detail.) "The Bower of Bliss is . . . a picture, one of the most powerful ever painted, of the whole sexual nature in disease. There is not a kiss or an embrace in the whole island: only male prurience and female provocation."

Of course it is not true, and it was on this topic that I wrote to Lewis in 1948. I pointed to Spenser's restrained but unequivocal account of Acrasia and Verdant in the Bower: the references to "his sleepie head," her "langour of her late sweet toyle," the sweat on her breasts, her "faire eyes sweet smyling in delight," the references to Verdant spending his body "in lewd loves, and wasteful luxuries." How did this square with Lewis's claim that there was "not a kiss or an embrace in the whole island: only male prurience and female provocation"? In his reply, which I have said was rather bullying in tone, he evaded the direct question, skipped sideways, and went on to say that he was not claiming that "intercourse never took place" but that I should concentrate on what Spenser actually presented, which was a semi-naked girl gazing at a sleeping lad. Of course, he went on, Spenser *couldn't* have presented intercourse. However, it was just this, the sexual congress of Venus and Adonis in the Garden of Adonis, which he had praised in *The Allegory of Love* because it was frank and natural. And in that same Garden, "Frankly each paramour his leman knowes" (III. 6.42). But Lewis was not prepared to yield, and I note that many years later, although he had modified his view somewhat, he was still guilty of inaccuracy of detail and held to his original point: "because the Bower is simply a place of sensuality, it is never shown in act. It presents no action, but only the sensual attractions that lead to action. Thus Verdant and Acrasia are never actually shown embracing, even if embraces may be supposed to have taken place between them outside the poem." (*Spenser's Images of Life,* ed. Alastair Fowler, Cambridge 1967, p. 46.)

Sex was possibly a kind of blind spot and stumbling block to Lewis. In his writing, there are much adulation and veneration of virginity. There is a hearty (but shy) bachelor admiration for womanly beauty provided it is known to be virtuous, and especially for presentation of motherliness and fruition. There is a hatred of sensuality and the indulgence of sexuality. The slangy style he adopted at times, for example with reference to Cissie and Flossie, is an indicator of fascination and recoil presented as jocular contempt. Yet he shared largely in the healthiness of imagination and response he rightly praises in Spenser. I wonder whether the Tintoretto, with its frank (but virtuous) sexuality wasn't chosen not so much because of Lewis's interest in the Renaissance and in mythology but because of its virtuous eroticism. Although the subject is strictly not erotic or even amatory, the picture is deeply erotic. Hera springs naked from her bed, one foot to the ground, her loins suggestively not quite bare. Over her cruises the strongly built figure of Alkmene; if you look at the muscular back and shoulders you might think the model was a man. Phallic shapes are prominent around the central figure. The infant Heracles is at one breast, and from both nipples spurts the heavenly milk. Lewis tells us of his dismissal of a young lady he once had to examine who "advanced the view that Charissa suckling her babies was a figure, in its own way, no less disgusting than Error vomiting (p. 316)." He is making it clear that he will have no truck with such prudish and unnatural fastidiousness, or "disdainefull nicetee." Tintoretto's robust Venetian candor and delight in the body clearly appealed to him. It is very like Spenser's (and Tintoretto died only four or five years before Spenser).

It was strange perhaps that Lewis, this powerfully emotional and imaginative man, lived as a bachelor until he was fifty-eight. The maleness of his worlds—schools, briefly the army, a man's college at Oxford—the custom of the time, his early loss of his mother, and the difficulties of relationship with his father (more than balanced by the affectionate ease of his relationship with his brother), his early shyness, perhaps his too-great dedication to scholarship and hard work, part legacy of his Protestant-Ulster origins, all no doubt contributed something to this prolonged bachelorhood.

Some years after the rebuffing letter ("Hoots!"), fairly soon after he had met Joy Davidman, I started seeing him again, originally by the mere chance of meeting them on a sunny Sunday morning when I found them having a drink before lunch at Studley Priory, an Elizabethan house in its own park six or seven miles north of Oxford, which was then a delightful private hotel. He seemed very different: much more muted, gentle, and relaxed. Even his voice and laugh seemed quieter. I felt that his sensitive nature had at last come through a carapace of tough masculine clubbability. I think perhaps by this time his health was not good (he had always before seemed a personification of rude health), and certainly Joy David-man was in poor health. But I do not think this alone could have accounted for the change I saw in him. Later he asked my wife and me with a number of others to a luncheon party in Magdalen to signalise their marriage. We had lunch in a room in the Chaplain's Quad, and after the pudding the men moved out into the sunny day and the ladies elsewhere while the table was cleared for dessert and coffee and brandy. I happened to stand talking with him and Nevill Coghill, and Lewis said: "Do you know, I am experi-encing what I thought would never be mine. I never thought to have at sixty what passed me by in my twenties." He was smiling and seemed gentle and jubilant with love. I like to think that the great interpreter of chivalrous, honourable, generous, and chaste love, in his palmary studies of Chaucer, other medieval writers, and Spenser, should have come toward the end of his life to such felicity.

Two years later Joy died, and in another three he followed her. My last memory is of his funeral at Headington Quarry, on a very cold, frosty but brilliantly sunny November morning. There was one candle on the coffin as it was carried out into the churchyard. It seemed not only appropriate but almost a symbol of the man and his integrity and his absoluteness and his faith that the flame burned so steadily, even in the open air, and seemed so bright, even in the bright sun.

# PART THREE
## *Colleague*

# 9
## *At the Breakfast Table*
### ADAM FOX

To become a fellow of an Oxford College for the first time when one was well on in middle life and then discover that, instead of having a quiet breakfast in their own rooms, the dons were expected to have it in the common room, was a shock from which I never really recovered all the twelve years I was at Magdalen. And yet this grisly practice certainly had its compensations. For it gave me the privilege of being at table a hundred times a year at least with three very interesting characters whom it gives me great joy to recollect.

The *doyen* among them was certainly Paul Benecke, the senior fellow, a grandson of Mendelssohn, a scholar of overwhelming modesty, utterly devoted to the college in which he had already spent thirty-six continuous years, a man of very great virtue and piety, yet with a touch of cynicism that was entertaining. Only once did I hear him say a word against a member of the college. That was when I had remarked that, while I was away, I had seen something of a certain bishop whom I named, and that he had told me that his father had been a Fellow; at which Benecke looked very grave and said, "Oh, he was the son of that man, was he? He was a very bad man." I would have liked very much to have probed the badness, but it was clear that the conversation was at an end; it was impossible to pursue it, it was too awful; he went on eating.

As the Senior Fellow, he had one gift that was of great value to the college. In my time we expended, and perhaps wasted, a great deal of our attention and ingenuity discussing new statutes. Benecke was always able to tell us how the old statutes ran that these new statutes were intended to replace, and what they had been held to mean on different occasions. He knew what objections had been raised to them that had called for change or redrafting. He knew also how any new statute was supposed to rectify the position, and on what grounds it had been criticised in the course of discussion and finally decided upon. And when the college seemed likely to be prevented by statute from doing what it would like to do, he would with the utmost diffidence suggest that under the circumstances a statute might be deemed to mean or to permit it, even if a more obvious interpretation lay in the opposite direction.

Benecke always affected or rather possessed instinctively the scholar's grace of assuming that you were bound to know anything that he knew, which was of course wildly untrue in my case, and not in mine alone. It was sometimes rather tiresome and made it difficult to know what he was talking about. I remember a morning when he suddenly said, "I see *Fury's* in trouble again." You had to think like lightning whether *Fury* was an old member of the college or an animal at the zoo (where, like God, he called all the animals by their names), or whether, as was actually the case this time, it was one of His Majesty's ships that had run ashore.

His rooms had nothing new in them and nothing of note except a rather stolid-looking piano, on which he played beautifully, if only he could be persuaded to play at all. One of his most persevering idiosyncracies was exhibited on the mantelpiece that was stocked up with pigs—china pigs, clay pigs, wooden pigs, ivory pigs—in great variety, none of them large.

I believe he spent almost nothing on himself. Beneath a handsome face, slightly touched by sadness, he habitually wore a very torn and ragged collar, and the rest of his clothes were more or less in keeping. He was bent on avoiding waste of time; his rapid gait was an indication of that. He would undertake the dullest jobs, long or short, make out a long list, hunt out a date, discover a reference. I asked one morning where the words *Securus judicat orbis* came from, and he gave me the reference to St. Augustine before 10:00 o'clock. As a matter of fact I suppose he knew it is given in Newman's *Apologia*.

I could willingly spend some more time on Benecke, but I must pass on to J. A. Smith, the Waynflete Professor of Moral and Metaphysical Philosophy. J. A., as he was called, partly to distinguish him from A. L. Smith, the Master of Balliol, was now some seventy years of age and a fine specimen of an old Scotsman who had devoted a long life to clearing up his own mind and other people's. He had been a real institution at Balliol as a successful tutor and a character, and to tell the truth his heart was still there. Appointment to the Waynflete Professorship had entailed a migration to Magdalen, and although he did not say it in so many words, he never ceased to reveal his lasting regret at the change. But quite unconsciously, for he was a benign and gracious person and would never have wished to offend; but truth will out when you have been her votary all your life.

At the time when I knew him, he had become in the main a philologist. Perhaps without knowing it he was a pioneer in the move to semantics so-called that has overtaken philosophy in recent years. Perhaps however this was not so, for he was not interested, I imagine, in the meaning of meaning, but just in the meaning of words. For his purposes I myself came in useful. My fellowship was attached to the office of Dean of Divinity, which meant what would better be described as Dean of Chapel, a title that seems to belong only to Cambridge. I used to have to confess that apart from the Bursars, I had, I believed, the last surviving fellowship in Oxford that was not specifically attached to learning. Among the other dons I was the man in the street.

Now J. A. had fallen into the way of speculating on odd little problems, which apparently assailed him in bed when sleep deserted him. I remember him coming down one morning and telling us that he had been thinking in the night what a dreadful thing it would be for a learned Chinese to go blind. I do not know if the other members of the party knew why it would be more dreadful for a Chinese than for any other learned person. I had no idea, but I knew my place, and when I asked why this was so, it appeared, according to J. A., that many of the ideograms that make Chinese writing so beautiful conveyed meaning to the eye but had no sound attached to them. Reading in Chinese was in part at least like looking at a picture book, and for that of course a blind man is fatally handicapped. I understand this really is so.

But J. A.'s speculations were not always so exotic. They were more in the way of combating accepted notions. One day he asked me at breakfast what I thought the common Greek word *cheir* meant. I never doubted from the age of ten, and I don't think anyone else ever doubted, that it means "a hand." "I'm not asking you for information," he said. "I don't want to know what you think. I only want to see what you will say." I quite understood this, and I dutifully obliged by saying "hand," and indeed I had no other answer ready. "No," he said triumphantly. "That is what I thought you would say. But my belief is that it means 'a forearm.' " He illustrated this with examples that I cannot now recall; several of them were from Homer. Some months or a year later he was still considering the same question. He asked me once more what I thought *cheir* meant. I had half a mind to say "forearm," but I hadn't the heart to do it.

I always regretted that he was a bit past his best when I came to know him. But he was still impressive, and very kind to me, though I stood for the Church, of which he had no great opinion. He once opined that Dr. Lang, the Archbishop of Canterbury, had in his early days wavered between a career in the Church or at the bar, and he thought he had made a wise choice and would certainly not have been Lord Chancellor.

I have now given some notion, I hope, of three of those (including myself) who formed our quartet at the breakfast table. But now comes in the fourth and in many ways most remarkable, C. S. Lewis, remarkable perhaps most of all because he was notably detached from this world and yet made so great an impact on it. His innocence and ignorance were unlimited. He took a very slight interest in what was going on around about him in our little academic world. Some current discussion about college or university affairs that had been in everybody's mind and on everybody else's lips passed him by, though when at last he heard of it, he often made a very sound observation slightly tinged with petulance. About some proposed change in the tutorial system that tended to exalt the faculties at the expense of the colleges, he remarked, "We shall soon be just the Staff," an anticipation not far from the truth. When proposals were first published in the press for a new kind of college, which ultimately issued in the foundation of Nuffield, and we four were discussing them, he said, with less prescience it may be, that a college like that would either disappear or more probably become like all the other colleges. It seems possible now that the other colleges will become more or less like it.

But petulance is always half amused at itself, and his was no exception. On Fridays our chapel service consisted of the Litany, which in the *Book of Common Prayer* contains three substantial suffrages for the sovereign and another for his family. As we came into common room one Friday,

Lewis commented, "That Litany makes one feel as if the Royal Family were not pulling their weight."

If my recollection is correct he never read the newspaper in Common Room himself. I seem to think that in the earlier years, when he was struggling out of atheism into the Church, he rarely came to breakfast at all. But from about 1933 he attended chapel regularly, and came in from it with Benecke and myself about 8:15 to join J. A. I always felt, I don't know why, that J. A. might have been there for an hour or two already or all night. Lewis at any rate was the first to leave us. There was a touch of haste without hurry about his attitude toward his breakfast. He was anxious to get back to his work and have a little time at something congenial before the pupils arrived. Not that the pupils were for the most part uncongenial, but few of them afforded any contest of wit, which was what he greatly loved in company of every kind. He sometimes regaled us with little anecdotes about them, as of one, who being questioned as to the matter of a date referred to his own manuscript and said with some assurance, "Well, it says so here." He took some pupils from outside, mainly from New College and University, and occasionally asked them to dinner in hall. One, Hone, a somewhat senior man and a Rhodes scholar, came once. It was in the summer term, and we were all delighted to hear Lewis inquire of him whether he played games, for he was in fact captain of one of the university cricket eleven at the time.

But we must come back to him at breakfast in common room. I think he had a great respect for Benecke, but he had a real reverence for J. A., though both respect and reverence were mingled with some amusement. He had not many interests in common with Benecke, nothing much to give or to receive about the college or about music or about ancient history, in which Benecke had been tutor for many years in the past; and Benecke was in any case too modest to sustain a lively debate. But Lewis was a philosopher as well as a man of letters, and as such able to bring out J. A. much better and make him show his paces. He asked him enticing questions and chaffed him not a little in an affectionate way. But I cannot recollect much of these small encounters or enough to retell them; what I could write down would have lost its savour.

In me Lewis found someone much devoted to poetry as a reader but not as a student. I looked to him for information and opinion, but I must often have asked the wrong question. He sometimes surprised me, as when he named Dante as the best example of "pure poetry." He did not often quote poetry, at any rate so early in the morning. I have sometimes wondered whether he really enjoyed it in the way I do. Certainly he admired some of it immensely and asked himself how it was significant in its own age and ours. His *Allegory of Love* I took up as a duty, not thinking to care greatly for it, since it ended with Spenser, which is just where I begin. But I found it fascinating; he had the art (which he shared with Lytton Strachey) of interesting one in authors one had never read. Personally, if I had ventured on anything but homage, I should have told him that for me he was too much concerned with what his author was meaning to say, and too little with the art of artifice with which he said it. He might have replied that he did not by any means neglect the art of poetry; he might just have thought me hopeless.

Among the acts and words of Lewis at the breakfast table was something that intimately concerned me, and its effect was so remarkable and unexpected that it entertains me and will perhaps entertain others if I tell my version of how I became Professor of Poetry in 1938. This shall close these random recollections. The faculty of English literature has always tended to try and make the professorship of use to itself, and the professor is in fact a member of the board of the faculty. But I always held that Mr. Henry Birkhead in leaving funds for founding the chair was proclaiming that poetry, since it is the art in which English indisputably reaches the heights, may be justly claimed as an interest of all who were bred at Oxford. The holder of the office was to address himself to the university at large and not to a group of specialised students only. The faculty in fact, since its foundation in 1904, has not notably diffused a love of letters, and perhaps that is not its aim.

The professorship falls vacant every five years, and on this occasion the first name put up was that of the late E. K. Chambers, a retired civil servant, aged seventy, a very learned man who had made Shakespeare his hobby and had written more than one learned volume about him. If you had asked him what was the cast at the first performance of *Love's Labour's Lost*, I think it is quite likely he would have told you out of his head. But he would not have been my choice; and when at breakfast one morning I read that Chambers was proposed, I said without any thought of being taken literally, "This is simply shocking; they might as well make me Professor of

Poetry." Whereupon, Lewis said instantly, "Well, we will." And they did.

Of course I had no claim to the appointment. I was known to all my intimates as a lover of poetry; the Oxford University Press had published at their expense a long and childlike poem of mine called *Old King Coel*, and I had won the Sacred Poem prize, though that achievement would have been a decided handicap if many had known of it. Nevertheless the faculty became somewhat alarmed at the weakness of their candidate, and with what Evelyn Waugh called the "innocent ineptitude of the don," they put up a second candidate of greater promise. Between them these two divided the votes of the learned, and I came in with the mob. For the whole body of the masters of arts of the university, estimated at that time at about 9000, are the electors, though of course most of them know nothing of it; and I expect I may have been known to a rather disproportionately large number of them. At any rate I had the majority, and the damage was done. Whether Lewis had ever expected me to be elected I don't know, but I think he did feel about Chambers as I did. And besides that he was always ready for an adventure, and often feeling fine at breakfast. My lectures were not very successful; if I were professor now, I should be much more outrageous, and I ought to have been then. But anyway the war came on, and I left Oxford and went to London. I really think I did some good, for those who have followed me in the chair have been men of distinction, and mostly successful.

But things are not what they were in the world of poetry. At the beginning of this century Andrew Bradley gave his lectures on Shakespearean tragedy to an audience reckoned at about 1400. I recollect that he had a high, not quite agreeable, but rather exciting voice, and we all hung on his words. The great bulk of the undergraduates in those days would have had some poetry on their shelves, and many of them were constant lovers of it. Lewis did more than a little to foster that love, but other influences have put poetry in the shade, the more's the pity. For it means that the most poetical nation on earth is not being true to itself.

Lewis and Benecke and J. A. Smith are dead. Their voices at breakfast in the Common Room at Magdalen thirty years ago linger only in my mind. And in the common room at breakfast now, I understand that no one speaks at all.

# 10

## *Orator*

### GERVASE MATHEW, o.p.

C. S. LEWIS HAS BEEN FORTUNATE in his two biographers: Walter Hooper was a son to him at the end, and Roger Lancelyn Green inspired the Narnia cycle and was responsible for his final idyll, the journey to Greece. They aimed at providing "a framework of straightforward fact not advancing psychological theories or passing philosophical judgments." The life story has been told quietly—but it is the quiet digestion of massive documentation. Still, perhaps because of the interests of both authors, it is primarily the life of C. S. Lewis the writer; each of his books is analyzed with sensitive perception. But his influence on his contemporaries was at least as much as orator as writer. This will be forgotten increasingly, and there is already some evidence of a strange popular image of him. One is this: "Lewis was popularly supposed to regard both lectures and tutorials as a complete waste of his valuable time and to hold undergraduates in the uttermost contempt." No travesty could be further from the truth. His willing audiences would never have enjoyed his lectures so much if he had not been so obviously enjoying them himself. He took a vivid, perhaps rather sporting, interest in the numbers who came to him, and he was depressed when he failed to repeat his Oxford triumphs at Cambridge. At times he lectured from skeleton notes, at times from a written text; on occasion he improvised; it was hard to tell which method he was following. But always he forged a personal link with those who heard him.

I can write with some authority on C. S. Lewis as a lecturer; for nine years my lectures for the English faculty were coordinated with his and, when he went to Cambridge, he arranged that I should take on his course "Prolegomena to Medieval Literature." I have no qualification to write on him as a tutor but, when I remember the vehemence of his belief in education as opposed to training, I find it impossible to conceive that he judged his tutorials to be a complete waste of his time. The suggestion that he had a contempt for undergraduates will seem patently absurd to any who remember the Socratic.

It seems likely that we are at the birth of equally bizarre popular images of Charles Williams and of J. R. R. Tolkien.

# II

## *In Cambridge*

### RICHARD W. LADBOROUGH

THE OLD MYTH STILL SURVIVES at Cambridge that an Oxford don in a Cambridge street feels that he is wearing patent-leather shoes, whereas a Cambridge don in Oxford feels that he is shod in heavy boots. In other words a product of Cambridge is rude and unsophisticated, whereas an Oxford man is elegant, witty, clever, and sleek. Cambridge, therefore, is afraid of Oxford, whereas Oxford despises Cambridge. The myth might be said to have had some origin in fact were it not true—so I've heard—that in Oxford it is told exactly the other way round.

The person who informed me of this was C. S. Lewis. But when he first arrived at Magdalene College, Cambridge, from, as he used to describe it "the other Magdalen," those who didn't know him whispered among themselves (and I was of their number) that he was "very Oxford." I suspect that we hadn't the faintest notion of what we really meant, except that we were in a vague kind of way frightened of him. Lewis was certainly witty and clever, but he was not at all elegant and sleek. Metaphorically, he wore heavy boots, not pumps. And even that tended to irritate us, for we were not accustomed, in our stereotyped way, to people appearing at high table literally in a tweed coat.

It was some time before he learned to conform. But, apart from that, with his booming voice and jolly-farmer appearance, he immediately dominated in conversation any group in which he happened to find himself. He couldn't help doing so, of course, but at first we thought it a conscious attitude. We thought that he was an example, pushed to an extreme degree, of Oxford donnery. There were two fallacies in this. First, there is no such thing, and we were guilty of silly generalizations. Secondly, Lewis was fundamentally—and here I know that some will disagree—a shy man. He had lived most of his life in Oxford. His friends, with one or two great exceptions, were Oxford men and women, and of Cambridge he knew almost nothing at all. I am convinced that his fundamental shyness (part of his modesty) caused him during the first years of his Cambridge career to appear more aggressive than he really was. It was not that he outshone us all in conversation, but that he felt that brilliance was expected. There was, perhaps, something of the poseur about him when he first arrived at his new college.

It was Lewis who first broke the ice. I remember how grateful I felt when I, perhaps among others, received a little note from him in his crabbed handwriting: "Dear Dick, May I call you that? Yours, Jack." Jack was the name he was known by, and Jack, of course, he always remained. This calling of his colleagues by their first names was one of his few unconservative traits. In at least one Cambridge college, the older generation, however long they have formed part of its society, to this day call one another by their surnames. I recall this trivial incident because it is one of the things, among many others, that contributed to Lewis's essential warmth of character. He was from the first anxious to be accepted, however hard he might find it to be so.

Lewis was frequently jovial and delighted not only in hearing funny stories but also was in telling them, and in this he was an expert. No one was less like the puritanical, tight-lipped moralist that some people thought he was after reading *The Screwtape Letters*. Some of his own stories were certainly not prudish, though never obscene. They were meant for men only and, indeed in certain respects, Lewis was what is sometimes known as "a man's man." He liked, for instance, to talk about his experiences in the army during World War I and to hear those of others.

His rooms in college, which with their paneling and antique appearance, could have been made attractive with little cost and even with little thought, were, it seemed to me, merely a laboratory for his work and his writings. Here he would sit with pen and ink in a hard chair before an ugly table and write for hours on end. Indeed, he seemed to be oblivious of his immediate surroundings, although I suppose that the beauty of them in both his universities must have had an effect upon him. It is always a matter of astonishment to me that during the whole of his period at Magdalene, Cambridge, he should only once have visited the Pepys Library, and that for only twenty minutes when incited to do so by two eminent Oxford visitors.

And yet he read the whole of Pepys's Diary with insight and, of course, with intelligence, and made one of the best speeches on Pepys I have ever heard. This was in hall at the annual dinner held to celebrate Pepys's birthday. Pepys in fact was a late acquaintance of his, and he took it for granted, with his usual modesty, that his hearers knew the text as well as *he* did. The same was true for most other authors. It is now common knowledge that his memory was prodigious and that he seemed to have read everything. The authors and books I liked hearing him talk about most were, I think, some of his own favourites: Dr. Johnson (with whom he had many affinities), Jane Austen, Steven's *The Wrong Box,* and—curiously perhaps—that pearl of schoolboy stories, Anstey's *Vice Versa.* I never tired of hearing him recite from memory the German lesson of the superbly humourless Herr Stohwasser.

The one author he was usually silent about was himself. Little did we know, or even guess when he dined with us in hall of an evening, that he had been engaged in penning during the daytime one of his magna opera. He was silent even when occupied in translating the Psalms into the new version. As is known, he had illustrious colleagues in this task, including, for example, T. S. Eliot. But he was unforthcoming about the whole enterprise. Again, I think that was partly due to his modesty and to his reticence. No man was less given to name-dropping, and no one was ever less of a snob. If a famous person happened to be staying with us, and even if that person were an eminent ecclesiastic, Lewis would *appear* uninterested. Ecclesiastical gossip, indeed gossip about people at all, was completely foreign to him. More often than not he would make a point of sitting next to the most junior person in the room. He was interested in ideas and things; though, when pressed, his judgment of character was sharp and penetrating.

Until his decline in health, Lewis would go for an afternoon walk. He was good with a map and soon had tracked down most of the footpaths in and around Cambridge. Just occasionally, he would start in the morning with a visit to a pub. He liked the atmosphere of a pub, and he liked beer.

He liked port, too, and he enjoyed one or two nightly glasses in the combination room. Incidentally, when he first arrived at Magdalene, he was technically its Junior Fellow, whose customary duty it is to fill the glasses of his colleagues. We tried to absolve our illustrious new professor from performing this menial task but, characteristically, he would not allow us.

He preferred to go for his walks alone, but just occasionally he would allow himself to be conveyed to some special spot by car, for he did not himself drive and was hopeless with any form of machine. Those of us who were privileged to accompany him on walks in the countryside were impressed by his intense enjoyment of scenery. I think that he had more feeling for Nature than for manufactured objects. He would often, for instance, rhapsodize about the "skyscapes"—as he called them—of East Anglia. And, curiously enough, at the end of a walk or drive in the country, he liked to drop in to a tearoom. Tea was as much a part of his routine as port or beer. He usually made himself some tea in his rooms before settling down to his work before dinner. And often he would make another pot before bedtime, which he would ask someone, whether colleague, undergraduate or guest, to share. In food and drink he had, on the whole, simple tastes, but he enjoyed well-cooked food and vintage wines. It was all the more remarkable that at the end of his life, when almost no alcohol was allowed, and he was on a horribly strict diet, he should make no complaint and draw no attention to the fact.

If Lewis were a man's man, it is also certain that he enjoyed female company. Even before he married, he used to give large luncheon or dinner parties in college. Naturally he enjoyed these most when his wife came over from Oxford and acted as hostess. I think he enjoyed these parties as much as we did. He even enjoyed dining out.

But he was essentially a college rather than a university man. He rarely seemed to be interested in the affairs of the university as a whole, or even (and this was a fault) in those of his own faculty. He never attempted to master regulations. He hardly ever read *The Reporter*, the university's official journal, and it was some time before he even discovered its existence. But as time went on, he became more and more interested in college affairs, in some, of course, more than others. He was ignorant of anything to do with finance, and during debates on figures his eyes closed and he was even known to snore. But it might surprise some people to know that, when genuinely interested, administration did not entirely pass him by. I suspect that few could guess that one passage in *The Reporter* on a particularly intricate subject dealing with the relationship between the university and the colleges was penned largely by the hand of C. S. Lewis.

Even the statement that he was above all a college man needs qualifying. Like Magdalene's former master, A. C. Benson, he disliked organized games. (Was it altogether bravado that caused him to make an exception of polo, a sport, I believe, he had never seen?) He quoted Benson on the subject with glee, and with typical overstatement used to say that some of the best cricketers he had met were the nastiest men. I don't think he really believed it; it was merely a hangover from his schooldays at Malvern, which he seemed to take a delight in hating, or pretending to hate, till the end of his days, though in fact he had been there only a year.

Among other college activities, he took an interest in our dramatic productions and was even known to praise a Restoration Comedy produced by undergraduates. He was really excited by a production in English of Tartuffe, which caused him to go back to the French text. By the end of his life he had read the whole of Molière.

Not many undergraduates got to know him; he was too shy to appear to want to be known and too modest to think that they wanted to know him. But he befriended some, particularly those on his own staircase. As there was no question of professional relationship between them, the talk ranged widely and freely and even settled on religion if, but only if, they introduced it. And there was an occasion when he was induced to accompany a party of us to the French Society's production of Racine's *Athalie*. This was a work he did not happen to have read. He did so before seeing the play. He came to lunch with us before we set out and asked the sort of questions I wish I had thought of when discussing the play with undergraduates. He thoroughly enjoyed the rather mediocre performance, and even went on to read some books and articles on Racine afterward. On another occasion, I asked him to be present at a discussion I was holding with undergraduates on Corneille's *Polyeucte*. The discussion lasted two hours, largely on the subject of whether or not a Christian should knowingly seek martyrdom. (Eliot, of course, was freely quoted by the undergraduates.) The volleying was fast and furious, with Lewis usually getting in the final slam.

From what I have heard, the college servants, some perhaps only vaguely aware that he was a great man, respected and admired him. He not only showed them great courtesy—"He was a *real* gentleman," I heard one of them remark—but also showed interest in their well-being. Some of them came voluntarily to attend his memorial service in the college chapel.

It seems needless to say that the chapel was the center of his life in college. He daily attended weekday matins at 8:00 o'clock and, when he was well enough, he walked in the Fellows's Garden beforehand. He was nearly always at Oxford at weekends and so rarely came to our choral services. But at a Sunday Evensong, soon after his arrival, he preached a short, but pithy sermon. I think he liked our chapel and the way things were there ordered. It is typical of him that he preferred a said service to a sung one. He hated hymn singing, and his unconsciously agonized face often showed his distaste when we did the singing. Of course there were often theological reasons for this as well as musical ones. But I think it true to say, as others have also noticed, that neither in conversation nor in his works did he show much interest in organized religion. He was orthodox in belief but seemed to have little sense of the Church. Some may see in this a weakness; others, in his lack of sectarianism, a sign of greatness. One thing is certain: he had little interest in ritual and, I think, did not pretend to understand it. But he liked things to be decently ordered and hated sloppiness. Of course, he was as disciplined in his religion, especially his prayers, as he was in everything else. And at his Oxford house there were grace before meals and fish on Friday.

I think that discipline, one of the keynotes of Lewis's life, goes far to explain how he accomplished so much. His normal existence followed an extremely orderly pattern: early rising, chapel, Communion at least once a week, early breakfast, and then attendance to his huge correspondence that came from all over the world. In Cambridge he had no secretary and answered most of his letters in his own hand. If time allowed he would also write his lectures or books, or else read till lunchtime. Then the afternoon walk and tea, and then more work both before and after dinner. That was, I suppose, his ideal program but, like most great men, he never seemed to be in a hurry and always had time to see people who wanted to consult him. There were many of these, and often strangers, but they were hardly ever turned away.

He rarely referred to these visits and indeed rarely referred to his own affairs or to ours. He seemed, in a sense, to lead a curiously detached life, even when undergoing mental or physical agony. When he learned that his wife was suffering from her deadly illness, he did not mention it at first. I heard of it myself in a rather untypical way. He was looking unusually strained one evening after dinner, and I ventured to ask if he were tired. He replied very suddenly: "I am in great mental agony. Please pray for us." and then was silent. It was some time later that he told me why he asked for my prayers.

He showed the same reticence about the illness that caused his retirement from Cambridge and which eventually killed him. He accepted it with a sort of saintly patience. Right to the end he was his usual gay and humorous self. Only about a fortnight before his death I received a card from him from Oxford: "Have been reading *Les Liaisons Dangereuses*. Wow what a book! Come to lunch on Friday (fish) and tell me about it." I'm glad to say that I went, and of course it was Jack who told *me* about it, and not the other way round.

But C. S. Lewis reading *Les Liaisons Dangereuses* when on the point of death! All in all, I don't think it uncharacteristic. I somehow felt that it was the last time we should meet and, when he escorted me, with his usual courtesy, to the door, I think he felt so too. Never was a man better prepared.

# PART FOUR
## *Transatlantic Ties*

# 12

## *A Chance Meeting*

### CHARLES WRONG

I WAS, FOR A SHORT WHILE in the 1930s, C. S. Lewis's student for political science at Magdalen (I was "reading" history) and was far too much in awe of him ever to have ventured, while a student, beyond deferential formality. He impressed me as an immensely formidable personality, and one who would not tolerate any falling off in scholarly standards. He was always perfectly courteous, but inaccurate statements and fallacious reasoning would be instantly and devastatingly exposed. Nor was he impressed by smart-aleck cleverness. A succession of adolescent wisecracks in an essay of mine was greeted with the observation, "Well, some of them came off and some of them didn't." Looking back on what I can remember of that essay, I think he was probably being too kind.

When I lunched *alfresco* with my friends W. R. Fryer and Norman Bradshaw, both of whom later came to be rather close to Lewis, we used sometimes to see him and his brother setting off for a walk. The brothers looked very much alike, and the sight of the two egg-shaped figures striding briskly along in animated conversation used to provoke amused comments from the three of us. None of us, however, would have ventured to speak to the walkers—although I don't suppose either of the brothers would have minded in the least if we had.

It was only during the war, while serving in Italy with the Royal Air Force, that I became an enthusiastic reader of Lewis. I had read *The Allegory of Love* and *The Pilgrim's Regress* while at Oxford, but I had not had the degree of commitment to Christianity necessary to appreciate the latter, nor the knowledge of medieval literature fully to understand the former. (In fact, more than a knowledge of literature was required. Years later I made a mild protest at the fact that in *The Allegory of Love* there is a lengthy quotation in Anglo-Saxon, which the author does not translate. Lewis simply could not see what I was complaining about.) Now, in Italy, I came across *The Screwtape Letters* and was fascinated. (I was surprised to learn later that, for reasons that he explained in his Introduction to the last edition, he greatly disliked this book.) From *Screwtape*, which remains one of my favorites, I went on to all the others I could find. I can now claim that I have read almost all his books at least twice and possess most of them.

Our paths occasionally crossed. At one time I thought of making a living by journalism, and I wrote to ask Lewis if I could interview him with a view to writing an article about him for publication. He was far from keen on the publication part but, with his never-failing courtesy, he not only consented but also invited me to lunch with him at Magdalen. We had an excellent lunch, but the article on Lewis, though duly written, was never submitted for publication and is now lost. I can remember only a few scraps. He revealed one or two of his strong dislikes: for the philosophy (or perhaps only for the personality, as exhibited in *The Confessions*) of Jean-Jacques Rousseau; and for the novels about King Arthur written by T. H. White. He expressed his surprise at my failure to understand why Ransome, in *Perelandra*, is wounded in the heel (and certainly the symbolism is obvious enough). He was astonished when I told him that I had searched *That Hideous Strength* in vain for a priest or minister, of whatever church, who was not one of the villains; he said this was not the result of anticlericalism, merely an accident. And it was at this lunch, when a friend dropped in to talk to him, that I learned that his name among his personal friends was Jack. This was not a thing that an undergraduate, in prewar Oxford, would ever have found out.

On another occasion we ran into each other at the Oxford railway station. I had been rereading *Perelandra*, and talked to him about it with great enthusiasm. He told me that somebody had written to complain that he couldn't read *Perelandra* because the description of the floating islands made him seasick. "I consider that a very great compliment," said Lewis. For my own part I did have one criticism to make of the book, that I found the conversation between the planetary intelligences rather unconvincing; and I was presumptuous enough to say so. "Oh well," said Lewis, "I don't think I'm very good at archangelese."

The last time I ever saw him was on August 8, 1959, when I happened to run into him in Broad Street, Oxford, which contains Blackwell's (probably the best bookshop in the world), several other bookshops, a pub or two, and three men's colleges—the intellectual heart of Oxford. It took him a moment to recognize me, but that was not surprising. I had no difficulty in recognizing him. He looked a little older than when I had last seen him, five years before; his face was red, as I always remembered its being, but the red was slightly faded. My memory of Lewis was always of somebody who, without being fat, gave the *impression* of enjoying food and drink and good living. He looked as if he still did.

I had recently read his essay on Kipling ("Kipling's World" in *They Asked for a Paper*); and I had a lot to say about it, none of which I remember, as we walked along to Hunt's, the stationery shop. The shop turned out to be very crowded. Suddenly Lewis turned to me and said, "If we get out of here—I say 'if' because it's beginning to seem rather doubtful—I should think we might go and have a pint." And this, shortly, we did.

His personality in conversation was very different from his writing style. Sometimes, and particularly in his scholarly works on aspects of language or literature, his massive erudition and his professional care always to use exactly the right words to convey his meaning made his writing seem a little heavy. It was never pompous, but it could be almost oppressively dignified and formal. His talk was not like this at all. It was friendly, brilliant, and fascinating—entirely suited to the company in which he found himself. In masculine company he used masculine words—coarse ones, if necessary.

We discussed a number of topics, which follow here in no special order. On his novel, *Till We Have Faces*, which I had recently read: "A complete flop," he said, "the worst flop I've ever had. I must admit it's my favorite of all my books, but I suppose that's because it's the last." To my great regret now, I did not pursue this topic; it would be of enormous interest now to know what Lewis had to say about what, failure or no failure, was in some ways his most challenging and interesting work of fiction. On *English Literature in the Sixteenth Century* he spoke with less enthusiasm: "When they asked me to do that, I was tremendously flattered. It's like a girl committing herself to marrying an elderly millionaire who's also a duke. In the end she finally has to settle down and live with the chap, and it's a hellish long time before he dies." On homosexuality: "The thing that you really find out from studying Greek pederasty is what an awful *bore* it must have been. . . . No, I don't think schoolboys pick up the habit from that sort of thing at school. After all, it was *faute de mieux*. You don't go on drinking Wincarnis [an English tonic wine] when you've been introduced to port."

On his books in general: "People complain because my books aren't all of the same sort. And you can't blame them. They expect an author's label to be a reliable guide to the contents. When you buy a bottle of wine with a Burgundy label, you don't want it to taste of hock" (Rhine wine). "Yes, it might have been a good idea to write different sorts of books under different pseudonyms, and I sometimes wish I had. It would have been interesting to see if people could spot that the books were all by the same author —I don't think they could. But of course if you do that, you start at the very bottom with the publisher as far as trade terms are concerned, and that's only fair. He's losing the advantage of your name."

I mentioned that the book critic in *The New Yorker*, reviewing *The Splendid Century* by W. H. Lewis, had referred to the author as "C. S. Lewis's worldly brother." This had surprised me because, though I did not know Major Lewis, it had seemed quite obvious to me that in matters of religion the two brothers held identical views. "Yes; and what's so remarkable is that we were converted about the same time, but quite independently. We weren't in touch. What converted him was, of all things in the world, the Buddha of Kamakura. It gave him an inescapable sense of the numinous. And he went on from that, all the way back to Christianity." I observed that Charles Williams struck me as a man for whom the question of religious denomination appeared almost irrelevant. "Yes," he said, "but I think that's true of *all* good Christians."

About his wife and her illness: "I don't know what you feel about miracles performed by infidels." (That last word has puzzled me. He may perhaps have thought that, as a Catholic, I regarded all non-Catholics as "infidels," which I don't.) "I got married three years ago. My wife was bedridden and dying of cancer; every bone was just eaten up with it. The doctors said her life would be measured in months. The nurses, who know these things far better, said weeks. A priest came and said a prayer. . . .

Well, it didn't happen all at once; but the bones started mending, knitting themselves together. Now—well, one leg is shorter than the other, but she walks, she gardens, she runs about the house. The doctors said it was, literally, miraculous. You know, it frightened me. St. Augustine, you remember, [I didn't, of course] records how he had toothache and prayed to be delivered from it, and when he was, his feeling was one of terror. That your prayers really should be answered—it's very frightening." He quoted Pascal: "The purpose of prayer is that man's efforts should attain the dignity of causality." And "I can't admire an extreme virtue unless the man who has it can show the extreme *opposite* virtue: can reach the two poles and cover all the ground in between." I have not myself read Pascal, and I don't know whether, in this latter observation, Lewis was giving his own opinion of Pascal or summing up one aspect of Pascal's thought.

Not being Irish, I felt no special animus against Oliver Cromwell and said something exculpatory, perhaps even laudatory, about him. Lewis caught me up at once: "I'm afraid I can't agree with you. You see, I'm an Irishman. Yes, Northern Irish, but that makes it worse; the offenders you can't forgive are the ones on your own side." (This would explain his utter detestation of the Black and Tans, who appear, in *That Hideous Strength* and elsewhere, as being much the same as Nazi storm troopers.) "For you to forgive him would be all right, but not for me. 'Forgiveness to the injured doth belong.' "

About suicide: "You know, there's nothing to condemn it in the Bible, in the Old or the New Testament. I think it must be a pagan idea; comes from Plato. I accept it purely on authority. But I remember once I said to a doctor that I didn't see why the incurably sick shouldn't be given release from pain; and I remember what he said: 'You've had no clinical experience, Lewis. Like most of the people who talk like that, you're in robust health. You'll find that it's hardly ever the incurably sick who want to be released, whatever the pain is like. It's their families, who hate to see them suffer, and can't stand the emotional strain (or, of course, the worry and expense), that start saying, "Doctor, he mustn't be allowed to suffer—far better to put him out of his misery".' "

I mentioned a book that had impressed me: Lael Tucker Wertenbacker's *The Death of a Man*. It is the account of how her husband, dying of cancer, killed himself, with her assistance. I don't remember his judgment on the rightness or wrongness of her action, and probably he didn't make one.

What he certainly thought was absolutely right was her decision, from the beginning, to tell her husband exactly what the doctor had told her, holding nothing back. "It's wicked," said Lewis, "to lie about a thing like that. And once you do, you become, in a sense, the enemy; you're trying to fool him. You're like two antagonists across a tennis net. Whereas, if you are honest from the start, when it comes you can face it together."

Everyone knows about his enthusiasm for Tolkien's great trilogy. He asked if Naomi Mitchison, the novelist, had liked it; as it happens, she had written a rave review of it, but he hadn't come across it. "I was so pleased," he said, "when the book was such a success. I thought it would only appeal to a few funny people here and there. . . . No, I agree with you, I'm not particularly fond of *The Hobbit*; but you must realize that *The Hobbit* is only a detached fragment of the whole work. Don't get it into your head that *The Lord of the Rings* is *The Hobbit* expanded; it's the other way about."

We returned to his brother's books: "I'm glad you liked them. You know, he never published a word before he was sixty. . . . Those fool publishers over in America told him, when he was doing his *Life of Louis XIV*, that he wasn't to put in any politics, and he wasn't to give any of his sources. As a result, of course, all the reviewers have been going at him for not giving his sources; and the book itself is entertaining, but it's light, it's history at the popular level. Those publishers always know exactly what they think the public will want, and they're nearly always wrong. . . . His spelling is utterly hopeless. Always has been. He spelled *hierarchy* as *heirarchy* through the whole book, and when I told him he said, 'I use *simplified* spelling!' "

On "Wyvern," his name for Malvern (the public, i.e., private, school where, unlike his brother, he was so unhappy), he mentioned X, a critic whose name I have forgotten: "He's never liked anything I've done, but he's an Old Wyvernian, so to speak, himself, and when *Surprised by Joy* came out he wrote to me and said, 'If we ever go to prison, our first reaction will be "Well, at least it's not as bad as school." That's what made the English great. Their school life was so unpleasant that whatever happened afterwards was enjoyable.' But he's no longer right about the prisons, I'm afraid. You've lost your privacy. It used to be the one great blessing that a prison offered you and a public school didn't. . . . At Malvern all the lavatories were connected, by a channel of water running underneath. It sloped downhill a little, and people used to roll up a vast quantity of bumf in the top one, shove it down, and set fire to it. Then there'd be a fireship passing under everybody's bottom, all the way down."

I remembered that somebody had once said that F. Anstey's Victorian classic, *Vice Versa*, was the only boys' school story that was really true to life; and I asked him if he knew who it was. "Me. Even in a good school, there's no escape from that feeling at the beginning of term: one of utter degradation. I remember once dreaming that I'd gone back to my prep. school [i.e., pre-prep.] as a master. I said to myself, 'All your dreams and your ambitions, and you've come down to this.' And then all of a sudden I wasn't a master: I was a boy. The masters' table in the dining room, which had seemed like hell, suddenly became a far-off paradise."

On the problems of authorship: "People haven't the faintest idea how to set about buying a book. They think the way to do it is to send the money to the author. Of course, some people won't pay money for a book whatever happens. As a friend of mine put it, they'd as soon think of buying a restaurant because they wanted to have a meal in it." On science fiction: He had corresponded with Anthony Boucher and admired him but did not know him personally. "*Fantasy and Science Fiction* (Boucher's magazine) "is the best of those magazines; there's sometimes some astonishingly good stuff in it.... It's getting to be too difficult a field for me. There's less and less fiction and more science."

I myself (like Tolkien) have always had a blind spot for his Narnia series of children's books. With the exception of *The Horse and His Boy,* I have never cared for them. I should not have expected children to enjoy them either, but I have been proved wrong more times than I can count. It turned out that Lewis himself had never been particularly interested in the genre in the first place. He happened to have had an idea that he wanted to try out, and by now, having worked it out to the full, he did not plan to write any more. "I had to write three volumes, of course, or seven, or nine. Those are the magic numbers."

I mentioned that, as an admirer of the books of the late Monsignor R. A. Knox, I had been disappointed in his monumental *Enthusiasm,* an account of the different heresies through eighteen centuries or so. "It's extraordinary," said Lewis, "what a bad book it is. I suppose an author's favorite often is; like *Till We Have Faces.* ——— [again I've forgotten the name] wrote to Knox pointing out fifteen major errors of fact; and

Knox replied very courteously and nicely, didn't try to defend himself. I think it's particularly bad on the Moravians. He was trying to treat them in the same way that he did the others, gently making them look foolish, and when he came to the point he couldn't manage it. There was nothing like that to say about them."

We finished our drinks and stood up to go. He asked me what my plans were. I told him I was about to leave for America, to settle there and teach. He grinned and said, "You, sir, are an adventurer!"

# 13
## *An Enduring Friendship*
### JANE DOUGLASS

I T WAS A BEAUTIFUL AUTUMN DAY, late in October 1954, when I went to Oxford to call upon C. S. Lewis at Magdalen College. I had written to him before going to England about making a dramatization of *The Lion, the Witch and the Wardrobe*, the first of the Narnia stories. He was not at all interested in this idea, but with his usual consideration of others, he said he would be glad to see me should I be in England and "Oxford, not out of the way." Thus the matter rested for several years until I did go to London in September 1954. Alas, I had not read his article "On Stories," included in the volume *Essays Presented to Charles Williams*, for which Professor Lewis was largely responsible and for which he wrote the Preface. Had I done so I should never have had the temerity to embark upon such a project as making a play of one of the Narnia stories.

In the end, I wrote to Professor Lewis, who did not withdraw his suggestion that we meet for a talk. So to Oxford I went, and we had a delightful afternoon in the famous study. Once inside Magdalen College, my courage began to fail me, until I met a young scholar, coming down the stairs, who inquired if I were looking for Professor Lewis. I said yes, adding nervously, "Does he like being addressed as Professor Lewis?" The youth replied with a smile, "Oh, yes, but I think he likes being called just Mr. Lewis better." This encouraging interlude was barely over when a door opened and I heard a cheery voice calling down, "Oh, yes, yes, Miss Douglass—do come up." And soon I was sitting on the sofa near the fireplace facing the windows, and a memorable—for me—conversation took place.

After a few remarks about his interest in Americans, I was soon quite at ease and rattled away as if I had known him always. I tried to explain how I felt about cheap programs for children on the radio and how I dreaded worse what was to come with the development of television. His reply was that he knew nothing of either radio or television and that the thought of such mass media filled him with horror. I think it was at this point that he said, with a wistful smile, "And of course if I should agree to what you want I should more than ever be accused of making propaganda for Christianity." "Well," I blurted out, "with the world in the state it's in, could that do any harm?"

This remark elicited a kind chuckle and, after a pause, he said with some firmness, "I'm the last person in the world with whom to discuss dramatizing anything. I know next to nothing about the drama, and I believe plays should be plays, poems, poems, novels, novels, stories, stories, and certainly the book you mention is pure narrative." Undaunted, I then inquired, "If that is the case, what are you going to do about *Romeo and Juliet?*"

There was another laugh from Mr. Lewis before he lit his pipe and said, "Well, you have me there." Another pause, and he said, "Now you see how little I know about these things." It was then my turn to laugh, and he stopped pacing up and down and sat down opposite me, and we began to discuss what might be done with *The Lion, the Witch, and the Wardrobe,* not for the stage or television, but for the radio. I explained that I thought this might be the ideal medium for it as the effect of the animals could be got by the use of carefully selected and trained voices in contrast to those of the humans. While not enthusiastic, he agreed that this might be possible except in the case of Aslan, who was, of course, God. I acknowledged that this *was* a problem, but I thought the difficulty would solve itself as we worked upon it.

I tried to assure him that I wanted to do nothing without his entire approval. He was very thoughtful before he finally said the only thing he could visualize was to have a narrator (and it would be difficult to cast) reading or telling the story accompanied by drawings (and they must not be cartoons) by a skillful and sensitive artist, as if moving across the pages of a book. He repeated his dread of such things as radio and television apparatus and expressed his dislike of talking films. I said I quite understood this, and that nothing would distress me more than that he should think that I had in mind anything like the Walt Disney shows; I hoped nobody had suggested the book to Mr. Disney. This seemed to relieve Mr. Lewis to such an extent that I thought perhaps Mr. Disney *had* been after the book, but of course I did not ask. And in his usual generous way, Mr. Lewis said, "Too bad we didn't know Walt Disney before he was spoiled, isn't it?"

Before I realized it the afternoon was nearly gone. And what an afternoon it was! The result was that Mr. Lewis agreed to read anything I sent in the way of a scenario, and thus began the correspondence that lasted for so many years.

While working on the scenario, I read everything I could find written by the best children's librarians about the Narnia stories and began the search for C. S. Lewis's own article "On Three Ways on Writing for Children." Excerpts could be located in New York, but I wanted the whole thing, hoping it would help me work out the portrayal of Aslan. Finally, I located the piece in the *Canadian Library Bulletin*, July 1958. The result of this was that I persuaded the Horn Book to publish it in October 1963, with Lillian H. Smith's *News from Narnia* and excerpts from *On Fairy Stories* by J. R. R. Tolkien, so highly regarded by Mr. Lewis. This proved so popular with Horn Book readers that it was re-issued in pamphlet form.

At long last, the suggested treatment of part one of *The Lion, the Witch, and the Wardrobe* was sent to Mr. Lewis. He did not like it at all, and when I saw how upsetting the whole scheme was to him, I dropped the matter at once. This however did not break off the friendship, as might have happened with anyone else. And through it I gained many interesting friends—the friends one makes through letters: Pauline Baynes, who illustrated the seven Narnia books; Professor Kilby; the Howards; and after the death of C. S. L., his brother, Major Lewis, who so faithfully and delightfully carried on my earlier correspondence with his brother. As brief as these letters were, typed on bits of paper, they were always prompt, and usually in answer to some question. It was almost like picking up a conversation with a friend one had recently seen or talked with on the telephone.

It was perhaps due to the experience with *The Lion, the Witch, and the Wardrobe* and its author that I turned to the fairy tales of George Mac-

Donald and began a work on him as a writer of fairy stories. In the midst of this research, I wrote my friend asking permission to use the passage about "Phantastes" in *Surprised by Joy.* The reply was: "Of course, use the reference to *Phantastes* in what I hope will be a very good book about MacDonald."

About this time I went to Cambridge to see the original drawings by Arthur Hughes for this lovely story, recently secured by The Houghton Library of Harvard. Philip Hofer introduced me to Professor Wolff (Robert Lee Wolff) who was then completing a book on George MacDonald, which (within a few months) would be published by The Yale University Press. This lengthy Freudian study of MacDonald, based upon his poorest work (his potboiling novels) appeared in 1961 under the title *The Golden Key,* one of the loveliest of George MacDonald's fairy tales. The Wolff book is another of these works seeking to destroy the reputation of an author long dead. Happily, it has met with a poor reception. Professor Wolff's underlying purpose is to attack Christianity, and his references to C. S. Lewis are extremely disagreeable.

Loyalty to Yale prompted me to accept the invitation of The Yale University Press, prior to its publication of *The Golden Key,* to attend a lecture there by Professor Wolff. His references to C. S. Lewis were even more scathing and unattractive when spoken than read, so I slipped out before he had finished, catching the five o'clock train from New Haven. I was so upset that before I retired, I poured out my feelings in a letter to Mr. Lewis. His answer (and it's the only letter I had from him from Magdalene College, Cambridge) is written in longhand. It has been one of my greatest treasures (and still is), and until recently I kept it in a safe-deposit box in a bank. I took it out once to show my friend, the late John Gordan, then Curator of the Berg Collection in The New York Public Library, who had told me the story of their acquisition of the manuscript of *The Screwtape Letters.*

While preparing the memoir, Major Lewis wrote asking me for any letters I had from his brother. I sent them at once and, while I did not say so, I hoped he would use this Magdalene College letter in the proposed volume. Major Lewis did not do so. I feel sure the reason was that he could not do anything that might make his brother appear, in the slightest way, vindictive. The Major is right of course, but I wish this letter might have been included in *The Letters of C. S. Lewis.*

After much thought, I gave to The Berg Collection, in memory of John Gordan, my first edition of *The Letters of C. S. Lewis*. In the front of it I placed two letters: the first, from Major Lewis giving me permission to do this, and the second the C. S. Lewis letter concerning the Wolff opus. (I thought the Major's letter a lovely one and, also, that it might be useful should any question of copyright ever arise.) This gift comforted Mrs. Gordan, who wrote most touchingly to thank me. She spoke of her husband's admiration of C. S. Lewis and said John Gordan had read aloud the Narnia stories to their children—another beautiful link with C. S. L.

Now when I feel frustrated and discouraged, instead of going to a bank, I can go to my palace on Forty-second Street and Fifth Avenue and read this letter, as indeed you may whenever you wish.

# 14

## *Good Cheer and Sustenance*

### NATHAN C. STARR

Ｍ Y FIRST READING in the works of C. S. Lewis was *The Screwtape Letters,* which my wife gave me, I believe, in 1944. I was completely captivated. Lewis's highly original fantasy, his barbed wit and satire in revealing the wiles of the devil attempting to seduce a Christian believer, were to me enthralling. Having thus made a start I began to explore *The Abolition of Man* and the planetary trilogy. These last so moved me that I wrote to Lewis an "arrow in the dark" on October 18, 1947, praising his insistence on "life made strong through divine grace" and his restoration of "authentic vision" in beauty and terror. In reply, I received a cordial letter of thanks, ending with an invitation to look him up if I ever came to England.

This invitation I was determined to accept, and the opportunity came soon. At the time, I was just embarking on a study of the twentieth-century Arthurian legend. The possibility of going to England and tapping the resources of the British Museum and the Bodleian Library stirred me into action. I was then teaching at Rollins College in Florida. Taking my resolution in both hands, I asked President Hamilton Holt if he would grant me leave of absence for a term. Like the generous friend he always was, he said yes, go with my blessing. In the fall of 1948, my wife and I and two of our daughters set sail for England.

I had already notified Lewis that I was coming. After we got settled in Oxford I sent him a note, saying in effect, "Here I am. When may I see you?" His reply, after an interval of perhaps four or five days, was slightly dashing. I had overlooked the fact that term was just beginning, a time when he was unusually busy. In addition, he had a cold. So there was nothing to do but wait. Meanwhile, my wife had an inspiration. Before we left America, on advice of friends who knew the rigors of British postwar rationing at firsthand, we had filled a small square trunk with all kinds of food that we knew would be very scarce in England. I then prepared a package for Lewis and sent it to him with the following presentation poem I had written in Chaucerian English:

> And now, with sorwe, at his beddes heed,
> Displacyng twenty bokes in blake and reed,
> An heep of boteles, whose bitre bote
> Constreyneth hym to wisshe a shorter throte.
> O curssed tyme, O wikke aspect grym
> Of Saturn whose forlevyng rageth hym.

I don't know whether it was Chaucer or the bacon that did the trick. Maybe it was only because his cold was gone. At any rate, very shortly I received an invitation to see him in his rooms at Magdalen College.

At the appointed hour, I went to his chambers and faced Lewis for the first time. He wore a tweed coat, much rumpled, and baggy grey trousers. I got the impression of a solidly built man, not at all fat, who moved lightly. It took me no time at all to realize that his mind moved as effortlessly as his body. There was no sense of the slight embarrassment that one sometimes feels on meeting a stranger. It seemed as if we had known each other a long time. I cannot now remember how we managed at once to get on such easy terms, what I said, what he answered, what caught us up so easily in friendship. I only know that the hour I spent in his rooms overlooking the Magdalen quadrangle was the most stimulating experience I had ever had—stimulating not through the sober discussion of weighty literary matters, though we had that, too, but chiefly because of the sheer joy of meeting a man of such enormous vitality, such electrical responses, such spontaneous wit, and such a generous outgiving of spirit to a stranger from across the Atlantic.

I was perhaps too bedazzled to remember all the matters we discussed. I told him, of course, about my projected Arthurian book, and I remember his referring with some amusement to his youthful encounter with Mark Twain's *Connecticut Yankee*. We also talked about Charles Williams. He had died, unfortunately, in 1945, three years before my meeting with Lewis, so that I missed the opportunity of knowing a man whose works I greatly admired. I told Lewis how much I valued Williams's novel *War in Heaven*, a profoundly moving story of the discovery of the Holy Grail by a country archdeacon in present-day England, and his Arthurian poems, *Taliessin Through Logres* and *The Region of the Summer Stars*, to my way of thinking the most distinguished poetic additions to the legend in the twentieth century. Lewis was delighted, because of his great love for Williams as a writer and as a person. He pleased me mightily by giving me a copy of Williams's *All Hallows Eve*.

We passed the hour as if it had been five minutes. As I left, he invited me to dine with him in hall at Magdalen. I accepted gladly, and on the day appointed met him in his rooms. We proceeded to the hall, where I was seated next to him at the high table—in the presence of the grave and reverend worthies of the college. This was a scene familiar to me because I had attended Christ Church, Oxford, for two years after World War I and saw such occasions many times. I learned, by the way, that Lewis and I had been undergraduates at Oxford at the same time; he at University College and I at Christ Church. How I wished that we had known each other then!

During that evening he told me about a gathering of friends he attended regularly at a pub in the town. He asked if I would join him at their next session. Would I indeed!

At noon on the day set I presented myself at a pub called The Eagle and the Child, the name vividly illustrated by a large sign on which was painted Ganymede being borne aloft by the eagle of Zeus. As far as I could discover, no one in Oxford ever called the pub The Eagle and the Child; it was known simply and affectionately as The Bird and Baby. I entered and, after ordering my pint of bitter at the bar, I was directed to the parlor, which the proprietor had set aside for the gathering of Lewis and his friends. Once there, I was told by Lewis that according to the established practice, I, as the latest comer, should take the seat nearest the fire, to be displaced by the next arrival. As I recall, there were about eight or ten gathered there. The only ones I remember surely, besides Lewis, were J. R. R. Tolkien and Lord David Cecil. I believe that Father Gervase Mathew was also present, but I cannot be sure. I remember meeting him later and having a valuable talk concerning his friend Charles Williams. The conversation at The Bird and Baby was rather casual and general; I do not recall any sustained serious discussion. It was almost entirely informal, friendly talk among men of like vocations and interests. More than anything else, I received the impression of Lewis as the catalyst, the animating element in the group.

After I returned to America, I felt strongly allied with Lewis. We corresponded quite often, and I greatly valued his letters. I have always remembered a statement in one of them reflecting his deep distress at the aberrations of mankind: "It is a terrible thing to live in a post-civilized world." His letters in their very physical form revealed the deprivations of a postwar period—a few lines on cutoff scraps of salvaged notepaper, mailed in used envelopes. Lewis was always meticulous about answering. For example, he was careful to acknowledge grateful letters from children who had loved the Narnia books; my young goddaughter was pleased beyond words by his reply. Sometimes, however, under press of urgent business, answers would come from his brother, Major Warren Lewis, a scholar who had written authoritative studies of the French ancien régime. We kept in touch, therefore, by considerable correspondence.

My next meeting with Lewis was in August 1960, when my wife and I planned to go from England to Bayreuth for the festival performance of *Parsifal*, and later to Vannes in Brittany for the triennial meeting of the International Arthurian Society. I had already written him, saying that we were coming to Oxford and that we very much hoped to see him and Mrs. Lewis. He had recently married Joy Davidman, an American widow who had been converted to Anglicanism through his influence. It was, alas, a doomed marriage. In one of his letters to me he wrote that he had married a dying woman—evidently a victim of cancer. Later, however, he described a miraculous remission when, after the doctors had done all that they could, and after prayers and laying on of hands administered by the church, the diseased bone began to knit, so that soon his wife was walking again. But the remission was short lived.

We had crossed the Atlantic on a slow ship, so missed hearing the news that stunned us the day after we arrived. As soon as we reached Oxford I telephoned Lewis, saying we would very much like to call. I was horrified to hear him say that his wife had died the week before. Naturally, I said that we would not think of intruding at such a time, but he replied that he very much wanted to see us and suggested that we meet the next day at the Eastgate Hotel on High Street.

So we met at the Eastgate, in the rather dark parlor, where we ordered beer and settled down for a memorable talk. There were two main topics: first Wagner, and second Lewis's wife and stepsons. My wife and I were on our way to hear *Parsifal*, the fulfillment of a lifelong ambition, and I was full of the subject. Lewis was an ardent Wagnerian, not surprising in view of his liking for romanticism and his "Northernness," his fondness for the heroic legends of the primitive Northern people. So we talked of the power and passion of Wagner.

My wife took several photographs of us in action, both of us very animated. Some months later, she sent him prints that she had developed and printed. For a while she struggled with the problem of how to address him. "Dear Mr. Lewis" seemed too stiff; "Dear Lewis" suggested the masculine informality he and I had observed in our letters: "Dear Lewis" and "Dear Starr." Finally she told him that after having spent many hours with him in the darkroom, she had settled on "Dear Jack," his boyhood nickname, as a good American solution. He replied in kind:

*Magdalene College*

CAMBRIDGE

1 Nov. 1960
Dear Nina

Thank you very much for the photos. I can't judge the likeness to myself of course, but if I've come out as well as Nathan it must be very good. Your own absence from the group is much to be regretted. The consolation is that it makes it a Problem Picture. WHOSE WAS THE THIRD GLASS? might well be engineered into a Research question!

I may some day accept your most kind offer of a duplicate or so.

It was a delightful meeting and I hope there may be others. Love to both,

Yours
Jack

We also spoke of his wife and the circumstances of his marriage. Lewis was extraordinarily frank. The marriage, he said, was at first simply one of convenience, arranged so that Mrs. Lewis could stay in England permanently. As time went on, however, the relationship developed into deep love. Joy Davidman was a woman of brilliant mind, of emotional and spiritual power. Her death was a shattering blow, as Lewis revealed poignantly in *A Grief Observed.* Yet I gathered the impression that it was a psychic relief to talk of her frankly to us, and I have always honored him for his confidence. He also told us of his two stepsons. That was the first time I had ever heard him use his familiar name Jack, which the boys called him. Apparently, he had never liked his name Clive as a young boy, and chose one of his own, saying, "Me Jack."

The next day we set out for the Continent and the festival at Bayreuth with a new awareness of depths of love and loyalty in Lewis, with sorrow for his cruel deprivation, and gratitude for his trust and friendship.

The last time we saw Lewis was in October 1963 at his home, The Kilns, in Headington, on the outskirts of Oxford. By then he had retired from the professorship at Cambridge because of ill health. Even though we knew this, we could see no sign of illness. He seemed as robust as ever and captivated us by his electric vitality, his friendliness, and the marvelous range of his mind. This last never ceased to amaze me. He was prodigiously learned, but he never paraded his knowledge. He used his learning dynamically, in the cut and thrust of good masculine argument, yet I never heard him in a contemptuous or malicious mood. He loved the form and the ethos of disputation too much for that.

As we left the snug house in Headington and said good-bye to both the Lewises (the Major was one of the added pleasures of the visit), it never occurred to us that we would never see C. S. Lewis again. Shortly thereafter we sailed for America and were appalled to read in the foreign edition of a New York newspaper that he had suddenly died. What a light was extinguished! And what an accumulation of sorrow for the world that the same day saw the death not only of Lewis but also of Aldous Huxley and John F. Kennedy.

I will always remember our first meeting in his rooms at Magdalen—the warm smile wrinkling up his eyes, his *joie de vivre,* his instantaneous outreach to an overseas visitor, his quick wit, his magnificent intellectual grasp. He was the greatest man I have ever known. Perhaps what has endeared him to me most, he was the best of companions.

# 15
## *Our Need For Such a Guide*
### EUGENE McGOVERN

TWENTY-FIVE YEARS AGO a good number of people were already saying that C. S. Lewis was the most effective apologist for Christianity in this century. The passage of time often has a way of making such judgments seem hasty, but this one could be made today with more confidence than ever. Enough new readers discover Lewis to keep very nearly all his large output in print and his sales at about two million copies per year.

I, for example, began reading Lewis shortly before he died. The impression he made was immediate and profound, and it has proved to be lasting. I am one of those who were fascinated by *Screwtape*, were soon pestering people with quotations from *The Problem of Pain*, and then were pressing *Perelandra* on those who would still patiently hear about the author we had found. Chad Walsh said it very well: "It was as though I had discovered a new ingredient in my intellectual, emotional, and spiritual diet that I had unconsciously desired but had not previously found." I have gone on to become one of those readers to whom Lewis's publishers are grateful: readers who have read very little Milton but have read *A Preface to Paradise Lost*; whose knowledge of English literature in the sixteenth century, whether including or excluding drama, is limited to Lewis's *Oxford History* volume; and who will die without having read Spenser, though they have read *The Allegory of Love*.

There are thousands upon thousands of readers around the world whose responses to Lewis have been the same as mine, and it is not surprising that many of us have come together in groups devoted to discussion of his work. The oldest of these is the New York C. S. Lewis Society, founded by those of us who responded to a brief note placed by Henry Noel in *National Review* in September 1969. Then a New Yorker and now living in France, Henry Noel provided most of the energy behind the society during the first eighteen months of its existence. The society has grown steadily over the years and now has members in almost all the states and in well over a dozen countries overseas. We have been fortunate to have had the co-operation and encouragement of those who knew or who wrote about Lewis. Our most memorable meetings have been those addressed by Owen Barfield and Walter Hooper, occasions for which some members traveled several hundred miles. Paul Holmer, Christopher Derrick, Thomas Howard, and Jane Douglass have also been among the guest speakers at the meetings, and the society's monthly *Bulletin* has had the privilege of publishing several of the essays that appear in this volume.

What might Lewis have had to say about this society? I am sure he would have tried to dissuade us and would have urged us to study instead Scripture, Malory, Hooker, Augustine, Vergil, Dante, Aquinas, and Milton. But after we insisted that it was to be his works we would be studying, I think he would be relieved to know that the society receives no support from any source other than its membership, and that its *Bulletin* accepts no advertising and stubbornly ignores inflation by maintaining the price of $7.00 per year that was set in 1970. And I suspect that he would be wryly amused to learn that the details of business are handled for the society by a committee titled the Eldila, and that for several years the monthly meetings were held at the Rudolf Steiner School.

More importantly, we like to think that Lewis would be gratified that the society exhibits certain characteristics that I mention only with some diffidence and hesitation: diffidence because they are delicate and subtle things; hesitation because they could be easily damaged. There is in the society a sense of community all too rare in most of our lives, and an acknowledgment that an interest in Lewis goes far toward establishing a friendship. There is, further, an example of Lewis's Principle of Inattention: we find that by coming together quite matter-of-factly to discuss an author in whom we share an interest we are led to the discovery that we are in agreement on the fundamental things. That is the kind of discovery that can best be made indirectly—by inferences, jokes, offhand remarks,

allusions, by what appear to be digressions from the topic under discussion
—and that will often elude the frontal approach in which we attempt to
make all presuppositions explicit. It is the kind of discovery we make about
one another not by giving formal statements of our beliefs, but by responding to such passages as, "No one is told any story but their own," "My name
also is Ransom," and "Sometimes it is hard not to say 'God forgive God.' . . .
But if our faith is true, He didn't. He crucified Him."

Is there an "explanation" for the continued interest in Lewis's work and
for the existence of such a thing as the New York C. S. Lewis Society? If
a sociologist were to write a monograph with the title "Literary Enthusiasm
Among the Nonliterary: Etiology and Symptomatology in Admirers of
C. S. Lewis," might there be someone, somewhere, who would be interested in reading it? Perhaps, but any such explanation would be one
obtained by looking *at* the phenomenon and so could not be as revealing
as one obtained by looking *along* it. And it is by looking along the continued
interest in Lewis that I will try to provide some reasons why so many of us
have reported that we owe far more to Lewis than we do to any teacher or
to any other author whom we have ever known.

The first thing to be said about the source of Lewis's appeal is that he is
a very fine writer. His scholarship, his storytelling, and his apologetics have
all been highly praised for the technical skill of their execution. Even
those readers who have no sympathy with the content of his work have
been ready to say that Lewis's meaning is always clear—all too clear for
some of them, it seems. His writing is, moreover, witty and provocative: the
reader is forced into either agreement or disagreement. His dialectical
skills are impressive, and he is as expert in advancing his own view as he is
willing to be fair to the opposition. Finally, there is a subtle quality by
which Lewis unobtrusively flatters his reader with unspoken encouragement: he allows us to feel, at least for the time we are reading him, that
*The Faerie Queene* is just what we would like to read next, or that Teu-
tonic myths are an important part of our intellectual landscapes.

But there has to be more to Lewis's extraordinary appeal than technical
skill, however polished. After all, there are a good number of faultless
stylists, some of them, though not enough, writing from the same Christian
standpoint as Lewis's. What is his special appeal?

A second source of Lewis's appeal is the simple reassurance that his
readers obtain from knowing that a distinguished career in secular learning

was comfortably combined with steadfast belief in orthodox Christianity. Lewis is a noteworthy example of the fact that an intelligent modern man can find Christian doctrine thoroughly credible, and such knowledge is useful when we are dealing with certain intellectual bullies. But quite a number of other authors provide examples of that fact, and few of them have won the following that Lewis has. So what was, and is, special about Lewis?

A third source lies in Lewis's ability to dissect various enthusiasms and follies of the twentieth century, and he not only did his share of this valuable work, but also went on to the next job: the one that Newman pointed to in his remark, "False ideas may be refuted indeed by argument, but by true ideas alone are they expelled." Walter Hooper has described Lewis's work in this area as follows:

Lewis's genuine and enduring value—that which continues to endear him to a growing number of readers—lies in his ability not only to do combat but to cleanse: to provide for the mind an authentic vision of the Faith which purges and replaces error, uncertainty and especially the presumptuousness of those who, as Lewis says . . . "claim to see fern-seed and can't see an elephant ten yards away in broad daylight."

Lewis insisted, of course, that the ideas that he enabled his readers to appreciate as they never had before were in no sense new, that they were very old and were not original with him. His readers knew this, and they knew that many other authors were trying to do the same thing. So why were Lewis's efforts so successful while other authors' are now forgotten?

These are some of the reasons Lewis continues to exert the influence he does. But I am not sure that, even taken together, they provide a satisfactory explanation for that influence. I am not sure they answer the questions, "Why are his readers so fervent?" "Why do they, learned or not, read and reread his books?" I would prefer to formulate the answer as follows: Lewis convinces his readers that he is the most reliable guide they have found on the subjects that matter most. Does God exist? Is there a spiritual reality that transcends the material world accessible to our senses? If so, what is our place in that spiritual reality? Other than scientific reasoning, is there any intellectually legitimate means of obtaining knowledge of the world we inhabit? Is moral reasoning only an expression of taste or opinion? What are we to make of Christ? There are no surprises in this list, and there are no surprises in the answers Lewis gave. His answers are the ones that have been given by thousands of expositors of Christianity since St. Paul.

The surprise comes from the responses his readers had, and have, to Lewis's conventional responses to these familiar questions. Great numbers of his readers have been stunned and awed and grateful to read Lewis's presentation of the beliefs they (many of them) had encountered in hundreds of sermons and classrooms and books. They find that he has encountered their difficulties and dealt with them, that he has anticipated their objections and has articulated them better than they could. It is not too much to say that (as has been said of Dr. Johnson) he convinces his readers that however far they go he has been there before them and they are meeting him on his way back, back from having addressed these subjects that matter most and having thought them through to the end, to "the absolute ruddy end."

It would, of course, be a mistake to suggest that Lewis applied himself only to theological questions. His incisiveness is displayed in his writings on secular subjects as well, and appeals to many who do not, finally, agree with his theological positions. I suspect that Jacques Barzun spoke for many when he recommended *God in the Dock* with the remark:

One need not be a believer in Lewis's church to profit from his candor and powers of reasoning on common predicaments. One of his most telling pieces is on National Repentance. Apply its teaching to any of the fashionable emotions and see how many survive. Then, the mind cleared of easy sophistication, start afresh to find out what you think with your whole being about the subjects he proposes to uncluttered mother wit.

This uncluttered mother wit is very useful in establishing what can be called a grammar for deciding what things are important or a prolegomenon to the selection of things that are worth paying attention to. Our lives are short, and every day we devote our time to some things and ignore the rest. The choice is very important, and we cannot afford to let anyone do our selecting for us—certainly not those in the news media, whose business it is to purvey a steady stream of material whose only claim on our attention is that it is the news; newspapers and television are the last places we should expect to find an admission that the subjects that most deserve our attention are what they always were.

In the face of endless discussions of politics, for example, it is at least a great timesaver to bear in mind Lewis's remark that

A sick society must think much about politics, as a sick man must think much about his digestion: to ignore the subject may be fatal cowardice for the one as for the other. But if either comes to regard it as the natural food of the mind—if either forgets that we think of such things only in order to be able to think of something else—then what was undertaken for the sake of health has become itself a new and deadly disease.

When we are dazzled by intellectual fashions, it is sobering to remember Lewis's depiction (worthy of *Rambler* Johnson) of the Artistic Soul who turns away from the Gates of Paradise because he has heard news of something more important:

Do you mean those damned Neo-Regionalists have won after all? I must be off at once. Damn it all, one has one's duty to the future of Art. I must go back to my friends. I must write an article. There must be a manifesto. We must start a periodical. . . .

Such examples of Lewis's trenchant advice on just what subjects are important could be multiplied to a great number and they constitute a valuable antidote for neophilia—that modern disease that Lewis called chronological snobbery. (Maritain's word for it was *chronolatry*.)

There is more, much more, to Lewis's appeal than I have mentioned. I have said nothing of his unequaled descriptions of Joy, of his superb Great Dance on a world that would not need a Redemption, of his breathtaking End of Narnia and the Beginning of the Real Story, or of his ability to stifle a raft of excited essays with a single phrase ("Christianity and Spelling Reform"), or of that prodigality exhibited in his telling the story of Ramadu as a part of a single episode, though it would serve a more frugal writer as the basis for an epic, and that will allow him to almost murmur, in a scholarly book, that "all except the best men would rather be called wicked than vulgar" as though this profound observation were a familiar commonplace.

There remains an aspect of the enthusiasm for this most reliable guide that should be mentioned: the fact that it often extends to a strong desire to learn about Lewis himself, to read about the kind of man he was, preferably from people who knew him. The New York C. S. Lewis Society does what it can to foster this interest. To an outsider, even a sympathetic one, there is perhaps something disquieting and even embarrassing about this interest in Lewis the man. Admiration for Lewis's literature, for his criticism or his apologetics, are all readily understandable, but can we say the same about the interest in Lewis himself? Can the enthusiasm, once it gives a large place to Lewis himself, avoid becoming narrow, precious, sticky, and cultish?

I think the answer to this question is easy. First, I think most admirers of Lewis have found that their reading and their interests are widened and expanded, rather than narrowed and confined, by reading Lewis. He is simply the wrong author for someone who wants an uneventful mental life. He is the wrong author also for those who like to have their thinking done for them; such readers might be surprised by the firm dissents from some of Lewis's views that are rather commonly made at meetings of the New York C. S. Lewis Society. Second, and more important, an interest in Lewis the man seems to be a perfectly natural and normal outgrowth of an appreciation of Lewis the writer. (Many readers who were stunned by the Gettysburg Address or the Second Inaugural have gone on to learn much about Lincoln; they are not foolish for having done so.) What can be more natural than wanting to know what we can of the man who seems to have dreamed our dreams before us? A nonchalant lack of interest would be an odd response to an opportunity to learn about an author who seems to be at once so profoundly like ourselves and yet so different from anyone we have ever met.

Those who are in a position to tell us about Lewis have been generous and informative in doing so, providing us with much that we are glad to know, much that enhances and deepens the knowledge we gain from Lewis's own writings. An example is an observation once made by Lewis's lifelong friend, Owen Barfield, who recorded, "for the sheer pleasure of it," his conviction that in his long years of friendship with Lewis,

I never recall a single remark, a single word or silence, a single look, the lightest flicker of an eyelid or hemi-demi-semitone of alteration in the pitch of his voice, which would go to suggest that he felt his opinion entitled to more respect than that of old friends he was talking with because, unlike theirs, it had won the ear of tens or hundreds of thousands wherever the English language is spoken and in a good many places where it is not.

This remark is worth pondering for what it tells us of the man who wrote so powerfully on The Great Sin; and we can wonder, with Mr. Barfield, of how many famous and not-so-famous persons it could be said.

Third, and most important of all, we need to know something of Lewis's life for the help such knowledge will give us in living as Christians in a world that is increasingly ignorant of, and uninterested in, Christianity. It is possible to exaggerate the uniqueness of our situation. We humans like to dramatize our positions and to imagine that we live at a hinge of history. Perhaps it is better to say that we are somewhere on a path that began at the top of a hill at a time when our civilization was called Christendom and are headed down and away from that toward something else. If there are doubters, let them compare the sources of rhetorical power that were used as recently as the last century, by the Abolitionists, with those used by advocates of social change today. On the one hand we have talk of immortal souls for whom Christ died and whose debasement would merit God's vengeance, and on the other we have . . . what? Or let the doubters imagine what a novelty it would be for a public figure to defend the hundreds of billions we spend on the health, education, and welfare of the citizenry by explaining that the citizens are worth such expense because they are destined for everlasting life, because they are, in Lewis's words, "possible gods and goddesses . . . immortal horrors or everlasting splendours," and because "Nations, cultures, arts, civilization—these are mortal, and their life is to ours as the life of a gnat."

There are many, including many Christians, who are convinced that Christianity must accommodate itself to the modern world and that such accommodation will have a salutary effect. Lewis was too prescient, too stable, too sane, to be so deluded. More than thirty years ago, while Christians who should have known better were often engaged in shameful sectarian bickering, he offered mere Christianity as a vast common ground that they could share and from which they could survey the gulf that separated them from most of the modern world. That gulf has widened perceptibly since then, and there is reason to believe the passage Lewis gave to his fictional Dr. Dimble: "the universe . . . is always hardening and narrowing and coming to a point. . . . Good is always getting better, and bad is always getting worse; the possibilities of even apparent neutrality are always diminishing. . . . Everything is getting more itself and more different from everything else all the time." Perhaps the hot/cold cleavage of either/or will force itself in the form of Augustine's dilemma: Christ was God, or he was a lunatic. In the past it was possible to demur, to talk around the problem, to refuse the dilemma and claim that Christ was only one of the best of the many moral teachers who have appeared in history. In the near future, I suspect, it will become increasingly common for those who believe that he was not God to urge upon us the logical alternative.

So problems and issues of the kind Lewis addressed will not grow fewer. What we can get from learning about Lewis the man is not simply his advice on how to regard the changes that will continue to occur in the world. His help in judging which changes are to be welcomed and defended, which are to be resisted and attacked, and which are to be ignored, can be obtained from his books. But by learning about the man himself we find that, for this most reliable guide on the subjects that matter most, the center remained unchanged; he really did believe what he wrote, and he practiced what he preached. Our need for such a guide will not diminish in the years ahead.

# PART FIVE
# *Much More Than a Tutor*

# 16
## *Oxford's Bonny Fighter*
### WALTER HOOPER

O<small>NE</small> <small>DAY</small> <small>DURING</small> <small>THE</small> M<small>ICHAELMAS</small> <small>TERM</small> of 1941 Miss Monica Shorten, an undergraduate at Somerville College (one of the five women's colleges in Oxford), complained that no one seemed ready to discuss the questions agnostics raised about God. She spoke to the right person—the indefatigable Stella Aldwinckle, who had been sent by the Oxford Pastorate to act in an advisory capacity to the ladies at Somerville, and who immediately put up a notice exhorting "all atheists, agnostics, and those who are disillusioned about religion or think they are" to meet in the Junior Common Room. There the ladies fulminated against the shortcomings of Oxford religious clubs and, after a few meetings with Stella Aldwinckle, it was concluded that what was much needed in Oxford was an "open forum for the discussion of the intellectual difficulties connected with religion and with Christianity in particular."[1]

The next problem was to find a president for the club that, it was hoped, would grow out of these meetings. According to Oxford's *Rules for University Clubs*: "The permission of the Proctors is required for the formation of any University Club, Society, or other organization whose undergraduate membership and meetings are not confined to one College. Application for permission to form such a 'Club' must be supported by a Senior Member of the University, who shall be a member of the Committee and must be kept fully informed of all the activities of the 'Club'."

---

[1] Stella Aldwinckle, *The Socratic Digest*, No. 1, (1942–43), p. 6.

Miss Aldwinckle had, then, to find a don, or senior member of the University, who would be willing to represent them. Ideally, the don ought to be a Christian and, further, one sympathetic to the questions unbelievers raise about God. About this same time Miss Aldwinckle picked up a copy of *The Problem of Pain* by C. S. Lewis, Magdalen College's English Tutor, and on reading the opening words "Not many years ago when I was an atheist..." she knew she had found the right man.

Lewis was not yet well known in America, but he was on the eve of becoming the most popular lay theologian in England. *The Problem of Pain* (1940) and the first of his interplanetary novels, *Out of the Silent Planet* (1938), had already been published, and his *Screwtape Letters* were appearing as weekly installments in *The Guardian*. He had twice preached in Oxford's University Church of St. Mary the Virgin, was lecturing on theology to members of the Royal Air Force, and had just completed his first series of radio broadcasts over the BBC. When Miss Aldwinckle wrote to him explaining the purpose of the club and asking if he would become its president, Lewis answered by return mail: "This club is long overdue! Come to coffee in my rooms on Tuesday, and we can talk it over."

Immensely excited by the idea, Lewis accepted the position of president, Miss Aldwinckle volunteered to act as chairman, and the Oxford Socratic Club was founded shortly before Christmas of 1941. Lewis's enthusiasm for logical disputation and his notion of what the purpose of the Club ought to be are clearly stated in the Preface he wrote for the first *Socratic Digest* (1942–43):

Socrates had exhorted men to "follow the argument wherever it led them": the club came into existence to apply his principle to one particular subject-matter—the *pros* and *cons* of the Christian religion. It is a little remarkable that, to the best of my knowledge, no society had ever before been formed for such a purpose. There had been plenty of organizations that were explicitly Christian ... and there had been plenty of others, scientific or political, which were, if not explicitly, yet profoundly anti-Christian in outlook. The question about Christianity arose, no doubt, often enough in private conversation, and cast its shadow over the aesthetic or philosophical debates in many societies; but an arena specially devoted to the conflict between Christian and unbeliever was a novelty. Its value from a merely cultural point of view is very great. In any fairly large and talkative community such as a university, there is always the danger that those who think alike should gravitate together into *coteries* where they will henceforth encounter opposition only in the emasculated form of rumour that the outsiders say thus and thus. The absent are easily refuted, complacent dogmatism thrives, and differences of opinion are embittered by group hostility. Each group hears not the best, but the worst, that the other group can say. In the Socratic all this was changed. Here a man could get the case for Christianity without all the paraphernalia of pietism and the case against it without the irrelevant *sansculottisme* of our common anti-God weeklies. At the very least we helped to civilise one another; sometimes we ventured to hope that if our Athenian patron were allowed to be present, unseen, at our meetings he might not have found the atmosphere wholly alien. . . .

It is (theoretically) a difficulty in the British Constitution that the Speaker of the House of Commons must himself be a member of one of the parties. There is a similar difficulty about the Socratic. Those who founded it do not for one moment pretend to be neutral. It was the Christians who constructed the arena and issued the challenge. It will therefore always be possible for the lower (the less Athenian) type of unbeliever to regard the whole thing as a cunningly—or not even so very cunningly—disguised form of propaganda. The Athenian type, if he had this objection to make, would put it in a paper and read that paper to the Socratic itself. He would be welcome to do so—though I doubt whether he would have the stomach if he knew with what pains and toil the committee has scoured *Who's Who* to find intelligent atheists who had leisure or zeal to come and propagate their creed. But when all is said and done, the answer to any such suspicion lies deeper. It is not here that the honesty of the Socratic comes in. We never claimed to be impartial. But argument is. It has a life of its own. No man can tell where it will go. We expose ourselves, and the weakest of our party, to your fire no less than you are exposed to ours. Worse still, we expose ourselves to the recoil from our own shots; for if I may trust my personal experience, no doctrine is, for the moment, dimmer to the eye of faith than that which a man has just successfully defended. The arena is common to both parties and cannot finally be cheated; in it you risk nothing, and we risk all. (pp. 3–4)

The club's program was planned a term or two in advance by a committee headed by Lewis, Stella Aldwinckle, and Dr. L. F. Grensted (the former Nolloth Professor of the Philosophy of the Christian Religion). From the beginning it was the practice of the club to have two speakers at each meeting, one to read a paper and another to "open the discussion" or "offer the first reply," after which it was thrown open to general discussion. Should the first speaker be a Christian, the reply would come from an atheist (if one could be found), and *vice versa* should the first speaker be an unbeliever. In fairness to both sides, the second speaker was usually allowed to see the other's paper in advance of the meeting in order that he might have a chance to frame his reply.

A number of American students whom I've met have expressed disapproval of the "undemocratic" tradition that only once a term did an Oxford undergraduate read a paper to the society. If the truth of Christianity were merely a matter of opinion, as some liberal theologians appear to think, Oxford students would have been pressed into more active service. As, however, the founders of the Socratic Club had no such fuzzy notions about the Christian Revelation, but believed in a full-blooded supernatural Christianity, they were anxious—as Lewis points out above—that both students and dons hear the best- and most-informed speakers it was possible to come up with. As a consequence, they naturally looked to those who were expert in their subject, atheists as well as Christians.

There are scores upon scores of college and university clubs in Oxford (about 250 the last time I tried counting them) catering to practically every conceivable interest: religion, literature, language, politics, history, sports, films, Bach, jazz—even tiddlywinks. Probably none of them has ever, and over so long a period, attracted so many undergraduates and dons as did the Socratic. From its beginning and up to the time that Lewis went to Cambridge in 1954, the club met every Monday evening in term from 8:15 to 10:30 P.M. Even then, some students remained behind talking into the small hours of the morning, with the result that they had to climb their college walls in order to get home to bed. There were usually between 60 and 100 members at every meeting, and unless one arrived early one was lucky to find a seat on the floor.

The first official meeting of the club was held in Somerville College on 26 January 1942, when Lewis's close friend and doctor, R. E. Havard, read a paper answering the question, "Won't Mankind Outgrow Christianity in the Face of the Advance of Science and Modern Ideologies?" Unfortunately, none of the minutes kept during the first two years of meetings have survived except those bits that found their way into the first two issues of the *Socratic Digest*. Of this first meeting, the secretary recorded (*Digest*, No. 1, pp. 9–10) that Miss Aldwinckle "opened the meeting with a brief description of the nature and aims of the club. She said it had been formed for those who do not necessarily wish to commit themselves to Christian views but are interested in a philosophical approach to religion in general and Christianity in particular." Following a brief resume of the main body of Dr. Havard's paper, the minutes end with this summary:

Talking of the so-called conflict between Science and Christianity, the speaker emphasised that they operated in different spheres. It was as if one man said: "It is very fine today"; and the other: "On the contrary, it is half-past four!" Hostility was more apparent between scientists and philosophers. On the subject of the Menace of Modern Ideologies to Christianity, Dr. Havard pointed out that although all theological fashions seem to be irresistible in their day they do not outgrow the Christian Creed. Christianity was very unpopular in the first and third centuries, and unfashionable in the eighteenth—but it continued to survive. In conclusion, the speaker gave it as his opinion that man's intellectual trust in the advances of science and in modern ideologies would not prove to be permanent.

Rather than attempt a full-scale summary of all the papers read to the Socratic Club during the years of Lewis's presidency, I've appended to the end of this essay as complete a list as I've been able to draw up of who read what paper. From this impressive list of speakers one can get a notion of how zealous and energetic the Socratic was in its program. My information comes from the five *Socratic Digests* published between 1942 to 1952, the two volumes of minutes kept from 1944 to 1960, and from Lewis and various others who have supplied me with their recollections.

As much as Lewis relished the cut-and-thrust of public debate, he was nonetheless anxious that the activities of the club not centre too closely upon himself, and he was the first speaker on only eleven occasions during the twelve years he was president. Despite this attempt to push others to the forefront, Lewis was, and remained, the chief attraction at most meetings. As president, it usually fell to him to open the discussions, and many hundreds of students came along with the express desire of watching him make mincemeat of those atheists who were intrepid enough to step into the ring with him. The great Anglo-Catholic theologian, Austin Farrer, who later became the Warden of Keble College, first came to know Lewis during the early years of the Socratic, and writing about him some years later he said: "The great value of Lewis as apologist was his many-sided-ness. So far as the argumentative business went, he was a bonny fighter. His writing gave the same impression as his appearances in public debate. I was occasionally called upon to stop a gap in the earlier program of Lewis's Socratic Club. Lewis was president, but he was not bound to show up. I went, in fear and trembling, certain to be caught out in debate and to let down the side. But there Lewis would be, sniffing the imminent battle and saying 'Aha!' at the sound of the trumpet. My anxieties rolled away. Whatever ineptitudes I might commit, he would maintain the cause; and nobody could put Lewis down."[2]

Before mentioning the papers Lewis read to the Socratic, I must salute another of his friends, Charles Williams, who addressed the society during its first term. Williams read a paper called "Are There Any *Valid* Objections to Free Love?" on 2 March 1942, and, as he has so many admirers on both sides of the Atlantic, I've decided to reproduce the entire *Digest* synopsis of it here (No. 1, p. 26):

Mr. Williams first discussed the phrase "Free Love," asking if it was to mean "unconditioned amorousness." This, he said, was a meaningless phrase, as the emotions were influenced by intellectual and physical conditions, if not by a spiritual attitude. The essence of emotional style lay in its capacity for definition. By following the immediate, momentary desires, instead of keeping in mind what he would call the "pattern," satisfaction was unlikely to be attained. (He pointed out that the Christian pattern need not necessarily be the one followed.) It was a question whether the Pragmatic or Metaphysical was to dictate to the emotional movements. Mr. Williams then discussed the other meaning of "Free Love," the right to seek for the most complete satisfaction by a series of trials. This theory assumes that there will be ultimately something satisfying for the individual. This does not guarantee that the same thing will be satisfying five minutes or five years later when the individual's views would have altered. It was impossible to be "adult" in love unless the emotions of the moment could be accepted or rejected at will. Fidelity was the mark of such a power of will. Unless it operates under fixed conditions all that we mean by love would cease to be. If "Freedom" in "Free Love" meant freedom to be ruled by the emotions of the moment, and the "love" meant the conscious pursuit of conscious felicity Mr. Williams emphasised that it was neither "Free" nor "Love."

    [2] "The Christian Apologist" in *Light on C. S. Lewis*, ed. Jocelyn Gibb (1965), pp. 25–26.

Lewis first addressed the Socratic on the 16th November 1942. His paper was entitled, "Christianity and Aesthetics, or 'The Company Accepts No Liabilities,' " but as no minute book was kept at the time, and as it received no mention in the *Digest*, there is little way of knowing what he said. I think it likely that the paper was a development of his two essays on "Christianity and Culture" that appeared during 1940 in the journal *Theology*, and that have since been reprinted in his *Christian Reflections* (ed. Walter Hooper, 1967). In these essays Lewis throws a good deal of cold water on the so-called spiritual values of culture. While admitting that literature and the arts afford a considerable amount of innocent pleasure, he nevertheless maintains that "culture" is no more than a "storehouse of the best sub-Christian values"—values that will save no man and that "resemble the regenerate life only as affection resembles charity or honour resembles virtue or the moon the sun"—for some a road into Jerusalem, but for some a road *out.*

By now enough had been said both at the Socratic meetings and elsewhere to indicate that a number of theologians and philosophers were seriously questioning whether there were any such thing as an objective moral law, a clear right and wrong about anything. When Lewis was invited to give the annual Riddell Memorial Lectures at the University of Durham on 24 February 1943, he chose as his subject a defense of the moral law. These lectures were eventually published as *The Abolition of Man* (1943) and are possibly the most lucid and able defense of the moral law ever written. Lewis did not attempt in this book to show the precise relationship between moral law and Christianity, but on 8 February 1943, he read a paper to the Socratic Club entitled, "If We Have Christ's Ethics, Does the Rest of the Christian Faith Matter?" in which he carried his argument further. As all we have of this paper is the précis in the *Socratic Digest* (No. 1, p. 23), I quote it here in full:

Mr. Lewis first demonstrated the existence of a massive and immemorial moral law by listing precepts from Greek, Roman, Chinese, Babylonian, ancient Egyptian, and Old Norse sources. By this account of the immutable laws of general and special beneficence, duties to parents and to children, of justice, good faith, and of the law of mercy, three illusions were dispelled; first, that the expression "Christian moral principles" means anything different from "moral principles"; secondly, the anthropological illusion that the crude and barbarous man is the natural and normal man; and, thirdly, that the great disease of humanity is ignorance and the great cure, education. On the contrary, it is only too obvious that while there is massive and immemorial agreement about moral law, there is also a massive and immemorial inability to obey it.

In considering the remedy for the cleavage between human nature and generally accepted moral law, Mr. Lewis first separated from normal humanity those faddists, whether Epicureans, Communists, or H. G. Wells, whose indefensible naiveté forbade them to understand the actual condition of Man. The remainder of humanity would be divided into the ordinary mass of pagan mankind and Christians. Both these classes of men know the moral law and recognise their own inability to keep it. Both endeavour to deal with this tragic situation. The pagan mysteries and Christianity are two alternative solutions, and whatever falls outside these two is simply naive. Now the *differentia* of Christianity, as against pagan mystery religions, lie in its survival, its historical core, its combination of the ethical and the sacramental, its ability to produce that "new man" which all rites of initiation premise and finally its restraining effect upon a community under its domination.

The datum is the complete cleavage between human behaviour and the code of morals which humanity acknowledges. And Christianity is the cure for this particular disease. For "excellent instructions" we have always had; the problem is how to obey them. To ask whether the rest of the Christian Faith matters when we have Christ's ethics presupposes a world of unfallen men with no need for redemption. "The rest of the Christian Faith" is the means of carrying out, instead of merely being able to discourse on, the ethics we already know.

Not a few of the papers read to the Socratic dealt with the issue raised by Dr. Havard—the so-called, and much exaggerated, conflict between science and Christianity. Though Lewis could not be said to have been overfond of the company of scientists, he nevertheless felt a greater respect for them than for those whose education had been neither scientific nor classical and who knew only enough popularized "science" to believe that in Nature we find the "whole show." Unluckily, no records have survived of his paper on "Science and Miracles" that he read to the Club on the 15th November 1943, but he has written at length on the subject, short articles such as those found in his *God in the Dock* (ed. Walter Hooper, 1970 and published in England as *Undeceptions*, 1971) and a full-length book called *Miracles* (1947). He believed, in short, that miracles are an interference with Nature by supernatural power and are, therefore, just as much a part of the same "show" as Nature herself.

Though few written records have come down to us from the first two years of the Socratic Club, many of those who were at the meetings have told me what an exciting figure Lewis cut in wartime Oxford. It was due in part to his influence that orthodox Christianity became so fashionable in the university, and the Socratic was by and far the most flourishing and influential of undergraduate societies. Every college lodge displayed one of the club's bright green posters announcing the topics and speakers for that term—and boldly stamped at the top of each poster were the words "President: C. S. LEWIS, M.A." Students turned out in vast numbers every Monday evening to watch Lewis's memorable knockdown-drag-out performances at the Socratic, all passionately wanting him to win.

The largest number ever to assemble was on the 24th January 1944 when 250 people crowded into Lady Margaret Hall (another of the ladies' colleges) to hear Lewis argue with that great erstwhile atheist, C. E. M. Joad, who had come down from London to read a paper called "On Being Reviewed by Christians." One of Lewis's pupils, John Wain, was at the meeting and, describing it in his autobiography, said that the atmosphere of the place was "positively gladiatorial":

Joad's last words were no longer out than the society's secretary, a formidable, crop-haired woman, was on her feet with the announcement, "Mr. C. S. Lewis will now ANSWER Dr. Joad." Lewis gently corrected her: "Open the discussion, I think, is the formula." But to this secretary and her like, these performances were no mere polite "opening" of "discussions." An enemy had invaded the very hearthstone of the faithful, and it was a matter of "Christian, up and smite them!"—Christian, in this case, being Lewis.[3]

The "crop-haired woman" is Stella Aldwinckle, who told me that, despite the freezing temperature outside, both Lewis and Joad were soon dripping with perspiration. Joad begged leave to remove his coat, but when Miss Aldwinckle suggested that Lewis do the same, he whispered to her that he had a large hole in his shirt. He was thus forced to carry on in his heavy tweed jacket. Though Miss Aldwinckle has forgotten it, Lewis told me of another occasion at which she became so infuriated by an atheist's violent

[3] John Wain, *Sprightly Running* (1962) p. 141.

attack on Christianity that, when he had sat down, she jumped up and, glancing from the atheist to Lewis, said, "Go get 'im, Jack!"

Lewis was a master of instant riposte. I have not been able to pinpoint the exact occasion, but Austin Farrer told me of a meeting at which the first speaker, who was a Relativist, ended his talk with the assertion: "The world does not exist, England does not exist, Oxford does not exist, and I am confident that *I* do not exist!" Lewis, standing up to reply, said, "How am I to talk to a man who's *not there?*"

He was later to remark to me how interesting it is that those people who don't believe in their own existence, nevertheless ask you, when at table, to pass them the salt. "Where do they put it?"

On the 7th February 1944, a week after Professor Joad's visit, Lewis entertained the Socratic with a paper entitled " 'Bulverism,' or The Foundation of 20th-Century Thought." In this lively address, the entire text of which was published in the *Socratic Digest* (No. 2, 1944) and is now available in *God in the Dock*, which I quote from here, Lewis points up the error of those Freudians and Marxists who attempt to invalidate thinking by claiming that it is psychologically or ideologically "tainted" at the source; or who, in other words, attempt to show *that* a man is wrong by explaining *why* they think he is wrong. Lewis wrote:

In the course of the last fifteen years I have found this vice so common that I have had to invent a name for it. I call it Bulverism. Some day I am going to write the biography of its imaginary inventor, Ezekiel Bulver, whose destiny was determined at the age of five when he heard his mother say to his father—who had been maintaining that two sides of a triangle were together greater than the third—"Oh you say that *because you are a man.*" "At that moment," E. Bulver assures us, "there flashed across my opening mind the great truth that refutation is no necessary part of argument. Assume that your opponent is wrong, and then explain his error, and the world will be at your feet. Attempt to prove that he is wrong or (worse still) try to find out whether he is wrong or right, and the national dynamism of our age will thrust you to the wall." This is how Bulver became one of the makers of the Twentieth Century.

On the 5th June 1944, at the last meeting of the academic year, Lewis spoke to the club on the question, "Is Institutional Christianity Necessary?" No minutes were preserved of the meeting, which is a pity because, while most of Lewis's books are intended to explain and defend the core of Christianity, he usually avoided references to anything of an autobiographical nature and to anything that tended to divide believers. However, he described his Christian profession (on the dust jacket of *Essays Presented to Charles Williams*) as "old-fashioned, square-rigged C. of E." and, despite his distaste for modernist priests, he was absolutely loyal to the Church of England. At another meeting of the club he maintained that "the core of Christian teaching has for centuries been preserved and handed down by the Church" and, considering his invariable practice of receiving Communion on Sundays and major feasts, as well as his practice of frequent confession (generally weekly), I think one must conclude that he most certainly believed "Institutional Christianity" to be necessary.

Although I do not think Lewis would have presumed to prescribe for those Christians outside the communions that share the Apostolic Succession, he was, interestingly, in the forefront of those who are fighting against the ordination of women. Long before so many Anglican bishops joined forces with the Women's Liberation movement to make this *the* issue, Lewis wrote an extraordinarily prophetic essay called "Priestesses in the Church?" (1948). In this he said: "To take such a revolutionary step at the present moment, to cut ourselves off from the Christian past and to widen the divisions between ourselves and other Churches by establishing an order of priestesses in our midst, would be an almost wanton degree of imprudence. And the Church of England would be torn in shreds by the operation."

By the time Miss Aldwinckle came to edit the second *Socratic Digest* in the summer of 1944, she was able to include in her editorial the following news: "The Socratic approach to the fundamental human questions evidently meets a need that is being felt beyond Oxford. Requests for last year's *Digest* were received from all over Britain, and even from the United States, Canada, and Australia."

One of those who had been reading the *Digest* and who had been down to Oxford to see the club in action was Lewis's friend, Miss Dorothy L. Sayers, the distinguished lay theologian and author of the popular Lord Peter Wimsey detective novels. So impressed was she by the club that she had an announcement put in *Digest No. 2* stating that she intended launching a London Socratic Club the following autumn. Though the interest was there on Miss Sayers's part, the chairman and secretary of the proposed London club resigned, and her plan was never realized. As a result, Miss Sayers became a "communicating member" and sometimes attended the meetings of the society in Oxford.

The club found another valuable acquisition in the person of Miss Valerie Pitt who, in the Michaelmas term of 1944, became a freshman at St. Hugh's College and secretary of the Socratic. It is she we have to thank for keeping a written record of the club's meetings: a practice that was continued by various secretaries, off and on, with varying degrees of quality and thoroughness, from 1944 to 1960.

On the 6th November 1944, Lewis spoke on "Is Theology Poetry?" which question had been put to him by some members of the society. This odd question, he said, might be more fully stated as "Does Christian theology owe its attraction to its power of answering and satisfying our imagination? Are those who believe it mistaking aesthetic enjoyment for intellectual assent, or assenting because they enjoy it?" In this talk, published in the *Socratic Digest* (No. 3, 1945) and now most easily accessible in the Fontana paperback, *Screwtape Proposes a Toast and Other Pieces* (London, 1965), which I quote from here, Lewis asserted that if theology is poetry, it is not very good poetry, having neither the monolithic grandeur of strictly Unitarian conceptions, nor the richness of polytheism. "If Christianity *is* only a mythology," he said, "then I find that the mythology I believe is not the one I like best. I like Greek mythology much better: Irish better still: Norse best of all" (p. 43).

In order to demonstrate that the construction of myths or "poetries" is not confined to avowedly religious men, Lewis—with obvious glee—condensed into a "world picture" the beliefs of those who, enamoured of popularized science, have given their beliefs aesthetic expression. This myth, believed in by H. G. Wells and other admirers of the scientific outlook (and named *Wellsianity* by a member of the Socratic) is itself, Lewis contends, one of the finest the modern folk imagination has yet produced:

The play is preceded by the most austere of all preludes: the infinite void and matter restlessly moving to bring forth it knows not what. Then, by the millionth millionth chance—what tragic irony—the conditions at one point of space and time bubble up into that tiny fermentation which is the beginning of life. Everything seems to be against the infant hero of our drama—just as everything seems against the youngest son or ill-used stepdaughter at the opening of a fairy-tale. But life somehow wins through. With infinite suffering, against all but insuperable obstacles, it spreads, it breeds, it complicates itself; from the amoeba up to the plant, up to the reptile, up to the mammal. We glance briefly at the age of monsters. Dragons prowl the earth, devour one another, and die. Then comes the theme of the younger son and the ugly duckling once more. As the weak, tiny spark of life began amidst the huge hostilities of the inanimate, so now again, amidst the beasts that are far larger and stronger than he, there comes forth a little naked, shivering, cowering creature, shuffling, not yet erect, promising nothing: the product of another millionth millionth chance. Yet somehow he thrives. He becomes the Cave Man with his club and his flints, muttering and growling over his enemies' bones, dragging his screaming mate by her hair (I never could quite make out why), tearing his children to pieces in fierce jealousy till one of them is old enough to tear him, cowering before the horrible gods whom he has created in his own image. But these are only growing pains. Wait till the next Act. There he is becoming true Man. He learns to master Nature. Science comes and dissipates the superstitions of his infancy. More and more he becomes the controller of his own fate. Passing hastily over the present (for it is a mere nothing by the time-scale we are using), you follow him on into the future. See him in the last Act, though not the last scene, of this great mystery. A race of demigods now rule the planet—and perhaps more than the planet—for eugenics have made certain that only demigods will be born, and psychoanalysis that none of them shall lose or smirch his divinity, and communism that all which divinity requires shall lie ready to their hands. Man has ascended his throne. Henceforward he has nothing to do but to practice virtue, to grow in wisdom, to be happy. And now, mark the final stroke of genius. If the myth stopped at that point, it might be a little pathetic. It would lack the highest grandeur of which human imagination is capable. The last scene reverses all. We have the Twilight of the Gods. All this time, silently, unceasingly, out of all reach of human power, Nature, the old enemy has been steadily gnawing away. The sun will cool—all suns will cool—the whole universe will run down. Life (every form of life) will be banished, without hope of return, from every inch of infinite space. All ends in nothingness, and "universal darkness covers all." The pattern of the myth thus becomes one of the noblest we can conceive. It is the pattern of many Elizabethan tragedies, where the protagonist's career can be represented by a slowly ascending and then rapidly falling curve, with its highest point in Act IV. You see him climbing up and up, then blazing in his bright meridian, then finally overwhelmed in ruin (pp.46–48).

Having described Christianity's chief rival—"Wellsianity" or the grand myth of evolution—Lewis concludes by pointing out that theology, far from defeating its rivals by a superior poetry, is far *less* poetical. This is because, when the essential meaning of all things comes down from the "heaven" of "myth" to the earth of history, it is emptied of glory and loses most of its poetic possibilities. When we move from the Old Testament to the New Testament, from myth to fact, "what is everywhere and always, imageless and ineffable, only to be glimpsed in dream and symbol and the acted poetry of ritual, becomes small, solid—no bigger than a man who can lie asleep in a rowing boat on the lake of Galilee" (p. 51).

Though it would not be obvious to those who have read Lewis's Socratic essays only in collections of his writings, many of them were answers to other papers read before the club. As an example of the continual crossfire that went on in the club, I must mention Professor H. H. Price (the retired Wykeham Professor of Logic in the University of Oxford) who on 23 October 1944 read a paper entitled "The Grounds of Modern Agnosticism," which was afterward published in *Socratic Digest* No. 3. In it the professor claimed that "the real crux of the quarrel between Religion and the Scientific Outlook" lay in the fact that man is *only* a body with "a consciousness that will be extinguished forever as soon as the body breaks up" (p. 17). The single comfort that Professor Price saw for the intellectually honest Theist is in—of all things—the findings of psychical research.

Spurred on by this naturalistic approach to man, and by way of an answer to those liberal clergy who deny the resurrection of the body, Lewis read a paper to the society on 14 May 1945 entitled "Resurrection." According to Miss Pitt's minutes, written at that time, "the President's paper was concerned with the possibility of other modes of being revealed at the Resurrection" and she goes on to quote Lewis as saying:

The Risen Christ appeared and disappeared like a ghost, yet He asserted that He was corporeal. It might be supposed that the Risen life was a spiritual life without space and without senses, but this was to regard the Resurrection as a return to Deity, an undoing of the Incarnation and to ignore the Risen Manhood. The Risen Body might have been a divine hallucination, but it was difficult to reconcile this with the fact that the Risen Christ was not at first recognisable by His disciples. If the story were true, however, if the Christ appeared and disappeared and yet was possessed of a natural body, then a new mode of being had appeared in the universe: a body inherently related to time and space but capable of animal operations and with a history before it. Then the Ascension, the going up of the body, and the abrupt ending of these appearances was an essential part of the same story. He passed not into a peculiarly negative spiritual life nor to a natural life but to a new nature and from that to create a new nature for His glorified saints ("I go to prepare a place for you"). He apparently passed into some spatial relationship with a new universe. The senses of His new body were responsive to multi-dimensional space and to a time that was not unilinear. The accounts of the Ascension were almost entirely metaphorical, but not quite so. From the local appearances, from the accounts of Christ's eating, it would seem that the new nature was at some points interlocked with the old. That to our view it was supernatural and yet it was natural. This to the modern habit of mind, conceiving of nothing real between the unconditioned and the world of our present senses, was shocking, but reality Mr. Lewis said, was like a skyscraper with several floors. God could create more systems than one, and there might be natures piled upon natures. The idea of there being several worlds did not obliterate spiritual apprehension of the Divine life; there was a union with it in the Sonship of Christ, and He was continually united with it not only at the Ascension but at every moment. . . .

Nature is not irrelevant to spiritual beatitude. Heaven is not merely a state of the spirit but a state of the body; we are never merely in a state of mind. Negative Spirituality is not Christianity, man is not to be unclothed but re-clothed. Bodily asceticism in this life is a training—but who would trust a man with a spiritual body if he could not control a material one?

As the Socratic was pretty regularly called upon to defend the Christian understanding of the Resurrection, I shall depart from chronological regularity to mention another meeting given to this subject. On 24 November 1947 a liberal Methodist, Rupert Davies, gave an impassioned address called "Did the Resurrection Happen?" in which he tried to show the Socratics how behind the times they were. Mr. Davies began by pointing out that the Apostles' account of the Resurrection must be discredited because of their "inaccurate memory," "unconscious interpretation," and "tendency to confuse symbolical and historical truth." It is indeed the very kind of modernist belittlement that, I think, must have led Austin Farrer to include in his university examinations the question "Just *how ignorant* was the first-century Jew?" From there the speaker went on to maintain that St. Paul *meant*, though he appears to say the opposite, that Christ rose as a disembodied ghost and that, like Him, the glorified saints will not have a body "in any material or physical sense."[4]

⁴ *Socratic Digest*, No. 4 (1948), pp. 107-13.

Mr. Davies had, presumably, not been warned that anyone brave enough to step into that prize ring was subject to the toughest grilling, from what were perhaps some of the most formidable and articulate theologians in England. Father T. M. Parker, then Chaplain of University College, opened the discussion with an extremely well-argued exegesis of the relevant biblical texts. The secretary goes on to record that: "In the remaining half hour of the discussion, Mr. Davies vigorously warded off sharp attacks from all sides, at the back of the room led by Mr. Vernon Rice, speaking as a Thomist, and also Professor Rogers, the Rev. E. L. Mascall, and others; while at close quarters he was besieged by the President, Father Parker, and others. . . . The President wanted to know what, in Mr. Davies's view, was the new element in Christianity, where was the novelty of the situation since, before Christ, ordinary ghosts had cropped up like mushrooms. . . . The argument raged in St. Giles (the road leading to Somerville College) long after the meeting had closed."

At the first meeting of Michaelmas term 1945, Lewis read another paper to the Socratic. Had the secretary known that his minutes would someday be published, he might have tried to capture with a bit more colour what it was like to both see and hear C. S. Lewis. As that, however, has proved a difficult task for some of Lewis's close friends, I don't feel we can legitimately blame a freshman at the university for doing no better. More important, the text of Lewis's paper has long since been lost, and I think we must be grateful that the young secretary's minutes are as full as they are:

The Socratic Club held the first meeting of the academic year at 8:15 P.M. on Monday, October 15, in St. Hilda's double Junior Common Room. The President, Mr. C. S. Lewis, presented a paper on "The Nature of Reason" to a very large audience.

We were said to be reasoning when the terms *must* and *must not* were used rather than *is* and *is not*, the language of observation. Thus in geometry we proved that if certain things were true, therefore other things *must be* true. Thus reason involved three things:

1. A field of material under consideration;
2. If certain things are true. These truths Mr. Lewis called the *data*;
3. Therefore, implying a principle by which to reason.

It was the third of these things that reason provided by the principle of non-contradiction. Reason was therefore defined as the application of self-evident principles to material which afforded a datum.

Three examples were given, one from geometry, one from history, and one from natural science. It was shown that the data usually came from sense experience, authority, or both. There was nothing essentially unreasonable about authority in general. But our datum was never certain, as authority and sense experience are both always open to doubt. Yet reason about uncertainties can be certain. If A is more probable than B, and B is more probable than C, A is more probable than C.

Some objections were considered. Firstly, might not reason itself be erroneous? This is more easily said than understood. We could say that a half may be greater than a whole, but could not even attach a meaning to this remark. Yet there were more serious attempts to undermine reason. Hegel showed that we entertained contradictory concepts, such as a tree simultaneously being and not being. These were reconciled by the concept of becoming. But this need for reconciliation showed that we believed in a law of non-contradiction. Then, we could not be sure of the existence of matter, which some people used as a *reductio ad absurdum* of reason. Mr. Lewis, however, saw no logical absurdity in the idealist position. Then again there were those who saw in economic or psychological conditions factors that invalidated all thought. But either this argument invalidated their own thought, or else it was untrue.

It was shown that so-called errors of reason were really errors of unreason, and that reason was competent to detect such errors. Reason was also universal, but it recognized its own limitations. It could not provide its own data, could not distinguish particular examples, for whose indication some form of "pointing" was necessary, and of itself provided no motive for action. Even if the existence of practical reason were granted, there was no logical connection between pure and practical reason. OUGHT could not be proved from IS.

In the ensuing discussion a gradual deification of Einstein was observed in some quarters, where the successive claims were advanced that relativity had disproved normal logic from a higher and unassailable plane, and that thought on this plane demanded entirely new faculties not possessed by the generality of men. It was objected that Mr. Lewis took too safe a position, refusing rational proofs of unreason as well as irrational. This pleased rather than dismayed Mr. Lewis. The discussion turned to the nature of truth, a quality which Mr. Lewis ascribed to the processes of reason, and of which he offered two alternative definitions, one of an external correspondence of statement and reality, and one of an internal coherence. Since Mr. Lewis had admitted that logic was only a more or less valuable tautology, and that a tautology must both correspond to and be coherent with itself, it was not generally admitted that any meaning could be ascribed to the truth of a logical proposition other than that such a proposition was, by definition, logical.

Hard on the heels of World War II there appeared a spate of Theosophists, dabblers in psychical research and the like, all anxious to climb into whatever "pulpits" were handy. The Socratics felt they ought to hear what they had to say and so invited them in, confident that Lewis would know how to answer their claims.

At the society's eighty-first meeting on 28 January 1946 Mr. Shaw Desmond spoke on "Religion in the Postwar World." According to the club secretary—of whose minutes I quote only a small portion—"The speaker touched on a wide range of subjects. His oratory was irresistible, and the account of his personal experiences a challenge even to the most credulous. Objects of his condemnation included Freud, Churchill, Stalin, pacifism, dogma, and the BBC. Lucifer was an object of pity. . . . Next he professed to believe in Reincarnation and claimed that immortality was irrefutably demonstrable by means of psychical research. He said that we made our own heaven and hell. . . . The churches could do nothing to save the world, but there was a purpose behind life. . . . Man was progressing, but in view of the insignificance of our world in comparison with the whole universe, we could not claim to know any final truths. Paul taught the opposite of Jesus. The religion of the future would be without dogma, priests, or an organized church. . . ."

Following this deluge the secretary had, it seems, only enough ink to summarize Lewis's reply before his pen ran dry:

Mr. Lewis in opening the discussion pointed out the trivial nature of the communications received in spiritualists' seances, and this Christians did not consider was as important as man's relation to something uncreated: to Christians salvation was an escape from Reincarnation, and they had the desire to meet what he called "the Other." In reply to the speaker's scepticism about Revelation, he suggested that the size of a creature was no criterion as to whether or not God should reveal Himself to it. The rest of Mr. Lewis's remarks took the form of a dialogue with the speaker. He ended by saying that the latest attempts to teach religion in schools without dogma seemed to him just the type of religion which the speaker recommended.

A few months later, on 6 May 1946 Mr. G. L. Wilson of the Society for

Psychical Research spoke to the club on "The Significance of Psychical Research." After regaling his hearers with descriptions of the levitation of tables, spirit possession, and telepathy, he concluded his talk by prophesying that the truths of psychical research "would have great influence upon belief in survival and resurrection, and so upon the acceptance of the beliefs of Christianity." Austin Farrer and several others went on to question Mr. Wilson minutely on his experiments, after which they were glad to turn the discussion over to the president. The secretary records that:

> Mr. Lewis contended that the results of such research, even where they did seem to prove survival, were of more *scientific* than religious interest. In itself survival was of no more religious significance than longevity. In fact the evidence as to the apparent conquest of time in the experiments in telepathy were sometimes embarrassing to proofs of survival. It was also an alarming fact that no message had yet been recorded as received from the spirits of the dead which had any value in itself. Perhaps here was confirmation of the Homeric view of the world of the dead, a world of fleeting ineffectual ghosts.

It was this widespread and growing enthusiasm for a minimal religion and for survival, of whatever quality, that led Lewis to write a detailed answer to what he considered very dangerous beliefs. On 20 May 1946 he read a paper to the society called "Religion Without Dogma?" which was a reply to these beliefs as they had been expressed in Professor Price's "Grounds of Modern Agnosticism." Lewis's paper was published in *Digest* No. 4, and later in *God in the Dock*, which version is quoted here.

Professor Price had argued: (1) that the essence of religion is belief in God and immortality, (2) that in most religions the "essence" is found in connection with "accretions of dogma and mythology" now rendered incredible by science, (3) that it would be desirable to retain the essence purged of the accretions, and (4) that our only hope in empirical evidence for the soul lay in the findings of psychical research.

Lewis began by disagreeing with the professor's first point. Judaism in its earliest stages had, he said, no belief in immortality, and in Christianity it has often had a subordinate position. The latter is certainly true of Lewis himself, who believed in God long before he believed in, or even cared about, everlasting life. He said:

> I cannot help thinking that any religion which begins with a thirst for immortality is damned, as a religion, from the outset. Until a certain spiritual

level has been reached, the promise of immortality will always operate as a bribe which vitiates the whole religion and infinitely inflames those very self-regards which religion must cut down and uproot. For the essence of religion, in my view, is the thirst for an end higher than natural ends; the finite self's desire for, and acquiescence in, and self-rejection in favour of, an object wholly good and wholly good for it. That the self-rejection will turn out to be also a self-finding, that bread cast upon the waters will be found after many days, that to die is to live—these are sacred paradoxes of which the human race must not be told too soon (p. 131).

He went on to say that, as he and Professor Price disagree about the "essence" of religion, they should probably disagree about the "accretions of dogma and mythology." Not only does the "essence" always coexist with other things, but he claimed that the similarities between Christianity and paganism strengthened his own belief in Christianity: "If my religion is erroneous, then occurrences of similar motifs in pagan stories are, of course, instances of the same, or a similar error. But if my religion is true, then those stories may well be a *preparatio evangelica*, a divine hinting in poetic and ritual form at the same central truth that was later focused and (so to speak) historicised in the Incarnation" (p. 132).

Such a minimal religion as Professor Price recommended is, he insisted, *impossible* to state without the introduction of dogma. This is because, to make it practicable, there must be some authoritive statements about truth, and Lewis suggested that such a theism really started with preconceived ideas whose familiarity hid their dogmatic shape. If, he suggested, the professor became its supreme head on earth, he would soon discover that "those who have come to his minimal religion from Christianity will conceive God in the Jewish, Platonic, Christian way; those who have come from Hinduism will conceive Him pantheistically; and the plain men who have come from nowhere will conceive Him as a righteous Creator in their moments of self indulgence. . . . The minimal religion in fact cannot, while it remains minimal, be acted on. As soon as you *do* anything you have assumed one of the dogmas. In practice it will not be a religion at all; it will be merely a new colouring given to all the different things people were doing already" (pp. 140–41).

Professor Price had stated in his essay that if civilization is to survive, which it can only do if it has a religious basis, the solution must lie in psychical research. As we have seen from the other meetings at which psychical research had been discussed, Lewis was extremely doubtful as to whether anything worth knowing could come from "spirit messages." He argued that if God is righteous, if He has purposes for us, if He is our leader in a cosmic battle—then the utterances of the mediums don't appear to help us. In what is his most complete and clearly articulated comment on spiritualism, he said:

As for the utterances of the mediums . . . I do not wish to be offensive. But will even the most convinced spiritualist claim that one sentence from that source has ever taken its place among the golden sayings of mankind, has ever approached (much less equalled) in power to elevate, strengthen, or correct even the second rank of such sayings? Will anyone deny that the vast majority of spirit messages sink pitiably below the best that has been thought and said even in this world?—that in most of them we find a banality and provincialism, a paradoxical union of the prim with the enthusiastic, of flatness and gush? (p. 142).

With young soldiers returning home from the war, the University of Oxford—which had been considerably depleted during 1939 to 1945—began to fill up again. Many of the new students, knowing more about world problems and politics than had the prewar students, felt less confident that "progress" was more or less inevitable. They wanted to talk as well as listen and they flocked to the Socratic (and other university clubs) in search of answers.

On the evening of 4 November 1946 the Socratic Club held a joint meeting with the Rationalist Society, the Socialist Club, and the Student Christian Movement in the enormous Debating Hall of the Oxford Union. C. S. Lewis was in the chair, and the two guest speakers, Mr. (now Sir) Arnold Lunn and Professor J. D. Bernal, debated the topic "Is Progress Possible Without Religion?"

Sir Arnold Lunn, after describing himself as a Roman Catholic and a liberal, viewed with satisfaction that Nazism had failed miserably to right the world, and from there he went on in a witty and vehement vein to identify Communism with apostasy. His speech soon deteriorated into a bitter political invective, with the result that he met with such rude and determined heckling that Lewis was forced to remind the audience that interruptions were not in keeping with the spirit of the meeting.

Professor Bernal, a dialectical materialist, opened the discussion by complaining that, instead of being told how progress was possible *with* religion, he had listened to a repetition of statements culled from the writings of bitter political enemies of the Soviet Union. From there he went on to view the last fifty years, not as a bad dream, but as the beginning of a free world. He claimed that the good changes of the last fifty years had been largely George Bernard Shaw's doing—which astonishing tribute many in the audience took as an insult. "Religion," Professor Bernal said, "is the concept that people make of the social forces of their time. . . . God is one of the finest creations of man. . . . The world view embodied in the Soviet system produced courage, goodwill and good sense." Finally, the professor applauded the recent appeal of the Archbishop of Canterbury for spiritual endeavor and asked Sir Arnold to join him in making a free world.

According to the Socratic secretary and a reporter for *The Cherwell,* an Oxford student magazine, the guest speakers interpreted both "religion" and "progress" too much in terms of their own narrow sympathies, and the general discussion was getting out of hand till Lewis intervened. Everyone seems to have been impressed by his ability to see the high, overarching truth that put into proper perspective the views of the other two men. Lewis, the secretary wrote, claimed that:

The meaning of the word *progress* depends on your world outlook. Why then did it seem possible for us to assume a fixed meaning? Because we inherit a common civilisation, with values not specifically Christian derived from several sources. To detach ourselves from this tradition we have to go to the abnormal, in modern systems, to something like the pessimism of Nietzsche. The word *religion* had no more meaning than the word *science*; in using it we were usually thinking of the *particular* religion and cultural tradition in which we stood. In the case of the transcendental religions, such as Platonism, Judaism, Islam, and Christianity, the individual must be infinitely more important than any group since, if you accept the immortality of the soul, nations, classes, and societies were ephemeral compared with men.

To put it more succinctly, it was recorded in *The Cherwell* of 13 November that Lewis stated that: "Marxists were not the only atheists, Catholics not the only Christians; that no nation emphatically *is* or is *not* a Christian nation; that moral man and immoral society were not always incompatible; that 'If you aim at Heaven, you get Earth as well; if you aim at Earth, you get nothing at all.' "

As there have recently been so many defections from orthodoxy by clergymen and others who have felt the stronger, and less exacting, pull of contemporary "ethics" and humanitarian ideals, it might be worthwhile glancing back to a discussion of this problem at the Socratic. On 19 May 1947 the philosopher, Dr. H. D. Lewis, read a paper on "Belief and Conduct" about which the secretary recorded: "Dr. Lewis had no doubt that participation in war was incompatible with the express teaching of Jesus. . . . Dr. Lewis then attacked what he called the 'perverted' and 'villainous' doctrine of original sin. To blame yourself for what happens independent of your own will is an irrational state of mind that only a psychiatrist can explain. From St. Augustine onward, this doctrine had been an excuse for disregarding the rigorous and exacting ethical principles of Jesus. Dr. Lewis protracted and enlarged upon these points, seeking to persuade, fervently but with prodigality of words rather than conciseness of argument."

Because most people will probably never read the Socratic record of this meeting, I quote the remaining minutes:

In reply, Mr. C. S. Lewis said that since there were strong motives for the individual Christian to abandon Christianity, he did not think Christians were to blame for other people's apostasy. While he would never use it as an argument against pacifism, he accepted the doctrine of original sin, because St. Augustine and St. Paul taught it, and to reject St. Paul meant rejecting the canon and so casting doubt on even the sayings of Jesus. As to the revolutionary character of Christian teaching, Mr. Lewis said that, while to loud-pedal this would be an advantage to a Christian apologist today, it might well be that, as Christianity was made feudal in a feudal age, and bourgeois in a bourgeois age, the world imposes upon it a revolutionary character in a revolutionary age. Christianity, in calling for repentance and offering forgiveness, assumes that a moral law has already been accepted, and its moral teaching only deepens . . . that of the Hebrews, and other pre-Christian civilisations. It offers, in a sense, an escape from the simple, ethical situation of man versus moral law by offering forgiveness and grace.

With regard to pacifism, Mr. C. S. Lewis said that it only became common with the rise of humanitarian, democratic ethics in general, and so may also have been imposed on Christianity by the world. He pointed out that our Lord did not condemn the militaristic history of Israel, that His injunctions about revenge and retaliation were the reversal of points in Jewish law which related only to personal life, that He commended a Roman sergeant major, and that St. Paul approved the use of the sword by civil magistrates. Mr. Lewis doubted whether it was possible or right to live permanently in a state of revolutionary tension: St. Paul taught Christians to be comformists until the real point of issue of their faith came in sight: there were dangers both in the direction of conformity and in the direction of crisis psychology.

Shortly after reading Kierkegaard's *Fear and Trembling* I was a little taken aback when, discussing the book with Lewis, he said, "What on earth is the man talking about?" Lewis had no use for the existentialists and once described the writings of Kierkegaard and Sartre to me as "philosophical moonshine." I have since come to agree with him, rather more than less, but it is more to the point that I mention the paper "A First Glance at Sartre" that Lewis read to the club on 3 November 1947.

The paper was an account and critique of Sartre's *Existentialism Is a Humanism* in which the writer's philosophy was summarized as follows: "Sartre's starting point is the same as Descartes', but with a plurality of consciousnesses. . . . He denies the existence of God, and also that there is any essence of Man: Man only creates his essence by acts of choice. To such choices a terrible responsibility is attached since each man, in choosing for himself, commits all humanity to that choice. The only actions are lucid and sincere ones, that is, ones that do not arise from conformity to any essence or any code of principles; and the one end of life is liberty."

Lewis's paper was lost, and I have not been able to find any more about it than this short account supplied by the club secretary:

Criticising these doctrines, Mr. Lewis said: firstly, that to speak of Man collectively or in the plural, implies an essence in any case: secondly, that I cannot be committing others to my choice, unless I know them to be beings of the same essence as myself: thirdly, that to define man's end as liberty is very like assuming a universal form of right conduct. These parts of Sartre seemed to Mr. Lewis to be undigested lumps of Kant; all the agony which Sartre, paradoxically, would have us accept leads us back only to the old principles of political liberty. Such an argument typifies the modern habit of exaggeration. What Sartre really hates is the idea of goodness as conformity, and he is a moral fanatic like Robespierre. Mr. Lewis then explained his view that conformity to a rule is not the essence, but only the accident of goodness. Thus there *can* be a measure of inventiveness, and freedom, in some moral actions. Sartre's illusion is his claim of total freedom, which leaves us in the dark at an endless trial, without a judge.

The secretary goes on to say that Fr. E. L. Mascall, who opened the discussion, "pointed out that Sartre's doctrine of the absurdity of the world was similar to the Christian doctrine of the contingency of the world, which implies that there can be no complete ethic without reference to a transcendental end." We are then told that, in the ensuing discussion, "Sartre underwent various transformations, and was chased into many tight corners. If, as it might have appeared, the President had only set fire to a man of straw, yet the effigy kept reappearing and being reburnt."

The Socratic was not intended to be a debating club, but it sometimes *looked* as though it was just that when the contestants hammered away at each other with more force than the issue in question would seem to justify. It continues to be maintained in some quarters that Lewis was "defeated" at a celebrated meeting of the Society on 2 February 1948 when Miss G. E. M. Anscombe, then the philosophy tutor at Somerville College, read a paper called "A Reply to Mr. C. S. Lewis's Argument That 'Naturalism' Is Self-Refuting," which was afterward published in the *Socratic Digest* (No. 4, pp. 7–15). I don't think Lewis was "defeated." However, as most of those who wish to take sides know so few of the facts involved, I give here all I've been able to discover, not only about the meeting itself, but also about the events that followed from it, all of which might collectively be called "The Case of Anscombe v. Lewis."

Miss Anscombe's paper was a reply to Chapter III ("The Self-Contradiction of the Naturalist") of Lewis's book *Miracles* (1947), where he used the *reductio ad absurdum* argument as a means of attacking the Naturalists. Believing, as many of them claim to do, he said, that Nature means "everything that happens," all of which came about by the blind working of chance, it must therefore follow that even their *thoughts* must also be the working of chance and the accidental by-products of atoms moving in their brains. That being so, he asked why the Naturalist should believe one thought to be more "valid" than another, and why it should give a correct account of all the others. To put it in its simplest

form, Lewis quotes that given by the late Professor J. B. S. Haldane in
his essay "When I Am Dead" from *Possible Worlds:*

If my mental processes are determined wholly by the motions of atoms in
my brain, I have no reason to suppose that my beliefs are true . . . and hence
I have no reason for supposing my brain to be composed of atoms.

Miss Anscombe's argument is much more complex than I am able to
present it here, but, insofar as I understand it, the crucial points are as
follows:

(1) Lewis had said in the suspect chapter of *Miracles* that "We may
in fact state it as a rule that *no thought is valid if it can be fully explained
as the result of irrational causes.*" Miss Anscombe insisted that, among
possible causes for human thought, a distinction must be made between
"irrational causes" (such things as passion, self-interest, obstinacy, and
prejudice) and "non-rational causes" (such things as brain tumours, tuber-
culosis, and mental fatigue). She agrees that if irrational causes supply a
satisfactory explanation for belief, that belief is discredited. But, she says,
Naturalism tries to supply an explanation on the basis of non-rational
causes, and such an explanation cannot impugn the validity of thought.

(2) She challenged Lewis to make as clear as he could what he meant
in his book by "valid" reasoning. "What *can* you mean by 'valid' beyond
what would be indicated by the explanation you would give for distin-
guishing valid and invalid, and what in the naturalistic hypothesis pre-
vents that explanation from being given and meaning what it does?"

(3) The Naturalist can be allowed, she claimed, to attempt to explain
a chain of reasoning as a result of "non-rational" causes—and in so doing
the meanings of the words *valid, invalid, rational* and *irrational* are left
intact. The reason they are left intact is that we are concerned, not with
*how* the Naturalist came to have such and such thoughts, but whether
*what he says* is "good" or "valid" reasoning.

(4) To clarify this further, she distinguishes between the "ground" of
a conclusion (the reasons a man would give if asked to explain why he
thinks such and such) and the "cause" of a conclusion (brain tumours,
prejudices, or whatever it is that makes him think as he does). All this
having been established, Miss Anscombe says that it is, nevertheless, true
that the conclusions a man reaches ought not to be finally judged by
whether they are the result of a "ground" or a "cause" but whether the

*piece of reasoning*, considered in itself, is valid or invalid. "A causal explanation of a man's thought only reflects on its validity as an indication
if we know that opinions caused in that way are always or usually unreasonable."

Such is the substance of Miss Anscombe's paper. The secretary
recorded in the minutes that:

In his reply Lewis agreed that the words *cause* and *ground* were far from
synonymous, but said that the recognition of a *ground* could be the *cause* of
assent, and that assent was only rational when such was its cause. . . . Miss
Anscombe said that Mr. Lewis had misunderstood her, and thus the first part
of the discussion was confined to the two speakers who attempted to clarify
their positions and differences. . . . The President finally admitted that the
word *valid* was an unfortunate one. From the discussion in general it appeared that Mr. Lewis would have to turn his argument into a rigorous,
analytic one, if his notion of "validity" as the effect of causes, were to stand
the test of all the questions put to him.

I think it may have been Miss Anscombe's rather bullying quality that
left Lewis low and dispirited afterward. His former pupil, Derek Brewer,
who dined with him two days later, says that he described the meeting
"with real horror." "His imagery was all of the fog of war, the retreat of
infantry thrown back under heavy attack." Some who were at the meeting contend that Lewis lost to Miss Anscombe; others that the lady came
out second best. Even the contestants said different things. Lewis told
me he did not lose the argument. A few years later when I met Miss
Anscombe in the common room of Somerville College and asked what
she remembered of the meeting, she removed a cigar from her mouth
only long enough to say, "I won."

But there is more to it than this. The important—the really valuable—
consequence of his disagreement with Miss Anscombe is that Lewis continued to think very hard about the problem of Naturalism. He inserted
a note in the same issue of the *Digest* (No. 4), and now reprinted in
*God in the Dock* (p. 146), in which he admitted that "valid" was an
unfortunate choice of words for what he wanted to convey. He suggested
"veridical," "verific" or "veriferous" as improvements, and he maintained,
as he had at the meeting, that the conclusion of an argument would be
the end point of a chain of "grounds" but also of a chain of "causes"

—which, he said, "is very much what I meant by the difficulty in Naturalism."

The matter rested there for some ten years until Fontana Books's decision to publish a paperback of *Miracles* provided Lewis with an opportunity to rewrite Chapter III. The new chapter, retitled "The Cardinal Difficulty of Naturalism," is three times the length of the earlier version and in it Lewis introduces two senses of the word *because*:

We can say, "Grandfather is ill to-day *because* he ate lobster yesterday." We can also say, "Grandfather must be ill to-day *because* he hasn't got up yet (and we know he is an invariably early riser when he is well)." In the first sentence *because* indicates the relation of Cause and Effect: The eating made him ill. In the second, it indicates the relation of what logicians call Ground and Consequent. The old man's late rising is not the cause of his disorder but the reason why we believe him to be disordered. There is a similar difference between, "He cried out *because* it hurt him" (Cause and Effect) and "It must have hurt him *because* he cried out" (Ground and Consequent). . . . The one indicates a dynamic connection between events or "states of affairs"; the other, a logical relation between beliefs or assertions.

After having shown that a "Ground to a Consequent" step in argument must also stand in a "Cause-Effect" relationship to its successor, his solution is that one thought can come to stand in a Cause-Effect relationship to another thought by *being seen to be* a ground for it. The "being seen to be" is accomplished by the "act of inference"—which "acts" he considers in two different lights. They are, on the one hand, subjective events or items in somebody's psychological history. They are, on the other hand, "insights into" or "knowledge of" something other than themselves:

When we are adopting the psychological point of view we may use the past tense. "B *followed* A in my thoughts." But when we assert the implication we always use the present—"B *follows* from A." If it ever "follows from" in the logical sense, it does so always. And we cannot possibly reject the second point of view as a subjective illusion without discrediting all human knowledge. For we can know nothing, beyond our own sensations at the moment, unless the act of inference is the real insight that it claims to be.

Lewis goes on to show that this "act of inference" cannot be explained on the Naturalist's terms: "Any thing that professes to explain our reasons fully without introducing an act of knowing thus solely determined by what is known, is really a theory that there is no reasoning." In contrast, the theist allows for exactly what is needed: "For him," says Lewis, 'reason—the reason of God—is older than Nature, and from it the orderliness of Nature, which alone enables us to know her, is derived. For him, the human mind in the act of knowing is illuminated by the Divine reason. It is set free, in the measure required, from the huge nexus of non-rational causation; free from this to be determined by the truth known. . . . It must break sufficiently free from that universal chain in order to be determined by what it knows."

Nine months after Lewis's clash with Miss Anscombe, a cool thrill of excitement—like the expectation of a vampire—was felt in Oxford when it was announced that the brilliant but perverse biologist, Professor J. B. S. Haldane, was coming to address the club. Professor Haldane hated Christianity intensely, and he had attacked Lewis's interplanetary novels in an article called "Auld Hornie" (Scottish for "the Devil") published in the *Modern Quarterly* (Autumn 1946). An enormous number of people met in the Taylorian Institute on the evening of 15 November 1948 to watch Haldane do battle with the Christians.

Professor Haldane's paper was, not unexpectedly, on "Atheism." After passing in review what he called the arguments "for" theism, but which were really not very cleverly disguised attempts at debunking it, he took a swipe at Lewis and went on to his arguments for atheism. According to the minutes:

Professor Haldane suggested first that atheism is more intellectually honest and less cramping than theism founded on insufficient evidence. Secondly, there were strong moral arguments. There were statistical arguments which show that religious people lead worse lives than non-religious the nearer they get to the Pope, and there is the perennial difficulty of reconciling a Good God with an evil world. If the Theist answers to this that free will is more valuable than an absence of evil, we must ask why; if eternal life is life without the possibility of sin, we should not have been thus created in the first place. In general the effect of a religious morality is to hamstring man's moral development. The true path lay in the use of each difficulty as it arose as a stepping stone to the next stage of moral advance.

Ian Crombie, the philosophy tutor at Wadham College, opened the discussion with a clearheaded reply on behalf of the Socratics. He objected to the professor's unanalyzed "statistics" (e.g., people lead worse lives the nearer they get to the Pope), which he thought proved nothing. "Atheism," he said, "may encounter fewer intellectual difficulties, but that is because it is not a hypothesis but a refusal to look for explanations of a certain type. There is something to be said for looking even if our answers are not free from difficulties."

It was understood that, immediately after Professor Haldane had answered Mr. Crombie, the meeting would be thrown open to general discussion. Professor Haldane clearly had no desire to confront Lewis and the other Socratics, and he ended his short reply to Mr. Crombie "with an impressive running panegyric of atheism of which the last word was perfectly timed to coincide with his exit."

Beginning in 1951 the club suddenly had a run of rather idle secretaries, some who kept scanty records of the meetings, and some who kept none. This explains why, even when I know what topics were discussed, I can give no record of what was said.

In 1952 Stella Aldwinckle edited the last *Socratic Digest* (No. 5, 1952), which contains a short contribution by Lewis called "Is Theism Important?" The blank pages in the minute book would suggest that it was read to the club sometime between November and December of 1951. This piece, now reprinted in *God in the Dock* (pp. 172–76), is a reply to Professor H. H. Price's paper of the same title.

Professor Price thought theism important, but he insisted pretty strongly that the philosophical "proofs of the existence of God" usually made men either atheists or agnostics. A surer way to God, he said, is through faith, which he defines as a "sense of the divine"—without which "sense" there would be no religion at all. There follows in his paper a very moving passage in which, after admitting to having a warm place in his heart for the ancient pagans, he insists that all men have an "awareness of God" however hard they try to repress it:

It is repressed, I think, because it does not fit in at all with the conception of the world and of human nature which is commonly accepted in the present secularistic phase of Western civilisation. To repress it is not very difficult. It does not have the urgency and the forcefulness of our primitive desires and passions. It is described in the Bible as "a still, small voice." All the same I do not think it will remain repressed for ever, any more than I think that the present phase of Western civilisation will last for ever. The time will come, and I think it may well come quite soon, when our modern Naturalistic Weltanschauung will seem topsy-turvy, a systematic attempt to put second things first and first things nowhere.

In summary, Professor Price claimed that faith is a combination of "belief in God" and "some direct and immediate religious experience." Finally, having confessed to being very muddled about the topic, he sat down to await Lewis's reply.

Lewis, as everyone who's read his books knows, also had a tender spot for paganism. "When grave persons," he replied, "express their fear that England is relapsing into Paganism, I am tempted to reply 'Would that she were.' For I do not think it at all likely that we shall ever see Parliament opened by the slaughtering of a garlanded white bull in the House of Lords or Cabinet Ministers leaving sandwiches in Hyde Park as an offering for the dryads. If such a state of affairs came about, then the Christian apologist would have something to work on. For a Pagan, as history shows, is a man eminently convertible to Christianity. He is, essentially, the pre-Christian, or sub-Christian, religious man. The post-Christian man of our own day differs from him as much as a *divorcée* differs from a virgin."

He goes on, with his characteristic clarity of thought and preciseness of expression, to distinguish between two senses of the word faith. The first—"Faith-A"—is not, he says, a religious state: "The devils who 'believe and tremble' have Faith-A. A man who curses or ignores God may have Faith-A. Philosophical arguments for the existence of God are presumably intended to produce Faith-A." The other sense—"Faith-B"—is defined as "a trust, or confidence, in the God whose existence is thus assented to." This involves an attitude of the will, and is more like our confidence in a friend.

But are the two so unconnected as Professor Price seemed to imply? We are told, says Lewis, that once we have Faith-A, to ask God Himself for the "gift" of Faith-B—which is what most people who have Faith-A would do anyway. The best way to put it, suggests Lewis, is to say that Faith-A "converts into religious experience what was hitherto only potentially or implicitly religious. In this modified form I would accept Professor Price's view that philosophical proofs never, by themselves, lead to religion. Something at least *quasi*-religious uses them before, and the 'proofs' remove an inhibition that was preventing their development into religion proper."

Those readers who have glanced at the list of speakers mentioned in the appendix to this paper will have noticed that a good many papers read during the 1950s were devoted to topics such as "Philosophical Muddles," "Linguistic Analysis," "Contemporary Philosophy," and the like. It was becoming clear to some of those in the Socratic, certainly to Lewis and Stella Aldwinckle, that the club was taking a dangerous trend, and one that could cause its days to be numbered. What was happening was that, whereas most members of the Socratic believed Christianity to be *true* in some ultimate sense, the new trend in philosophy at Oxford and Cambridge was to break away from theology and devote itself to the study of language. Philosophy was no longer metaphysics, but logical analysis, and, to reduce the Socratic's problem into the simplest form possible, the question now was not "Does God exist?" but "What do we mean by the word 'God'?"

The chasm that was beginning to divide theology and philosophy was specially noticeable to Austin Farrer and Basil Mitchell (another Socratic) as they were trained in both disciplines. A good starting point for understanding the new trend in philosophy is Basil Mitchell's essay "Modern Philosophy and Theology," which was published in the *Socratic Digest* (No. 5, 1952, pp. 3–10). In the same issue (pp. 35–38) can be found Austin Farrer's highly entertaining "Theologian's Point of View," which begins:

I had a dream. There were Theology and Philosophy, clothed in both the moral and the academic dignity of female professors. Theology held several slips of paper in her hand, with a single sentence written upon each: "God exists" on one, "The world was created" on another. Philosophy displayed several baskets on a table, marked with tickets describing sentences of different logical kinds. "Moral Commands," "Empirical Statements," "Truths of Definition," and so forth. "Into which of my baskets, dear Theology," she said, "would you like to put your statements?"

Theology looked at the baskets and hesitated. "Do I have to?" she replied. "I mean, is it certain that the right basket for my statements is on your table at all? Of course, if it were demonstrable that all the possible sorts of logical baskets were represented here. . . ."

"Dear me, no," said Philosophy, "we can't claim to be sure of that. But don't you find some of these baskets rather alluring? Here is a brand new one, delivered only this morning by Logical Baskets Limited (limited, you know, or virtually so, to Oxford and Cambridge). It is called 'Expressions of Attitude to Life.' Isn't that what you want? Now be reasonable."

"No, I'm afraid not," Theology replied. "You see, when I say, 'God loves what He has made,' I do not mean that John Christian takes up, or would be well advised to take up, a benevolent attitude to things in general or to his neighbour in particular; nor that he either does or should view them in the rosy light cast upon them by association with the creator-God image. No, I mean what I say; I mean that the actual creator is doing this actual loving."

"Good God!" said Philosophy. "You don't say so! . . ."

Lewis told me that he'd have made an effort to keep up with the new developments in philosophy if only he'd had time. As far back as 1935 he had promised the Oxford University Press to write the volume on sixteenth-century literature for their *Oxford History of English Literature* series. Having allowed this formidable task to slide for some years, he spent the greater part of his spare time in the late 1940s and early 1950s writing his *English Literature in the Sixteenth Century,* which was published in 1954.

Simultaneous with the publication of his mammoth "O. H. E. L." volume—to use his favourite abbreviation—came Lewis's election in 1954 to the Professorship in Medieval and Renaissance English Literature at Cambridge. This meant living in Cambridge most of term time. Though he returned to his home in Oxford for the weekends and vacations, it was impossible for him to attend all the Socratic meetings. His eventual resignation of the presidency made a hole in the society from which it never recovered.

Lewis did not want to let his friends down with too much of a bump, and he did not officially retire as president till after he'd been in Cambridge for a year. He was still in Oxford to welcome Dorothy L. Sayers, who read a paper to the society on 3 June 1954. It was called "Poetry, Language, and Ambiguity" and, as the entire text of the essay can be found in her book *The Poetry of Search and the Poetry of Statement,* I shall say no more about it here.

Lewis was also present, and in the chair, when the friend he called the "wisest and best of my unofficial teachers"—Owen Barfield—addressed the society. Austin Farrer was invited to open the discussion, and

Mr. Barfield, though he can't recall the date of the meeting except that it was before 1957, has said: "The interesting thing is that a brief exchange between Austin and myself was the very first germ of *Saving the Appearances.* I distinctly remember, not just afterwards, but the moment he had made the remark, the thought flashing through my mind—'That might make a good position from which to write a book.'"

There are so many blank pages in the minute books that I have been unable to pinpoint the exact date on which it was read to the Socratic. However, it is worth knowing that this chance comment by Austin Farrer led to what is, in the opinion of many, Owen Barfield's "wisest and best" book—*Saving the Appearances: A Study in Idolatry* (1957).

Lewis read his last paper to the Socratic Club on 30 April 1953, at their 218th meeting. It was called "Faith and Evidence," and Professor Price opened the discussion afterward. No minutes, other than these bare facts, were recorded. Again, we don't fare too badly as the paper was published later under the title "On Obstinacy in Belief" in the columns of *The Sewanee Review,* vol. LXIII (Autumn 1955). It has been reprinted in the collection of Lewis's essays, *The World's Last Night and Other Essays* (1960), which is quoted from here.

This truly brilliant paper arose out of a contrast that had many times been drawn at meetings of the Socratic between a supposedly scientific attitude to "belief" and a supposedly Christian one. Scientists had been represented as thinking it their duty to proportion the strength of the belief exactly to the evidence, and Christians as regarding it positively praiseworthy to believe without evidence, or in excess of it. "If this were a fair statement of the case," said Lewis, "then the co-existence within the same species of such scientists and such Christians would be a very staggering phenomenon" (p. 13).

Lewis began by clarifying the various senses of the word *believe.* There is, he said, the phrase "I believe" as uttered by a Christian when he does not usually claim to have demonstrable proof but assents to a proposition that he thinks so overwhelmingly probable that there is a psychological exclusion of doubt though not a logical exclusion of dispute. This kind of belief (or disbelief)—which is an entirely different thing from *knowing*—is used about things other than theological propositions. "The scientist himself," Lewis claims, "has beliefs about his wife and friends that he holds, not indeed without evidence, but with more certainty than the evidence, if weighed in the laboratory manner, would justify" (p. 16).

After dispelling the notion that Christians and non-believing scientists use their minds very differently, he attempted to show that the Christian's "obstinacy" in belief, which is praised when it holds out against any evidence whatever, is analogous to the faith we have in our friends. Such "obstinacy" is, he said, a *logical conclusion* from the original belief itself:

This can be done best by thinking for a moment of situations in which the thing is reversed. In Christianity such faith is demanded of us; but there are situations in which we demand it of others. There are times when we can do all that a fellow creature needs if only he will trust us. In getting a dog out of a trap, in extracting a thorn from a child's finger, in teaching a boy to swim or rescuing one who can't, in getting a frightened beginner over a nasty place on a mountain, the one fatal obstacle may be their distrust. We are asking them to trust us in the teeth of their sense, their imagination, and their intelligence. We ask them to believe that what is painful will relieve their pain, and that what looks dangerous is their only safety. We ask them to accept apparent impossibilities: that moving the paw farther back into the trap is the way to get it out—that hurting the finger very much more will stop the finger hurting—that water, which is obviously permeable, will resist and support the body—that holding onto the only support within reach is not the way to avoid sinking—that to go higher and onto a more exposed ledge is the way not to fall. To support all these *incredibilia* we can rely only on the other party's confidence in us—a confidence certainly not based on demonstration, admittedly shot through with emotion, and perhaps, if we are strangers, resting on nothing but such assurance as the look of our face and the tone of our voice can supply, or even, for the dog, on our smell. Sometimes, because of their unbelief, we can do no mighty works. But if we succeed, we do so because they have maintained their faith in us against apparently contrary evidence. No one blames us for demanding such faith. No one blames them for giving it. . . . Mark, I am not saying that the strength of our original belief must by psychological necessity produce such behaviour. I am saying that the content of our original belief by logical necessity entails the proposition that such behaviour is appropriate (pp. 23–24).

Anticipating the possible objections to such "obstinacy," Lewis goes on to point out that the demand for our confidence that a friend makes is exactly the same that a confidence trickster would make. The difference is that the refusal to trust, though sensible in replying to a trickster, is ungenerous and ignoble to a friend. To be aware of the possibilities that we could be wrong, and then to reject them, is, Lewis insists, the only mode in which our response to God can establish itself. This "ambiguity," said Lewis, "is not something that conflicts with faith so much as a condition that makes faith possible. When you are asked for trust you may give it or withhold it; it is senseless to say that you trust if you are given demonstrative certainty. There would be no room for trust if demonstration were given" (p. 28).

The happiest result of this "obstinacy in belief" is that thus, and not otherwise, do we move from variations in opinions to variations of conduct by a person to *the* Person—"the increasingly knowable Lord."

After his move to Cambridge in 1954, Lewis was unable to give much time to the Socratic Club, and in February 1955 the club chose as its new president the philosopher, Mr. (now Professor) Basil Mitchell. So determined, however, was the club to hang on to Lewis that they made him, by unanimous vote, their "Honorary President."

The club found it hard to survive the loss of Lewis. For the first few years following his resignation as President, it continued its practice of weekly meetings. Then, its attendance dropping off more and more, by 1960 it was possible for an undergraduate to spend three years in Oxford without having heard of the Socratic. This was not because anything like a clear and emphatic anti-Christian movement was underfoot. In his "Interim Report," comparing life in Cambridge with that in Oxford, Lewis said "Over there [Oxford] I know scores of people who did not believe in the existence of God. But they were no more on their toes about it than about their disbelief in leprechauns or flying saucers. The subject hardly ever came up. Their skepticism was relaxed, unemphatic, taken for granted. I doubt if you could then have founded a society or 'Movement' based on agreement in that single negative proposition." [5] It was, then, this slow, seeping, dangerous, and highly contagious indifference that played a very significant part in the spiritual paralysis of Oxford at this time. Other factors were at work as well. Weakened by the uncertain relationship between theology and philosophy, Lewis's death in 1963, the publication of Bishop J. A. T. Robinson's *Honest to God*, and the sub-

[5] *The Cambridge Review* (21 April 1956), p. 468.

sequent wave of apostasy and doubt that has followed in its wake, the Socratic declined until, in the summer of 1972, it came to an end.

But Lewis's great example was never lost sight of. Among the tributes offered him in Oxford after his death, the most moving one I attended was a Socratic gathering in the parlour of Wesley Memorial Church in New Inn Hall Street on the evening of 17 February 1964. No one had expected such a huge attendance of undergraduates, many of whom—though they knew him only by his books—were in tears as tributes were paid by Owen Barfield, Austin Farrer, and Colin Hardie. An equally impressive salute should be paid the still-active Stella Aldwinckle, who conceived the idea of the Socratic and guided it tirelessly and modestly through its whole history. If a full account of all her efforts on behalf of the Socratic is ever recorded, she will be a famous person.

Finally, when Christians are more smitten than smiting, and the Church seems to be fighting a rear-guard action, what is to be made of the Oxford Socratic Club? Though the Everlasting Gospel has been somewhat obscured by those who ought to be defending it, Christians and the enemies of the faith will have to go on battling till the end of this world. So shouldn't there be—*ought* there not be—other Socratics, not only in Oxford but also in many other places as well?

I was never more stunned in my life than the other day. A Christian, of what Lewis called the "Christianity-and-water" type, asked if I thought Lewis—had he lived longer—would have been too intimidated by the "trend of the times" to propound the apostolic faith as he once did. Would he not have fled into retirement? The appalling decadence of the times, the "enlightened" ignorance of the intelligentsia, and the shameless cowardice of the clerics who have bartered sacred truth and tradition for a mess of secular tastes and thus led the Anglican Communion into a state of schism—all of this, admittedly, is enough to make us at least *feel* that we are living in a madhouse.

But the answer to the liberal Christian just mentioned is No. Lewis knew what was wrong with the world. First, he did not believe in linear, or automatic, progress—the notion that things just somehow went on getting better and better and better. If such a thing as linear progress *is* true, then it is the liberals, not Lewis, who ought to feel stunned at the appearance of "progress." Second, Lewis believed in the Devil, and devils, and he seemed astutely aware of their continuous influence in the world. Third, he believed in the full revelation of God in Jesus— the ultimate Victor King whose glory and power just *cannot* be conquered.

Much of what the fainthearted suppose could have deterred Lewis from continuing as a "bonny fighter" was answered by Lewis years ago in his article "The Decline of Religion" in *God in the Dock* (pp. 218–23). He wrote "The 'decline of religion' becomes a very ambiguous phenomenon. One way of putting the truth would be that the religion that has declined was not Christianity. It was a vague theism with a strong and virile ethical code, which, far from standing over against the 'World,' was absorbed into the fabric of English institutions and sentiment and demanded churchgoing as (at best) a part of loyalty and good manners or (at worst) a proof of respectability. Hence a social pressure, like the withdrawal of the compulsion, did not create a new situation. The new freedom first allowed accurate observations to be made. . . . The decline of 'religion,' thus understood, seems to me in some ways a blessing. . . . The fog of 'religion' has lifted; the positions and numbers of both armies can be observed; and real shooting is now possible."

*Papers and Speakers*

*at the*

*Oxford University Socratic Club*

*(Hilary Term, 1942)*

| | | |
|---|---|---|
| Jan. 26: | Won't Mankind Outgrow Christianity in the Face of the Advance of Science and of Modern Ideologies? | R. E. HAVARD |
| Feb. 2: | Is God a Wish Fulfillment? | WILLIAM STEVENSON C. S. LEWIS |
| Feb. 9: | Was Christ Really Any More Than a Great Teacher and Prophet? | STELLA ALDWINCKLE |
| Feb. 16: | Skepticism and Faith | W. B. MERCHANT C. S. LEWIS |
| Feb. 23: | Is Christian Obscurantism Hindering Social Progress? | LORD ELTON |
| Mar. 2: | Are There Any *Valid* Objections to Free Love? | CHARLES WILLIAMS |
| Mar. 9: | Is Prayer Auto-suggestion? | L. W. GRENSTED |

### (*Trinity Term, 1942*)

| | | |
|---|---|---|
| Apr. 29: | Some Ambiguities in the Use of the Word *Rational* | D. M. MacKinnon |
| May 6: | Is It Rational to Believe in a "Personal" God? | W. G. De Burgh |
| May 13: | Did Christ Rise from the Dead? | Austin Farrer<br>Robert Eisler |
| May 20: | Can Science Render Religion Unnecessary? | H. A. Hodges |
| June 3: | Has Man a Special Place in the Universe? | R. W. Kosterlitz |

### (*Michaelmas Term, 1942*)

| | | |
|---|---|---|
| Oct. 12: | Purpose and Design in Nature | J. Z. Young |
| Oct. 19: | Is a "Mechanistic" View of the Universe Scientifically Tenable? | Hans Motz |
| Oct. 26: | The Concept of Revelation | D. M. MacKinnon |
| Nov. 2: | How Was Jesus Divine? | Austin Farrer |
| Nov. 9: | Christianity and Other World Faiths | E. O. James |
| Nov. 16: | Christianity and Aesthetics, or "The Company Accepts No Liabilities" | C. S. Lewis |
| Nov. 23: | Is Christian Sexual Morality Narrow-minded and Out of Date? | Gerald Vann |

### (*Hilary Term, 1943*)

| | | |
|---|---|---|
| Jan. 18: | Does Christianity Foreclose Philosophical Enquiry? | D. M. MacKinnon |
| Jan. 25: | What Is Prayer? | F. C. Bryan |
| Feb. 1: | Free Will and Predestination? | O. C. Quick |
| Feb. 8: | If We Have Christ's Ethics, Does the Rest of the Christian Faith Matter? | C. S. Lewis |
| Feb. 15: | Can the Existence of God Be Proved? | M. C. d'Arcy |
| Feb. 22: | Science and Faith | Frank Sherwood-Taylor |
| Mar. 1: | The Political Relevance of Christian Metaphysics | V. A. Demant |

## (Trinity Term, 1943)

| May 3: | Is the New Testament Reliable Evidence? | RICHARD KEHOE |
| May 10: | Immortality | AUSTIN FARRER |
| May 17: | The Fall and the Unconscious | R. SCOTT-FRAYN |
| May 24: | Conscience and Moral Freedom | WILLIAM STEPHENSON |
| June 14: | Marxism and Christianity | JOHN MACMURRAY |
| | | V. E. COSSLETT |
| June 21: | Mysticism | B. C. BUTLER |

## (Michaelmas Term, 1943)

| Oct. 16: | Morals Without Faith | D. FALK |
| | | C. S. LEWIS |
| Oct. 25: | Reason and Faith | M. C. D'ARCY |
| Nov. 1: | Can We Know That God Exists? | AUSTIN FARRER |
| Nov. 8: | Christianity and Philosophy | L. W. HODGSON |
| Nov. 15: | Science and Miracles | C. S. LEWIS |
| Nov. 22: | Buddhism | G. E. HARVEY |
| Nov. 29: | Inspiration in Art in Scripture | RICHARD KEHOE |

## (Hilary Term, 1944)

| Jan. 17: | The Concept of Reason | W. A. PICKARD-CAMBRIDGE |
| Jan. 24: | On Being Reviewed by Christians | C. E. M. JOAD |
| | | C. S. LEWIS |
| Feb. 7: | *Bulverism,* or The Foundation of 20th-Century Thought | C. S. LEWIS |
| Feb. 14: | Materialism and Agnosticism | J. K. WHITE |
| | | G. B. PRESTON |
| Feb. 21: | Christianity and Psychoneurosis | JOHN LAYARD |
| Feb. 28: | Can Science Provide Our Ethics? | DAVID WHITTERIDGE |
| Mar. 3: | The Significance of Reinhold Niebuhr for Contemporary Thought | D. M. MACKINNON |

## (Trinty Term, 1944)

| Apr. 24: | Socrates | J. K. SPALDING |
| May 1: | "Explaining" the Universe | P. D. MEDAWAR |
| | | AUSTIN FARRER |
| May 8: | Free Will and Determinism | L. A. MANNHEIM |
| | | G. H. L. ANDREW |
| May 15: | Philosophy Today | H. A. HODGES |

| | | |
|---|---|---|
| May 22: | Concerning the Question: Jesus, Prophet or Son of God? | STELLA ALDWINCKLE |
| May 29: | Duty and Delight | P. J. THOMPSON BARBARA FALK |
| June 5: | Is Institutional Christianity Necessary? | C. S. LEWIS |

## *(Michaelmas Term, 1944)*

| | | |
|---|---|---|
| Oct. 23: | The Grounds of Modern Agnosticism | H. H. PRICE |
| Oct. 30: | Is Belief in a Personal God Compatible with Modern Scientific Knowledge? | DAVID EVANS AUSTIN FARRER |
| Nov. 6: | Is Theology Poetry? | C. S. LEWIS |
| Nov. 13: | Has Psychology Debunked Sin? | L. W. GRENSTED BARBARA FALK |
| Nov. 20: | Is Christian Sex-Morality Out of Date? | GERALD VANN |
| Nov. 27: | Rational and Irrational | M. C. D'ARCY |
| Dec. 4: | Life and Matter | V. P. WHITTAKER |

## *(Hilary Term, 1945)*

| | | |
|---|---|---|
| Jan. 29: | The Gospels: History or Legends? | J. N. D. KELLY |
| Feb. 5: | Poetry and Truth | MICHAEL DALGLISH ANTONY CURTIS |
| Feb. 12: | Natural Law | RICHARD KEHOE |
| Feb. 19: | The Problem of Suffering | FRITZ PRINGSHEIM B. K. MALLIK |
| Feb. 26: | The Significance of Berdyaev | E. W. LAMBERT C. S. LEWIS |
| Mar. 5: | It and Thou (Scientific Knowledge and Personal Knowledge) | DOUGLAS VICARY |
| Mar. 12: | Faith and History | D. M. MACKINNON |

## *(Trinity Term, 1945)*

| | | |
|---|---|---|
| May 7: | Justification by Faith | J. P. HICKINBOTHAM T. M. PARKER |
| May 14: | Resurrection | C. S. LEWIS |
| May 21: | Reason and Faith | H. H. W. KRAMM |
| May 28: | Can Myth Be Fact? | AUSTIN FARRER |

June 4:     Christian and Non-Christian Mys-   GERVASE MATHEW
            ticism

### (Michaelmas Term, 1945)

Oct. 15:    The Nature of Reason              C. S. LEWIS
Oct. 22:    The Nature of Faith              ALEC WHITEHOUSE
Oct. 29:    The Existence of God             E. L. MASCALL
                                             JOHN MARSH
Nov. 5:     Was Christ Divine?               L. W. HODGSON
Nov. 12:    Has Man a Soul?                  H. H. PRICE
                                             AUSTIN FARRER
Nov. 19:    The Empirical Basis of Moral     ROBERT EISLER
            Obligation                       E. F. CARRITT
Nov. 26:    Marxist and Christian Views of   ARCHIBALD ROBERTSON
            the Nature of Man                EMILE CAMMAERTS
Dec. 3:     The Atomic Bomb—and After        DAVID EVANS

### (Hilary Term, 1946)

Jan. 28:    Religion in the Post-War World   SHAW DESMOND
                                             C. S. LEWIS
Feb. 11:    Can Science Provide a Basis for  C. H. WADDINGTON
            Ethics?                          AUSTIN FARRER
Feb. 18:    Superstition and Faith           L. W. GRENSTED
Feb. 25:    A Reply to Historicism           F. W. HEINEMANN
Mar. 4:     Rehabilitation—and Then?         ELEANOR PLUMMER
Mar. 11:    Religion and the Evolution of Man  R. W. KOSTERLITZ

### (Trinity Term, 1946)

May 6:      The Significance of Psychical Re-  G. L. WILSON
            search
May 13:     Buddhism                         G. E. HARVEY
May 20:     Religion Without Dogma?          C. S. LEWIS
                                             H. H. PRICE
June 2:     The Problem of Evil              J. L. EVANS
June 9:     Morals and Religion              D. M. MACKINNON
                                             D. FALK
June 17:    Spiritualism as a Religion       JOHN ROSSER

## (Michaelmas Term, 1946)

| Oct. 14: | Belief and Reason in Philosophy | MICHAEL FOSTER |
| | | A. J. AYER |
| Oct. 21: | The Limits of Positivism | FRIEDRICH WAISMANN |
| Oct. 28: | The Existence of God | A. D. HOWELL-SMITH |
| | | E. L. MASCALL |
| Nov. 4: | Is Progress Possible Without Religion? | ARNOLD LUNN |
| | | J. D. BERNAL |
| Nov. 11: | The Deity of Christ | R. NICOL CROSS |
| | | T. M. PARKER |
| Nov. 18: | Scientific World Outlook | FRANK SHERWOOD-TAYLOR |
| Dec. 2: | Kierkegaard | LORD LINDSAY OF BIRKER |

## (Hilary Term, 1947)

| Jan. 20: | The Objectivity of the Christian Revelation? | T. M. PARKER |
| | | H. R. TREVOR-ROPER |
| Jan. 27: | Is Dogma the Shackling of Thought? | AUSTIN FARRER |
| | | R. NICOL CROSS |
| Feb. 10: | The Nature of Man | DOUGLAS VICARY |
| Feb. 17: | Is Conscience More than a Sociological Phenomenon? | WILLIAM BROWN |
| | | J. C. FLUGEL |
| Feb. 24: | Is Pain Evil? | J. H. SCOBELL-ARMSTRONG |
| Mar. 3: | Sex and Religion | SHAW DESMOND |
| Mar. 10: | Myth, Pagan and Christian | RICHARD KEHOE |

## (Trinity Term, 1947)

| May 5: | The Rationality of the Incarnation | E. L. MASCALL |
| May 12: | Losing One's Faith | F. L. MacCARTHY |
| May 19: | Belief and Conduct | H. D. LEWIS |
| | | C. S. LEWIS |
| May 26: | The Oedipus Myth | COLIN HARDIE |
| June 9: | Christianity and Other Faiths | J. N. MICKLEM |

## (Michaelmas Term, 1947)

| Oct. 13: | Does God Exist? | AUSTIN FARRER |
| | | W. H. WALSH |
| Oct. 20: | Toynbee's Study of History | MICHAEL FOSTER |
| | | J. F. GOODRIDGE |

| Oct. 27: | Design and the Existence of God | F. L. MacCarthy |
| | | C. S. Lewis |
| Nov. 3: | A First Glance at Sartre | C. S. Lewis |
| | | E. L. Mascall |
| Nov. 10: | Existentialism | Ronald Grimsley |
| | | F. C. Copleston |
| Nov. 10: | Time | John Marsh |
| | | D. E. Nineham |
| Nov. 24: | Did the Resurrection Happen? | R. E. Davies |
| | | T. M. Parker |
| Dec. 1: | Rationalism | A. D. Howell-Smith |
| | | I. M. Crombie |

## (Hilary Term, 1948)

| Jan. 19: | Can the Existence of God be Demonstrated? | Vernon Rice |
| | | Gerd Sommerhoff |
| Jan. 26: | Political Faiths | T. D. Weldon |
| | | H. A. Glegg |
| Feb. 2: | "Miracles"—A Reply to Mr. C. S. Lewis | G. E. M. Anscombe |
| | | C. S. Lewis |
| Feb. 9: | Rudolf Steiner and the Scientific Outlook | Alfred Heidenreich |
| | | Frank Sherwood-Taylor |
| Feb. 16: | Theism and Personal Relationships | Gabriel Marcel |
| | | L. W. Grensted |
| Feb. 23: | Plato and Christianity | Leslie Walker |
| | | A. G. N. Flew |
| Mar. 1: | Aristotle and Christianity | F. C. Copleston |
| | | W. C. Kneale |
| Mar. 8: | The Concept of Salvation in Analytical Psychology and Religion | Basil de Mel |
| | | Leycester King |

## (Trinity Term, 1948)

| Apr. 26: | Our Political Predicament Theologically Considered | V. A. Demant |
| | | T. D. Weldon |
| May 3: | Psychic Research and Its Bearing on the Christian Faith | L. S. Grensted |
| | | B. Babington Smith |
| May 10: | The Necessity of Christian Mysticism | Conrad Pepler |
| | | T. M. Parker |
| May 17: | Aesthetics and Moral Standards | N. J. P. Brown |
| | | C. S. Lewis |

| May 31: | Karl Barth on Faith and Reason | DANIEL JENKINS |
| | | THOMAS CORBISHLEY |
| June 7: | Biblical Thought and the Language of Philosophy | AUSTIN FARRER |
| | | P. J. THOMPSON |

## *(Michaelmas Term, 1948)*

| Oct. 18: | A Scientific View of Ethics | J. D. BERNAL |
| | | FRANK SHERWOOD-TAYLOR |
| Oct. 25: | Is Religion Doomed? | R. W. KOSTERLITZ |
| | | VINCENT TURNER |
| Nov. 1: | The Truth and Error of Agnosticism | E. L. MASCALL |
| | | G. A. PAUL |
| Nov. 15: | Atheism | J. B. S. HALDANE |
| | | I. M. CROMBIE |

## *(Trinity Term, 1949)*

| Apr. 25: | Can Science Create Values? | J. BRONOWSKI |
| | | BASIL MITCHELL |
| May 2: | Some Remarks on Analysis, Personality, and Religion | G. J. C. MIDGLEY |
| May 9: | Christianity, the Church, and the Churches | OLIVER TOMKINS |
| | | T. M. PARKER |
| May 16: | Psychoanalysis and Religion | ANITA KOHSEN |
| | | R. S. LEE |
| May 30: | Value Judgments | R. M. HARE |
| June 6: | The Morality of Dangerous Devices | I. M. CROMBIE |
| | | N. J. P. BROWN |

## *(Michaelmas Term, 1949)*

| Oct. 10: | Are Tautologies Really Necessary? | P. J. FITZGERALD |
| | | C. S. LEWIS |
| Oct. 17: | Agreement and Disagreement in Ethics | A. C. EWING |
| | | R. M. HARE |
| Oct. 24: | Philosophy and Psychoanalysis | JOHN WISDOM |
| | | LEYCESTER KING |
| Oct. 31: | Some Displaced Questions | E. L. MASCALL |
| | | A. G. N. FLEW |
| Nov. 7: | Hindu Speculation and Jung | BASIL DE MEL |
| | | VERNON KATZ |

| Nov. 21: | Can Science Be Creative? | C. H. WADDINGTON |
|  |  | FRANK SHERWOOD-TAYLOR |
| Nov. 28: | Physics and Philosophy | LORD CHERWELL |
|  |  | J. C. STUART |

### (Hilary Term, 1950)

| Jan. 23: | The Nature of Faith | J. P. HICKINBOTHAM |
|  |  | E. L. MASCALL |
| Feb. 6: | Certainty | L. A. GRINT |
|  |  | C. D. ROLLINS |
| Feb. 13: | Grounds for Disbelief in God | ARCHIBALD ROBERTSON |
|  |  | C. S. LEWIS |
| Feb. 20: | Freudian Psychology and Christian Faith | B. A. FARRELL |
|  |  | R. S. LEE |
| Feb. 27: | The Relation of Psychical Research to the Scientific Method | N. M. TYRELL |
|  |  | L. W. GRENSTED |
| Mar. 6: | Marxism | DOUGLAS HYDE |
|  |  | V. A. DEMANT |

### (Trinity Term, 1950)

| May 1: | Can We Trust the Gospels? | D. E. NINEHAM |
|  |  | G. E. F. CHILVER |
| May 8: | Biology and Theism | A. RENDLE SHORT |
|  |  | A. C. HARDY |
| May 15: | Theology and Verification | A. G. N. FLEW |
|  |  | BERNARD WILLIAMS |
| May 22: | The Spirit of Religious Intolerance | GERVASE MATHEW |
|  |  | H. C. CARPENTER |
| May 29: | Criteria in Ethical Judgment | G. E. HUGHES |
|  |  | S. E. TOMLIN |
| June 5: | Personalism | J. B. COATES |

### (Michaelmas Term, 1950)

| Oct. 16: | God and History | MICHAEL FOSTER |
|  |  | C. S. LEWIS |
| Oct. 30: | Explanation: Scientific and Philosophical | DAVID MITCHELL |
|  |  | S. F. MASON |
| Nov. 7: | Is Theology a Science? | G. C. STEAD |
|  |  | AUSTIN FARRER |
| Nov. 13: | Reason and Rationalism in Religion | R. S. LEE |
|  |  | A. P. D'ENTREVES |

## (*Hilary Term, 1951*)

| | | |
|---|---|---|
| Jan. 22: | The Problem of Freedom | J. WARD-SMITH |
| Jan. 29: | On Clearing Up Philosophical Muddles | BERNARD WILLIAMS |
| Feb. 12: | Psychopathology and Sin | SEYMORE SPENCER<br>VICTOR WHITE |
| Apr. 30: | The Philosophical Basis of Marxism | MARCUS WHEELER<br>S. F. MASON |

## (*Michaelmas Term, 1951*)

| | | |
|---|---|---|
| Oct. 22: | Appreciation of Linguistic Analysis | I. T. RAMSEY |
| Nov. 5: | Do the Mystics Know? | THOMAS CORBISHLEY |

## (*Hilary Term, 1952*)

| | | |
|---|---|---|
| Jan. 28: | *Imago Dei* and the Unconscious | OSWALD SUMMER<br>R. W. KOSTERLITZ |
| Feb. 4: | The Buddhist Approach to Philosophy | AUGUSTE PURFURST<br>BASIL MITCHELL |
| Feb. 25: | The Gospels—History or Myth? | CHRISTOPHER EVANS<br>P. H. NOWELL-SMITH |
| Mar. 3: | Rational Existentialism | E. L. MASCALL<br>IRIS MURDOCH |
| Mar. 10: | Cosmology and Theism | G. J. WHITROW<br>E. L. MASCALL |

## (*Trinity Term, 1952*)

| | | |
|---|---|---|
| Apr. 28: | The Notion of Development in Psychology and Its Bearing upon Religion | R. S. LEE |
| May 5: | Creation Never Was | MICHAEL SCRIVEN |
| May 12: | Christianity and Humanism in Western Culture | CHRISTOPHER DAWSON<br>I. T. RAMSEY |
| May 19: | What Is Theology? | H. D. LEWIS<br>J. J. HARTLAND-SWANN |
| May 26: | Subjective and Objective Language | J. Z. YOUNG<br>GILBERT RYLE |
| June 2: | The Stability of Beliefs | MICHAEL POLANYI<br>C. T. W. CURLE |
| June 9: | Guilt and Freedom | JOHN WISDOM<br>J. L. AUSTIN |

### (*Michaelmas Term, 1952*)

| | | |
|---|---|---|
| Oct. 17: | Contemporary Philosophy and Christian Faith | BASIL MITCHELL |
| Oct. 24: | The Logic of Personality | BERNARD MAYO R. M. HARE |
| Nov. 3: | A Living Universe | D. E. HARDING C. S. LEWIS |
| Nov. 10: | A New Humanist Alternative to Christ and Mary | H. J. BLACKHAM IRIS MURDOCH |
| Nov. 17: | The Ethic of Belief | BRAND BLANHARD H. H. PRICE |
| Nov. 24: | ? | J. N. FINDLAY |
| Dec. 1: | Soloviev and His Idea of Good and Evil | NICHOLAS ZERNOV E. W. LAMBERT |

### (*Hilary Term, 1953*)

| | | |
|---|---|---|
| Jan. 19: | The Epistemology of the Act of Faith | VINCENT TURNER BASIL MITCHELL |
| Jan. 26: | "Very God and Very Man": Why Talk Like This? | AUSTIN FARRER DAVID EDWARDS |
| Feb. 9: | Ethics and Instinct | CONRAD LORENZ C. S. LEWIS |
| Mar. 2: | Scientific Beliefs | MICHAEL POLANYI JOHN LUCAS |
| Mar. 9: | Spirits | STEPHEN TOULMIN MICHAEL DUMMETT |

### (*Trinity Term, 1953*)

| | | |
|---|---|---|
| Apr. 30: | Faith and Evidence | C. S. LEWIS H. H. PRICE |
| May 11: | Common Ground Between Christian and Scientist | C. A. COULSON MICHAEL FOSTER |
| May 21: | The Logic of God's Infinity | CHARLES MARTIN PETER GEACH |
| May 28: | The Problem of Knowledge of God | PETER HERBST |
| June 11: | A Primitive People's Conception of God | E. EVANS-PRITCHARD J. N. MICKLEM |

### (*Michaelmas Term, 1953*)

| | | |
|---|---|---|
| Oct. 15: | What Is a Rational Proof of God's Existence | PETER GEACH VINCENT TURNER |

| Oct. 22: | Myth and Meaning | RENFORD BAMBROUGH |
| | | BERNARD WILLIAMS |
| Oct. 29: | Is Theology Possible? | CHESLYN JONES |
| | | D. E. NINEHAM |
| Nov. 12: | The Gospels: Myth or History? | R. CREHAM |
| | | A. R. C. LEANEY |
| Nov. 19: | Creation Models | I. T. RAMSEY |
| | | BASIL MITCHELL |
| Nov. 26: | Creation Myths | P. H. NOWELL-SMITH |
| | | AUSTIN FARRER |

### (Hilary Term, 1954)

| Jan. 28: | A Non-Empirical Element in Linguistic Empiricism | MICHAEL FOSTER |
| | | J. O. KINNON |
| Feb. 13: | Meaning in History | W. H. WALSH |
| | | C. S. LEWIS |
| Feb. 18: | The Need for Metaphysics | C. P. MACKOR |
| | | MICHAEL DUMMETT |
| Feb. 25: | Religion and Ethics | R. M. HARE |
| Mar. 4: | Is Science Skeptical? | JOHN ROBERTSON |
| | | STEPHEN TOULMIN |

### (Trinity Term, 1954)

| Apr. 29: | The Anatomy of Atheism | E. W. LAMBERT |
| | | JOHN LUCAS |
| May 6: | Tertullian's Paradox | BERNARD WILLIAMS |
| | | BRIAN McGUINESS |
| May 13: | Psychoanalysis and Value Judgments | ANTHONY QUINTON |
| May 21: | Incarnation—Christian and Non-Christian | R. C. ZAEHNER |
| | | I. T. RAMSEY |
| June 3: | Poetry, Language and Ambiguity | DOROTHY L. SAYERS |
| | | AUSTIN FARRER |

# 17
## *To the RAF*
### CHARLES GILMORE

To a point, I have small title to a place among the distinguished contributors to this collection of essays on C. S. Lewis for I knew him for a shorter time than many of them and less closely than quite a number of the rest. I met him briefly once when he was a young don and I an undergraduate in the late twenties at Oxford, and not again until 1941, after which we met reasonably often till the end of the war. Then, regrettably, our ways parted. At the same time, I met with, and walked with, this amazing polymath through a brief period of our lives.

To explain. The Battle of Britain had had an extraordinary effect on the nation and a quite miraculous effect on the status of the Royal Air Force. One cannot analyse the interplay of emotion and events in this short essay, but for some considerable time afterward the feeling of many men was that this was the service to join as a volunteer rather than to wait for call-up on conscription, where one might well be drafted into one of the other two services without being given a choice. Only those who lived through those days can understand this feeling. For quite a time, the RAF received into its ranks more than its fair share of the cream of the nation. It was this sort of attitude that led the Dean of St. Paul's to offer a lectureship in his gift to the Chaplain-in-Chief of the RAF with the proposal that C. S. Lewis should fill it and help with his great intellect some of the finest youth in the country.

Before continuing I must ask those who knew him more closely and for a longer time than I to bear with one who can write only of the Lewis he knew. My life has not been spent in the academic mainstream, although the wise men who guided me at Oxford half a century ago gave me a love for learning so that I have always had some worthwhile book open on the desk. But I am "distinctly unacademic" and have never claimed to be anything else. I had a feeling that Lewis knew this and consequently relaxed with me more than he would have done with someone endeavouring to disply academic attainments he did not really possess. "You must learn to hold your reading like a gentleman," said my father once to me, and after fifty-odd years I have found it to be good advice.

So on a rainy night in 1941, the Chaplain-in-Chief of the Royal Air Force took me as his adviser to Magdalen College, Oxford, to talk with Lewis about the possibility of his giving lectures to the men and women of the Royal Air Force disposed in the many camps and training establishments in the United Kingdom. He was interested but diffident. He thought that he should not embark on a project of this nature if in his age group (he was, I think, forty-two at the time) he should be called up a few months later. However, we went ahead in our negotiations, and I can well remember Lewis slowly but surely "taking off" and promising to soar.

One has to remember two vitally important things about these plans, very obvious at the time but very likely to be obscured nearly forty years later. This assignment represented a new task for Lewis. He was a teacher to his bones, he could even be termed the teacher's teacher, but I don't think that he was, for all his kindness, the plodder's teacher. How would it all work out when he was talking to an audience who had never, for the most part, contemplated an academic life at university level?

The second point is that his hearers, well over three-quarters of them, were civilians in uniform, men and women now with time to think, knowing it to be important to get it right if they should survive into the postwar world. This applies, of course, only to those who came to his lectures. Obviously, the nonthinkers didn't come.

The first venture was at Abingdon, some five miles from Oxford, almost a "home fixture," described by Jack as a complete flop, but I think he was wrong. At any rate, he quickly grasped the position and, at some of the great training stations where he met with people, some of whom were the equals of his own undergraduates, I know that he had a profound effect. It was neither striking nor startling; he was not that kind of person. There were, so to speak, no headlines in the morning papers, but as a result of hearing Lewis there were handfuls of young people all gaining quite new concepts of how they fitted into the life that immediately lay before them. I had this direct from a friend who commanded a large training school.

The effect he made is hard to describe a generation later, and I doubt whether even a contemporary diary could quite convey it. He never showed any emotion, although I think that his listeners knew instinctively that his thoughts had been hammered out in the furnace rather than stored inside a glacier. His subject matter varied most wonderfully and, considered as such, was not always very interesting to ordinary people, but he could light it up with such grace and clarity that, long after what he actually said had been forgotten, the memory of many who heard him was that he had shown to them a sterling and direct purpose, where before they had found only the confusion of a whirlpool. How he did this, whether he knew that he did it, I have no idea but, although I went to only a few of his lectures, I saw the same result, sharp and clear as a diamond with many lights, whether he was speaking to a hundred or to a dozen.

I had charge of the RAF Chaplains School at that time, together with the RAF Leadership Courses. Both were accommodated at Magdalene College, Cambridge, to where Lewis some ten years later was to migrate from Magdalen Oxford to his professorial chair. It was well within the terms of his lectureship (which had been renewed) that he should come and talk to the chaplains. But there were doubts.

Just as with the lay men and women, the great majority of the chaplains were civilians in uniform. They varied in age from about twenty-six to forty-six. Quite a few had served in World War I as combatants or as chaplains. Their backgrounds before ordination were widely divergent. There were about twenty ex-pilots, one or two doctors, an ex-corporal who was a V.C. [Victoria Cross holder], and a few journalists and bankers, besides those who had known only school, university, and theological college. A formidable crowd for even Lewis to address!

All were by definition volunteers, and a new world had opened to many of them. They met in the services men and women whom they would never encounter in a lifetime of parish work, and the effect on them was seismic. Some were shaken in the whole idea of their calling; a greater number were finding a larger, much larger, vocation for the first time. They were being asked questions by the friends of those who left in the evening for enemy targets and didn't come back. And they were asking themselves yet deeper questions. In both events, no nonsense, no equivocation, would do. Some had returned from the field, some were facing a baptism of fire on a near but unknown D-day. They were free men indeed, needed indeed. One particular course had already given a visiting dignitary a rough ride because he offered only stock answers with the thunder of Sinai and would listen to no one else. I knew that Lewis could be hurt, and I did not want him to be hurt. He was far too good for that.

I need not have worried. At first, however, my worst fears looked as if they were being confirmed. To these men, probing life in the raw and trying to do something about it, he chose to speak on "Linguistic Analysis in Pauline Soteriology." Worse, if you can imagine it, he seemed to be feeling for words. Clive Staples Lewis feeling for words! He hummed, and the ill-mannered coughed. A future bishop secretly got on with *The Times'* crossword. But Lewis knew his men. He suddenly said something about prostitutes and pawnbrokers being "Pardoned in Heaven, the first by the throne," and the rest of the morning was full of the clang of steel on steel and the laughter of good fellows, and answers that belonged to life. Regrettably, as I remember, linguistic analysis was an early casualty, but Jack had done his job.

He came often to the school after this. He usually lectured on the last day of each course, would stay the night in college, and return to Oxford the next morning. The course being over, I normally made my way to the Air Ministry for a day to discuss and report on the provenance and general administration of the school. One such day Lewis and I walked in the gardens of Magdalene before ambling to the station, for we had much time to catch our respective trains. I put my briefcase on a garden bench where I could see it easily from almost any point. I told him that I had to keep it in sight because it contained a bottle of whiskey, which in those days resembled a virtuous wife whose price was above rubies. I remember his riposte to this day. "I don't think that to be a very safe remark," he said, "We are alone in this garden, I am bigger than you, and the inference is appalling."

In the gardens and on our way to the railway station, to which we nearly always walked unless the weather was impossible, we spoke of a dozen different matters and on a dozen different topics. I have never kept a diary save in a romantic youthful period, so that after thirty-five years one remembers but little; on the other hand what one does remember must be the things most worth remembering. I am not really sorry that he never said to me: "The tablets, boy, the tablets!"

It was never difficult to get Lewis to talk, but I admit to being flustered when he asked me my opinion of a writer. I had then (as now) a great opinion of G. K. Chesterton, whom I had mentioned to him as being one of the writers who had never really acquired his rightful niche. That really started him off! I didn't then know that, some twenty years before, *The Everlasting Man* had helped pilgrim Lewis to a logical view of the outline of Christian history. We agreed that Chesterton's paradoxes were not really paradoxes at all. I was to study *The Everlasting Man* again, and Chesterton, like most of the great writers, would be rediscovered and revalued about fifty years after his death.

He taught me on those walks never to try to judge the achievements of one generation by the standards of another. He did not live to hear the modern phrase "generation gap," but he would surely have lighted it up for us. He begged me on several occasions to forget only at my peril that the ancients had every whit as fine brains as modern man, and that we should never really understand old mythologies, allegories, or much of history until this became an automatic assumption on the part of the scholar.

He had a deep love for the Church of England and asked me whether I thought she would survive. He thought that if England survived, the Church of the Nation would survive but afterward, that is, after we had won the war, "Can you keep a democracy armed in peacetime?" he asked. No bad observation.

This, as I hinted in the beginning, is one man's Lewis, and I could be well out in my judgments. I admired him immensely and, let anyone say what he will, this great polemicist needed sympathy, even empathy, as a part of his diet.

Somewhere Gilbert Murray, a great hero to Lewis, says that at the end of his life Plato had not quite solved his philosophical world problem and that Plato knew it. I am left with the impression that Lewis had the answers, and I think that he knew it. On his own estimate, it will be about A.D. 2013 before this is resolved. I shall not, alas, attend the debate.

On a purely personal note, I have to admit to an instant affinity with Lewis. If he were the last of the dinosaurs, then I am a throwback. Long before I had met or even heard of him, my old headmaster told me that the unmistakable signs of a scholar and a gentleman were that he wore old tweeds, pronounced his diphthongs correctly, worked briefly in his dressing gown, and discovered the great answers to life using only the stub of a pencil on the back of an old envelope. It is quite remarkable that every one of these characteristics applied to Lewis. He often worked out—hammered is a better word—his theology on the back of an old envelope as he tells us, old tweeds were a part of him, and he was wearing a dressing gown when I went to see him in 1941.

I plead at the close to be permitted an irrelevancy that will harm none and interest many. I have met during a considerable lifetime three Oxford men who gained professorial chairs at Cambridge; A. E. Housman, Arthur Quiller-Couch, and C. S. Lewis. Each had a mind of crystal, each wrote in a style that varied from the exquisite to the abrasive. (There is here material for some young man's doctoral thesis.) But if, beneath it all, Lewis, as I think, had the longest reach and the deepest thrust of the three, I would suggest that it was because he came to the Honours School of English already a double first and that. when he made the final commitment, it was that of a man whose treasury was bursting.

> From cloister, desk, and grove you proved the skies;
> Oft in your words great Homer spoke again;
> You loved the Galilean, in His eyes,
> You harmonised the overtones of pain.
> Your accents, borne from ancient regions far,
> Were sometimes pitched beyond the human bound,
> But Smith of England hailed a star,
> In the Soul of Smith, which you had found!

# 18

## *A Christian Gentleman*

### CLIFFORD MORRIS

As an ordinary person with no special qualifications, save that he called himself my friend, I want to share with you some of my memories of the late Clive Staples Lewis, Master of Arts, Doctor of Literature, Doctor of Divinity, Fellow of the Royal Society of Literature, Fellow of the British Academy, holder of a Gollancz Memorial Prize, and a Carnegie Medal for Literary Achievements, Honorary Fellow of Magdalen College, Oxford, and sometime Professor of Medieval and Renaissance Literature at the University of Cambridge. And I must begin with a confession: I find it difficult to do, adequately, what I have set out to do—not because there is little to say, but because there is far too much! He was my friend, my very dear friend, and I loved him greatly.

That is not said in any sickly sentimental spirit—which he would have hated anyway—but as a simple statement of fact. C. S. Lewis was very similar in many ways to the late William Edwin Sangster, the famous Methodist minister of the London Westminster Central Hall. They both included me in their circle of friendship; they both treated me with affectionate comradeship; they both talked with me freely on a great variety of subjects; they were both dedicated and devoted disciples of Jesus Christ; and they both desired passionately to let others see and know what it means to be a Christian. But I had a somewhat closer relationship with C. S. Lewis, and when he was taken from us, I suffered (as did so many others) an irreparable loss.

Like Dr. Sangster, Dr. Lewis was a man to whom one would go in any sort of trouble and be sure that one would receive *all that could possibly be given* of Christian love, understanding, and helpfulness. Lewis, like Sangster, was a dear man, a lovable man, a true friend, and a splendid companion. Clive Staples Lewis, like William Edwin Sangster, was a Christian warrior of the highest order. There have been many, many occasions since his passing when I would have consulted him, when I wanted, above all else, to hear his voice and see his smile, when I have wished for his wise and loving counsel. But he has gone from us, and we can—indeed, we *must*—thank God for every remembrance of him.

His influence upon me has not come from his early days nor, indeed, chiefly from his many writings, but from the days when I knew him personally. "Jack" Lewis—and all his friends were invited to call him Jack—is a difficult man to describe, and although Chad Walsh in his book *C. S. Lewis: Apostle to the Skeptics,* and Clyde Kilby in his volume *The Christian World of C. S. Lewis,* have both attempted it, the results fall far short of the reality. Both Walsh and Kilby feel this and admit their difficulties. Their words form small snapshots of the man, taken from slightly different angles, both good, but neither the complete picture. I suppose that is not possible—witness the essays in a book called *Light on C. S. Lewis*—and I will not be so foolish as to pretend that *I* can be any more successful. But I do want to add my own personal touches to the snapshots, if I can.

When I was first asked, by my private car-hire business predecessors, to take a car and meet Professor Lewis, it was to be at Oxford station. I was told to look for a portly gentleman who would be wearing a thick overcoat and a trilby hat turned down all around; he would also be carrying a walking stick, have a grey haversack on his back, would be wearing horn-rimmed glasses, and would look like a prosperous farmer! Well, that was a good few years ago, and after becoming the proprietor of the car-hire business, I was privileged to drive the "prosperous farmer" some hundreds of miles, enjoy with him some hundreds of conversations on all sorts of subjects, and share with him scores of times of fellowship over meals.

When I first knew Dr. Lewis, he was a Fellow of Magdalen College, Oxford, and the journeys he required me to do for him were mostly local ones. Then he occupied the Chair of Medieval and Renaissance Literature at Cambridge, and his journeys were to and from that university town at the beginning and ending of terms, and to and from Oxford station when he came home at weekends. So I saw him and enjoyed his company every week. There were also, of course, the other odd occasions when he and Mrs. Lewis went out to dinner or to see friends or for drives in the country. Unfortunately ill-health forced his premature retirement, and then I did not see him quite so frequently.

Naturally you will find some of his books on my shelves, several of which he gave me, and which bear his cordial regards and signature therein. I remember one of my friends, seeing one of these books one day, said, "Oh, so you know C. S. Lewis! Do tell me what he's really like!" *That,* as I have already indicated, is no simple task. Dr. Lewis has been described as one of the greatest Christian apologists of the last hundred years and, again, as one of the wittiest and most penetrating thinkers of this present century. *The Screwtape Letters* is probably the most popular of his books, and I think that *Mere Christianity* would come a close second. Here are a few sentences of the kind you will find in his work:

Until you have given yourself up to Christ, you will not have a real self.

Nothing that you have not given away will ever be really yours. Nothing in you that has not died will ever be raised from the dead. Look for yourself, and you will find that in the long run only hatred, loneliness, despair, rage, ruin, and decay will be yours. But look for Christ, and you will find Him, and with Him everything else thrown in.

All that is not eternal is eternally out of date.

I believe in Christianity as I believe that the sun has risen; not only because I can see it, but because by it I see everything else.

Don't bother much about your feelings. When they are humble, loving, brave, give thanks for them; when they are conceited, selfish, cowardly, ask to have them altered. In neither case are they *you,* but only a thing that happens to you. What matters is your intention and your behaviour.

Yes, I am impressed by his writing. I am impressed by his concise and logical reasoning, I am impressed by his cogent arguments; but I am *more* impressed—because I have been in a position to be more impressed—by the man himself.

First and foremost, Clive Staples Lewis was a Christian gentleman. Having been converted from a very real atheism to a very real Christianity, he was a man who knew what he believed and was ever ready to give a reason for the hope that was in him. If he were discussing religious matters, it would be in the same manner as he wrote about these things: there would be no platitudes, no shallow optimism about the world getting better and better, there would be nothing stereotyped; whatever he said would have a welcome freshness, a new viewpoint, an attractive difference of approach. And if he were speaking of ordinary, humdrum, everyday matters, you would find that, as in all his conversations, there would be an exactness and a precision in all he said. In fact, if he knew you well enough, he might suddenly pull you up for some looseness of expression! I remember one occasion when I was driving him through Oxford, and somebody unexpectedly dashed into the roadway immediately in front of the car, so that we had to stop sharply. I muttered something about "blessed pedestrians," and the professor right away took me to task on the expression; he began to enquire the exact meaning of the word *blessed* and, further, what the word meant as used by me in those particular circumstances! He looked at me, with that well-known twinkle in his eye, and said, "I suspect that what you *really* meant was *damned pedestrians*—just the opposite to what you said! You certainly didn't hope that they were exceedingly happy now, and that presently they will enjoy the bliss of the celestial realms!" Oh yes, he could be very academic, very professorish; but, on the other hand—and I hasten to adjust the balance—he could be, and usually was, the truest of friends, the finest of companions, and the most excellent of conversationalists. He never "talked religion," except in the sense that a real Christian never talks anything else.

I very much enjoyed our drives to and from Cambridge. After Dr. Lewis died, I wrote to his brother (also a personal friend), and in the letter sent to me in return Warren Lewis said that Jack often spoke of me with affection, and that those journeys to and from Cambridge were among the greatest pleasures of his latter years. I am so glad to know that. If it were in wintertime, we generally found a snug little inn, somewhere on the way, and had a meal there; if it were in the summer, we generally took sandwiches and picnicked where we fancied. I made a little personal pilgrimage not long ago to a certain tree and the patch of grass surrounding it, not far from a certain Bedfordshire village; Jack and I sat under that tree a good many times and ate our food and talked; and I felt a strange desire to go and see the place once more. So I went and stood under the tree and looked at the grass and the thicket and saw the same old cottage in the distance—and I felt very near to my friend as I stood under the tree that day.

It was on one of those picnics that the Cambridge professor lost his hat! Now there are many stories about this famous hat, and Major Lewis recalls one of them in his Memoir prefacing the *Letters*. He writes:

Jack's clothes were a matter of complete indifference to him: he had an extraordinary knack of making a new suit look shabby the second time he wore it. One of his garments has passed into legend. It is said that Jack once took a guest for an early morning walk on the Magdalen College grounds, in Oxford, after a very wet night. Presently the guest brought his attention to a curious lump of cloth hanging on a bush. "That looks like my hat," said Jack; then, joyfully, "*It is my hat.*" And, clapping the sodden mass on his head, he continued his walk.

That same hat was lost on one of our picnics, coming back from Cambridge at the end of a term. On the way *to* Cambridge, at the beginning of the next term, we looked inside the field gate where we had picnicked, and there was the hat, under the hedge, being used as a home for field mice. Jack retrieved it, of course, and later on continued to wear it. Sometime after that, that same hat spent a week under the front seat of my car; and the very last time I drove the professor, the same hat sat squarely on his head.

Dr. Lewis was a great lover of the natural scene, and he was always delighted to be taken through Woburn Park, where the herds of deer and other animals come wandering down to the public highway; and where, in its season, the magnificent rhododendron drive is a sight to behold. It was on one of these country journeys that an amusing incident took place. We had called at a little wayside inn for a midday drink and some bread and cheese, and the landlord's wife (a very highly made-up and peroxided female of uncertain age) addressed Jack several times using the endearing word "ducks"! After we came out, I noticed that he was smiling, and then, digging me in the ribs, he said, "You know, old Morris, there must still be *something* about me! Did you notice that that good lady called me 'ducks' three times in as many minutes?"

I often found myself envying his students, for it must have been an inestimable privilege to have had such a lecturer: every point made with careful accuracy so that there could never be any possibility of mistaking the meaning; the voice always clear, the pronunciation distinct. I once had to take him to Cambridge for just one lecture and then bring him home again, and he invited me to "sit in," which I did with great interest and pleasure. He began by going briefly over all the ground already previously covered for, as he put it, "the weaker brethren," but the point was put in such a way that the "weaker brethren" would have been eternally grateful to him for his kindness and consideration. This clarity and distinction were also manifest whenever he spoke on the radio or appeared on television.

Jack Lewis loved a joke—either to tell one or to hear one. He often related humorous stories to me during our drives together, and I have seen him roar with laughter many times over something I thought would amuse him. He often laughed at my own propensity for suddenly delivering little bits of out-of-the-way information. One day I noticed on the side of a Harris Sausage delivery van the words, "Established 1770"; I remarked on this and then said, "So Mr. Harris began making his sausages in the year that George Whitefield died!" My companion burst into laughter, and then he said, "You know, Morris, if I met you on top of the Alps I should expect you to tell me that John Wesley or somebody preached a sermon there!" He was never dull. The only time I have known him morose was when he was not feeling up to the mark, and which of us is not a bit edgy at such times? It was then best to keep quiet and not attempt to engage him in conversation. I might also add that I have known Jack Lewis to be very wide awake indeed when he appeared to be fast asleep!

I shall always consider myself fortunate to have been included in his circle of friendship. This I valued tremendously. It has meant a very great deal to me—more than I can ever put into words. I want to say this deliberately: *Jack Lewis was the greatest man I have ever known.* He was never, as Professor Kilby said, an intellectual snob, and he was willing to talk with anyone on any subject, having the ability to put the other person, or persons, at their ease.

In the book to which I have already referred—*Light on C. S. Lewis*—one of the essayists said that Lewis always took good care that he performed, or contested, on ground of his own choosing; and another said that he was a formidable character. I would most strongly disagree with both these statements. His *learning* may have been formidable, but not the man himself; he was one of the most approachable men I have ever met; and he was, as I have said, always and ever ready and willing to talk with anybody on any subject. I have been with him in the company of Oxford and Cambridge professors, intellectual and learned men, and I have overheard some of their conversation—conversation that I, personally, was totally unable to share; but I have also been with him, sitting in the midst of a crowd of long-distance truck drivers in a transport cafe, while he enthralled them with his wit and conversational powers. After one of these occasions one of the men came to me and said, "Hy, mate, who's the guv'nor?" And when I told him, he expressed surprise, and then he said, "Blimey, he's a toff, he is! A real nice bloke!" When I told Jack about this later, he took it as a compliment, and I was glad because I think it is the greatest compliment I ever heard paid him. C. S. Lewis was indeed "a toff" and "a real nice bloke." I have never known his like, anywhere, or at any time.

I remember that I once wanted to speak to him about something that was in the nature of a very personal and delicate matter, and he must have sensed my diffidence. I shall never forget—never—how he turned to me, how he smiled at me, and how he then said with tremendous affection, "My dear old Morris, *friends* can say *anything* to one another, and be quite sure that no confidence will be broken." His written words—so deservedly popular—and his spoken words to private individuals—so remembered and cherished—were freely given, but not without care.

Some of his books I was acquainted with from the time of their writing, and one or two of his manuscripts I had the honour of putting into typescript for him. I was also instrumental in introducing him to the works of the great Alexander Whyte, the famous Puritan preacher of Free St. George's, Edinburgh, and this fact I see he has graciously acknowledged in his posthumously published volume, *Letters to Malcolm*.

There were occasions when Jack used me as a kind of sounding board when he was trying out some new ideas or some new way of putting an old idea or some fresh outline or even, now and again, some striking phrase. As we might be sitting over a glass of beer, or as we were quietly driving along, he would suddenly say, "Friend Morris, listen to this, and tell me if it means anything to you," or, "How does this strike you?" And if I didn't "catch on" at once, I have known him to scrap the whole idea, phrase, sentence, or whatever it was, and then begin all over again from another angle or in another way. He took tremendous trouble to say, in plain words, just what he meant, and it was always an imperative duty with him to write good English, as concisely as possible, coherently, forthrightly, leaving no loose ends, evading no difficulties, dodging no awkward questions.

There are many memories of him that come to me as I think of him now, some of which may be told, some of which will never be told. On one occasion I went to fetch him back from the Acland Nursing Home, in Oxford, where Mrs. Lewis was at that time a patient. When I arrived in the driveway I saw him pacing up and down, up and down, up and down, slowly and deliberately, his eyes upon the ground, utterly oblivious to anything that was going on around him. I sat in the car and waited for a moment or two, and then he looked up and saw me. He came straight to the car and, as he got in, he apologized for keeping me waiting, and then said, very simply, "I was just saying my prayers." He told me afterward that he often prayed in this fashion, while walking or waiting anywhere; and once, at the beginning of a journey to Cambridge, he asked me not to speak to him for a while because he wanted to say his prayers.

I shall always remember, too, the night that Mrs. Lewis died. I have not said much about Jack's wife, because this is chiefly about him, and I did not know her until after they were married. He himself has said that, marrying late in life as he did, he was fortunate to find in his latter years what he had missed in his younger days. Joy Davidman was a very charming lady, with a brain that matched his own, and a great sense of humour and fun. As Major Lewis has said, "She was a woman of great charity, with unbounded contempt for the sentimental. Setting herself high standards, she could laugh at the seeming absurdities to which they sometimes carried her. With all this, she was intensely feminine." She suffered from cancer, and they were married at the bride's bedside in the Wingfield Hospital, at Headington, the civil ceremony having taken place earlier. They both knew that she had not long to live, but they were allowed three years of what I can only call unbounded happiness together.

She died in 1960, and that night they telephoned me from the Radcliffe Infirmary, in Oxford, asking me to bring the car to take him home. It was very late—after midnight—but I got there as quickly as possible and so was the first person (apart from the hospital staff) to see him and speak with him after Joy's death. He did not wish to go straight home, and so we sat in the car and talked—for a long time. We talked about the things that good friends do talk about on such occasions, and I shall always count it a privilege to have seen—and shared, in some measure—his Christian faith and confidence, both of which were so manifest behind and beyond the tears of personal sorrow and loss.

The theologian Kierkegaard, speaking of his own writings on the Christian religion, said, "I firmly resolved to employ all my powers in the defense of Christianity, or at any rate to present it in its true form." And that is just exactly what C. S. Lewis tried to do, for many years, and in many volumes, and in every possible way. The first time I heard Jack preach was in St. Mary the Virgin Church, in Oxford, and, although at that time I did not know him personally, I have never forgotten it: it was, indeed, a never-to-be-forgotten hour of worship. The great building was packed, with many people sitting and standing in the aisles and on the window ledges. The title of the sermon was, "The Weight of Glory." I know that this idea of the divine in man—the image of Christ in every man—was an ever-present idea in the last years of Jack Lewis's life. He spoke about it often, and it goes a long way toward explaining his attitude to other people, especially those who were his inferior in learning and intellectual capabilities.

I don't think he ever "looked down" on anybody, and he was always willing to learn from anybody. It always seemed to me a great pity he did not preach more often, until I learned the reason for his reluctance to do this; he told me one day that after he had delivered a sermon and had received the kind words and the congratulations of all and sundry—as always happened when he spoke in public—he began to think what a jolly fine and clever fellow Jack Lewis was and, said he, "I had to get to my knees pretty quickly to kill the deadly sin of pride!"

Jack Lewis ministered to all of us, and there was healing in his touch. We shall not look upon his like again. Jack and I talked together, drove together, laughed together, wept together—he was my friend. And when he died I wrote a little memorial poem, in which I tried to express my feeling of utter loss and desolation. My own words I prefaced with four lines from William Watson's poem, "The Glimpse":

> Just for an hour you crossed my life's dull track,
> Put my ignoble dreams to sudden shame,
> Went your bright way, and left me to fall back
> On my own world of poorer deed and aim. . . .

> So you, my friend, have gone upon your
> own bright way, and I have never
> missed a dear friend more: I miss
> your face, your voice, your smile, the
> twinkle in your eye, your
> presence at my side. . . .

> You never failed me once, nor did you
> ever let me down; you met my need; but
> now—ah now—you are, in truth,
> gone far upon the brightest way
> of all: a gallant Christian
> warrior indeed.

I said at the beginning that C. S. Lewis was a Christian gentleman, and that is what I have been saying all through. It must suffice. I have tried to show you something of the man as I knew him. He thought so little of himself and did so much for others—not only by his speech and in this teaching, but also in secret charities and in other unsuspected ways. When I think of him—and it is very often—I remember the face, the voice, the smile, the clear-cut arguments, the calculated precision, the fun and laughter, the persuasive eloquence, the rugged exterior of form, and the vast intellectual power and drive; and I always find in my heart a great and loyal affection for my revered teacher, my invaluable counselor, and my dearly beloved friend.

> And we, who knew him well,
> and loved him much, are
> poorer, sadder, and so sore
> bereft by this, so great a loss. . . .

# 19
## *Jack On Holiday*
### GEORGE SAYER

THE MEMORY OF HIS UNHAPPY YEARS at school in Malvern did not prevent C. S. Lewis from often visiting the little straggling town. He stayed on one of two occasions with Lady Dunbar, and once in her absence on holiday took over her house with his brother Warren ("Warnie"), J. R. R. Tolkien ("Tollers" always to Jack), and Dr. R. E. Havard ("Humphrey") as fellow guests. But usually he came to my house and was our sole guest. My wife invited him during every school or university holiday, and he usually came twice a year, except during the period of his marriage to Joy Davidman, when we saw much less of him. His acceptances of my wife's invitations (always by letter or postal card, for he hated the telephone), were amusing and imaginative but often left out practical information of the sort that every hostess wants. Thus:

15/8/1951
Dear George & Moira,
    You are treasures. Yes, I'd love to. The 15th Sept week end (i.e. arrive 14th) if I may. Lovely. I've just been having mumps. Humphrey kept on quoting me bits out of *The Problem of Pain*, which I call a bit thick. Love and deep thanks to both.
                                        J.

Of course we had to write back to find out by which train he was coming. He always came by train unless I went to bring him over by car, because although for many years he possessed a car, he never succeeded in learning to drive it although, as he once said, it was not for want of trying. He also tended to be uncertain about time, because during the period I knew him he never wore a watch. "They never seem to go on me," or "I always forget to wind it up" were the reasons he gave, but I think he also disliked the idea of having to spend an unnecessarily large sum of money on himself. He liked to arrive very early at Oxford station, to walk up and down the platform saying his prayers, and then to catch the first *slow* train to Malvern. He and his brother, Warnie (who also often came to stay with us, but never with Jack) preferred slow trains to fast ones and liked most of all to sit in the very front of the little rail motorcars that stopped at every station on the Oxford-Worcester line.

Much of the journey is through lovely unspoiled country on the fringe of the Cotswolds. If the weather were fine and he had the seat he wanted, he would enjoy the changing scenery. Otherwise he would read in the little book that he would have brought with him. This would probably be a classic, perhaps a volume of Vergil or of his favourite poet, Dante, in the Temple Classics Edition. He would never buy a newspaper because he had, as he would put it, better things with which to occupy his mind. "You don't need to read the news. If anything important happens, far too many people are sure to tell you about it."

He always seemed dressed in much the same way when he stepped off the train at Malvern Link station: an old grey Harris tweed jacket, often with leather patches on the elbows; trousers of thickish grey flannel or brown corduroy, old, uncreased, and very out at the knees; an open-necked white shirt; stout brown walking shoes; an old grey felt hat; and often a walking stick. His luggage was contained in a simple, much-stained khaki rucksack that looked old enough to have been in his possession when he was a boy before World War I. He always called it "the pack"; later in the visit it would be used to hold the food, raincoats, and everything else that we took with us on the walks that would be the main activity during his stay.

As we were making a late start on our first day, we took it easy. We allowed my wife to drive us either to the Wyche or to the British Camp, the two nearest of the three passes over the Malvern Hills, climbed to the ridge, and then walked along it until at the right time we came to a place suitable for eating the sandwiches that Moira had prepared for us.

The Malvern Hills consist of a single ridge about ten miles long that falls away very steeply on either side. Because of its isolation and steepness it produces the impression of a range of far greater height—in one of his letters Horace Walpole went so far as to call it "a monstrous great mountain." It commands one of the longest and best views in England, with the Welsh mountains on one hand, Bredon and the Cotswolds on the other, and to the south the Somerset hills with perhaps a glimpse of the Severn estuary. Jack loved these long views and often praised the scenery. Only water was missing, and there was some of that on the eastern side of the fine Iron Age Hill Fort, called the British Camp.

Our routine was always the same. One of us would shoulder the pack, and we would walk for half an hour (I with the watch had to time this). We would then change packs but, if it were warm enough, as it usually seemed to be, we would have first of all what Jack called "a soak." This meant lying down while Jack smoked a cigarette. We would get up as soon as the cigarette was finished, and the other man would take the pack. "Turn and turn about," as he put it.

We would continue in this way until we came to a pub of the sort that we both liked—fortunately we had much the same taste in pubs. Ideally it should be small, simple, old, and preferably in the black-and-white style. It must serve what would be now called "real ale," that is, bitter beer drawn from the wood, not pasteurised and stored under pressure in metal drums, as is now all too common in England. Jack and Warnie would not drink this, and both disliked bottled and, still more, tinned beer. The interior of the pub should not be "tarted up"; the furniture should be traditional and, if it were at all cold, there should be a coal or wood fire burning in the grate. If there were a switched-on radio, Jack would want to give the place a miss. He disliked radio, though not as much as he disliked television. Fortunately this and jukeboxes were menaces not to be found in the country pubs of those days. With our pints of beer, we ate the sandwiches Moira had made for us, usually of cheese, ham, or cold beef. After this Jack would certainly smoke a cigarette and perhaps have a second pint of beer.

Our aim would probably now be to walk home to my house, which was near the northern end of the hills. If we were not there by about 5:00 P.M., Jack would like to find a cottage where we could have a pot of tea. He liked it made strong in the Irish manner.

Back home Jack would wash all over in his bedroom (he rarely had a bath when he was staying with me and still less often in his own house, The Kilns, because of the rather inadequate water supply there), read in the Bible, "in any translation, which I had put by his bed," and say his prayers. He found this the best time of day for religious devotions. He explained that if he left them until later he often felt too sleepy to say them properly. We dined at half past seven or a quarter to eight, so at about seven Jack came down to sip a glass or two of sherry over a cigarette and, unless she was preparing food, to chat with my wife about our adventures during the day (he usually managed to make these amusing) and about her own very wide reading.

His taste in food was for the plain, solid, and traditional. He liked roast meat of any sort, perhaps beef and chicken particularly, served with the conventional trimmings. I don't think he appreciated in the least the rather subtle French recipes that my wife, who had no liking for plain food, tended to follow, and he liked still less the dishes of the excellent Italian servant that we at one time had. He had little use for vegetables, except new potatoes, for puddings or for fruit, but much enjoyed good cheese, especially ripe Stilton or cheddar. These narrow tastes in food are less surprising if one remembers that, apart from the short time he was in France during World War I, he had never been abroad, and that in Ireland restaurants very often served roast beef, hot or cold, at almost every meal.

What made him a difficult guest at the dinner table, especially for my wife, who ate very slowly, was the tremendous speed with which he ate his food. He would often have finished a second helping before my wife and I were halfway through our first. He was well aware of the fault ("I'm afraid I gobble") and once explained how it had caused him to alter a tradition at Magdalen College, Oxford, where at the senior common room dining table the vice-president (or president, if he were there) was served first. Jack found that this meant that he had finished each course before some of his colleagues had been served at all. To eliminate the awkward gap, which he could not fill with a cigarette, which he sometimes did with us, Jack, when he was vice-president, asked to be served last of all.

With his meal Jack liked to drink a couple of glasses of red wine. Although we both preferred claret, we generally gave him burgundy, for he considered it a far superior wine. He rarely drank white wine, but he would take cider or draught beer with pleasure. His taste for port at the end of a meal with cheese, fruit, and nuts had been formed by an Oxford college where only vintage port was served, so he did not much care for the tawny that was all I could offer him. As a matter of fact, he once told me that his favorite after-dinner drink was not port at all, but brown sherry. He had a robust rather than a sensitive palate.

Of course he talked all the time—literary, anecdotal, fantastic, usually light hearted, and nearly always amusing in one way or another. But when the coffee or tea had been cleared away (I think he preferred tea), he liked to settle down to an hour or two of silent reading. He would choose a book from my shelves, usually a novel, and often one that he had read before, for he held the view that the qualities of a good book could not be appreciated at the first reading. Books that he read with us included some children's stories such as *Harding's Luck* by E. Nesbit, *The Midnight Folk* by John Masefield, and a book that we introduced to him, *The Slowcoach* by E. V. Lucas. We also introduced him to *The Valley Beyond Time* by Vaughan Wilkins, *The Little Flowers of St. Francis,* I think, *Alec Forbes of Howglan,* one of the realistic novels of George MacDonald, and Mrs. Gaskell's *Wives and Daughters.* But of course in the matter of literary introductions our debt to him is far greater than his to us. Without him we should never have found, for instance, Eddison's great romance, *The Worm Ouroboros,* nor even perhaps the novels of Charles Williams. He read very fast and if the book were a humourous one (he pronounced that word with an *h*) often chuckled or laughed aloud. At about half past ten, he liked to be brought another cup of tea, after which he went to bed, falling asleep almost at once.

I think he was always awake when I took him a cup of tea at about half past seven the next morning. He dressed and shaved very quickly and then if it were fine strolled around our garden or up and down our suburban street until breakfast was ready. When we first knew him, he ate what the hotel trade calls a full English breakfast, that is, eggs, bacon, toast, and marmalade, but he came to prefer bread to toast, and in his later years was put on a diet that allowed him only tea and crisp bread.

I have described the ordinary routine; there were of course many variations. We sometimes drove to the Black Mountains on the borders of England and Wales and walked a ridge there. We once arrived at the Abbey Hotel at Llanthony, a building constructed out of the ruins of the twelfth- and thirteenth-century priory there, and asked if we could have lunch. The landlady's reply was severe: "I cannot have you in the dining room, for I have gentry staying in the house, but if you like to go to the back kitchen and have money in your pockets I'll see if I can find you a plate of cold meat. And mind you wipe your feet well before coming in." Jack took it like a lamb and actually removed his shoes before entering. Over the cold meat and what he maintained was home-brewed ale, he whispered: "You know I rather enjoy being ordered about like this. What would the psychologists make of it?" I think that he probably felt the same way he did about Mrs. Moore who, although in my experience kind and hospitable, was certainly autocratic.

The ruins of Llanthony Abbey are of great beauty, but Jack took almost no interest in them or in any other buildings apart from pubs and occasionally country cottages of the picture post card sort. Such a building induced in him what we called the pastoral delusion. "Don't you feel that you would be quite happy and almost entirely virtuous if only you could live in a place like that?" He never wanted to go inside the village churches that are one of the main glories of the English countryside and was unmoved by beauty spots such as Goodrich Castle and Tintern Abbey. Of the latter he remarked that Wordsworth's description seemed remarkably inaccurate, but that was probably because our conception of wildness has altered.

He enjoyed wild flowers, although he knew little about them, birds, butterflies, and animals of all sorts. Once when we were walking on Bredon Hill we met a fox that looked bedraggled and exhausted. "Oh, poor thing!" said Jack. "What shall we do when the hunt comes up? I can already hear them. Oh, I know, I have an idea." He shouted with cupped hands: "Hallo, yoicks, gone that way," and pointed in the opposite direction to the one in which the fox had gone. The trick worked, and he went home to boast delightedly to my wife that he had saved the life of a poor fox.

Although most of our tramps were hill walks, if the sun were really hot we sought the woods and valleys. If then we came to a river or a brook, Jack would, if there were no one else about, strip off his clothes and bathe and swim delightedly in the cool water. Both he and his brother loved bathing, and he had an old-fashioned, partly Greco-Roman, partly donnish attitude toward nakedness. He was fond of pointing out that in the English coastal resorts of the nineteenth century it was common for men to bathe naked. "As Kilvert wrote, 'If women don't like the sight, let them look the other way.'"

All the time we walked, we talked in the frankest way as friends should.

I have never known a man more open about his private life. He spoke about his personal temptations, his spiritual difficulties, and worries about other people. He spoke about Mrs. Moore, who was ailing in mind and body, about his brother, who often had to go for treatment to a nursing home in North Oxford, to the Warneford Hospital, or if on a binge while in Ireland to the hospital at Drogheda of the Medical Missionaries of Mary. Warnie was the most constant and long-lasting of his anxieties because "he is not merely my brother, but my greatest friend." He spoke of the growth of his relationship with Joy Davidman, "an odd but very intelligent person. I am not sure if I like her and pretty sure that you wouldn't."

I remember vividly the August in which he told me of his civil marriage the April before to Joy, contracted so that she should not have to go back to America with her two sons. He emphasized that the marriage was purely formal and that he had no intention at all of living with her as man and wife. After the religious ceremony we saw much less of Jack although he came once or twice when Joy was on holiday with the boys at Solva in Pembrokeshire, "where the air is good and the drinks are strong." He consulted me about the education of his stepsons, David and Douglas. They were at a preparatory boarding school called Dane Court. Joy at one time wanted them to go on to Bryanston, but probably to save money (Jack was inclined to imagine that he was about to go bankrupt) they went in the end to Magdalen College School, Oxford. Jack did not naturally like boys (or children at all, although he was a most successful writer of stories for them) and this perhaps made him over-anxious to do his duty as their stepfather.

He usually had a stock of stories about his friends with which to entertain me, but none was ever malicious or the least indiscreet. Indeed no one could have been more certain than Jack not to betray a confidence. He maintained that if you knew that a friend of yours had done something discreditable and were asked about it ("Is it true that X was fined £50 for shoplifting?"), the only proper course was to deny it at once, for any hesitation would be taken as an admission that the charge was true. As examples of his little stories, here are two about Tom Stevens, a colleague at Magdalen. To a pupil who had arrived for a tutorial and knocked on the door of his rooms: "You can't come in. I'm saying my prayers. Kneel down and pray for me." The pupil did. And to another pupil who called to say: "I'm sorry, sir, but I'm afraid that I shan't be able to finish your essay by tomorrow," "Oh, that's quite all right, my dear boy, quite all right, but you must bring me a suitable bribe." Again the pupil did. He turned up with a bottle of whiskey.

Of course much of his conversation was literary. He was often amusing as well as perspicacious about the work of other writers. For instance on D. H. Lawrence, whose novels he did not care for: "A pity the man had no sense of humour. Really if you think about them, those great long clinches of his are terribly funny. I suppose sex is meant to be a good clean joke."

He particularly enjoyed talking not about the books he had written but about those that he was writing or planning to write. Alas, a good many never came to be written. There was for instance a version of the Faust story in which the man sells his soul for a trip into the future; a romance in which the journey was to the middle of the earth, and a sequel to *Surprised by Joy*. On our walks a very small incident would sometimes suggest a story to him. Thus, we once passed a field of pigs, one of which came away from the herd and showed a great interest in us. Jack rubbed its back with his stick for a time and then said: "George, this is no ordinary pig. It is too intelligent. It is transformed. You and I are privileged to meet not a pig but the first pog. Let us move away before we corrupt it." Then later: "*The Pig and the Pog*. That's not a bad title. I wonder if I can write the story to go with it. I must think about it."

The delights of his visit were not over when I had seen him off on the slow, stopping train that would take him back to Oxford. There were his thank-you letters. The first one started: "There's no disguising a roofer [bread-and-butter letter]." But Jack did succeed in disguising a roofer or at least turned it into a work of art. All were witty. Several were pastiches, perhaps of the style of Sidney or Eddison or Sir Thomas Browne; a few were parodies (one began "Blest pair of sirens") or original verses. No two were in the least alike.

The roofers were usually addressed to Moira, as was appropriate, but for me there was yet another pleasure to come, Jack's invitation to a return visit, and the visit itself often to Oxford, where there might be a meeting of The Inklings.

# 20

## *In the Evening*

### ROGER LANCELYN GREEN

How DIFFICULT IT IS for those who knew C. S. Lewis at all well to write about him. Quite apart from the poignancy of loss that returns so strongly when such an attempt is being made, there is at once the feeling of that overwhelmingly vital presence still so near, and at the same time a numbing sense of something too big to grasp and come to terms with.

In life Lewis had something of this effect on those of only average intelligence and learning. My many tête-a-tête evenings with him in his rooms at Oxford or Cambridge stand out as supremely precious memories. But I also remember the feeling of living for those evenings on an exalted plane, of "drawing up every spirit to its full height," sometimes of speaking a language that I was hardly aware that I knew—and of the utter but blessed weariness as of a complete mental and spiritual catharsis as I made my way across moonlit quad or court to the many chimes of midnight.

It was almost as if Lewis Carroll's nonsense theory about "tiring out the muscles of the mind" were a serious reality. When I came to think over those evenings, though I remembered what we talked about, I remembered little of what Lewis had said—and on such occasions I regretted deeply that I was not possessed of Boswell's type of memory and could not reproduce any of the wonderful discussions of the evenings and had been able to write in my diary something more illuminating than: "*10 March 1950*. To dinner with C. S. Lewis at Magdalen—excellent meal and pleasant common room thereafter. Then to Lewis's room, and talk till midnight:

romance, Arthurian legend, fairy tales, children's books, recollections of childhood, visual memories in stories and in dreams. A wonderful evening, really good talk; how exceptionally kind Lewis is to spare whole evenings to me like this. I wonder if he realizes what they mean to me."

Or the following year, when we were much more intimate, and deep in *The Chronicles of Narnia*: "*31 May 1951*. To Magdalen: dinner with Jack Lewis, and thereafter walked round Addison's Walk and the private garden beyond the Cherwell, and then sat in his rooms until 11:45. Talk very various: nymphs and river gods—what they would be like, sub- or super-human, their origin. The characters of Troilus and Thersites (comparing Quintus Smyrnaeus and Shakespeare, etc.). The Black Mass, Giles de Retz—the possibility of Jeanne d'Arc being really a witch and no saint. The greatness of Boswell; biography in general. Then suddenly Jack asked if I would like to write his biography, assuming that I survive him. . . ."

There are many, many more such tantalizing notes—but usually the dimmest of recollections as to what Lewis actually said on the majority of these and many other subjects. We hardly ever talked about religion—only twice that I can remember: once when I stayed with him a few months after his wife Joy's death, and once many years earlier when we talked "about prayer and about books that end well and those that don't or can't." As far as I remember this was the occasion when I think we had been talking about the Faust legend and Faust's summoning of Helen of Troy as the most beautiful woman who ever lived.

"I'm sure I couldn't resist her if she appeared 'in a coming-on mood,' however much I knew that I should," I said.

"Yes, you would," said Lewis firmly. "You would be given strength if you truly wished it and prayed for it."

This led to a discussion of sexual temptation, and he said that he regretted having been so uncharitable about it in *Mere Christianity*, having since had letters from sincere Christians who were apparently pathologically oversexed. This led to homosexuality, and he said that he now realised that it was sometimes an ailment rather than a sin, and had nothing but pity for homosexuals provided they tried honestly not to give way to their unnatural desires but considered themselves in the same position as a man sworn to celibacy.

What Lewis said of Nevill Coghill—"He spoke much 'ribaldry' but never 'vileinge' "—was true of himself. As Walter Hooper writes in our

*Biography,* "By 'bawdy,' Lewis did not mean what are commonly called dirty stories. He disliked stories containing smut or that bordered upon the blasphemous and, when told in his presence, he did not disguise his annoyance." By his own definition, bawdy ought to be outrageous and extravagant, but it must not have anything cruel or pornographic about it, and he proceeds to give a very mild example.

I can remember Lewis telling only one such story, to a gathering of the later Inklings in The Bird and Baby—and that with many apologies if anyone found anything objectionable about it: he felt it was so funny as to cancel out any such possibility.

"There was a new waiter being instructed in a hotel by an old waiter as to his duties who finished up, "And the most important thing, my boy, is tact."

"How do you mean—tact?" asked the new waiter.

"Well, I'll give you an example," said the old waiter. "A few days ago I went up to the bathroom to leave a fresh cake of soap—and there was a lady in the bath, who had forgotten to lock the door. So I said: 'A fresh cake of soap, *sir'*—and went straight out as if nothing were wrong."

A week or two later the two waiters were again talking, and the old waiter said: "And how are you getting on—particularly in the matter of tact?" "Oh, splendidly," answered the young waiter. "I'll give you an example. A few mornings ago I took a tray of tea into the bridal suite, and there were the bride and bridegroom in bed together—in the very act. So I put down the tray by the bed and said, as I turned to go: 'Your early morning tea, gentlemen'. . . ."

This was the only "bawdy" story I remember hearing Lewis tell, and it was toward the end of his life when his supremely happy marriage had eased many tensions and broadened his outlook. Some years earlier I remember offering him a hard-boiled egg when we stopped for refreshments in a railway buffet on the way from Oxford to Cambridge, and he refused it, saying: "No, no, I mustn't. It's supposed to be an aphrodisiac. Of course its all right for you as a married man—but I have to be careful." In some ways he was extraordinarily innocent, and the young lady (the daughter of the head of an Oxford college) who seems to have represented his only thought of marriage in his twenties or thirties spoke with amusement of his awkwardness in the role of a wooer.

After his conversion Lewis was inclined to speak of his unregenerate days as given over to the sins of the flesh. But I have always thought that this was an understandable exaggeration on his part—or that his readers have been too ready to read "sex" for "sin." On the occasion when we discussed the irresistibility of Helen of Troy, he surprised me by saying that our strongest temptations were obviously different, and he would be well able to resist the desire to be "made immortal by a kiss" from the lips of the daughter of Leda. His earlier letters to his closest friend Arthur Greeves contain occasionally crude references to women whom he had seen and lusted after, but no suggestion of actual affairs. And it seems fairly certain that John's fornication with the Brown Girls in *The Pilgrim's Regress* represents solitary vice and unchaste thoughts rather than any heterosexual sin. Even during his short spell in the army and on active service, he recorded that he could afford to buy books because he did not waste his pay "on prostitutes, restaurants, and tailors."

But part of a dream recorded in his diary on 26 April 1922 is relevant here: ". . . The next thing I remember was coming back from Malvern. On the way I met a big cart driven by a girl who had no clothes on. She had very light brown hair: but dark skin, pink-brown like sand. I smiled at her in the confidential way one might smile at a girl when you'd seen a hole in her stocking, and she smiled back in just the same way, as much as to say, "Yes, I know. Isn't it a scream!" Then I went back to Malvern and woke up—having seen the girl again, this time in the distance beyond the river, with other people in the cart." This may well be the origin of the Brown Girls, just as the vivid dream of a visit to the moon, quoted on page 181 of the *Biography*, must have given him the setting at least for his short science-fiction story "The Forms of Things Unknown."

Lewis confessed to drawing many ideas for scenes and characters in his stories from mind pictures that came to him either waking or asleep, and it is a pity that more have not been recorded. When we were discussing dreams and the imaginative literary use to be made of them, I complained that though I dreamed frequently, I seldom remembered anything from my dreams. I shall never forget the vehemence with which he turned on me and exclaimed: "Then you may thank God that you don't!" And he went on to explain that he had suffered most of his life from appalling nightmares—which he remembered only too well when he awakened. This personal trial he turned to very good and convincing use in the chapter called "The Dark Island" in *The Voyage of the "Dawn Treader."*

A typical nightmare that Lewis recorded appears in his diary for 27 April, 1923: "I dreamed first that I was sitting in the dark on Magdalen Bridge and there met Jenkin; then I went up a hill with a party of people. On the top of the hill stood a window—no house, a window standing alone, and in the sashes of the window a sheep and a wolf were caught together and the wolf was eating the sheep. The wolf disappeared from my dream, and one of my friends began to cut up the sheep, which screamed like a human being but did not bleed. Afterward we proceeded to eat it." Another nightmare, which came to him later the same year, is fully quoted in the *Biography* (page 175), and may have had some influence on "The Head" kept alive in *That Hideous Strength*. But unfortunately no dreams that came to Lewis after his conversion (1931) seem to have been recorded, and he was too obviously anxious to change the subject for me to ask for an example—although he later confessed that the nightmare chapter in the third chronicle of Narnia was based on actual experience.

But how much we would like to be told some of the "good many dreams about lions about that time," which he felt may have brought Aslan into his growing vision of Narnia. May we not hope that one day, when "the term is over," we may hear that great, booming voice again as he answers this, and many another questions?

# 21

## *Philia: Jack at Ease*

### ROBERT E. HAVARD

C. S. LEWIS FIRST SENT FOR ME one day in 1934 or 1935 when he had an attack of influenza. He had been the patient of Dr. W. Wood, who had a practice in Headington, a growing suburb to the east of Oxford. Dr. Wood had died early in 1934 and I had taken over his practice. Then Fellow and Tutor at Magdalen College, Lewis was living at The Kilns, which he owned. This is a large rambling house built, as its name suggests, on the site of an old brick kiln. There were extensive grounds running up into a wood on the southern slopes of Shotover and containing a shallow, mysterious-looking pool surrounded by bushes and young trees. Shotover itself is an open space forming part of the Oxford Heights and rising a few hundred feet above the level of Headington. It is some three miles east of Oxford itself, whose suburbs sprawl up to its western margin. It is kept as an open space by a preservation trust, and beyond it is open country. By English standards it forms an extensive park land, some two to three miles east to west and a mile or so north to south. Some of this hillside was cultivated farm land, but about half of it was an open common and also woodland belonging to the trust.

Lewis, always very fond of the countryside, used it a great deal. Its presence on one side of his house, with the Oxford suburbs on the other, illustrates two sides of his nature. The university don, the popular lecturer and scholar who packed his university lecture halls with undergraduates, as during the war he later packed lecture halls all over the country with audi-

· ences from the Forces, and who established a world reputation as a writer on Christianity, was always in appearance and practice a lover of the English and Irish countrysides. He enjoyed country walks and country pubs and country people.

On my first visit we spent some five minutes discussing his influenza, which was very straightforward, and then half an hour or more in a discussion of ethics and philosophy. Lewis was something of a Berkleyan and had returned to Christianity via idealism, as he describes in his autobiography, whereas I, as a scientist of sorts, had been attracted to the realism of St. Thomas Aquinas. Our differences laid the foundation of a friendship that lasted, with some ups and down, until his death nearly thirty years later, always with The Kilns and Shotover in the background.

## THE INKLINGS

Not very long after this Lewis invited me to a meeting of a group of his friends who met informally in his rooms in Magdalen College, usually on Thursday evenings. His brother Major W. H. Lewis, then living with him at the Kilns, dispensed drinks. There were several members of the University English School—Professor Tolkien, later of Hobbit fame; Nevill Coghill, who translated *The Canterbury Tales* into modern English and was active in the University Dramatic Society; Professor Wren, returned to Oxford from teaching Egyptians in Cairo; and Lord David Cecil, Fellow of New College and author of *The Stricken Deer* and later of many other moving biographies. From time to time Hugo Dyson was there. He was then teaching English at Reading University and later became a Fellow of Merton. Colin Hardie, a classics Fellow of Magdalen and an authority on Dante, was a regular member. Dr. Adam Fox, the College Chaplain, occasionally looked in until later he left the college to become Dean of Westminster Abbey.

Charles Williams, a close friend of Lewis's, worked in the University Press. He was a man of great charm with a gift for friendship, who had already published imaginative novels with a highly original flavour. He was a member of the Inklings from 1939 until his death in 1945. At this time he was writing *Taliessin Through Logres*, a poem of epic dimensions, very Welsh, and of an obscurity beyond belief. He read parts of it to us, and I believe Lewis was really the only one of us who understood a word of it. He was the chief commentator, and even he complained that Charles seemed at times to be intentionally obscure. This, coming from Lewis, whose own writings have such pellucid clarity, was a generous comment, but typical. He was always very generous in criticizing his friends' writings.

The usual procedure, after drinks and gossip had been exchanged, was to settle into armchairs and then for someone to be invited to read a recent manuscript. The rest then commented, led nearly always by Lewis. Criticism was frank but friendly. Coming from a highly literate audience, it was often profuse and detailed. The universal complaint from the speaker actually holding the floor was that everyone else spoke so much that it was barely possible to get his own ideas in edgeways. True enough, the informality of the group led occasionally to several trying to speak at once. As the only nonliterary and nonteaching member, my chief contribution was to listen. The talk was good, witty, learned, high hearted, and very stimulating. We all felt the itch to join in.

It was in this way that the early *Screwtape Letters* first saw daylight. They were greeted hilariously. We heard several of Lewis's poems, including "Le Roi S'Amuse" (*Poems*, p. 23) and chapters from the *Problem of Pain* and *Miracles*. Later many evenings were spent listening to Tolkien reading the *Lord of the Rings*. I came into this halfway through, as I had been to war, and it was difficult to pick up the thread of the story. In those days the meetings were in Tolkien's rooms in Merton, overlooking the meadow. This is an open, low-lying, fogbound stretch of riverside grassland that was immortalised by Max Beerbohm in *Zuleika Dobson*. It was a good background to Tolkien's unearthly and heroic tale. Later on he lent me a typescript copy, and I was better able to savor its compulsive character. At first hearing, its reception was mixed. Lewis himself was loud in its praise, but his view was not shared by everyone. Time has supported Lewis's judgment, and Tolkien has added Hobbits to folklore. Still there have always been those who have found it hard to take.

The group was referred to as the Inklings from an obvious association of ideas, but I do not know how the term first arose. Their outlook was broadly traditional Christianity, taking their tone largely from Lewis himself, but the membership was indifferently distributed between Church of England and Roman Catholic. The Oxford don of that day has been described as having positive philosophy, comparative religion, and superlative conceit, a reputation not perhaps entirely undeserved. The Inklings achieved some notoriety in the university as being in wholehearted opposition to this spirit of the age.

Lewis has given, in *The Four Loves,* a description of his own delight in his friends, but he could give no adequate account of the entertainment and warmth that his friends received from him. He was the link that bound us all together. When he was no longer able to meet us, the link was snapped, and regular meetings came to a swift end, although many friendships remained.

## THE UPPER THAMES

Lewis's brother had a small, two-berth cabin cruiser he called the *Bosphorus,* which was based at Salter's Boatyard at Folly Bridge. He had planned to take his brother and Hugo Dyson on a holiday up river toward the end of August 1939, but the war clouds over Europe grew heavier, and his army commitments prevented him from keeping his promise. Lewis asked me whether I would replace his brother and act as navigator. A colleague arranged to look after my practice, and the three of us met at Folly Bridge midday on Saturday, August 26. The Russo-German pact had just been signed and all feared the consequences. Yet our spirits were high at the prospect of a temporary break with politics and daily chores.

The river above Oxford is well known and has been described by A. P. Herbert in his book *The Thames.* It winds its way between fields, remote from towns or villages, which have settled a mile or more away from the river's verge, above the level of winter floods. It is navigable for small crafts as far as Lechlade, some thirty miles upstream, and its level of water is held up by a series of weirs and locks. There are half a dozen road bridges, and at each an inn provides refreshment for travelers by either land or water. Newbridge, built in the fourteenth century, has two, one in Oxfordshire, one in Berkshire. Few of these escaped a visit from us.

We were fortunate in our weather and motored slowly along the placid waterway between the flower-covered banks of late summer. The conversation of my learned, loquacious friends was sparkling. Talk turned on the Renaissance. A call at the Trout at Godstow just before closing time stimulated both to a vigorous discussion as we circumnavigated Wytham Wood. Dyson tried to pin Lewis down to a date for the onset of the Renaissance. Was it at the fall of Constantinople, or was it earlier? Lewis said that the closer you looked into the evidence, the earlier it seemed to appear. Like all movements of the kind, it was a continuous process without a clearly marked beginning or end. "All periods are periods of transition." Later they are split up for the convenience of historians and pedagogues; the term *Renaissance* did not appear until the eighteenth century. Lewis, who had read everything and who seemed to remember everything he had read, supported his thesis with inexhaustible quotations. Dyson did his best but was talked down in the end.

The argument was less dry and academic than you might suppose, lit by flashes of wit and imaginative reconstruction of events. It was so stimulating that when at last they retreated for the night into the Rose Revived at Newbridge, I remained on board and, in spite of the peaceful river outside, I found it hard to get to sleep.

The next morning, Sunday, we moved on to the Tadpole Bridge and separated on foot to our respective churches in Buckland a mile or so away. That afternoon after lunch we went on upstream and met, coming down, Robert Gitting in a canoe, naked to the waist. His bearded figure was greeted rapturously by Lewis with a quotation:

> Have sight of Proteus rising from the sea;
> Or hear old Triton blow his wreathed horn.

At this Gitting picked up an enormous conch from the bottom of his canoe and attempted to blow a fanfare on it. After some lively talk each craft went on its way. Gitting later put some of the canoe trip into his book *Sweet Thames Run Softly*.

We saw no papers and were cut off from all news except what Lewis and Dyson gathered from the inns where they slept at night. I remember an hour on a riverside lawn waiting for lunch to be ready at Radcot and an evening meal at Lechlade and an expedition upstream for half a mile to Inglesham and the ruined opening into the disused Thames and Severn Canal; but I remember little of the return downstream except that the engine broke down, as engines of small boats often do. Lewis and Dyson shared a tow rope on the river bank. I offered my own share, but neither of the other two seemed able to keep the boat out of the bank while it was being towed. So after a short spell ashore I was voted back again to the helm. About this time also the weather broke. Fortunately for tempers, the engine recovered and returned to duty. Our spirits revived until we heard at midday on the first or second of September that Hitler had invaded Poland. We knew then that war was imminent. The news broke on us, I think, at Godstow. In any case the return to Oxford from Godstow was in an unnatural silence. Depression was profound and tempers were short. We left *Bosphorus* at Salter's and agreed to meet for a final dinner at the Clarendon in Cornmarket—since replaced by a Woolworth store. At dinner Lewis tried to lift the gloom by saying, "Well, at any rate, we now have less chance of dying of cancer." It was a well-judged attempt in spite of it being at least semi-serious, and it won the best laugh of the evening.

The outbreak of war depressed Lewis deeply. He remembered the slaughter of World War I, which he had been close to. The university was expected to close, and Lewis spent many days of hard work moving books from his rooms in college to the basement and then, plans being changed, returning them again. He remarked that it was a blow, having spent so many years in preparing himself to write, that he should now find himself prevented from doing so. Events proved he was mistaken, but at the time he expected all academic work to become impossible. One evening after the fall of France, all were expecting an invasion. The Inklings were remembering passages in their work likely to prove obnoxious to the Nazis. Lewis remembered *The Pilgrim's Regress* and dwarfs of "a black kind with shirts." He affected to be apprehensive of their effect, given a Nazi occupation, but it was generally agreed that he was relatively safe because his work was not very political. But it was not our happiest evening.

## WARTIME

It was, I think, early in the war that Lewis asked me to write an appendix to *The Problem of Pain*. I was glad to do so and took some trouble over it. Lewis had suggested about a thousand words. When he saw it, he seemed pleased. He edited it, shortened it (for I had overrun my allowance), and one evening read it to the Inklings, winning for me some appreciation. I was impressed by the trouble he took to get it right.

Also around this time there was some discussion on the ethics of writing. "The first duty of an author is to entertain," said Lewis. "The *first* duty?" I queried. "Well," he said, "it's not much use writing if no one is going to read it!" He advised writers, especially beginners, to avoid ornament, but to set down as simply and clearly as possible what it was they had to say, then to go through it and remove all purple passages or anything that seemed to be particularly fine writing. All the Inklings had learned by experience that passages valued most by the writer appealed least to the reader. It is a hard saying but worth remembering.

He also thought it was vital for a writer to be interested in what he was trying to say. "If you write about something of absorbing interest to you, you may or may not succeed in communicating your interest to your reader. But if you yourself are not interested, then you have no chance at all."

Lewis had clear ideas on the art of letters. He had read widely and had thought deeply and professionally on its technique, as appears in his *Preface to Paradise Lost*, Chapter 7. He enjoyed the physical act of writing, and he did not use a typewriter. He used to say that one of his greatest pleasures was to sit down to fill a virgin sheet of foolscap. His script was clear and there were few corrections.

Often when I had occasion to visit The Kilns professionally, he would be busy writing. He would break off without hesitation, show me in to my patient, and then return to his desk. On my leaving he would break off again to ask a few questions about the visit and to say good-bye. Before I was well out of the room he would be back again at work, yet he never betrayed any impatience at the interruptions. He seemed to have his creative faculty under almost perfect control. I asked him how he managed to do this and he replied, "I suppose it comes with practice like anything else."

Major works such as books grew from a painful period of gestation. He described this state as being "in book," and the process of actual writing as akin to parturition—painful but enlivening. *The Screwtape Letters*, once he had the idea, were easy to write. The most difficult, at least the one he complained of most, was his contribution to the *Oxford History of English Literature,* or Oh Hell as he called it. He had been asked to write the section on sixteenth-century literature, excluding drama. He lent me a copy on the assumption that I might find his Introduction of interest, and indeed I found fascinating and masterly his resume of the background of the Renaissance and the Reformation. But what impressed me most was the way he described really very dull poets and their work so that they became more interesting to read about than to read.

On the fall of France in 1940 Lewis joined the Home Guard, a form of militia hurriedly organized from among those unsuitable for ordinary military service in response to the apparent threat of a German invasion, and had many good stories to tell. One was of the tough workingman who said at the time that invasion was threatened, "Well, it looks as if we are for the Final and that it will be on the home ground." By this time his spirits had recovered from the depression we all felt at the outbreak, and he enjoyed these contacts with men with a simple straightforward outlook. His insights into their ways of thought and of speech may well have contributed to his great success later on as a speaker to RAF men up and down the country. He faced some discomfort travelling in Britain in overcrowded wartime trains and in often barely adequate Service accommodations. His brother arranged his journeys and often accompanied him. He claimed, in fact, that he managed and produced him. I never heard that he ever received payment for these talks apart from a contribution to his expenses.

On one of his visits to Liverpool in 1944, I was stationed there as a surgeon lieutenant and saw something of him. He was evidently enjoying his experiences with his usual zest for life. He regarded the actual talks as another chore and approached them mainly from a sense of duty. But he seemed to enjoy the measure of fame that they brought him, and his experiences at this time no doubt contributed to his overwhelming success as a religious broadcaster and writer later on.

In 1943 I had taken advantage of a spell at sea to grow a beard, which came out ruddy in hue. On my appearing one day at Magdalen College while on leave, Lewis promptly labeled me The Red Admiral. I was addressed also as The U.Q. (Useless Quack) and referred to once in pure error as Humphrey. But the name stuck, and under it Lewis, so he told me, put me into *Perelandra*. He had a fertile imagination for literary nicknames. Edward Robinson, a friend of mine and an occasional visitor, was known as Little Pig Robinson after a character in the Beatrix Potter books. His family cat was known as Pushkin.

There were periods in the war when civilian food rationing was strict. Lewis received many food parcels from admirers in the United States. One of these, who must be called Dr. X, sent him a series of magnificent hams, which Lewis often shared with his friends. They were greatly appreciated, and when we heard that one evening the donor, Dr. X, would be present, our anticipation was acute.

It turned out to be a memorable night. Dr. X was revealed as an academic of great charm, courage, and generosity. He told us a hair-raising story of a rescue from behind the iron curtain. It seemed that the wife of one of Dr. X's colleagues was in Russia and was not allowed to leave except in company with her husband. For some reason, I don't remember if it were unsafe for her husband to return to Russia. Dr. X had a visa for Russia on other business. While there he used a forged passport and, pretending to be the lady's husband, succeeded in restoring her to her real husband in America. We were stunned at the dangers he ran, which seemed to have been perhaps not only political. Dr. X appears to have taken them very calmly. We tried to express our thanks for the many treats he had given us. Even now it may be better not to give his real name.

About this time Christopher Dawson wanted to meet Lewis, and one evening I brought him round to Magdalen. Dawson was a physically frail, shy, disappointed man, in every way a contrast to Lewis. He was a historian but at that time had no academic appointment. He had written much on the philosophy and history of religion. (*The Making of Europe* is perhaps his best-known book.) In comparison with Lewis his style is tortuous, full of qualifications and abstractions. If, as has been said, "The style is the man," the contrast between the two could not have been greater. Lewis did his best to draw Dawson out; but he shrank from our vigorous humour and casual manners. For once the evening was a frost and it was not repeated.

On another frosty evening my wife had invited Lewis to dinner to meet Elizabeth Anscombe. Miss Anscombe, a disciple of Witgenstein, and a philosopher then a tutor at Somerville College and a Catholic, now a Professor of Philosophy at Cambridge, had perhaps the most acute intelligence of anyone in Oxford. She out-argued Lewis, who remarked later, "Of course, she is far more intelligent than either of us." But it cannot be said that they got on really well together.

A lunch party just before the war had more success, when we asked Lewis to meet Monsignor Ronald Knox, chaplain to the university Catholics. Lewis started well by greeting him as possibly the wittiest man in Europe. After that the party flourished, and both afterward expressed their delight with the other. Each was witty, humourous, very widely read; each had an unobtrusive but profound Christian faith. They had much to say to each other, and it was a pity that Monsignor Knox left Oxford and that they had few further opportunities to meet. Each of them later told me of their admiration and liking for the other.

Writing this brings forcibly to mind Cory's lines that Monsignor Knox quoted in his Romanes lecture on translation, in Oxford's Sheldonian Theater. He used them as illustration of a perfect translation, but he knew, and he knew that we knew, that he himself was under notice of death at the time. Perhaps it is pardonable to quote them again.

> They told me, Heraclitus, they told me you were dead;
> They brought me bitter news to hear and bitter tears to shed.
> I wept, as I remembered, how often you and I
> Had tired the sun with talking and sent him down the sky.
> And now that thou art lying, my dear old Carian guest,
> A handful of grey ashes, long long ago at rest,
> Still are thy pleasant voices, thy Nightingales, awake;
> For Death, he taketh all away, but them he cannot take.

## POSTWAR

A change in the pattern of life followed Lewis's appointment as Professor of English in Cambridge. The Chair carried with it a Professional Fellowship in Magdalene College, Cambridge. He was happier in his new surroundings, especially in his new college. Magdalene, Cambridge, is a small intimate college, and he felt at home there. He used to refer to it as the Penitent Magdalene, the other as the Impenitent.

So the meetings in his rooms in college were discontinued, but morning meetings held in The Eagle and the Child in St. Giles, Oxford, went some way to take their place. On Tuesday mornings we virtually took over an inner room, to the discomfiture of the occasional uninformed visitor. Following a snack lunch at the bar, he usually drove with me to the station to catch the train for Cambridge. Commander Dundas-Grant, who had by then joined the circle, came with us, and we would sit talking in the train until it was due out. His comments on affairs in general and British Rail in particular were often embarrassingly frank. He had a strong antipathy to all nationalized institutions. Once or twice we drove out to Islip, five miles or so on his way, to pick up his trains there; once or twice I drove him all the way to Cambridge.

On one occasion, while driving Lewis and his brother back from Cambridge, we nearly ran into trouble. We were approaching cross roads in Bedford when just in front of us an unhappy youth on a bicycle rammed, in a moment of hesitation, an inspector of police, also on a bicycle. Both fell off, and the inspector's bicycle became a twisted wreck. No other injury was done except to his feelings, which found eloquent expression. We had to pull up to avoid running over them and so had a front-seat view of the drama while they disentangled themselves from the wreckage and picked up the pieces. We could not hear the inspector's speech, but this was little loss. His gestures and the demeanour and expression of his partner in woe told us that it was good value, effectively delivered. For some unkind reason the sudden downfall of dignified authority is always funny. We kept painfully straight faces until at last the inspector reached his peroration and irritably signed us on. We laughed continuously for the next ten miles.

Lewis usually returned to The Kilns on Fridays for the weekend. On the Sunday mornings, after attending our respective duties in religion, we commonly drove out a few miles into the country to an old priory now made into a residential hotel with a bar. Sometimes we were alone, sometimes with his brother, sometimes with other friends. These were carefree, enjoyable events. During vacations he lived on at The Kilns, and we often arranged a midweek meeting as well. This pattern continued with minor modifications until he was overtaken by his final illness.

Seeing him so regularly two or three times a week, I came to know him well in all his moods. He was a "magnanimous" man in the Aristotelian sense of the word. He was, as we say, a "big" man. I was aware that I shared only one side of him, and that many others were out of my reach. Similarly, with large areas of my own life he had no contact or indeed apparent interest. Perhaps this is the case in any friendship. The areas we did share were large and were varied enough to sustain continual warmth and interest over many years, at any rate on my side. For he had many other friends in many other walks of life who admired him and loved him. But we all had to take him on his own terms.

He could be intolerant, he could be abusive, and he made enemies. He was being discussed one day in the course of a general conversation among a group of scientists. "He is a dangerous man," said one of his Magdalen colleagues. "Dangerous to whom?" I asked. "Dangerous to his own side," he replied after a short hesitation; a quick and effective recovery if not a wholly honest one, for the speaker, a scientific agnostic, had clearly meant something quite different originally. When I later related the incident to Lewis, he dismissed it, remarking that he never minded hostility from "the enemy." But in fact, although his moral courage was very great, he did mind criticism, much as we all do. He was unhappy at his Oxford college. At dinner there I sensed the occasional whiff of hostility from some of his colleagues. The academic mind is a master of the politely barbed shaft. The college was pervaded by an abrasive anti-Christian humanism at that time, which gave Lewis a good deal of painful opposition.

His religious outlook is well known. We had many discussions, nearly all of them very amicable. He had many Roman Catholic friends and admired Catholic writers such as St. Thomas and St. Francis de Sales. But there were certain areas of Catholic teaching and practice that he would never discuss or indeed understand. In a man of such wide reading and sympathies, these "blind spots," as they appeared to be, were surprising. One was reminded of his Ulster Protestant upbringing. He had travelled far from those days, but there were times when traces of their influence seemed to survive.

His political views were described by an interviewer in *Time* as "those of his class and times," by which he seemed to mean that Lewis was a staunch Conservative. He supported capital punishment, he took a strong line on issues of law and order and on the defense of property. He disliked intensely the age into which we seemed to be moving. In his "Inaugural Lecture" at Cambridge he described himself as "the last of the antediluvians." He was a supporter of the *philosophia perennis,* especially in ethics. He regarded these as common to all ages and many creeds, as in his *Abolition of Man.* He was an opponent, not of science as such, but of much popular scientism, and of nearly all the consequences of the Industrial Revolution. But he had no hesitation in using trains, cars, and even airplanes when occasion offered. He had in The Kilns an old-fashioned gramophone with an enormous horn filling one corner of the room. But he had no use for electronics and never listened to radio or viewed television. He seldom read newspapers, saying that it always gave his friends pleasure to keep him up to date with the news. He prefered the slow, local train to a main-line express. His favourite form of locomotion was on foot.

He was most at ease among a few friends, acquaintances, or admirers in informal surroundings. He described with admiration approaching awe a meeting he had once had with Yeats. There was a morning of brilliant conversation with Roy Campbell in The Eagle and the Child. Campbell, a colourful figure, had not long before achieved some notoriety in the press by horsewhipping a critic of a friend on the steps of the Athenaeum in

London. We were all in some dread of this fiery poet, who had fought in the Spanish Civil War and also, I believe, in the bullring. But Lewis, in no way disconcerted, was on top of his form and drew Campbell out so that he was soon rather shyly describing some of his experiences and defending his views expressed in *The Flowering Rifle*. On more formal occasions also, Lewis was a competent host, although less relaxed, and he seemed to enjoy them less.

In his enjoyment of a holiday, he was like a schoolboy. There was a week's holiday with his brother in a friend's house that was lent to us. We did our own cooking and housework, as Major Lewis was a good cook. We spent our days walking on the Malvern Hills, which have been described as pocket mountains, reaching about fourteen hundred feet and dropping steeply down to the Severn Valley to the east. On the west there is the rolling wooded countryside of Hereford, and beyond, the distant Welsh hills. Lewis, who disliked precipitous cliffs, revelled in views from the top of these old, rounded hills; the depth of his love for nature and the countryside was very clear.

There was another short holiday when we drove down for a long weekend in a small village hotel in Corris, south of Cadar Idris in central Wales. We went into the mountain, which, although just under three thousand feet, is wild and craggy. His dislike of heights prevented him from tackling a steepish slope to the summit. So we separated, and he explored a narrow track round a mountain tarn. Apart from this phobia, he enjoyed mountains and was a tireless walker.

He was intrigued by the Welsh spoken in the bar on the Saturday night but was not happy about the "dry" Welsh Sunday that followed. (At that time, though we were unaware of it, total prohibition reigned over the Welsh sabbath.) We drove ten miles or so to plead that we were "bonafide travellers." This would have earned us a drink in Scotland but was no go in Wales. We tried to plead a residential qualification in our own little hotel in Corris, but to no purpose. The licensing laws in Britain are complex, rigorous, and frustrating. We had to obey, but we grumbled. A week's holiday was spent in a hotel perched on a promontory of rock overlooking St. Ives harbour in Cornwall. On the train journey down Lewis was reading *1984* by George Orwell. Later he lent it to me. Although depressing for holiday reading, we both enjoyed it.

In the hotel it was quickly apparent that in booking our rooms there because of its site I had overlooked the fact that it was "dry." The discovery was followed by one of the most eloquent silences I have ever listened to. It was long before I lived it down. However the damage was quickly repaired after dinner by a visit to the nearest inn. Old St. Ives is a fishing village invaded by an artists' colony, which has expanded into a modern seaside watering place. The combination gives it character and interest. We walked the neighbouring rockbound coastline. We spent one long morning in a sailing dinghy with a local "salt" as guide and pilot. I was introduced to a lobster lunch. We called on the local parish priest, whom I knew, and entertained him to dinner one evening in another hotel, properly licensed. He later informed the local newspaper of Lewis's arrival in St. Ives, and he was listed among the distinguished visitors. We bathed in the Atlantic rollers thundering on the westward beach.

We had often bathed in an open-air man's bathing stretch of river in Oxford, where bathing trunks were not usually worn. While we were drying off one afternoon, Maurice Bowra came up to Lewis to congratulate him on the recent publication of his volume in the *Oxford History of English Literature*. The scene was incongruous, as there was not a stitch of clothing among the three of us. These swims were brief and the weather usually warm. In St. Ives, however, Lewis showed himself a strong swimmer, playing in and out of the rollers like a dolphin, undeterred by cold.

Lewis always said that a writer's reputation should depend only on his works. Biographical details should be irrelevant. He would have objected to the motives underlying these memoirs, superficial as they are. With regard to some events for example, his marriage, his last illness, these views of his should surely be respected.

# 22

## *From An "Outsider"*

### JAMES DUNDAS-GRANT

I GINGERLY OPENED THE DOOR of the senior common room of Magdalen College, Oxford, one October morning in 1944. I had just been appointed to take over the command of the University Naval Division, and Magdalen had very kindly offered me accommodations during my appointment.

It was a square room, panelled, and lit by two tall windows on the far side; dimly lit because they looked onto a small cloister. To the right a log fire roared and flickered. To the left a long sideboard held silver-covered dishes and a tureen of porridge. In the centre was a round mahogany table set for some ten places. The bells from the nearby and famous tower rang out eight o'clock.

At the far side of the table I saw a baldish head deeply ensconced in *Punch,* so I helped myself to porridge, picked up *The Times,* and sat down. There was a rustle of *Punch,* and I found a pair of merry, friendly eyes looking at me. "I say," then in a whisper, "do you talk at breakfast?" "By training, no; by nature, yes," I replied. Down went *Punch.* "Oh, good," he said. "I'm Lewis." "Not 'Screwtape?' " I blurted out. "I'm afraid so; yes." That was my first meeting with C. S. Lewis, known to his friends as Jack. There was a step outside; the door was flung open; a tall, gaunt figure stalked in. Up went *Punch;* up went *The Times.* We ate in silence.

To the outsider—such as I considered myself—Jack was an essentially kindly man; as a Christian, he had the plenitude of charity. He could, I heard, be trying at council meetings. Dogged in his opinions when he thought he was right. Irritating to the ponderous with his sotto-voce quips. He was kindness itself to the ignoramus and even the fool, but the affected, the poseur, was anathema to him. I took at once to this genial "gentleman farmer," for that is what he looked like to me. High complexion; wind-swept face. To say he looked like a scarecrow might be unkind—to the scarecrow! Old, tattered jacket, bulging pockets, rough tweed fisherman's hat, and baggy corduroy trousers. He invariably walked with an ash stick. And walk he did, from his house in Headington Quarry to college and back each day. Up hill one way; down hill the other. This was the dear chap who eased me through from ship's wardroom to the senior common room of one of the oldest Oxford colleges. Rather a steep dive or a rapid ascent, according to how you look at it.

My four officers and I felt that it was rather wasting a wonderful opportunity if, plunged into the seat of learning, we took no advantage of it. Our young cadets were all taking short courses (six months) in a variety of subjects at the same time that they were carrying out their basic naval training, each one hoping to be commissioned at the end of the course. Some subject not readily available outside we thought would be best, so we chose philosophy. One morning, then, when our period of conversation was likely to be rather more prolonged, I asked Jack about a possible tutor. "I'm your man," he said, without hesitation. Thus began a more intimate acquaintance.

We met in his rooms once a week, were given set reading in books available from college libraries, and had to submit an essay each week. He couldn't have taken more trouble with us had we been graduates reading for a doctorate. True, he tore our essays to pieces but so gently that he could put the pieces together again in proper form and solve the argument. The great thing was he made us *think*.

During this time he sometimes received a large ham and groceries from Ireland. He would approach me with a conspiratorial glint in his eye. "D. G.," he said, using the nickname he had given me, "I've got a rather nice ham in my room. Would you care to come up tonight and have some?" It was thus I came to meet his great friend Tolkien: tall, sweptback grey hair, restless. He read to us parts of his manuscript for *Lord of the Rings*, asking for criticism. Colin Hardie was there and sometimes our doctor friend Havard, known as Humphrey. His brother, too, was usually in attendance. It was at these sessions that I found out how much one learned just sitting and listening.

The war over, my wife and I decided to live in Oxford, so I left the sheltering walls of Magdalen. I kept in touch with Jack because Humphrey Havard used to pick him up sometimes in his car and whisk him out to some little hostelry in the country for lunch. Humphrey would call for me and off we went. He was such good company, never "talked down" to me but probed gently for what I knew of literature and fed me back, usually through Humphrey, with what I didn't know—and that was a lot! The essential teacher in him always came out but so effortlessly that one didn't realize that one was being fed.

Then one day Jack said to Humphrey: "Don't you think that D. G. should join us at The Bird and Baby on Tuesday?" I should explain that this was the name given by us to a small pub in St. Giles. Actually it was The Eagle and the Child. Thus began my real acquaintance with Jack—perhaps I should say that acquaintance turned to friendship. We met every Tuesday morning over a glass of beer. Warnie, his brother, was there; MacCallum of Pembroke; Father Gervase Mathew, O. P., from Blackfriars; Tolkien of Merton and Havard. Others came and went. We sat in a small back room with a fine coal fire in winter. Back and forth the conversation would flow. Latin tags flying around. Homer quoted in the original to make a point. And Tolkien, jumping up and down, declaiming in Anglo-Saxon. Sometime, in the summer, after we had dispersed, Havard would run Jack and me out to The Trout at Godstow, where we would sit on the wall with the Isis flowing below us and munch cheese and French bread.

One thing very noticeable at our Bird and Baby meetings was Jack's unobtrusive leadership. He sat there in a corner with his beer and just seemed to "stoke the fire" of conversation. When tragedy struck him, the death of his wife, he was absent from our meetings for a time. Attendance dropped and, to me at least, stars ceased to sparkle. When he did come back, he was the same old Jack. Our spirits rose; attendance rose. He was quite determined that his private grief should not impinge on us. Though what that grief was became obvious on the anonymous publication of *A Grief Observed*.

Time slid gently on until he was elected to the Chair of Medieval and

Renaissance English at Magdalene, Cambridge. I heard of this with dismay; what would become of our meetings, our country walks, the weekly topping up or sharpening of my brain cells? But all was to be well. Jack decided to spend his weekends at his home in Oxford, and we simply transferred our meetings to Monday.

Lunch now became the regular thing. Either at the Bird and Baby or The Trout or—more rarely—at the little inn at Wytham. Havard would drive the two of us to the station, where we always arrived at least a quarter of an hour before the train was due to start as Jack had a horror of hastening for a train. It started from a terminal platform on the far side of the station, and we would climb into the carriage with him and continue our chat. The train would start without any whistle, shouts, or flag-wagging, and Havard averred that it was Jack's fond hope that we would be carried off with him. It was a tedious cross-country journey, and I asked him once how he wiled away the time. "Oh, I say my prayers," he replied without any hesitation, as if nothing were more natural.

Leaping ahead a little in time, I remember when I visited him in the Oxford nursing home. I leaned over the end of the bed and watched him, obviously under drugs. One eye opened. "Hullo, D. G. Nice to see you." He drowsed off again, and as I was about to slip out I heard him say, "Not going yet, are you?" and he stirred up fully awake.

After a brief chat I said, "Jack, I wish you'd write us a book about prayer." "I might," he said, with a twinkle. Then he dozed off again. I'm sure many people must have suggested this, but his last book, published posthumously, was *Letters to Malcolm*.

He introduced me to Mary Renault—as an author, not personally—saying, "There's someone you ought to read, D. G." They had been discussing the Theseus legends, and this was one of the many ways he would bring an outsider into the conversation.

Next day I found one of her books in the public library: *The Charioteer*. I was surprised and disappointed when I found it was a contemporary novel dealing with the problem of homosexuality in the last war. When I mentioned this to Jack, he said, "How boring; haven't read it. Try *The Last of the Wine*. This I did and was happily launched into that classical world with whose legends I had wrestled, in the original, in my schooldays.

His home at Headington Quarry was quite typical of him. An old, rambling house built in a copse and approached by a muddy lane that might once have been a tree-flanked drive. The two kilns, after which the house was named, were on the right at the top as you circled around to the back of the house to find the front door. Inside, the rooms had low ceilings and were dark. The sitting room was, of course, lined with books, and there was a slightly dusty smell reminiscent of a second-hand bookshop or the sort of smell one gets when taking a very old book from the top shelf and opening it. He loved the view from his window; through spindly trees to the quarry—long abandoned—but very quiet and full of wild life.

Time came when we decided we must leave Oxford, and it was with a heavy heart I went down to the last meeting. Jack's last words to me were, "You'll have to come up each Monday, D. G. We can always find you a bed for the night." Ten days later, as we had just got settled into our new house, the news came over the radio: Professor C. S. Lewis had died. We hadn't even had a phone connected, so I had to hurry round to our daughter's flat and ring my good friend Humphrey Havard at Oxford. He confirmed the news, gave me a few details, and immediately offered me a bed for the night so that I could attend the funeral. On that morning, early, Tolkien, Havard, and I attended a requiem Mass for the repose of his dear soul, we three being Catholics. At eleven we went up to the little Anglican church, beautifully situated in a well-kept graveyard. Not many were there. The memorial service with which the university would honour him would follow later. A sad sight was his younger stepson following the coffin; Warnie, his brother, didn't feel he could bear the burial. Certainly we had lost a friend but, as Havard said quietly, "Only for a time, D.G."

# PART SIX
# *The Essence That Prevails*

# 23
# *A Toast To His Memory*
## A. C. HARWOOD

Wнен I наve неаrd previous speakers on these occasions, they have mostly spoken of some aspect of Lewis's works in which they have taken the greatest delight or from which they have most benefited. And there is God's plenty to choose from. Far more than Oliver Goldsmith did Lewis deserve the epitaph composed by Samuel Johnson: *Nullum fere scribendi genus non tetigit: nullum tetigit quod non ornavit.* Literary and historical criticism, verse of many kinds, allegory, history, theology, Christian ethics and practice, planetary fiction, children's books—all came from his pen with equal readiness and forcefulness and in equal abundance. He had a teeming mind. When his fellow undergraduates were producing perhaps one exquisite lyric (now well forgotten) in a month, he was writing a young epic; and when he was told that one of its cantos was not up to standard, he went away and produced another in the space of a few days.

Like all who read his books—or were privileged to enjoy his conversation—I learned very much from him, though others have made more profound studies of his works and been more deeply influenced by them. My own great debt to him—it could not have been greater—was that of an abiding friendship, which defied all differences of opinion, outlook, and interests. I find that many of the experiences that live most vividly in my memory are those I shared with him.

I remember one of my early sojourns at The Kilns, when there had been a heavy fall of snow in the night with no wind. We went out in the morning into a world transformed. Everything bore its replica in white. We tried to find words to express the beauty—and the silence—of this new world but ended speechless before it. At the other end of our meetings, on the last occasion when he was well enough to pay a visit to my home in Sussex, we were assailed after sunset by one of those tremendous storms when thunder and lightning were almost instantaneous and the whole house was wrapped in blinding flashes of light. We sat in a darkened room with open windows, overwhelmed by the sheer power of the elements. Jack said afterward he had rarely been so frightened and had never so much enjoyed being frightened.

An almost equally memorable occasion was when I spent a weekend with him in Magdalen during the war. He had just discovered the works of that incomparable novelist of high life, Mrs. Amanda Ross. We read one of her books to each other in turn until convulsions overcame the reader, and we ended by—literally—rolling together on the floor in one of those paroxysms of painful laughter that rarely visit one (alas) after one grows up.

He was at his best on walking tours when his delight in Nature met with his enjoyment of conversation, in which of course he took a leading part. The day's walk had to be carefully planned so that we reached an inn about one o'clock—he held sandwiches in anathema, as one of his printed letters testifies. There were grand tours with a muster of six or seven, but I remember well two or three walks we took alone. One was down the Wye Valley —then still a pretty remote place. As we came down from the hills to Tintern Abbey, he shouted for joy that the hedges were still just as Wordsworth had described them:

> These hedge-rows, hardly hedge-rows,
> Little lines of sportive wood run wild:

Whenever I read those lines, I hear Jack declaiming them as we strode down the hill.

In earlier years, when he often stayed with me in London, there were many visits to theatres and picture galleries. I remember especially walking with him to the charming little gallery in Dulwich and his delight in the classical landscapes of Poussin. There was one terrible occasion, of which I was recently reminded on looking through his letters, when—I suppose through dilatoriness—I had failed to secure tickets for *The Ring*. On my confessing my failure, I received the following in Johnsonian style, of which he was almost as eloquent a master as the great Doctor himself.

Magdalen College
May 7th '34

Sir,

I have read your pathetical letter with such sentiments as it naturally suggests, and write to inform you that you need expect from me no ungenerous approach. It would be cruel if it were possible, and impossible if it were attempted, to add to the mortification which you must now be supposed to suffer. Where I cannot console, it is far from my purpose to aggravate; for it is part of the complicated misery of your state that while I pity your sufferings I cannot innocently wish them lighter. He would be no friend to your reason or your virtue, who would wish to pass over so great a miscarriage in heartless frivolity or brutal insensibility. . . .

As soon as you can, pray let me know through some respectable acquaintance in what quarter of the globe you intend to sustain that irrevocable exile, and perpetual disgrace to which you have condemned yourself. Do not give in to despair. Learn from this example the fatal consequences of error, and hope in some humbler station and some distant land that you may yet become useful to your species.

Later I received a letter of forgiveness in the same vein, calculated to wither any part of me that the earlier letter had left unscathed.

He was a wonderful guest to have in the house, and always wrote the most charming bread-and-butter letters to his hostess. He is said to have regretted that he had had so little to do with children and indeed never felt at home with them. All I can say is that my own children adored him. He entered with complete seriousness into their concerns, swung with them on their swing, and went swimming with them, and delighted them by discoursing volubly on some philosophical subject the moment his head appeared after he had dived into the muddy Sussex water. He played with them the noble game of heads, bodies, and tails, and excelled everyone in his sketches or, when more literary games succeeded, his contributions (one, at least, of which has survived) were of course masterly.

All this illustrates the fact that he lived in the present moment. No one was less given to reminiscences—or to repining. I can hear him heartily deprecating all I have ventured to tell you about him this afternoon. He wrote me once that I should not be sorry for him because his illness deprived him of many things he had loved to do, because "you soon cease to want to do the things you know you can't do." And his interest was in people, not in institutions. That, I think, is why, when I read his works, I seem to hear him speaking to me. His benefactions, which were very great, were mostly to individuals, not to societies. He had enormous sympathy for the "little man." On one occasion, when I was deprecating some modern housing estate, he said: "But if you could see not the houses, but the souls of the people in them, it might look very different." Indeed we shall never be true men "till we have faces." But I believe he felt that the simple man with his simple virtues might often be nearer that achievement than the sophisticated savant.

I would like to end with a brief anecdote. Some months ago I had to visit the North of England, and I had secured not a compartment to myself—progress has deprived us of such amenities—but at least reasonable breathing space, when at the last minute a naval petty officer entered with his wife and children, to whom he had plainly been giving a treat in town, perhaps on returning from some voyage. Each child had been given some hideous toy, a doll as big as the child herself, or some monstrous Walt Disney creation, and each was flourishing a comic of unbelievable vulgarity. The eldest, a girl about fourteen, had received an elaborate manicure and make-up set—plainly not the first she had used. But she was a friendly child, and when I began to read she looked up and asked, "Is that a nice book?" I said it was a very nice book, and in return inquired if she were fond of reading and what she liked best to read. "Oh," she said, "far the best I like the Narnia tales of C. S. Lewis. I read them again and again." So we talked about C. S. Lewis, and she was amazed to think she was talking to someone who had actually known him. It happened that I had just received the current excellent *Bulletin* of The New York C. S. Lewis Society, and I had brought it with me to read in the train, so of course I produced it for her to see. She was astounded that people in America knew about Lewis. "If they know about him there, he must be a great man," she said. (I present the compliment to their country to my American friends.)

All the rest of the journey I was thinking of what Jack had done for that little girl. What a window he had opened from her banal and vulgar surroundings into the world of imagination. Indeed he opened windows for many people into realms hitherto unknown to them. No doubt he would have felt his greatest achievement was to open the windows of Christianity in a way no one else had done in his generation. But I rather think he would have been on another level as delighted by the tribute of the little girl in the train. He has indeed opened windows for us all, or he would not be here. Let us drink his memory, in gratitude for what each one of us has received from him.

# 24
## *In His Image*
### AUSTIN FARRER

A FAMILIAR PRAYER in commemoration of benefactors declares that God is to be praised as well in the dead as in the living; and to praise God in the dead is to honour the excellence of his handiwork in them. It is no business of ours to sit in judgment or to strike the balance of merit; how much of the virtue we praise was the gift of fortune, how much the product of effort or self-discipline is a question with which we have nothing to do. God is the supreme cause of every positive effect, whatever the means he employs to bring it about; we glorify the Creator when we mark the glory in his creature.

Every human mind is a marvel, for is it not a focus into which the world is drawn? Yet minds differ vastly in force or range, and spirits in life or feeling; and the first thing I am moved to say about the man we commemorate is that he had more actuality of soul than the common breed of men. He took in more, he felt more, he remembered more, he invented more. The reflections on his early life right up to manhood, which he has left us in his writings, record an intense awareness, a vigorous reaction, a taking of the world into his heart, which must amaze those whose years have offered them a processional frieze in several tints of grey. His blacks and whites of good and evil and his ecstasies and miseries were the tokens of a capacity for experience beyond our scope. And yet he was far from the aesthetic type as commonly conceived—this burly man was no overstrained neurotic, whatever he was.

Someone wrote to me yesterday that Lewis was a split personality because the imaginative and the rationalistic held so curious a balance in his mind; and he himself tells us how his imaginative development raced away in boyhood and was afterward called to order by logic. Yet I will not call a split personality one brave enough both to think and to feel, nor will I call it integration, which is achieved by halving human nature. Certainly reason struggled in him with feeling and sometimes produced bizarre effects; but no one who conversed with him and listened to the flow of that marvellous speech could wish to talk of a split between powers so fruitfully and so mutually engaged. No doubt many intellectuals keep a life of feeling somewhere apart, where it will not infect the aseptic purity of their thoughts. If it is a crime to think about all you strongly feel and feel the realities about which you think, then the crime was certainly his.

It was this feeling intellect, this intellectual imagination that made the strength of his religious writings. Some of those unsympathetic to his convictions saw him as an advocate who bluffed a public eager to be deceived by the presentation of uncertain arguments as cogent demonstrations. Certainly he was a debater and thought it fair to make the best of his case; and there were those who were reassured by seeing that the case could be made. But his real power was not proof; it was depiction. There lived in his writings a Christian universe that could be both thought and felt, in which he was at home and in which he made his reader at home. Moral issues were presented with sharp lucidity and related to the divine will and, once so seen, could never again be seen otherwise. We who believe will ask no more. Belief is natural, for the world is so. It is enough to let it be seen so.

The impact of his writings sufficiently shows that he had a fundamental sympathy with the public for which he wrote, a sympathy based partly on the experience of teaching, partly on a scrupulous attention to the letters that readers, sane or mad, simple or sophisticated, wrote him from all over the world. He answered them all in his own hand.

His characteristic attitude to people in general was one of consideration and respect. He did his best for them, and he appreciated them. He paid you the compliment of attending to your words. He did not pretend to read your heart. He was endlessly generous. He gave without stint, to all who seemed to care for them, the riches of his mind and the effort of his wit; and where there was need, he gave his money. I will not say what I know about his charities. When he had entered into any relationship, his patience and his loyalty were inexhaustible. He really was a Christian—by which I mean, he never thought he had the right to stop.

As he gave, so he took. Everything went into that amazing capacity of mind, his living friends as much as the authors on his shelves. Not to name those who are still with us, his debts in personal wisdom and in literary inspiration to his wife and to Charles Williams were visible to all. He had no affectation of originality. He did not need it.

I must not let myself be led into a panegyric, still less a critique, of his writings. You will estimate them, and are free to estimate them very variously; and what another generation will say, who can guess? Perhaps the force of his style, the concreteness of his invention, and the solidity of his scholarship are unlikely to lack appreciators. But it is not the work of Lewis's pen; it is the work of God's fingers that we are to praise. Truly he had made man in his image, and where the lineaments are visible we will glorify the Maker.

The life that Lewis lived with zest he surrendered with composure. He was put almost beside himself by his wife's death; he seemed easy at the approach of his own. He died at the last in a moment. May he everlastingly rejoice in the Mercy he sincerely trusted.

# A Bibliography of the Writings of
# C. S. Lewis

### Revised and Enlarged

## WALTER HOOPER

I F IT COULD TALK, C. S. Lewis's wastepaper basket might tell the perfect bibliographical story. Lewis tossed almost every copy of his own books and all his contributions to periodicals into the W.P.B., as he called it. And just as promptly forgot what he had written.

When I became his secretary, I had already compiled an enormous collection of his writings. I showed Lewis my bibliography, which surprised him. "Did *I* write all these?" he asked, and thereafter named me his Pseudo-Dionysius on the grounds that I had invented most of them. But I could never change his habit of dealing with his own works. One day, on entering the sitting room, I discovered him dumping *my* copies of his books into the wastepaper basket.

Even though I suspect that Lewis was gratified, my collector's habit continued a standing joke between us. So much so, that during one of his last illnesses, as I was taking the tea tray out, he said, shaking his finger, "I know what the divine joke on you would be. One day, as soon as the door is closed behind you, I will utter my last immortal words and *you* shan't get to hear them!" I remember suggesting that he keep a pencil and pad close by.

Lewis had a marvellous memory. Following his retirement from Cambridge, he sent me to Magdalene College with seven pages about the care and disposal of every book in his library. The only order respecting his own works was, "All my own books W.P.B. or apply to your own use." Needless to say, the W.P.B. went empty.

There would be many in my position who would wish their bibliography to be complete. But with various letters, oddments, and uncollected pieces still cropping up, such a claim for this one would obviously be untrue. But what of it? If an archangel informed me that there were still many major works missing from this bibliography, then, far from being sad, I would rejoice with the rest.

This is, however, the work of more than twenty years and includes everything I have been able to find. From the beginning it seemed important to establish, as it were, something of a Lewis "canon" so that it can be known what "Lewisiana" there is. And while I cannot claim to have had any archangelical assistance, the bibliography has grown considerably since it first appeared in 1965 in *Light on C. S. Lewis*. This new edition of the bibliography contains eleven books that have been published since that time and more than seventy other items that were not in the edition of 1965.

Not being a collector of his own works, Lewis could never remember a single item to add to my list. My usual method was to sit down in the Bodleian with bound issues of, say, *The Oxford Magazine,* and search each page from 1917 onward. Besides its vast acquisitions from abroad, that great library automatically receives a copy of every book and periodical published in Britain. Thus, when you are attempting to examine everything from the Salvationists' *War Cry* to *The Magazine of Fantasy and Science Fiction* you are bound to peer into some very strange places.

Seeing me eternally poring over magazines, a youngish don who had known Lewis told me that he very definitely recalled seeing a contribution from Lewis in *Men Only*. I had somehow got it into my head that this monthly was about deep-sea fishing and the like, and I promptly ordered up every copy covering 1935–63. An hour later, a young assistant in the Upper Reading Room appeared at my desk, wheeling on a trolley vast stacks of *Men Only*. "Father's 'journals,' " she whispered, blushing scarlet, "and there are more when you've finished these." Even as she heaped them upon my desk, I saw at once that this "journal" has little connection with deep-sea fishing. Despite the astonished stares of those who observed me, I spent a fortnight turning over thousands of pages of *Men Only*. Although I discovered articles by many notable writers, including C. Day-Lewis, I found nothing by C. S. L. But other equally unlikely sounding periodicals yielded happier results—and, all told, it has been a profitable quest.

Still . . . much as I hang on every word that Lewis wrote, I would happily exchange all for one more conversation with him over tea in the sitting room of the Kilns. But content we must all remain with the huge legacy he has left us.

# A Note on the Use of the Bibliography

THIS BIBLIOGRAPHY IS DIVIDED into eight sections in which the items are arranged and numbered chronologically. They are

A. Books
B. Short Stories
C. Books edited or with Prefaces by C. S. Lewis
D. Essays, Pamphlets, and Miscellaneous Pieces
E. Single Short Poems
F. Book Reviews by C. S. Lewis
G. Published Letters
H. Books Containing Numerous Small Extracts from Lewis's Unpublished Writings

Section H, which includes only six books, did not appear in the first edition. It had to be included because, though it would not have been impossible to catalogue the many quotations from Lewis's unpublished letters and other manuscripts, such a catalogue would be hopelessly complex. In any case, the books referred to are more readily available than are the original manuscripts.

The Index, which follows, is designed to help locate items by title. For instance, *Perelandra*, a book in Section A, is numbered 13. Thus, in the Index one finds the combination, *Perelandra*, A13. The same method is used throughout except for "Books Reviewed" and "Letters to Editors, Publishers, and Individuals," which are grouped separately.

One will also find some cross-references. For example "The Personal Heresy in Criticism" (D6) was originally published as an essay. Later it became the first chapter of *The Personal Heresy* (A7). Consequently, in the Index one finds the entry *Personal Heresy in Criticism, The*, D6, A7. However, the converse is not the same: D6 is *part* of A7, but A7 is *not* part of D6.

This bibliography includes only the original issues of Lewis's published writings as well as their reappearance in collections of his own essays and poems. In every case I have given the full title of each piece in expectation that the bibliography may be useful to librarians and scholars.

I should mention that *The Guardian* (1846–1951) in which *The Screw-tape Letters* originally appeared was a religious newspaper, now out of print, and not to be confused with *The Guardian* (formerly, *The Manchester Guardian*) in print today. *The Cherbourg School Magazine,* the rarest item on my bibliography, was published by Cherbourg School, Malvern, Worcestershire, when Lewis was a pupil there. It is, in fact, the same school that he calls Chartres in *Surprised by Joy.* It has since become a girls' school, Ellerslie. The items from *The Cherbourg School Magazine* are the only ones I have never seen. I should have thought it wrong to include them except that I have seen the items reproduced in the eleven unpublished volumes of *Lewis Papers: Memoirs of the Lewis Family 1850–1930* (edited by W. H. Lewis). The original of these is in Wheaton College, Wheaton, Illinois, and there is a copy in the Bodleian.

# A Bibliography of the Writings of C. S. Lewis

(The American editions, where they exist, are in brackets except when they preceded their English counterparts. Place of publication is London or New York, respectively, if no place is given. Although descriptions have been kept to a minimum, the main titles of the books have been printed in capitals to distinguish them from the subtitles. In order that the reader may know what the title pages of the original editions of the books looked like, the virgule (/) is used to indicate the arrangement of the words on the title pages. Thus, in the fifth book in this section the words OUT OF THE SILENT appear together on one line, and they are followed by the word PLANET, which appears beneath it on the next.)

## A. BOOKS

1. *SPIRITS IN BONDAGE/ A Cycle of Lyrics.* London: William Heinemann, 1919 (under the pseudonym of Clive Hamilton).
2. *DYMER.* London: J. M. Dent, 1926 (under the pseudonym of Clive Hamilton); reprinted with a new Preface, as by C. S. Lewis, 1950 [E. P. Dutton, 1926; Macmillan, 1950].
3. *THE/ PILGRIM'S REGRESS/ An Allegorical Apology/ for/ Christianity, Reason and Romanticism.* London: J. M. Dent, 1933; Sheed and Ward, 1935; Geoffrey Bles, 1943, with the author's important new Preface on Romanticism, footnotes, and running headlines [Sheed and Ward, 1944; Grand Rapids, Michigan: Eerdmans, 1958].
4. *THE ALLEGORY/ OF LOVE/ A Study in/ Medieval Tradition.* Oxford: Clarendon Press, 1936; reprinted with corrections, London: Oxford University Press, 1938 [Oxford University Press, 1958].
5. *OUT OF THE SILENT/ PLANET.* London: John Lane the Bodley Head, 1938 [Macmillan, 1943].
6. *REHABILITATIONS/ And Other Essays.* London: Oxford University Press, 1939. (Contents: *Preface,* "Shelley, Dryden, and Mr. Eliot," "William Morris," 'The Idea of an 'English School'," "Our English Syllabus," "High and Low Brows," "The Alliterative Metre," "Bluspels and Flalansferes: A Semantic Nightmare," "Variation in Shakespeare and Others," "Christianity and Literature").
7. (With E. M. W. Tillyard) *THE/ PERSONAL HERESY/ A Controversy.* London: Oxford University Press, 1939.
8. *THE PROBLEM OF PAIN.* London: The Centenary Press, 1940 [Macmillan, 1943]. The French edition of this book, *Le Problème de la*

*Souffrance,* Traduit de l'anglais par Marguerite Faguer, Préface le Maurice Nédoncelle, Paris: Desclée de Brouwer, 1950, contains a footnote (ch. ix, p. 163) and preface written specially for it by Lewis.

9. *THE/ SCREWTAPE LETTERS.* London: Geoffrey Bles, 1942 [Macmillan, 1943]; reprinted with a new Screwtape letter as *THE SCREWTAPE LETTERS/ AND/ SCREWTAPE PROPOSES A TOAST,* with a new and additional Preface, London: Geoffrey Bles, 1961 [Macmillan, 1962].

10. *A PREFACE TO/ "PARADISE LOST"/ Being the Ballard Matthews Lectures/ Delivered at University College, North Wales, 1941/ Revised and Enlarged.* London: Oxford University Press, 1942.

11. *BROADCAST TALKS/ Reprinted with some alterations from two series/ of Broadcast Talks ("Right and Wrong: A Clue to/ the Meaning of the Universe" and "What Christians/ Believe") given in 1941 and 1942.* London: Geoffrey Bles: The Centenary Press, 1942 [As *The Case for Christianity,* Macmillan, 1943].

12. *CHRISTIAN BEHAVIOUR/ A further series of Broadcast Talks.* London: Geoffrey Bles: The Centenary Press, 1943 [Macmillan, 1943].

13. *PERELANDRA.* London: John Lane the Bodley Head, 1943. Also published as *VOYAGE TO VENUS/ (PERELANDRA).* London: Pan Books, 1953 (a paperback) [First title, Macmillan, 1944].

14. *THE ABOLITION OF MAN/ or/ Reflections on Education with Special/ Reference to the Teaching of English/ in the Upper Forms of Schools.* Riddell Memorial Lectures, Fifteenth Series. London: Oxford University Press, 1943; London: Geoffrey Bles: The Centenary Press, 1946 [Macmillan, 1947].

15. *BEYOND PERSONALITY/ The Christian Idea of God.* London: Geoffrey Bles: The Centenary Press, 1944 [Macmillan, 1945].

16. *THAT/ HIDEOUS/ STRENGTH/ a modern fairy-tale for grown-ups.* London: John Lane the Bodley Head, 1945. A paperback specially abridged by the author, with a different Preface, as *THE/ TORTURED/ PLANET/ (THAT HIDEOUS STRENGTH).* New York: Avon Books, 1946; this same abridgement published as *THAT HIDEOUS/ STRENGTH* London: Pan Books, 1955 [First title, Macmillan, 1946].

17. *THE/ GREAT DIVORCE/ A Dream.* London: Geoffrey Bles: The Centenary Press, 1945 [Macmillan, 1946].

18. *MIRACLES/ A Preliminary Study.* London: Geoffrey Bles: The Centenary Press, 1947 [Macmillan, 1947]. With revision of Chapter III, London: Collins-Fontana Books, 1960 (a paperback). [An abridgement with a specially written preface by the author, New York: The Association Press, 1958].

19. *ARTHURIAN TORSO/ Containing the Posthumous Fragment of/ The Figure of Arthur/ by/ Charles Williams/ and/ A Commentary on The Arthurian Poems of/ Charles Williams/ by/ C. S. Lewis.* London: Oxford University Press, 1948 [Contained in *Taliessin Through Logres/ The Region/ of the Summer Stars/ by Charles Williams/ and Ar-*

*thurian Torso/ by Charles Williams/ and C. S. Lewis.* Introduction by Mary McDermott Shideler, Grand Rapids, Michigan: Eerdmans, 1974].

20. *TRANSPOSITION/ And Other Addresses.* London: Geoffrey Bles, 1949. (Contents: *Preface*, "Transposition," "The Weight of Glory," "Membership," "Learning in War-Time," "The Inner Ring") [As *The Weight of Glory and Other Addresses,* Macmillan, 1949].

21. *THE LION, THE WITCH/ AND/ THE WARDROBE/ A Story for Children.* Illustrations by Pauline Baynes. London: Geoffrey Bles, 1950 [Macmillan, 1950].

22. *PRINCE CASPIAN/ The Return to Narnia.* Illustrations by Pauline Baynes. London: Geoffrey Bles, 1951 [Macmillan, 1951].

23. *MERE CHRISTIANITY/ A revised and amplified edition, with a/ new introduction, of the three books/ "Broadcast Talks," "Christian Behaviour," and "Beyond Personality."* London: Geoffrey Bles, 1952 [As *Mere Christianity: A revised and enlarged edition, with a new introduction, of the three books "The Case for Christianity," "Christian Behaviour," and Beyond Personality,"* Macmillan, 1952].

24. *THE VOYAGE OF THE/ "DAWN TREADER."* Illustrations by Pauline Baynes. London: Geoffrey Bles, 1952 [Macmillan, 1952].

25. *THE SILVER CHAIR.* Illustrations by Pauline Baynes. London: Geoffrey Bles, 1953 [Macmillan, 1953].

26. *THE HORSE AND HIS BOY.* Illustrations by Pauline Baynes. London: Geoffrey Bles, 1954 [Macmillan, 1954].

27. *ENGLISH LITERATURE/ IN THE/ SIXTEENTH CENTURY/ EXCLUDING DRAMA.* The Completion of "The Clark Lectures," Trinity College, Cambridge, 1944 (*The Oxford History of English Literature,* Vol. III). Oxford: Clarendon Press, 1954.

28. *THE/ MAGICIAN'S NEPHEW.* Illustrations by Pauline Baynes. London: The Bodley Head, 1955 [Macmillan, 1955].

29. *SURPRISED BY JOY/ The Shape of My Early Life.* London: Geoffrey Bles, 1955 [Harcourt, Brace & World, 1956].

30. *THE LAST BATTLE/ A Story for Children.* Illustrations by Pauline Baynes. London: The Bodley Head, 1956 [As *The Last Battle,* Macmillan, 1956].

31. *TILL WE HAVE FACES/ A Myth Retold.* London: Geoffrey Bles, 1956 [Harcourt, Brace & World, 1957].

32. *REFLECTIONS ON THE PSALMS.* London: Geoffrey Bles, 1958 [Harcourt, Brace & World, 1958].

33. *THE FOUR LOVES.* London: Geoffrey Bles, 1960 [Harcourt, Brace & World, 1960].

34. *STUDIES IN/ WORDS.* Cambridge: Cambridge University Press, 1960 (Contents: *Preface*, "Introduction," "Nature," "Sad," "Wit," "Free," "Sense," "Simple," "Conscience and Conscious," "At the Fringe of Language, *Index.*) The Second Edition includes three new and additional chapters on "World," "Life," and "I Dare Say," 1967.

35. *THE WORLD'S LAST NIGHT/ And Other Essays.* New York: Harcourt, Brace & Co., 1960. (Contents: "The Efficacy of Prayer," "On

Obstinacy in Belief," "Lilies that Fester," "Screwtape Proposes a Toast," "Good Work and Good Works," "Religion and Rocketry," "The World's Last Night.")

36. *A GRIEF OBSERVED.* London: Faber and Faber, 1961 (under the pseudonym of N. W. Clerk); reprinted, as by C. S. Lewis, 1964 [Greenwich, Connecticut: Seabury Press, 1963 (under the pseudonym of N. W. Clerk)].

37. *AN/ EXPERIMENT IN/ CRITICISM.* Cambridge: Cambridge University Press, 1961.

38. *THEY ASKED FOR A PAPER/ Papers and Addresses.* London: Geoffrey Bles, 1962. (Contents: Acknowledgements, *"De Descriptione Temporum,"* "The Literary Impact of the Authorised Version," "Hamlet: The Prince or the Poem?," "Kipling's World," "Sir Walter Scott," "Lilies that Fester," "Psycho-analysis and Literary Criticism," "The Inner Ring," "Is Theology Poetry?," "Transposition" (an expanded version of the one in A20), "On Obstinacy in Belief," "The Weight of Glory").

39. *BEYOND/ THE BRIGHT BLUR.* New York: Harcourt, Brace & World, 1963. (On the flyleaf: *"Beyond the Bright Blur* is taken from *Letters to Malcolm: Chiefly on Prayer* [Chapters 15, 16, 17] by C. S. Lewis, which will be published in the year 1964. This limited edition is published as a New Year's greeting to friends of the author and his publisher.")

40. *LETTERS TO MALCOLM:/ CHIEFLY ON PRAYER.* London: Geoffrey Bles, 1964 [Harcourt, Brace & World, 1964].

41. *THE/ DISCARDED IMAGE/ An Introduction to/ Medieval and Renaissance/ Literature.* Cambridge: Cambridge University Press, 1964.

42. *POEMS.* Edited by Walter Hooper. London: Geoffrey Bles, 1964 [Harcourt, Brace & World, 1965].

43. *SCREWTAPE/ PROPOSES A/ TOAST/ and other pieces.* A paperback with a Preface by J. [ocelyn] E. [aston] G. [ibb]. London: Collins—Fontana Books, 1965. (Contents: *Preface* by J. E. G., "Screwtape Proposes a Toast," "On Obstinacy in Belief," "Good Work and Good Works," "The Inner Ring," "Is Theology Poetry?," "Transposition," "The Weight of Glory," "A Slip of the Tongue").

44. *STUDIES IN MEDIEVAL/ AND RENAISSANCE/ LITERATURE.* Collected by Walter Hooper. Cambridge: Cambridge University Press, 1966. (Contents: *Preface* by Walter Hooper, *"De Audiendis Poetis,"* "The Genesis of a Medieval Book," "Imagination and Thought in the Middle Ages," "Dante's Similes," "Imagery in the Last Eleven Cantos of Dante's *Comedy*," "Dante's Statius," "The *Morte Darthur*," "Tasso," "Edmund Spenser, 1552–99," "On Reading *The Faerie Queene*," "Neoplatonism in the Poetry of Spenser," "Spenser's Cruel Cupid," "Genius and Genius," "A Note on *Comus*," *Additional Editorial Notes, Index*).

45. *LETTERS OF/ C. S. LEWIS.* Edited, with a Memoir, by W. H. Lewis. London: Geoffrey Bles, 1966 [Harcourt, Brace & World, 1966].

46. *OF OTHER WORLDS/ Essays and Stories.* Edited by Walter Hooper.

London: Geoffrey Bles, 1966. (Contents: *Preface* by Walter Hooper; ESSAYS: "On Stories," "On Three Ways of Writing for Children," "Sometimes Fairy Stories May Say Best What's to be Said," "On Juvenile Taste," "It All Began with a Picture . . . ," "On Criticism," "On Science Fiction," "A Reply to Professor Haldane," "Unreal Estates"; STORIES: "The Shoddy Lands," "Ministering Angels," "Forms of Things Unknown," *After Ten Years* (fragment of a novel), *Notes* on *After Ten Years* by Roger Lancelyn Green and Alastair Fowler)[Harcourt, Brace & World, 1967].

47. *CHRISTIAN REFLECTIONS*. Edited by Walter Hooper. London: Geoffrey Bles, 1967. (Contents: *Preface* by Walter Hooper, "Christianity and Literature," "Christianity and Culture," "Religion: Reality or Substitute?," "On Ethics," "*De Futilitate*," "The Poison of Subjectivism," "The Funeral of a Great Myth," "On Church Music," "Historicism," "The Psalms," "The Language of Religion," "Petitionary Prayer: A Problem Without an Answer," "Modern Theology and Biblical Criticism," "The Seeing Eye") [Grand Rapids, Michigan: Eerdmans, 1967].

48. *SPENSER'S/ IMAGES OF LIFE*. Edited by Alastair Fowler. Cambridge: Cambridge University Press, 1967.

49. *LETTERS TO/ AN AMERICAN LADY/* [Mary Willis Shelburne]. Edited by Clyde S. Kilby. Grand Rapids, Michigan: Eerdmans, 1967 [London: Hodder and Stoughton, 1969].

50. *A MIND AWAKE/ An Anthology of C. S. Lewis*. Edited by Clyde S. Kilby. London: Geoffrey Bles, 1968 [Harcourt, Brace & World, 1969].

51. *NARRATIVE POEMS*. Edited by Walter Hooper. London: Geoffrey Bles, 1969. (Contents: *Preface* by Walter Hooper, *Dymer, Launcelot, The Nameless Isle, The Queen of Drum*, Notes) [Harcourt Brace Jovanovich, 1972].

52. *SELECTED/ LITERARY/ ESSAYS*. Edited by Walter Hooper. Cambridge: Cambridge University Press, 1969. (Contents: *Preface* by Walter Hooper, "*De Descriptione Temporum*," "The Alliterative Metre," "What Chaucer Really Did to *Il Filostrato*," "The Fifteenth-Century Heroic Line," "Hero and Leander," "Variation in Shakespeare and Others," "Hamlet: The Prince or the Poem?," "Donne and Love Poetry in the Seventeenth Century," "The Literary Impact of the Authorised Version," "The Vision of John Bunyan," "Addison," "Four-Letter Words," "A Note on Jane Austen," "Shelley, Dryden, and Mr. Eliot," "Sir Walter Scott," "William Morris," "Kipling's World," Bluspels and Flalansferes: A Semantic Nightmare," "High and Low Brows," "Metre," "Psycho-analysis and Literary Criticism," "The Anthropological Approach," *Index*).

53. *GOD IN THE/ DOCK/ Essays on Theology and Ethics*. Edited by Walter Hooper. Grand Rapids, Michigan: Eerdmans, 1970. (Contents: *Preface* by Walter Hooper, "Evil and God," "Miracles," "Dogma and the Universe," "Answers to Questions on Christianity," "Myth Became Fact," "'Horrid Red Things'," "Religion and Science," The Laws of Nature," "The Grand Miracle," "Christian Apologetics," "Work and Prayer,"

"Man or Rabbit?," "On the Transmission of Christianity," " 'Miserable Offenders'," "The Founding of the Oxford Socratic Club," "Religion without Dogma?," "Some Thoughts," " 'The Trouble with "X" . . .'," "What Are We to Make of Jesus Christ?," "The Pains of Animals," "Is Theism Important?," "Rejoinder to Dr. Pittenger," "Must Our Image of God Go?," "Dangers of National Repentance," "Two Ways with the Self," "Meditation on the Third Commandment," "On the Reading of Old Books," "Two Lectures," "Meditation in a Toolshed," "Scraps," "The Decline of Religion," "Vivisection," "Modern Translations of the Bible," "Priestesses in the Church?," "God in the Dock," "Behind the Scenes," "Revival or Decay?," "Before We Can Communicate," "Cross-Examination," " 'Bulverism', or, The Foundation of 20th-Century Thought," "First and Second Things," "The Sermon and the Lunch," "The Humanitarian Theory of Punishment," "Xmas and Christmas: A Lost Chapter from Herodotus," "What Christmas Means to Me," "Delinquents in the Snow," "Is Progress Possible?: Willing Slaves of the Welfare State," "We Have No 'Right to Happiness'," LETTERS: "The Conditions for a Just War," "The Conflict in Anglican Theology," "Miracles," "Mr. C. S. Lewis on Christianity," "A Village Experience," "Correspondence with an Anglican Who Dislikes Hymns," "The Church's Liturgy, Invocation, and Invocation of Saints," "The Holy Name," "Mere Christians," "Canonization," "Pittenger-Lewis and Version Vernacular," "Capital Punishment and Death Penalty," *Index*) [As *Undeceptions: Essays on Theology and Ethics*, London: Geoffrey Bles, 1971].

54. *FERN-SEED/ AND ELEPHANTS/ and Other Essays on Christianity.* Edited by Walter Hooper. London: Collins—Fontana Books, 1975. (Contents: *Preface* by Walter Hooper, "Membership," "Learning in War Time," "On Forgiveness," "Historicism," "The World's Last Night," "Religion and Rocketry," "The Efficacy of Prayer," "Fern-Seed and Elephants") (A paperback).

55. *THE DARK TOWER/ And Other Stories.* Edited by Walter Hooper. London: Collins, 1977. (Contents: *Preface* by Walter Hooper, *The Dark Tower*, Note on *The Dark Tower* by Walter Hooper, "The Man Born Blind," "The Shoddy Lands," "Ministering Angels," "Forms of Things Unknown." *After Ten Years*, Notes on *After Ten Years* by Roger Lancelyn Green and Alastair Fowler) [Harcourt Brace Jovanovich, 1977, hardback and paperback].

56. *THE JOYFUL CHRISTIAN/ 127 Readings from C. S. Lewis.* With a Foreword by Henry William Griffin. New York: Macmillan, 1977.

57. *GOD IN THE/ DOCK/ Essays on Theology.* Edited by Walter Hooper. London: Collins—Fount Paperbacks, 1979. (Contents: *Preface* by Walter Hooper, "Miracles" [D28], "Dogma and the Universe," "Myth Became Fact," "Religion and Science," "The Laws of Nature," "The Grand Miracle," "Man or Rabbit?," "What are We to Make of Jesus Christ?," "Must Our Image of God Go?," "Priestesses in the Church?," "God in the Dock," "We Have No 'Right to Happiness' ").

58. THEY STAND/ TOGETHER/ *The Letters of/ C. S. Lewis to Arthur Greeves/ (1914–1963).* Edited by Walter Hooper. London: Collins, 1979. (Contents: *Introduction* and *Editor's Note* by Walter Hooper, 296 letters from C. S. Lewis to Arthur Greeves, 2 letters from W. H. Lewis to Arthur Greeves, 1 letter from Joy Davidman to Arthur Greeves, and 4 letters from Arthur Greeves to C. S. Lewis, *Index*) [Macmillan, 1979].

## B. SHORT STORIES

1. "The Shoddy Lands," *The Magazine of Fantasy and Science Fiction*, X (Feb. 1956) pp. 68–74.

2. "Ministering Angels," *The Magazine of Fantasy and Science Fiction*, XIII (Jan. 1958) pp. 5–14.

3. "Forms of Things Unknown," *Fifty-Two: A Journal of Books & Authors* [from Geoffrey Bles], No. 18 (Autumn 1966) pp. 3–9. (An abridgement of the story that appears in *Of Other Worlds* and *The Dark Tower*.)

4. "The Man Born Blind," *Church Times*, No. 5947 (4 Feb. 1977) pp. 4–5.

## C. BOOKS EDITED OR WITH PREFACES BY C. S. LEWIS

1. St. Athanasius, *The Incarnation of the Word of God: Being the Treatise of St. Athanasius' "De Incarnatione Verbi Dei"* with an Introduction by C. S. Lewis. (Translated and edited by A Religious of C.S.M.V. [R. P. Lawson].) London: Geoffrey Bles, 1944 (Lewis's Introduction was reprinted as "On the Reading of Old Books" in *God in the Dock*.)

2. *George MacDonald: An Anthology.* Edited by C. S. Lewis. London: Geoffrey Bles, 1946. (Preface by C. S. Lewis and 365 brief excerpts from the works of George MacDonald.)

3. B. G. Sandhurst, *How Heathen is Britain?* with a Preface by C. S. Lewis. London: Collins, 1946. (Lewis's Preface was reprinted as "On the Transmission of Christianity" in *God in the Dock*.)

4. Eric Bentley, *The Cult of the Superman: A Study of the Idea of Heroism in Carlyle and Nietzsche, with Notes on Other Hero-Worshippers of Modern Times* with an Appreciation by C. S. Lewis. London: Robert Hale, 1947.

5. J. B. Phillips, *Letters to Young Churches: A Translation of the New Testament Epistles* with an Introduction by C. S. Lewis. London: Geoffrey Bles, 1947. (Lewis's Introduction was reprinted as "Modern Translations of the Bible" in *God in the Dock*.)

6. C. S. Lewis and others, *Essays Presented to Charles Williams.* London: Oxford University Press, 1947. (With a Preface and an essay, "On Stories," by C. S. Lewis.)

7. D. E. Harding, *The Hierarchy of Heaven and Earth: A New Diagram of Man in the Universe,* Preface by C. S. Lewis. London: Faber and Faber, 1952.

8. Joy Davidman, *Smoke on the Mountain: An Interpretation of the Ten Com-*

*mandments in Terms of To-day* with a Foreword by C. S. Lewis. London: Hodder and Stoughton, 1955.
9. Austin Farrer, *A Faith of Our Own* with a Preface by C. S. Lewis. Cleveland, Ohio: World Publishing Co., 1960.
10. Layamon, *Selections from Layamon's "Brut"* with an Introduction by C. S. Lewis. (Edited by G. L. Brook.) Oxford: Clarendon Press, 1963.

## D. ESSAYS, PAMPHLETS, AND MISCELLANEOUS PIECES

1. "The Expedition to Holly Bush Hill," *Cherbourg School Magazine* (Nov. 1912).[1]
2. "Are Athletes Better than Scholars?," *Cherbourg School Magazine*, No. 2 (1913).
3. "The Expedition to Holly Bush Hill," *Cherbourg School Magazine* (July 1913). (A different Expedition than that described in D1.)
4. "A Note on *Comus*," *The Review of English Studies*, VIII (April 1932) pp. 170–6.
5. "What Chaucer Really Did to *Il Filostrato*," *Essays and Studies by Members of the English Association*, XVII (1932) pp. 56–75.
6. "The Personal Heresy in Criticism," *Essays and Studies by Members of the English Association*, XIX (1934) pp. 7–28; cf. E. M. W. Tillyard, "The Personal Heresy in Criticism: A Rejoinder," *ibid.*, XX (1935) pp. 7–20; C. S. Lewis, "Open Letter to Dr. Tillyard," *ibid.*, XXI (1936) pp. 153–68. (These three essays form the first half of *The Personal Heresy: A Controversy*.)
7. "A Metrical Suggestion," *Lysistrata*, II (May 1935) pp. 13–24. (Reprinted as "The Alliterative Metre" in *Rehabilitations* and *Selected Literary Essays*.)
8. "Genius and Genius," *The Review of English Studies*, XII (April 1936) pp. 189–94.
9. "Donne and Love Poetry in the Seventeenth Century," *Seventeenth Century Studies Presented to Sir Herbert Grierson*. Oxford: Clarendon Press, 1938, pp. 64–84.
10. "From Johnson's *Life of Fox*," *The Oxford Magazine*, LVI (9 June 1938) pp. 737–78. (Unsigned.)
11. "The Fifteenth Century Heroic Line," *Essays and Studies by Members of the English Association*, XXIV (1939) pp. 28–41.
12. "None Other Gods: Culture in War Time," mimeographed by the Church of St. Mary the Virgin, Oxford, 22 Oct. 1939. (Reprinted in pamphlet form as *The Christian in Danger*, London: Student Christian Movement, 1939; reprinted as "Learning in War Time" in *Transposition and Other Addresses*.)

---

[1] I have not been able to find any issues of the *Cherbourg School Magazine*, but Lewis's contributions to the magazine are reproduced in the unpublished *Lewis Papers: Memoirs of the Lewis Family 1850–1930* (in 11 vols.), the original of which is in Wheaton College, Illinois, and a copy of which is in the Bodleian Library. D1 is in the *Lewis Papers*, vol. III, pp. 310–11; D2 is in vol. III, pp. 318–19; and D3 is in vol. IV, p. 51.

13. "Christianity and Culture," *Theology*, XL (March 1940) pp. 166–79; cf.
    S. L. Bethell and E. F. Carritt, "Christianity and Culture: Replies to
    Mr. Lewis," *ibid.*, XL (May 1940) pp. 356–66; C. S. Lewis, "Chris-
    tianity and Culture" (a letter), *ibid.*, XL (June 1940) pp. 475–77;
    George Every, "In Defence of Criticism," *ibid.*, XLI (Sept. 1940) pp.
    159–65; C. S. Lewis, "Peace Proposals for Brother Every and Mr.
    Bethell," *ibid.*, XLI (Dec. 1940) pp. 339–48.

14. "Dangers of National Repentance," *The Guardian*, (15 March 1940) p.
    127.

15. "Two Ways with the Self," *The Guardian*, (3 May 1940) p. 215.

16. ["The Necessity of Chivalry"],[2] "Notes on the Way," *Time and Tide*, XXI
    (17 Aug. 1940) p. 841. (Reprinted as "Importance of an Ideal," *Liv-
    ing Age*, CCCLIX (Oct. 1940) pp. 109–11.)

17. "Meditation on the Third Commandment," *The Guardian*, (10 Jan. 1941)
    p. 18.

18. "Evil and God," *The Spectator*, CLXVI (7 Feb. 1941) p. 141.

19. "Edmund Spenser," *Fifteen Poets*. London: Oxford University Press, 1941,
    pp. 40–43. (Reprinted as "On Reading *The Faerie Queene*" in *Studies
    in Medieval and Renaissance Literature.*)

20. "Notes on the Way," *Time and Tide*, XXII (29 March 1941) p. 261.
    (Reprinted, and expanded, as " 'Bulverism', or, The Foundation of
    20th Century Thought," *The Socratic Digest*, No. 2 (June 1944) pp.
    16–20.)

21. "The Screwtape Letters," *The Guardian*: (2 May 1941) pp. 211–2; (9
    May 1941) pp. 223–4; (16 May 1941) pp. 235–6; (23 May 1941)
    pp. 246, 249; (30 May 1941) pp. 259–60; (6 June 1941) pp. 270,
    273; (13 June 1941) p. 282; (20 June 1941) pp. 291–2; (27 June
    1941) pp. 307–8; (4 July 1941) pp. 319–20; (11 July 1941) pp.
    331–2; (18 July 1941) pp. 343–4; (25 July 1941) pp. 355–6; (1
    Aug. 1941) pp. 367–8; (8 Aug. 1941) pp. 378, 382; (15 Aug. 1941)
    pp. 391–2; (22 Aug. 1941) p. 402; (29 Aug. 1941) pp. 417–8; (5
    Sept. 1941) p. 426; (12 Sept. 1941) pp. 443–4; (19 Sept. 1941) pp.
    451–2; (26 Sept. 1941) p. 465; (3 Oct. 1941) pp. 475–6; (10 Oct.
    1941) p. 490; (17 Oct. 1941) pp. 498, 502; (24 Oct. 1941) p. 514;
    (31 Oct. 1941) p. 526; (7 Nov. 1941) p. 531; (14 Nov. 1941) p.
    550; (21 Nov. 1941) p. 558; (28 Nov. 1941) p. 570. (These install-
    ments are published, with some alterations, in book form as *The
    Screwtape Letters*.)

22. "Religion: Reality or Substitute?," *World Dominion*, XIX (Sept.–Oct.
    1941) pp. 277–81.

23. "The Weight of Glory," *Theology*, XLIII (Nov. 1941) pp. 263–74. (Re-
    printed as a pamphlet, London: S.P.C.K., 1942.)

24. "Psycho-analysis and Literary Criticism," *Essays and Studies by Members
    of the English Association*, XXVII (1942) pp. 7–21.

---

[2] Lewis had titles of his own for some of his articles in the series "Notes on the
Way," and these are given in brackets whenever they occur.

25. *Hamlet: The Prince or the Poem?* Annual Shakespeare Lecture of the British Academy, 1942, *The Proceedings of the British Academy*, XXVIII, London: Oxford University Press, 1942, 18 pp.

26. "Notes on the Way," *Time and Tide*, XXIII (27 June 1942) pp. 519–20. (Reprinted as "First and Second Things" in *God in the Dock*.)

27. "Miracles," *The Guardian* (2 Oct. 1942) p. 316.

28. "Miracles," *Saint Jude's Gazette*, No. 73 (Oct. 1942) pp. 4–7. (Published by St. Jude on the Hill Church, Golders Green, London. This version of "Miracles" that was reprinted in *God in the Dock* is an expansion of D27.)

29. Preface to *The Socratic Digest*, No. 1 (1942–3) pp. 3–5. (Reprinted as "The Founding of the Oxford Socratic Club" in *God in the Dock*.)

30. "Dogma and the Universe," *The Guardian*, (19 March 1943) p. 96; this article concluded as "Dogma and Science," *The Guardian*, (26 March 1943) pp. 104, 107. (Both parts reprinted as "Dogma and the Universe" in *God in the Dock*.)

31. "The Poison of Subjectivism," *Religion in Life*, XII (Summer 1943) pp. 356–65.

32. "Equality," *The Spectator*, CLXXI (27 Aug. 1943) p. 192.

33. ["My First School"], "Notes on the Way," *Time and Tide*, XXIV (4 Sept. 1943) p. 717.

34. "Is English Doomed?," *The Spectator*, CLXXII (11 Feb. 1944) p. 121.

35. "The Map and the Ocean," *The Listener*, XXXI (24 Feb. 1944) p. 216; "God in Three Persons," *ibid.* (2 March 1944) p. 244; "The Whole Purpose of the Christian," *ibid.* (9 March 1944) p. 272; "The Obstinate Tin Soldiers," *ibid.* (16 March 1944) p. 300; "Let us Pretend," *ibid.* (23 March 1944) p. 328; "Is Christianity Hard or Easy?," *ibid.* (30 March 1944) p. 356; "The New Man," *ibid.* (6 April 1944) p. 384. (These installments are published, with some alterations, in book form as *Beyond Personality: The Christian Idea of God*.)

36. ["The Parthenon and the Optative"], "Notes on the Way," *Time and Tide*, XXV (11 March 1944) p. 213.

37. *Answers to Questions on Christianity*. Electric and Musical Industries Christian Fellowship, Hayes, Middlesex, [1944], 24 pp. (From the Preface: "A 'One Man Brains Trust' held on 18 April 1944, at the Head Office of Electric and Musical Industries, Ltd." H. W. Bowen, Question-master.)

38. ["Democratic Education"], "Notes on the Way," *Time and Tide*, XXV (29 April 1944) pp. 369–70.

39. "A Dream," *The Spectator*, CLXXIII (28 July 1944) p. 77.

40. "Blimpophobia," *Time and Tide*, XXV (9 Sept. 1944) p. 785.

41. "The Death of Words," *The Spectator*, CLXXIII (22 Sept. 1944) p. 261.

42. "Myth Became Fact," *World Dominion*, XXII (Sept.–Oct. 1944) pp. 267–70.

43. " 'Horrid Red Things'," *Church of England Newspaper*, LI (6 Oct. 1944) pp. 1–2.

44. "Who Goes Home? or The Grand Divorce," *The Guardian*: (10 Nov.

1944) pp. 399–400; (17 Nov. 1944) pp. 411, 413; (24 Nov. 1944) pp. 421–2; (1 Dec. 1944) pp. 431–2; (8 Dec. 1944) pp. 442, 445; (15 Dec. 1944) pp. 453–4; (22 Dec. 1944) pp. 463–5; (29 Dec. 1944) pp. 472–4; (5 Jan. 1945) pp. 4, 8; (12 Jan. 1945) pp. 15, 18; (19 Jan. 1945) pp. 25–6; (26 Jan. 1945) pp. 34, 37; (2 Feb. 1945) 45, 48; (9 Feb. 1945) p. 52; (16 Feb. 1945) pp. 63–4; (23 Feb. 1945) pp. 73, 77; (2 March 1945) p. 84; (9 March 1945) pp. 95–6; (16 March 1945) p. 104; (23 March 1945) pp. 114, 117; (29 March 1945) p. 124; (6 April 1945) p. 132; (13 April 1945) p. 141. (These installments are published in book form as *The Great Divorce: A Dream*.)

45. "Private Bates," *The Spectator*, CLXXIII (29 Dec. 1944) p. 596.
46. "Religion and Science," *The Coventry Evening Telegraph* (3 Jan. 1945) p. 4.
47. "Who Was Right—Dream Lecturer or Real Lecturer?," *The Coventry Evening Telegraph* (21 Feb. 1945) p. 4. (Reprinted as "Two Lectures" in *God in the Dock*.)
48. "The Laws of Nature," *The Coventry Evening Telegraph* (4 April 1945) p. 4.
49. Recollection of George Gordon's "Discussion Class" in M.[ary] C. G. [ordon], *The Life of George S. Gordon 1881–1942*. London: Oxford University Press, 1945, p. 77.
50. "The Grand Miracle," *The Guardian* (27 April 1945) pp. 161, 165.
51. "Charles Walter Stansby Williams (1886–1945)," *The Oxford Magazine*, LXIII (24 May 1945) p. 265. (An obituary)
52. "Work and Prayer," *The Coventry Evening Telegraph* (28 May 1945) p. 4.
53. "Membership," *Sobornost*, No. 31, New Series (June 1945) pp. 4–9.
54. "Hedonics," *Time and Tide*, XXVI (16 June 1945) pp. 494–5.
55. "Oliver Elton (1861–1945)," *The Oxford Magazine*, LXIII (21 June 1945) pp. 318–19. (An obituary)
56. "Meditation in a Toolshed," *The Coventry Evening Telegraph* (17 July 1945) p. 4.
57. "Addison," *Essays on the Eighteenth Century Presented to David Nichol Smith*. Oxford: Clarendon Press, 1945, pp. 1–14.
58. "The Sermon and the Lunch," *Church of England Newspaper*, No. 2692 (21 Sept. 1945) pp. 1–2.
59. "Scraps," *St James' Magazine* (Dec. 1945) pp. [4–5]. (Published by St James' Church, Birkdale, Southport.)
60. "After Priggery—What?," *The Spectator*, CLXXV (7 Dec. 1945) p. 536.
61. "Is Theology Poetry?," *The Socratic Digest*, No. 3 (1945) pp. 25–35.
62. *Man or Rabbit?* Student Christian Movement in Schools [n.d.], 4 pp. (A pamphlet, probably published in about 1946.)
63. Sermon in *Five Sermons by Laymen*. S. Matthew's Church, Northampton, (April-May 1946) pp. 1–6. (Reprinted, with slight alterations, as "*Miserable Offenders*": *An Interpretation of Prayer Book Language*, Advent Paper No. 12. Boston: Church of the Advent [n.d.], 12 pp.)
64. "Notes on the Way," *Time and Tide*, XXVII (25 May 1946) p. 486.

65. "Notes on the Way," *Time and Tide*, XXVII (1 June 1946) pp. 510–11.
66. "Talking about Bicycles," *Resistance* (Oct. 1946) pp. 10–13.
67. ["Period Criticism"], "Notes on the Way," *Time and Tide*, XXVII (9 Nov. 1946) pp. 1070–71.
68. "The Decline of Religion," *The Cherwell*, XXVI (29 Nov. 1946) pp. 8–10.
69. "A Christian Reply to Professor Price," *Phoenix Quarterly*, I, No. 1 (Autumn 1946) pp. 31–44; cf. H. H. Price, "The Grounds of Modern Agnosticism," *ibid.*, pp. 10–30. (Despite the fact that "Religion Without Dogma?"—D74—was published later, "A Christian Reply to Professor Price" is Lewis's final *revision* of "Religion Without Dogma?.")
70. "On Stories," *Essays Presented to Charles Williams*. London: Oxford University Press, 1947, pp. 90–105.
71. Vivisection [with portrait], and a Foreword by George R. Farnum. Boston: New England Anti-Vivisection Society, [1947], 11 pp. (Reprinted, with portrait, and a Foreword by R. Fielding-Ould. London: National Anti-Vivisection Society, [1948], 11 pp.)
72. "Kipling's World," *Literature and Life: Addresses to the English Association*, I. London: Harrap and Co., 1948, pp. 57–73.
73. "Some Thoughts," *The First Decade: Ten Years' Work of the Medical Missionaries of Mary*. Dublin: At the Sign of the Three Candles, [1948], pp. 91–4.
74. "Religion without Dogma?," *The Socratic Digest*, No. 4 [1948], pp. 82–94; cf. H. H. Price, "Reply," *ibid.*, No. 4, pp. 94–102; G. E. M. Anscombe, "A Reply to Mr. C. S. Lewis's Argument that 'Naturalism' is Self-refuting," *ibid.*, No. 4, pp. 7–15; C. S. Lewis, "Reply," *ibid.*, No. 4, pp. 15–16. (Both Lewis's essay and "Reply" are found in *God in the Dock*.)
75. "The Trouble with 'X' . . . ," *Bristol Diocesan Gazette*, XXVII (Aug. 1948) pp. 3–6.
76. "Notes on the Way," *Time and Tide*, XXIX (14 Aug. 1948) pp. 830–1. (Reprinted as "Priestesses in the Church?" in *God in the Dock*.)
77. "Difficulties in Presenting the Christian Faith to Modern Unbelievers," (English text with French translation), *Lumen Vitae*, III (Sept. 1948) pp. 421–26. (Reprinted as "God in the Dock" in *God in the Dock*.)
78. "Note" on Programme of Owen Barfield's play *Orpheus*, produced by the Sheffield Educational Settlement at The Little Theatre, Shipton Street, Sheffield, on 25 Sept. [1948], p. 8.
79. "On Church Music," *English Church Music*, XIX (April 1949) pp. 19–22.
80. "The Humanitarian Theory of Punishment," *20th Century: An Australian Quarterly Review*, III, No. 3 (1949) pp. 5–12; ct. Norval Morris and Donald Buckle, "A Reply to C. S. Lewis," *ibid.*, VI, No. 2 (1952) pp. 20–26.

These two articles are reprinted in *Res Judicatae*, VI (June 1953) pp. 224–30 and pp. 231–37, respectively.

The controversy continues with the following articles: J. J. C. Smart,

"Comment: The Humanitarian Theory of Punishment," *Res Judicatae,* VI (Feb. 1954) pp. 368–71; C. S. Lewis, "On Punishment: A Reply," *ibid.,* (Aug. 1954) pp. 519–23.

81. (With C. E. M. Joad) "The Pains of Animals: A Problem in Theology," *The Month,* CLXXXIX (Feb. 1950) pp. 95–104.

82. *The Literary Impact of the Authorised Version,* The Ethel M. Wood Lecture delivered before the University of London on 20 March 1950. London: The Athlone Press, 1950, 26 pp.

83. "What are we to make of Jesus Christ?," *Asking Them Questions* (Third Series). Edited by Ronald Selby Wright. London: Oxford University Press, 1950, pp. 48–53.

84. "Historicism," *The Month,* IV (Oct. 1950) pp. 230–43.

85. "Christian Hope—Its Meaning for Today," *Religion in Life,* XXI (Winter 1951–52) pp. 20–32. (Reprinted as "The World's Last Night" in *The World's Last Night and Other Essays.*)

86. *Hero and Leander,* Wharton Lecture on English Poetry, British Academy, 1952. *The Proceedings of the British Academy,* XXXVIII. London: Oxford University Press [1952], 15 pp.

87. "Is Theism Important? A Reply," *The Socratic* [*Digest*], No. 5 (1952) pp. 48–51; cf. H. H. Price, "Is Theism Important?," *ibid.,* pp. 39–47. (Reprinted as "Is Theism Important?" in *God in the Dock.*)

88. "On Three Ways of Writing for Children," *Library Association. Proceedings, Papers and Summaries of Discussions at the Bournemouth Conference 29 April to 2 May 1952.* London: Library Association (1952) pp. 22–8.

89. "Edmund Spenser, 1552–99," *Major British Writers, Vol. I.* Edited by G. B. Harrison. New York: Harcourt, Brace & Co., 1954, pp. 91–103.

90. Reminiscence of P. V. M. Benecke in Margaret Deneke, *Paul Victor Mendelssohn Benecke 1868–1944.* Oxford: Privately printed by A. T. Broome and Son, [1954], pp. 9, 31–34.

91. "A Note on Jane Austen," *Essays in Criticism,* IV (Oct. 1954) pp. 359–71.

92. "Xmas and Christmas: A Lost Chapter from Herodotus," *Time and Tide,* XXXV (4 Dec. 1954) p. 1607.

93. "George Orwell," *Time and Tide,* XXXVI (8 Jan. 1955) pp. 43–4.

94. "Prudery and Philology," *The Spectator,* CXCIV (21 Jan. 1955) pp. 63–4.

95. *De Descriptione Temporum,* An Inaugural Lecture by the Professor of Medieval and Renaissance English Literature in the University of Cambridge. Cambridge: Cambridge University Press, 1955, 22 pp.

96. "Lilies That Fester," *Twentieth Century,* CLVII (April 1955) pp. 330–41.

97. "On Obstinacy in Belief," *The Sewanee Review,* LXIII (Autumn 1955) pp. 525–38.

98. [A toast to] "The Memory of Sir Walter Scott," *The Edinburgh Sir Walter Scott Club Forty-ninth Annual Report, 1956.* Edinburgh, 1956, pp. 13–25. (Reprinted as "Sir Walter Scott" in *They Asked for a Paper.*)

99. "Critical Forum: *De Descriptione Temporum,*" *Essays in Criticism,* VI (April 1956) p. 247.

100. "Interim Report," *The Cambridge Review* (21 April 1956) pp. 468–71.

101. "Sometimes Fairy Stories May Say Best What's to Be Said," *The New York Times Book Review, Children's Book Section* (18 Nov. 1956) p. 3.

102. "Behind the Scenes," *Time and Tide*, XXXVII (1 Dec. 1956) pp. 1450–51.

103. "Is History Bunk?," *The Cambridge Review*, LXXVIII (1 June 1957) pp. 647, 649.

104. "Dante's Statius," *Medium Aevum*, XXV, No. 3 (1957) pp. 133–9.

105. "What Christmas Means to Me," *Twentieth Century*, CLXII (Dec. 1957), pp. 517–18.

106. "Delinquents in the Snow," *Time and Tide*, XXXVIII (7 Dec. 1957) pp. 1521–2.

107. "Will We Lose God in Outer Space?," *Christian Herald*, LXXXI (April 1958), pp. 19, 74–6. (Reprinted as *Shall We Lose God in Outer Space?* London: S.P.C.K., 1959, 11 pp.; and as "Religion and Rocketry" in *The World's Last Night*.)

108. "Revival or Decay?," *Punch*, CCXXXV (9 July 1958) pp. 36–8.

109. "Is Progress Possible?—2: Willing Slaves of the Welfare State," *The Observer* (20 July 1958), p. 6; cf. C. P. Snow, "Is Progress Possible?—1: Man in Society," *ibid.* (13 July 1958) p. 12.

110. "The Psalms as Poetry," *Fifty-Two: A Journal of Books & Authors* [from Geoffrey Bles], No. 3 (Autumn 1958) pp. 9–12. (Part of the Introductory chapter to *Reflections on the Psalms*)

111. "Rejoinder to Dr. Pittenger," *The Christian Century*, LXXV (26 Nov. 1958) pp. 1359–61; cf. W. Norman Pittenger, "Apologist Versus Apologist: A Critique of C. S. Lewis as 'defender of the faith'," *ibid.*, LXXV (1 Oct. 1958) pp. 1104–7.

112. "On Juvenile Tastes," *Church Times, Children's Supplement* (28 Nov. 1958) p. i.

113. "The Efficacy of Prayer," *The Atlantic Monthly*, CCIII (Jan. 1959) pp. 59–61.

114. "*Molliter Ossa Cubent*," *The Campbellian* (the School Magazine of Campbell College, Belfast), XIV, No. 9 (July 1959) pp. 692–3. (An obituary of Jane Agnes McNeill.)

115. *A Series of Ten Radio Talks on Love*, Atlanta, Georgia: The Episcopal Radio-TV Foundation, 1959. (These ten individual pamphlets are the radio scripts Lewis recorded onto tape in 1958, which tapes were issued in 1970 on four cassettes called *Four Talks on Love*. The scripts served as a basis for Lewis's book *The Four Loves*.)

116. "Affection—Friendship—Eros—Charity," *Fifty-Two: A Journal of Books & Authors* [from Geoffrey Bles], No. 4 (Autumn 1959), p. 20. (An extract from the Introduction to *The Four Loves*.)

117. "Screwtape Proposes a Toast," *The Saturday Evening Post*, CCXXXII (19 Dec. 1959), pp. 36, 88–9.

118. "Good Work and Good Works," *Good Work*, XXIII (Christmas 1959), pp. 3–10.

119. "Metre," *A Review of English Literature*, I (Jan. 1960), pp. 45–50.

120. "Undergraduate Criticism," *Broadsheet* (Cambridge University), VIII, No. 17 (9 March 1960).

121. "It All Began with a Picture . . .". *Radio Times, Junior Radio Times*, CXLVIII (15 July 1960), p. [2].
122. "Haggard Rides Again," *Time and Tide*, XLI (3 Sept. 1960), pp. 1044–5.
123. "Four-letter Words," *The Critical Quarterly*, III (Summer 1961), pp. 118–22.
124. "Before We Can Communicate," *Breakthrough*, No. 8 (Oct. 1961), p. 2.
125. "The Anthropological Approach," *English and Medieval Studies Presented to J. R. R. Tolkien on the Occasion of his Seventieth Birthday.* Edited by Norman Davis and C. L. Wrenn. London: Allen and Unwin, 1962, pp. 219–30.
126. "Sex in Literature," *The Sunday Telegraph*, No. 87 (30 Sept. 1962), p. 8.
127. "The Vision of John Bunyan," *The Listener*, LXVIII (13 Dec. 1962), pp. 1006–08.
128. "Going into Europe: A Symposium," *Encounter*, XIX (Dec. 1962), p. 57.
129. "Thoughts of a Cambridge Don," *The Lion* (The magazine of St. Mark's Dundela, Belfast) (Jan. 1963), pp. [11–21]. (Reprinted in an enlarged form as "A Slip of the Tongue" in *Screwtape Proposes a Toast and Other Pieces.*)
130. "The English Prose 'Morte'," *Essays on Malory.* Edited by J. A. W. Bennett. Oxford: Clarendon Press, 1963, pp. 7–28.
131. "Onward, Christian Spacemen," *Show*, III (Feb. 1963), pp. 57, 117. (Reprinted as "The Seeing Eye" in *Christian Reflections.*)
132. "Must Our Image of God Go?," *The Observer* (24 March 1963), p. 14; cf. J. A. T. Robinson, "Our Image of God Must Go," *ibid.* (17 March 1963), p. 21. (Lewis's article is reprinted in *The Honest to God Debate: Some Reactions to the Book "Honest to God" with a new chapter by its author, John A. T. Robinson, Bishop of Woolwich.* Edited by David L. Edwards, London: S. C. M. Press, 1963, p. 91, and in *God in the Dock.*)
133. "I Was Decided Upon," *Decision*, II (Sept. 1963), p. 3. (Answers to questions when interviewed by Sherwood E. Wirt of the Billy Graham Evangelistic Association on 7 May 1963.)
134. "Heaven, Earth and Outer Space," *Decision*, II (Oct. 1963), p. 4. (Answers to questions when interviewed by Sherwood E. Wirt on 7 May 1963. D132 and D133 are parts of a single interview and are reprinted as "Cross-Examination" in *God in the Dock.*)
135. A Note on the meaning of Civilisation in the *Chronicles of Narnia* found in Roger Lancelyn Green, *C. S. Lewis* (A Bodley Head Monograph). London: The Bodley Head, 1963, p. 51.
136. "We Have No 'Right to Happiness'," *The Saturday Evening Post*, CCXXXVI (21–28 Dec. 1963), pp. 10, 12.
137. "Heaven?—It's a Venture," *Fifty-Two: A Journal of Books & Authors* [from Geoffrey Bles], No. 13 (Spring 1964), pp. 3–5. (An extract from ch. 22 of *Letters to Malcolm*)
138. " 'The establishment must die and rot . . .': C. S. Lewis Discusses Science Fiction with Kingsley Amis," *SF Horizons*, No. 1 (Spring 1964), pp. 5–12. (An informal conversation between C. S. Lewis, Kingsley Amis, and Brian Aldiss recorded on tape in Lewis's rooms in Magdalene Col-

lege, Cambridge, on 4 Dec. 1962. It was reprinted as "Unreal Estates" in *Encounter*, XXIV (March 1965), pp. 61–65, and under this last title in *Of Other Worlds*.)

139. "Dante's Similes," *Nottingham Mediaeval Studies* (Dante Centenary Number), IX (1965), pp. 32–41.

140. *Mark vs. Tristram: Correspondence between C. S. Lewis and Owen Barfield.* Edited by Walter Hooper. Cambridge, Massachusetts: The Lowell House Printers. A hand-printed edition limited to 126 copies, Nov. 1967, 11 pp.

141. Boxen and Narnian Manuscripts quoted in Walter Hooper's "Past Watchful Dragons," *Imagination and the Spirit*. Edited by Charles A. Huttar. Grand Rapids, Michigan: Eerdmans, 1971, pp. 279–80, 286, 291, 302–07.

142. "Outline of Narnian history so far as it is known," in Walter Hooper's "Past Watchful Dragons," *Imagination and the Spirit*. Edited by Charles A. Huttar. Grand Rapids, Michigan: Eerdmans, 1971, pp. 298–301.

143. Martlet Society Minutes of 31 Jan. and 14 June 1919, in Walter Hooper's "To the Martlets" in *C. S. Lewis: Speaker & Teacher*. Edited by Carolyn Keefe. Grand Rapids, Michigan: Zondervan, 1971, pp. 43, 44.

144. Diary of 9 Feb. 1923, about Martlet Society meeting quoted in Walter Hooper's "To the Martlets" in *C. S. Lewis: Speaker & Teacher*. Edited by Carolyn Keefe. Grand Rapids, Michigan: Zondervan, 1971, pp. 47–50.

145. Passage from Oxford lecture on Philosophy (1924) quoted in Walter Hooper's "To the Martlets" in *C. S. Lewis: Speaker & Teacher*. Edited by Carolyn Keefe. Grand Rapids, Michigan: Zondervan, 1971, p. 52.

146. "Professor J. R. R. Tolkien: Creator of Hobbits and Inventor of a New Mythology," *The Times* (3 Sept. 1973), p. 15. (An unsigned obituary)

147. Sole paragraph, that is the earliest known manuscript (1939) of *The Lion, the Witch and the Wardrobe,* quoted in Walter Hooper's Preface to Kathryn Ann Lindskoog, *The Lion of Judah in Never-Never Land*. Grand Rapids, Michigan: Eerdmans, 1973, p. 12.

148. Passage from fragment of a novel written about 1927, quoted in Walter Hooper's Preface to Kathryn Ann Lindskoog, *The Lion of Judah in Never-Never Land*. Grand Rapids, Michigan: Eerdmans, 1973, p. 9.

149. Excerpts from unpublished *Clivi Hamiltonis Summae Metaphysices contra Anthroposophos,* quoted in Lionel Adey, "The Barfield-Lewis 'Great War'," *CSL: The Bulletin of the New York C. S. Lewis Society*, VI, No. 10 (Aug. 1975), pp. 10–13.

## E. SINGLE SHORT POEMS

(Lewis wrote most of his poems over the pseudonym Nat Whilk, or the initials N. W., as marked in this section. Even though many were revised and given new titles by the author, all the following appear in *Poems* with the exceptions of Nos. 1, 2, 3, 4, 16, 22, 24, 63 and 74.)

1. *"Quan Bene Saturno," Cherbourg School Magazine* (July 1913).[1]
2. "Death in Battle," *Reveille*, No. 3 (Feb. 1919), p. 508 (Clive Hamilton). (Reprinted in *Spirits in Bondage*.)
3. "Joy," *The Beacon*, III, No. 31 (May 1924), pp. 444–5 (Clive Hamilton).
4. (With Owen Barfield) "Abecedarium Philosophicum," *The Oxford Magazine*, LII (30 Nov. 1933), p. 298.
5. "The Shortest Way Home," *The Oxford Magazine*, LII (10 May 1934), p. 665 (Nat Whilk). (Revised and retitled "Man is a Lumpe Where All Beasts Kneaded Be" in *Poems*.)
6. "Scholar's Melancholy," *The Oxford Magazine*, LII (24 May 1934), p. 734 (Nat Whilk).
7. "The Planets," *Lysistrata*, II (May 1935), pp. 21–24. (A portion of the poem is quoted in Lewis's essay "A Metrical Suggestion.")
8. "Sonnet," *The Oxford Magazine*, LIV (14 May 1936), p. 575 (Nat Whilk).
9. "Coronation March," *The Oxford Magazine*, LV (6 May 1937), p. 565 (Nat Whilk).
10. "After Kirby's *Kalevala*," (a translation), *The Oxford Magazaine*, LV (13 May 1937), p. 505 (Nat Whilk).
11. "The Future of Forestry," *The Oxford Magazine*, LVI (10 Feb. 1938), p. 383 (Nat Whilk).
12. *"Chanson D'Aventure," The Oxford Magazine*, LVI (19 May 1938), p. 638 (Nat Whilk). (Revised and retitled "What the Bird Said Early in the Year" in *Poems*.)
13. "Experiment," *The Spectator*, CLXI (9 Dec. 1938), p. 998. (Revised and retitled "Pattern" in *Poems*.)
14. "To Mr. Roy Campbell," *The Cherwell*, LVI (6 May 1939), p. 35 (Nat Whilk). (Revised and retitled "To the Author of *Flowering Rifle*" in *Poems*.)
15. "Hermione in the House of Paulina," *Augury: An Oxford Miscellany of Verse and Prose*. Edited by Alec M. Hardie and Keith C. Douglas. Oxford: Basil Blackwell, 1940, p. 28. (Revised in *Poems*.)
16. "Essence," *Fear No More: A Book of Poems for the Present Time by Living English Poets*. Cambridge: Cambridge University Press, 1940, p. 4.[2]
17. "Break, Sun, my Crusted Earth," *Fear No More: A Book of Poems for the Present Time by Living English Poets*. Cambridge: Cambridge University Press, 1940, p. 72. (A revised version of the last three stanzas of "A Pageant Played in Vain" in *Poems*.)
18. "The World is Round," *Fear No More: A Book of Poems for the Present Time by Living English Poets*. Cambridge: Cambridge University Press, 1940, p. 85. (A revised version of "Poem for Psychoanalysts and/or Theologians" in *Poems*.)

[1] This poem is reproduced in the unpublished *Lewis Papers*, Vol. IV, pp. 51–2.
[2] All the poems in *Fear No More* are published anonymously. There are, however, six copies containing an additional leaf giving the names of the authors of the poems, and one of these is in the Bodleian Library, Oxford.

19. "Arise my Body," *Fear No More: A Book of Poems for the Present Time by Living English Poets*. Cambridge: Cambridge University Press, 1940, p. 89. (A revised version of "After Prayers, Lie Cold" in *Poems*.)

20. "Epitaph," *Time and Tide*, XXIII (6 June 1942), p. 460. (Retitled "Epigrams and Epitaphs, No. 11" in *Poems*.)

21. "To G. M.," *The Spectator*, CLXIX (9 Oct. 1942), p. 335. (Revised and retitled "To a Friend" in *Poems*.)

22. "Awake, My Lute!," *The Atlantic Monthly*, CLXXII (Nov. 1943), pp. 113, 115.

23. "The Salamander," *The Spectator*, CLXXIV (8 June 1945), p. 521; see erratum: "Poet and Printer," *ibid.* (15 June 1945), p. 550.

24. "From the Latin of Milton's *De Idea Platonica Quemadmodum Aristoteles Intellexit*" (a translation), *English*, V, No. 30 (1945), p. 195.

25. "On the Death of Charles Williams," *Britain To-day*, No. 112 (Aug. 1945), p. 14. (Revised and retitled "To Charles Williams" in *Poems*.)

26. "Under Sentence," *The Spectator*, CLXXV (7 Sept. 1945), p. 219. (Revised and retitled "The Condemned" in *Poems*.)

27. "On the Atomic Bomb (Metrical Experiment)," *The Spectator*, CLXXV (28 Dec. 1945), p. 619.

28. "On Receiving Bad News," *Time and Tide*, XXVI (29 Dec. 1945), p. 1093. (Retitled "Epigrams and Epitaphs, No. 12" in *Poems*.)

29. "The Birth of Language," *Punch*, CCX (9 Jan. 1946), p. 32 (N. W.). (Revised in *Poems*.)

30. "On Being Human," *Punch*, CCX (8 May 1946), p. 402 (N. W.). (Revised in *Poems*.)

31. "Solomon," *Punch*, CCXI (14 Aug. 1946), p. 136 (N. W.). (Revised in *Poems*.)

32. "The True Nature of Gnomes," *Punch*, CCXI (16 Oct. 1946), p. 310 (N. W.).

33. "The Meteorite," *Time and Tide*, XXVII (7 Dec. 1946), p. 1183.

34. "Pan's Purge," *Punch*, CCXII (15 Jan. 1947), p. 71 (N. W.).

35. "The Romantics," *The New English Weekly*, XXX (16 Jan. 1947), p. 130. (Revised and retitled "The Prudent Jailer" in *Poems*.)

36. "Dangerous Oversight," *Punch*, CCXII (21 May 1947), p. 434 (N. W.). (Revised and retitled "Young King Cole" in *Poems*.)

37. "Two Kinds of Memory," *Time and Tide*, XXVIII (7 Aug. 1947), p. 859. (Revised in *Poems*.)

38. "*Le Roi S'Amuse*," *Punch*, CCXIII (1 Oct. 1947), p. 324 (N. W.). (Revised in *Poems*.)

39. "Donkeys' Delight," *Punch*, CCXIII (5 Nov. 1947), p. 442 (N. W.). (Revised in *Poems*.)

40. "The End of the Wine," *Punch*, CCXIII (3 Dec. 1947), p. 538 (N. W.). (Revised and retitled "The Last of the Wine" in *Poems*.)

41. "*Vitrea Circe*," *Punch*, CCXIV (23 June 1948), p. 543 (N. W.). (Revised in *Poems*.)

42. "Epitaph," *The Spectator*, CLXXXI (30 July 1948), p. 142. (Revised and retitled "Epigrams and Epitaphs, No. 14" in *Poems*.)

43. "The Sailing of the Ark," *Punch*, CCXV (11 Aug. 1948), p. 124 (N. W.). (Revised and retitled "The Late Passenger" in *Poems*.)

44. "The Landing," *Punch*, CCXV (15 Sept. 1948), p. 237 (N. W.). (Revised in *Poems*.)

45. "The Turn of the Tide," *Punch* (Almanac), CCXV (1 Nov. 1948) (N. W.). (Revised in *Poems*.)

46. "The Prodigality of Firdausi," *Punch*, CCXV (1 Dec. 1948), p. 510 (N. W.). (Revised in Poems.)

47. "Epitaph in a Village Churchyard," *Time and Tide*, XXX (19 March 1949), p. 272. (Retitled "Epigrams and Epitaphs, No. 16" in *Poems*.)

48. "On a Picture by Chirico," *The Spectator*, CLXXXII (6 May 1949), p. 607. (Revised in *Poems*.)

49. "Adam at Night," *Punch*, CCXVI (11 May 1949), p. 510 (N. W.). (Revised and retitled "The Adam at Night" in *Poems*.)

50. "Arrangement of Pindar," *Mandrake*, I, No. 6 (1949), pp. 43–45. (Revised and retitled "Pindar Sang" in *Poems*.)

51. "Epitaph," *The Month*, II (July 1949), p. 8. (Retitled 'Epigrams and Epitaphs, No. 17" in *Poems*.)

52. "Conversation Piece: The Magician and the Dryad," *Punch*, CCXVII (20 July 1949), p. 71 (N. W.). (Revised and retitled "The Magician and the Dryad" in *Poems*.)

53. "The Day with a White Mark," *Punch*, CCXVII (17 Aug. 1949), p. 170 (N. W.). (Revised in *Poems*.)

54. "A Footnote to Pre-History," *Punch*, CCXVII (14 Sept. 1949), p. 304 (N. W.). (Revised and retitled "The Adam Unparadised" in *Poems*.)

55. "As One Oldster to Another," *Punch*, CCXVIII (15 March 1950), pp. 294–5 (N. W.). (Revised in *Poems*.)

56. "A Cliché Came Out of its Cage," *Nine: A Magazine of Poetry and Criticism*, II (May 1950), p. 114. (Revised in *Poems*.)

57. "Ballade of Dead Gentlemen," *Punch*, CCXX (23 March 1951), p. 386 (N. W.).

58. "The Country of the Blind," *Punch*, CCXXI (12 Sept. 1951), p. 303 (N. W.).

59. "Pilgrim's Problem," *The Month*, VII (May 1952), p. 275.

60. "Vowels and Sirens," *The Times Literary Supplement*, Special Autumn Issue (29 Aug. 1952), p. xiv. (Revised in *Poems*.)

61. "Impenitence," *Punch*, CCXXV (15 July 1953), p. 91 (N. W.).

62. "March for Drum, Trumpet, and Twenty-one Giants," *Punch*, CCXXV (4 Nov. 1953), p. 553 (N. W.). (Revised in *Poems*.)

63. "To Mr. Kingsley Amis on His Late Verses," *Essays in Criticism*, IV (April 1954), p. 190; cf. Kingsley Amis, "Beowulf," *ibid.* (Jan. 1954), p. 85.

64. "*Odora Canum Vis* (A defence of certain modern biographers and critics)," *The Month*, XI (May 1954), p. 272. (Revised in *Poems*.)

65. "Cradle-Song Based on a Theme from Nicolas of Cusa," *The Times Literary Supplement* (11 June 1954), p. 375. (Revised and retitled "Science-Fiction Cradlesong" in *Poems*.)

66. *"Spartan Nactus,"* *Punch,* CCXXVII (1 Dec. 1954), p. 685 (N. W.). (Revised and retitled "A Confession" in *Poems.*)
67. "On Another Theme from Nicolas of Cusa," *The Times Literary Supplement* (21 Jan. 1955), p. 43. (Revised and retitled "On a Theme from Nicolas of Cusa" in *Poems.*)
68. "Legion," *The Month,* XIII (April 1955), p. 210. (Revised in *Poems.*)
69. "After Aristotle," *The Oxford Magazine,* LXXIV (23 Feb. 1956), p. 296 (N. W.).
70. "Epanorthosis (for the end of Goethe's *Faust*)," *The Cambridge Review,* LXXVII (26 May 1956), p. 610 (Nat Whilk). (Revised and retitled "Epigrams and Epitaphs, No. 15" in *Poems.*)
71. "Evolutionary Hymn," *The Cambridge Review,* LXXIX (30 Nov. 1957), p. 227 (N. W.).
72. "An Expostulation (against too many writers of science fiction)," *The Magazine of Fantasy and Science Fiction,* XVI (June 1959), p. 47.
73. "Re-Adjustment," *Fifty-Two: A Journal of Books & Authors* [from Geoffrey Bles], No. 14 (Autumn 1964), p. 4.
74. "The Old Grey Mare," Quoted in Roger Lancelyn Green, "C. S. Lewis," *Puffin Post,* IV, No. 1 (1970), pp. 14–5.

## F. BOOK REVIEWS BY C. S. LEWIS

(Some reviews were given titles, and wherever this occurs the title follows the name of the book reviewed.)

1. Evelyn Waugh, *Rossetti: His Life and Works. The Oxford Magazine,* XLVII (25 Oct. 1928), pp. 66, 69. (Unsigned)
2. Hugh Kingsmill, *Matthew Arnold. The Oxford Magazine,* XLVII (15 Nov. 1928), p. 177.
3. W. P. Ker, *Form and Style in Poetry.* (Edited by R. W. Chambers.) *The Oxford Magazine,* XLVII (6 Dec. 1928), pp. 283–4.
4. H. W. Garrod, *Collins. The Oxford Magazine,* XLVII (16 May 1929), p. 633.
5. Ruth Mohl, *The Three Estates in Medieval and Renaissance Literature. Medium Aevum,* III (Feb. 1934), pp. 68–70.
6. E. K. Chambers, *Sir Thomas Wyatt and Some Collected Studies. Medium Aevum,* III (Oct. 1934), pp. 237–40.
7. T. R. Henn, *Longinus and English Criticism. The Oxford Magazine,* LIII (6 Dec. 1934), p. 264.
8. Dorothy M. Hoare, *The Works of Morris and of Yeats in Relation to Early Saga Literature.* "The Sagas and Modern Life: Morris, Mr. Yeats and the Originals," *The Times Literary Supplement* (29 May 1937), p. 409. (Unsigned)
9. J. R. R. Tolkien, *The Hobbit: or There and Back Again.* "A World for Children," *The Times Literary Supplement* (2 Oct. 1937), p. 714. (Unsigned)
10. J. R. R. Tolkien, *The Hobbit: or There and Back Again.* "Professor Tolkien's 'Hobbit'," *The Times* (8 Oct. 1937), p. 20. (Unsigned)

11. Charles Williams, *Taliessin Through Logres*. "A Sacred Poem," *Theology*, XXXVIII (April 1939), pp. 268–76.

12. A. C. Bouquet (Editor), *A Lectionary of Christian Prose from the Second Century to the Twentieth Century*. *Theology*, XXXIX (Dec. 1939), pp. 467–8.

13. D. de Rougemont, *Passion and Society* (Translated by M. Belgion); Claude Chavasse, *The Bride of Christ*. *Theology*, XL (June 1940), pp. 459–61.

14. Lord David Cecil (Editor), *The Oxford Book of Christian Verse*. *The Review of English Studies*, XVII (Jan. 1941), pp. 95–102.

15. Helen M. Barrett, *Boethius: Some Aspects of His Times and Work*. *Medium Aevum*, X (Feb. 1941), pp. 29–34.

16. Logan Pearsall Smith, *Milton and His Modern Critics*. *The Cambridge Review* (21 Feb. 1941), p. 280.

17. Dorothy L. Sayers, *The Mind of the Maker*. *Theology*, XLIII (Oct. 1941), pp. 248–49.

18. Andreas Capellanus, *The Art of Courtly Love* (with introduction, translation, and notes by John Jay Parry). *The Review of English Studies*, XIX (Jan. 1943), pp. 77–79.

19. J. W. H. Atkins, *English Literary Criticism: The Medieval Phase*. *The Oxford Magazine*, LXII (10 Feb. 1944), p. 158.

20. Owen Barfield, *Romanticism Comes of Age*. " 'Who gaf me Drink'," *The Spectator*, CLXXIV (9 March 1945), p. 224.

21. Charles Williams, *Taliessin Through Logres*. *The Oxford Magazine*, LXIV (14 March 1946), pp. 248–50.

22. Douglas Bush, *"Paradise Lost" in Our Time: Some Comments*. *The Oxford Magazine*, LXV (13 Feb. 1947), pp. 215–17.

23. Sir Thomas Malory, *The Works of Sir Thomas Malory* (Edited by E. Vinaver). "The Morte Darthur," *The Times Literary Supplement* (7 June 1947), pp. 273–74. (Unsigned)

24. G. A. L. Burgeon (= Owen Barfield), *This Ever Diverse Pair*. "Life Partners," *Time and Tide*, XXXI (25 March 1950), p. 286.

25. Howard Rollin Patch, *The Other World, According to Descriptions in Mediaeval Literature*. *Medium Aevum*, XX (1951), pp. 93–94.

26. Alan M. F. Gunn, *The Mirror of Love: A Reinterpretation of "The Romance of the Rose."* *Medium Aevum*, XXII, No. 1 (1953), pp. 27–31.

27. J. R. R. Tolkien, *The Fellowship of the Ring* (being the First Part of *The Lord of the Rings*). "The Gods Return to Earth," *Time and Tide*, XXXV (14 Aug. 1954), pp. 1082–83.

28. J. R. R. Tolkien, *The Two Towers* (being the Second Part of *The Lord of the Rings*); *The Return of the King* (being the Third Part of *The Lord of the Rings*). "The Dethronement of Power," *Time and Tide*, XXXVI (22 Oct. 1955), pp. 1373–74.

29. W. Schwarz, *Principles and Problems of Biblical Translation*. *Medium Aevum*, XXVI, No. 2 (1957), pp. 115–17.

30. R. S. Loomis (Editor), *Arthurian Literature in the Middle Ages: A Collaborative Study*. "Arthuriana," *The Cambridge Review*, LXXXI (13 Feb. 1960), pp. 355, 357.

31. M. Pauline Parker, *The Allegory of the "Faerie Queen." The Cambridge Review,* LXXXI (11 June 1960), pp. 643, 645.
32. John Vyvyan, *Shakespeare and the Rose of Love. The Listener,* LXIV (7 July 1960), p. 30.
33. Robert Ellrodt, *Neoplatonism in the Poetry of Spenser. Etudes Anglaises,* XIV (April–June 1961), pp. 107–16.
34. George Steiner, *The Death of Tragedy.* "Tragic Ends," *Encounter,* XVIII (Feb. 1962), pp. 97–101.
35. David Loth, *The Erotic in Literature.* "Eros on the Loose," *The Observer* (Weekend Review), No. 8905 (4 March 1962), p. 30.
36. Sir John Hawkins, *The Life of Samuel Johnson* (Edited by B. H. Davis). "Boswell's Bugbear," *Sunday Telegraph,* No. 61 (1 April 1962), p. 8.
37. Homer, *The Odyssey* (Translated by Robert Fitzgerald). "Odysseus Sails Again," *Sunday Telegraph,* No. 84 (9 Sept. 1962), p. 6.
38. John Jones, *On Aristotle and Greek Tragedy.* "Ajax and Others," *Sunday Telegraph,* No. 98 (16 Dec. 1962), p. 6.
39. Harold Bloom, *The Visionary Company: A Reading of English Romantic Poetry.* "Poetry and Exegesis," *Encounter,* XX (June 1963), pp. 74–76.
40. Dorothy L. Sayers, *The Poetry of Search and the Poetry of Statement.* "Rhyme and Reason," *Sunday Telegraph,* No. 148 (1 Dec. 1963), p. 18.

## G. PUBLISHED LETTERS

1. "The Kingis Quair," *The Times Literary Supplement* (18 April 1929), p. 315.
2. "Spenser's Irish Experiences and *The Faerie Queene,*" *The Review of English Studies,* VII (Jan. 1931), pp. 83–85.
3. "The Genuine Text," *The Times Literary Supplement* (2 May 1935), p. 288; cf. J. Dover Wilson, *ibid.* (16 May 1935), p. 313; C. S. Lewis, *ibid.* (23 May 1935), p. 331; J. Dover Wilson, *ibid.* (30 May 1935), p. 348; J. Dover Wilson, *ibid.* (13 June 1935), p. 380.
4. "On Cross-Channel Ships," *The Times* (18 Nov. 1938), p. 12.
5. "The Conditions for a Just War," *Theology,* XXXVIII (May 1939), pp. 373–74.
6. "Christianity and Culture," *Theology,* XL (June 1940), pp. 475–77.
7. "The Conflict in Anglican Theology," *Theology,* XLI (Nov. 1940), p. 304.
8. Open Letter, *The Christian News-Letter,* No. 119 (4 Feb. 1942), p. 4.
9. "Miracles," *The Guardian* (16 Oct. 1942), p. 331.
10. Letter to the Publisher on dust cover of C. S. Lewis, *Perelandra.* New York: Macmillan, 1944.
11. "Mr. C. S. Lewis on Christianity," *The Listener,* XXXI (9 March 1944), p. 273; cf. W. R. Childe, *ibid.* (2 March 1944), p. 245; W. R. Childe, *ibid.* (16 March 1944), p. 301.
12. "Basic Fears," *The Times Literary Supplement* (2 Dec. 1944), p. 583; S. H. Hooke, *ibid.* (27 Jan. 1945), p. 43; C. S. Lewis, *ibid.* (3 Feb. 1945), p. 55; S. H. Hooke, *ibid.* (10 Feb. 1945), p. 67.
13. "Above the Smoke and Stir," *The Times Literary Supplement* (14 July 1945), p. 331; cf. B. A. Wright, *ibid.* (4 Aug. 1945), p. 367; C. S.

Lewis, *ibid.* (29 Sept. 1945), p. 463; B. A. Wright, *ibid.* (27 Oct. 1945), p. 511.

14. "A Village Experience," *The Guardian* (31 Aug. 1945), p. 335.
15. "Socratic Wisdom," *The Oxford Magazine*, LXIV (13 June 1946), p. 359.
16. "Poetic Licence," *The Sunday Times* (11 Aug. 1946), p. 6.
17. Letter to the Publisher on dust cover of *Essays Presented to Charles Williams* (Edited by C. S. Lewis). London: Oxford University Press, 1947.
18. "A Difference of Outlook," *The Guardian* (27 June 1947), p. 283; cf. A Correspondent, "Adult Colleges," *ibid.* (30 May 1947), pp. 235, 240.
19. "Public Schools," *Church Times*, CXXX (3 Oct. 1947), p. 583.
20. "The New Miltonians," *The Times Literary Supplement* (29 Nov. 1947), p. 615.
21. (With Erik Routley) "Correspondence with an Anglican who Dislikes Hymns," *The Presbyter*, VI, No. 2 (1948), pp. 15–20. (The two letters from Lewis, dated 16 July 1946 and 21 Sept. 1946, are printed over the initials "A. B.")
22. "Charles Williams," *The Oxford Magazine*, LVXI (29 April 1948), p. 380.
23. "Othello," *The Times Literary Supplement* (19 June 1948), p. 345.
24. "The Church's Liturgy," *Church Times*, CXXXII (20 May 1949), p. 319; cf. E. L. Mascall, "Quadringentesimo Anno," *ibid.* (6 May 1949), p. 282; W. D. F. Hughes, "The Church's Liturgy," *ibid.* (24 June 1949), p. 409; C. S. Lewis, *ibid.* (1 July 1949), p. 427; Edward Every, "Doctrine and Liturgy," *ibid.* (8 July 1949), pp. 445–46; C. S. Lewis, "Invocation," *ibid.* (15 July 1949), pp. 463–64; Edward Every, "Invocation of Saints," *ibid.* (22 July 1949), pp. 481–82; C. S. Lewis, *ibid.* (5 Aug. 1949), p. 513.
25. "Text Corruptions," *The Times Literary Supplement* (3 March 1950), p. 137; cf. J. Dover Wilson, *ibid.* (10 March 1950), p. 153.
26. Letter on "*Robinson Crusoe* as a Myth," *Essays in Criticism*, I (July 1951), p. 313; cf. Ian Watt, "*Robinson Crusoe* as a Myth," *ibid.* (April 1951), pp. 95–119; Ian Watt, *ibid.* (July 1951), p. 313.
27. "The Holy Name," *Church Times*, CXXXIV (10 Aug. 1951), p. 541; cf. Leslie E. T. Bradbury, *ibid.* (3 Aug. 1951), p. 525.
28. "Mere Christians," *Church Times*, CXXXV (8 Feb. 1952), p. 95; cf. R. D. Daunton-Fear, "Evangelical Churchmanship," *ibid.* (1 Feb. 1952), p. 77.
29. "The Sheepheard's Slumber," *The Times Literary Supplement* (9 May 1952), p. 313.
30. Letter to Dorothy L. Sayers quoted in Miss Sayer's "Ignorance and Dissatisfaction," *Latin Teaching*, XXVIII, No. 3 (Oct. 1952), p. 91. (The article is reprinted as "The Teaching of Latin" in Miss Sayers's *The Poetry of Search and the Poetry of Statement*. London: Victor Gollancz, 1963.)
31. "Canonization," *Church Times*, CXXXV (24 Oct. 1952), p. 763; cf. Eric Pitt, *ibid.* (17 Oct. 1952), p. 743.
32. Letter to the Publisher on dust cover of A Religious of C. S. M. V. [R. P. Lawson], *The Coming of the Lord: A Study in the Creed*. London: A. R. Mowbray, 1953.

33. Letter to the Publisher on dust cover of J. R. R. Tolkien, *The Fellowship of the Ring*. London: George Allen and Unwin, 1954.

34. Letter to the Publisher on dust cover of A. C. Clarke, *Childhood's End*. London: Sidgwick and Jackson, 1954.

35. Letter to the Milton Society of America, *A Milton Evening in Honor of Douglas Bush and C. S. Lewis*. Modern Language Association (28 Dec. 1954), pp. 14–15.

36. Open Letter to Fr. Berlicche, *L'Amico die Buoni Fanciulli*, No. 1 (1955), Verona, p. 75.

37. (With Dorothy L. Sayers) "Charles Williams," *The Times* (14 May 1955), p. 9.

38. "Portrait of W. B. Yeats," *The Listener*, LIV (15 Sept. 1955), p. 427.

39. Letters to the Publisher on the dust cover (a portion of one letter on the inside front flap and the portion of another on the back flap) of C. S. Lewis, *Till We Have Faces: A Myth Retold*. London: Geoffrey Bles, 1956. (The letter or "Note" from the back flap is printed in full in the Time Special Edition of *Till We Have Faces* published in paperback in New York by Time Inc., 1966, pp. 273–75.

40. Letter to J. B. Phillips [of 3 Aug. 1943], quoted in *Fifty-Two: A Journal of Books & Authors* [from Geoffrey Bles], No. 1 (Autumn 1957), p. 9.

41. Letter to the Publisher on dust cover of E. R. Eddison, *The Mezentian Gate*. London: Printed at the Curwen Press, 1958.

42. (With others) "Mgr. R. A. Knox," *Church Times*, CXLI (6 June 1958), p. 12.

43. "Books for Children," *The Times Literary Supplement* (28 Nov. 1958), p. 689; cf. "The Light Fantastic," *ibid.*, *Children's Books Section* (21 Nov. 1958), p. x.

44. Letter to the Publisher on dust cover of Mervyn Peake, *Titus Alone*. London: Eyre and Spottiswoode, 1959.

45. "Spelling Reform," *The Times Educational Supplement* (1 Jan. 1960), p. 13.

46. Letter to the Publisher on dust cover of David Bolt, *Adam*. London: J. M. Dent, 1960.

47. Letter to Charles Moorman in Charles Moorman, *Arthurian Triptych: Mystic Materials in Charles Williams, C. S. Lewis, and T. S. Eliot*. Berkeley and Los Angeles: University of California Press, 1960, p. 161.

48. Letter to Mahmoud Manzalaoui quoted in M. Manzalaoui's "Lydgate and English Prosody," *Cairo Studies in English* (1960), p. 94.

49. Letter to the Editor, *Delta: The Cambridge Literary Magazine*, No. 23 (Feb. 1961), pp. 4–7; cf. The Editors, "Professor C. S. Lewis and the English Faculty," *ibid.*, No. 22 (Oct. 1960), pp. 6–17; C. S. Lewis, "Undergraduate Criticism," *Broadsheet* (Cambridge), VIII, No. 17 (9 March 1960), p. [1].

50. Letters to "A Member of the Church of the Covenant" quoted in the pamphlet, *Encounter with Light*. Lynchburg, Virginia: Church of the Covenant [June 1961], pp. 11–16, 20. (The three letters from C. S. Lewis were written [14 Dec. 1950; 23 Dec. 1950; 17 April 1951] re-

spectively.) Reprinted, as by Sheldon Vanauken, by Wheaton College, Wheaton, Illinois [1976].

51. "Capital Punishment," *Church Times*, CXLIV (1 Dec. 1961), p. 7; cf. Claude Davis, *ibid.* (8 Dec. 1961), p. 14; C. S. Lewis, "Death Penalty," *ibid.* (15 Dec. 1961), p. 12.

52. "And Less Greek," *Church Times*, CXLV (20 July 1962), p. 12.

53. Letter to the Editor, *English*, XIV (Summer 1962), p. 75.

54. "Wain's Oxford," *Encounter*, XX (Jan. 1963), p. 81.

55. Letter quoted in Rose Macaulay, *Letters to a Sister* (Edited by Constance Babington Smith). London: Collins, 1964, p. 261 n. (Quotations from a letter C. S. Lewis wrote to Dorothea Conybeare, who had asked him to explain the title of his book *Till We Have Faces*.)

56. Letter to the Publisher on flyleaf of Austin Farrer, *Saving Belief: A Discussion of Essentials*. London: Hodder and Stoughton, 1964.

57. Letters to Clyde S. Kilby (of 10 Feb. 1957, 7 May 1959 and 11 Jan. 1961) and Thomas Howard quoted in Clyde S. Kilby, *The Christian World of C. S. Lewis*. Grand Rapids, Michigan: Eerdmans (1964), pp. 58, 136, 153–54, 189–90.

58. Letter to John Warwick Montgomery (of 29 Aug. 1963) in J. W. Montgomery, *History and Christianity*. Donner's Grove, Illinois: Inter-Varsity Press (1964), pp. 6–7.

59. "Conception of 'The Screwtape Letters'," *Fifty-Two: A Journal of Books & Authors* [from Geoffrey Bles], No. 14 (Autumn 1964), p. 3. (A letter C. S. Lewis wrote to his brother on 20 July 1940 which divulges the original idea for *The Screwtape Letters*. Reprinted in *Letters of C. S. Lewis*.)

60. "Two letters from C. S. Lewis," *Fifty-Two: A Journal of Books & Authors* [from Geoffrey Bles], No. 17 (Spring 1966), pp. 18–19. (Letters to his father about the writing of *The Allegory of Love* on 20 July 1928 and his visit to Cambridge in 1920. Reprinted in *Letters of C. S. Lewis*.)

61. A letter to James E. Higgins of 2 Dec. 1962 in J. E. Higgins, "A Letter from C. S. Lewis," *The Horn Book Magazine*, XLII (Oct. 1966), pp. 533–34.

62. Letter to Walter Hooper [of 30 Nov. 1954] in "Prof. Burton's Class," *The Greensboro Daily News*, North Carolina (8 Oct. 1967), p. 4.

63. Letters to Peter Milward, S. J. of 22 Sept., 17 Dec. 1955; 9 May, 22 Sept., 10 Dec. 1956; 24 Sept., 25 Dec. 1959; 7 March 1960 quoted in Peter Milward, "C. S. Lewis on Allegory," *Bigo Seinen: The Rising Generation*, Tokyo, CXIV, No. 4 (April 1968), pp. 227–31.

64. Letter to the Publisher on dust cover of Francis Warner, *Poetry of Francis Warner*. Philadelphia: Pilgrim Press, 1970.

65. Letters to Anthony Boucher (of 5 Feb. 1953) and Susan Salzberg (of 5 Feb. 1960) in *CSL: The Bulletin of the New York C. S. Lewis Society*, II, No. 10 (Aug. 1971), p. 3.

66. Letters to J. S. A. Ensor (of 13 March, 31 March and 28 April 1944), Owen Barfield (of 1943), and the Rt. Rev. Henry I. Louttit (of 5 Jan. 1958) quoted in *C. S. Lewis: Speaker & Teacher* (Edited by

Carolyn Keefe). Grand Rapids, Michigan: Zondervan Publishing Co. (1971), pp. 17–18, 102–03, 123, 132.

67. Letters to Arthur Greeves (of 12 Oct. 1916) and Pauline Baynes (of 21 Jan. 1954) quoted in Walter Hooper, "Past Watchful Dragons," *Imagination and the Spirit* (Edited by Charles A. Huttar). Grand Rapids, Michigan: Eerdmans (1971), pp. 282, 312.

68. "Letters of C. S. Lewis to E. Vinaver" (Edited by Richard C. West), *Orchrist* (Special C. S. Lewis Issue), No. 6 (Winter 1971–1972), pp. 3–5. (Contained are five letters to Professor Eugène Vinaver and one to Mrs. Vinaver.)

69. Letter to Nina Howell Starr (of 1 Nov. 1960) in Nathan C. Starr, "C. S. Lewis: A Personal Memoir," *Unicorn*, II, No. 2 (Spring 1972), p. 11.

70. Letter to an American Girl quoted in Kathryn Ann Lindskoog, *The Lion of Judah in Never-Never Land*. Grand Rapids, Michigan: Eerdmans (1973), p. 16.

71. Letter to Kathryn Ann Lindskoog [of 29 Oct. 1957] quoted on the back cover of her book *The Lion of Judah in Never-Never Land*. Grand Rapids, Michigan: Eerdmans, 1973.

72. Letters to Arthur Greeves quoted in Douglas Gilbert and Clyde S. Kilby, *C. S. Lewis: Images of His World*. Grand Rapids, Michigan: Eerdmans (1973), pp. 18, 20–21, 24, 34, 37, 58, 62, 70, 74, 75, 93, 119–35, 136, 138, 139, 145, 158, 162, 168, 169, 170, 171, 173, 178.

73. Letters to A. C. Harwood (of 28 Oct. 1926) and Daphne Harwood (of 28 March 1933 and March 1942) quoted in A. C. Harwood, "C. S. Lewis and Anthroposophy," *Anthroposophical Quarterly*, XVIII, No. 4 (Winter 1973), pp. 40–42.

74. Letters to Arthur Greeves and Owen Barfield quoted in Lionel Adey, "The Light of Holiness: some comments on Morris by C. S. Lewis," *The Journal of the William Morris Society*, III, No. 1 (Spring 1974), pp. 11, 12, 13, 14, 15, 16.

75. Letters to Corbin Scott Carnell (of 13 Oct. and 10 Dec. 1958) quoted in Corbin Scott Carnell, *Bright Shadows of Reality: C. S. Lewis and the Feeling Intellect*. Grand Rapids, Michigan: Eerdmans (1974), pp. 69, 71, 79.

76. Letter to John Warwick Montgomery (of 21 Jan. 1960) in *Myth, Allegory and Gospel: An Interpretation of J. R. R. Tolkien, C. S. Lewis, G. K. Chesterton, Charles Williams* (Edited by John Warwick Montgomery). Minneapolis: Bethany Fellowship (1974), pp. 145–47.

77. Letters to Arthur Greeves [of 8 June 1915, 12 Oct. 1915, 22 April 1923, 25 March 1933, 1 June 1930, 26 Dec. 1945, 24 July 1915, Dec. 1935, 5 Nov. 1933, 26 Dec. 1934, 4 May 1915, 17 July 1918, 29 Dec. 1935, 17 June 1918, 17 Aug. 1933, 5 Sept. 1931, 1 Feb. 1931] quoted in Clyde S. Kilby and Linda J. Evans, "C. S. Lewis and Music," *Christian Scholar's Review*, IV, No. 1 (1974), pp. 1, 11, 12, 13, 14, 15.

78. Letter to Lucy Matthews [of 11 Sept. 1958] quoted in *Amon Hen: The Bulletin of the Tolkien Society of Great Britain*, No. 14 (Feb. 1975), p. 2.

79. Letters to R. W. Ladborough quoted in R. W. Ladborough, "C. S. Lewis in

Cambridge," *CSL: The Bulletin of the New York C. S. Lewis Society*, VI, No. 9 (July 1975), pp. 8, 10.

80. Letter to A. C. Harwood (of 7 May 1934) quoted in A. C. Harwood, "A Toast to the Memory of C. S. Lewis proposed at Magdalen College, July 4th 1975," *CSL: The Bulletin of the New York C. S. Lewis Society*, VI, No. 11 (Sept. 1975), p. 2.

81. Letters to J. R. R. Tolkien [of 7 Dec. 1929, 27 Oct. 1949, 13 Nov. 1952, 7 Dec. 1953] quoted in Humphrey Carpenter, *J. R. R. Tolkien: A Biography*. London: Allen and Unwin (1977), pp. 145, 204, 215, and 219 respectively.

82. Letters to Owen Barfield (undated) on p. 216; to Gracia Fay Bouman (of 19 July 1960), on p. 3; to Arthur Greeves (of 4 Feb. 1933, 22 Sept. 1931, 8 Nov. 1931 [1 July 1930], 1 June 1930, 18 Oct. 1931, 1 Oct. 1931, 12 Sept. 1933 [18 Oct. 1916]) on pp. 137, 138, 141, 142–43, 155, 221, 173; to Dom Bede Griffiths (of 8 Jan. 1936, 1934) on pp. 143, 221; to Mr. Lennox (of 25 May 1959) on pp. 40–41; to Ruth Pitter (of 16 April 1952) on p. xv, quoted in *The Longing for a Form: Essays on the Fiction of C. S. Lewis* (Edited by Peter J. Schakel). Kent, Ohio: Kent State University Press, 1977.

83. Letters to Sheldon Vanauken in Sheldon Vanauken, *A Severe Mercy: C. S. Lewis and a pagan love invaded by Christ, told by one of the lovers.* London: Hodder and Stoughton, 1977. (The book contains 19 entire letters from Lewis written between 1950–57 including the three from *Encounter with Light*–G50–and excerpts from 6 others written between 1958–62.)

84. Letter to Bernard Acworth [of 5 March 1960] quoted in Malcolm Bowden, *Ape-men—Fact or Fallacy?* London: Sovereign Publications (1977), p. 35.

## H. BOOKS CONTAINING NUMEROUS SMALL EXTRACTS FROM LEWIS'S UNPUBLISHED WRITINGS

1. Roger Lancelyn Green and Walter Hooper, *C. S. Lewis: A Biography*. London: Collins, 1974 [Harcourt Brace Jovanovich, 1974].
2. Lionel Adey, *C. S. Lewis's "Great War" with Owen Barfield*. English Literary Studies Monograph Series No. 14. Victoria, B. C., Canada: University of Victoria, 1978.
3. Humphrey Carpenter, *The Inklings: C. S. Lewis, J. R. R. Tolkien, Charles Williams, and Their Friends*. London: Allen and Unwin, 1978 [Boston: Houghton Mifflin, 1978].
4. James T. Como (Editor), *"C. S. Lewis at the Breakfast Table" and Other Reminiscences*. New York: The Macmillan Publishing Company, 1979 [London: Collins, 1979].
5. Chad Walsh, *The Literary Legacy of C. S. Lewis*. New York: Harcourt Brace Jovanovich, 1979.
6. Walter Hooper, *Past Watchful Dragons: The Narnian Chronicles of C. S. Lewis*. New York: The Macmillan Publishing Company, 1979 [London: Collins, 1979].

# Supplement to Bibliography

## NEW ENTRIES

### A. BOOKS

59. *OF THIS/ AND/ OTHER WORLDS.* Edited by Walter Hooper. Collins, 1982. (Contents: *Preface* by Walter Hooper, "On Stories," "The Novels of Charles Williams,"* "A Tribute to E. R. Eddison," "On Three Ways of Writing for Children," "Sometimes Fairy Stories May Say Best What's to Be Said," "On Juvenile Tastes," "It All Began with a Picture . . . ," "On Science Fiction," "A Reply to Professor Haldane," "The Hobbit," "Tolkien's *The Lord of the Rings*," "A Panegyric for Dorothy L. Sayers,"* "The Mythopoeic Gift of Rider Haggard," "George Orwell," "The Death of Words," "The Parthenon and the Optative," "Period Criticism," "Different Tastes in Literature," "On Criticism," "Unreal Estates") [As *On Stories: and Other Essays on Literature:* Harcourt Brace Jovanovich, 1982]. This book contains all the essays that were in *Of Other Worlds* (A46).

60. *THE BUSINESS/ OF HEAVEN.* Edited by Walter Hooper. Collins—Fount Paperbacks, 1984. (Contents: *Preface* by Walter Hooper, *365 Readings for the Year, Movable Fasts and Feasts*) [Harcourt Brace Jovanovich, 1984].

61. *BOXEN/ The Imaginary World of/ the Young/ C. S. Lewis.* Edited by Walter Hooper. Collins, 1985. (Contents: *Introduction* by Walter Hooper, ANIMAL-LAND STORIES: "The King's Ring," "Manx Against Manx," "The Relief of Murry," "History of Mouse-Land from Stone-Age to Bublish I," "History of Animal-Land," "The Chess Monograph," "The Geography of Animal-Land," BOXEN STORIES: "Boxen: or Scenes from Boxonian City Life," "The Locked Door and Than-Kyu," "The Sailor"; *Encyclopedia Boxoniana*) [Harcourt Brace Jovanovich, 1985].

62. *LETTERS TO/ CHILDREN.* Edited by Lyle W. Dorsett and Marjorie Lamp Mead, with a Foreword by Douglas H. Gresham. New York: Macmillan, 1985 [London: Collins, 1985].

63. *FIRST AND/ SECOND THINGS: Essays on Theology and Ethics.* Edited by Walter Hooper. Collins—Fount Paperbacks, 1985. (Contents: *Preface* by Walter Hooper, "Bulverism," "First and Second Things," "On the Reading of Old Books," " 'Horrid Red Things,' " "Work and Prayer," "Two Lectures," "Meditation in a Toolshed," "The Sermon and the Lunch," "On the Transmission of Christianity," "The Decline of Religion," "Vivisection," "Modern Translations of the Bible," "Some Thoughts," "The Humanitarian

---

* Published for the first time.

Theory of Punishment," "Xmas and Christmas," "Revival or Decay?" "Before We Can Communicate").

64. *PRESENT CONCERNS*. Edited by Walter Hooper. Collins—Fount Paperbacks, 1968. (Contents: *Introduction* by Walter Hooper, "The Necessity of Chivalry," "Equality," "Three Kinds of Men," "My First School," "Is English Doomed?," "Democratic Education," "A Dream," "Blimpophobia," "Private Bates," "Hedonics," "After Priggery—What?," "Modern Man and His Categories of Thought,"* "Talking about Bicycles," "On Living in an Atomic Age," "The Empty Universe," "Prudery and Philology," "Interim Report," "Is History Bunk?," "Sex in Literature") [Harcourt Brace Jovanovich, 1987].

65. *TIMELESS AT HEART/ Essays on Theology*. Edited by Walter Hooper. Collins—Fount Paperbacks, 1987. (Contents: *Preface* by Walter Hooper, "Christian Apologetics," "Answers to Questions on Christianity," "Why I Am Not a Pacifist," "The Pains of Animals," "The Founding of the Oxford Socratic Club," "Religion Without Dogma?," "Is Theism Important?," "Rejoinder to Dr. Pittenger," "Willing Slaves of the Welfare State," Letters).

66. *LETTERS/ C. S. LEWIS/ DON GIOVANNI CALABRIA/ A study in friendship*. Translated and edited by Martin Moynihan. Collins, 1988. [Ann Arbor: Servant Books, 1988.] This is a correspondence in Latin between C. S. Lewis and Don Giovanni Calabria, founder of the Casa Buoni Fanciulli in Verona. When Don Calabria died the correspondence with Lewis was continued by Don Luigi Pedrollo. The book contains 28 letters from Lewis and 7 from Don Calabria, who was beatified by Pope John Paul II in 1988.

67. *THE/ ESSENTIAL/ C. S. LEWIS*. Edited with an introduction by Lyle W. Dorsett. New York: Collier Books, Macmillan, 1988. This anthology contains the complete texts of *The Lion, the Witch and the Wardrobe*, *Perelandra* and *The Abolition of Man* as well as representative selections from Lewis's other writings.

68. *THE/ QUOTABLE/ LEWIS*. Edited by Wayne Martindale and Jerry Root. Wheaton, Illinois: Tyndale House, 1989.

69. *CHRISTIAN/ REUNION/ And Other Essays*. Edited by Walter Hooper. Collins—Fount Paperbacks, 1990. (Contents: *Introduction* by Walter Hooper, "Christian Reunion,"* "Lilies that Fester," "Evil and God," "Dangers of National Repentance," "Two Ways with the Self," "Meditation on the Third Commandment," "Scraps," "Miserable Offenders," "Cross-Examination," "Behind the Scenes," "What Christmas Means to Me," "Delinquents in the Snow").

70. *ALL MY ROAD/ BEFORE ME: The Diary of C. S. Lewis 1922–1927*. Edited by Walter Hooper. London: HarperCollins [Harcourt Brace Jovanovich], 1991.

71. *DAILY READINGS WITH/ C. S. LEWIS*. Edited by Walter Hooper. London: HarperCollins—Fount Paperbacks, 1992.

## NEW EDITIONS OF OLD BOOKS WITH ADDED MATERIAL

9. *THE/ SCREWTAPE/ LETTERS/ WITH/ SCREWTAPE/ PROPOSES A TOAST.*

*Published for the first time.

*Revised Edition*. This edition contains a hitherto unpublished piece by C. S. Lewis, that here serves as a Preface to "Screwtape Proposes a Toast." New York: Macmillan—Macmillan Paperbacks Edition, 1982.

20. *THE WEIGHT/ OF GLORY/ And Other Addresses*. Revised and Expanded Edition. Edited by Walter Hooper. New York: Macmillan—Macmillan Paperbacks Edition, 1980. (Contents: *Introduction* by Walter Hooper, "The Weight of Glory," "Learning in War-Time," "Why I Am Not a Pacifist,"* "Transposition" [expanded version], "Is Theology Poetry?," "The Inner Ring," "Membership," "On Forgiveness," "A Slip of the Tongue").

23. *MERE/ CHRISTIANITY/ An Anniversary Edition of/ The Three Books/ "The Case for Christianity," "Christian Behaviour,"/ and/ "Beyond Personality."* Edited by Walter Hooper. New York: Macmillan, 1981. This edition contains the original broadcasts of those talks entitled "Some Objections" and "Sexual Morality," as well as part of a programme called "The Anvil" in which Lewis took part.

45. *LETTERS OF/ C. S. LEWIS/ Edited, with a Memoir/ by W. H. Lewis*. Revised and Enlarged Edition. Edited by Walter Hooper. London: Collins—Fount Paperbacks, 1988.

## D. ESSAYS, PAMPHLETS, AND MISCELLANEOUS PIECES

150. "Three Kinds of Men," *The Sunday Times*, No. 6258 (21 March 1943), p. 2. (Reprinted in *Present Concerns*.)

151. "On Living in an Atomic Age," *Informed Reading*, VI (1948), pp. 78–84. (Reprinted in *Present Concerns*.)

152. *A Cretaceous Perambulator (The Re-examination of)*, by Owen Barfield and C. S. Lewis. Edited by Walter Hooper. Oxford: Oxford University–C. S. Lewis Society, 1983. This 18-page pamphlet is in a limited edition of 100 copies.

153. "Commentary on the Lay of Leithian" in J. R. R. Tolkien, *The Lays of Beleriand*. Edited by Christopher Tolkien. London: George Allen & Unwin, 1985, pp. 315–29.

154. "Eric Bentley: An Appreciation" in *The Play and Its Critic: Essays for Eric Bentley*. Edited by Michael Bertin. Lanham, Maryland: University Press of America, 1986, pp. 4–7. The "Appreciation" consists of two letters of recommendation that Lewis wrote about his pupil Eric Bentley in 1938 and 1940.

155. "This Was a Very Frank Talk—Which We Think Everyone Should Read," *Daily Mirror* (13 Oct. 1942), pp. 6–7. This broadcast on "Sexual Morality" was published illegally before its appearance in *Christian Behaviour*.

156. Boxen Manuscripts quoted in Walter Hooper's Preface to C. S. Lewis, *Of Other Worlds: Essays and Stories*. Edited by Walter Hooper. Geoffrey Bles, 1966 [Harcourt, Brace & World, 1967], pp. vii, viii.

157. Wynyard School Diary (Nov. 1909) in Walter Hooper, "C. S. Lewis," *The Franciscan*, IX, No. 4 (Sept. 1967), p. 163.

158. Oxford Diary [14 Feb. 1923] quoted in Walter Hooper's Preface to C. S. Lewis, *Selected Literary Essays*. Edited by Walter Hooper. Cambridge: Cambridge University Press, 1969, p. xii.

159. Oxford Diary quoted in Walter Hooper's Preface to C. S. Lewis, *Narrative Poems*.

Edited by Walter Hooper. Geoffrey Bles, 1969 [Harcourt, Brace & World, 1972], pp. x–xiii. (2 April 1922) on p. x; (23 Nov. 1922) on p. xi; (9 Sept. 1923) on p. xi; (16 and 21 Jan. 1927) on pp. xii–xiii.

160. Definition of Myth, in Walter Hooper, "Past Watchful Dragons: The Fairy Tales of C. S. Lewis," in *Imagination and the Spirit*. Edited by Charles A. Huttar. Grand Rapids: Eerdmans, 1971, p. 286.

161. Fragment of a Story, quoted in Walter Hooper, "Past Watchful Dragons: The Fairy Tales of C. S. Lewis," in *Imagination and the Spirit*. Edited by Charles A. Huttar. Grand Rapids: Eerdmans, 1971, p. 291.

162. Holograph of "To Mars and Back," the fragment of a story written by Lewis when a child, in Douglas Gilbert and Clyde S. Kilby, *C. S. Lewis: Images of His World*. Grand Rapids: Eerdmans, 1973, p. 104.

163. Little Lea Diary ("My Life During the Exmas Holadys of 1907") quoted in Roger Lancelyn Green and Walter Hooper, *C. S. Lewis: A Biography*. Collins [Harcourt Brace Jovanovich], 1974, p. 24.

164. Wynyard School Diary (Nov. 1909) quoted in Roger Lancelyn Green and Walter Hooper, *C. S. Lewis: A Biography*. Collins [Harcourt Brace Jovanovich], 1974.

165. Oxford Diary, quoted in Roger Lancelyn Green and Walter Hooper, *C. S. Lewis: A Biography*. Collins [Harcourt Brace Jovanovich], 1974. (24 May 1922) on pp. 69–70; [11 June 1922] on p. 71; [9–23 Sept. 1922] on p. 71; [13, 15, 17 Oct. 1922] on p. 72; (18 Oct. 1922) on p. 72; [7 Nov. 1922] on p. 72; [15 Nov. 1922] on p. 72; [18 Jan. 1923] on p. 73; (26 Jan.; 2 Feb. 1923) on p. 73; (11 Feb. 1923) on pp. 73–4; (1 June 1923) on p. 75; (10 July 1923) on p. 75; [13–25 July 1923] on p. 76; [17–25 March 1924] on p. 76; (8 Sept. 1923) on p. 77; [13 Sept. 1923] on p. 77; (29 Feb. 1924) on pp. 78–9; [21–24 June 1924] on p. 80; [3, 4 July 1924] on .p. 80; (10 Feb. 1925) on pp. 81–2; [5 Feb. 1927] on p. 86; [5 May 1926] on p. 87; [10 May 1926] on p. 88; (11 May 1926) on p. 88; [10 June 1926] on pp. 88–9; [6 July 1926] on p. 89; (18 Jan. 1927) on p. 90; (8 Feb. 1927) on pp. 90–1; [1 March 1927] on p. 91; (24 Jan. 1927) on pp. 90–1; (12 Sept. 1923) on p. 175; (27 April 1923) on p. 250; (9 Sept. 1923) on p. 261; (23 Nov. 1922) on p. 161. (Reprinted in *All My Road Before Me*.)

166. Pen portraits from "The Lewis Papers," quoted in Roger Lancelyn Green and Walter Hooper, *C. S. Lewis: A Biography*. Collins, 1974 [Harcourt Brace Jovanovich], 1974.
Of Arthur Greeves's family on p. 40;
of Arthur Greeves on p. 98.

167. Early Prose Autobiography (the story of "Joy") quoted in Roger Lancelyn Green and Walter Hooper, *C. S. Lewis: A Biography*. Collins [Harcourt Brace Jovanovich], 1974, p. 113.

168. Passages from "The Dark Tower" quoted in Roger Lancelyn Green and Walter Hooper, *C. S. Lewis: A Biography*. Collins [Harcourt Brace Jovanovich], 1974, pp. 166–8. (Reprinted in *The Dark Tower and Other Stories*.)

169. Testimonial for Frank Goodridge (*c.* 1952) quoted in *CSL: The Bulletin of the New York C. S. Lewis Society*, Whole No. 75 (Jan. 1976), p. 13.

170. "Great War" Documents: Excerpts from *Clivi Hamiltonis Summae Metaphysices contra Anthroposophos Libri II*, quoted in Lionel Adey, "Enjoyment, Contemplation, and Hierarchy in *Hamlet*," in *Evolution of Consciousness: Studies in*

*Polarity.* Edited by Shirley Sugerman. Middletown, Connecticut: Wesleyan University Press, 1976, p. 151.

171. Annotations to Shakespeare quoted in Lionel Adey, "C. S. Lewis's Annotations to His Shakespeare Volumes," *CSL: The Bulletin of the New York C. S. Lewis Society,* VIII, No. 7 (May 1977), pp. 1–8.

172. Little Lea Diary ("My Life During the Exmas Holadys of 1907") quoted in Humphrey Carpenter, *The Inklings: C. S. Lewis, J. R. R. Tolkien, Charles Williams, and their friends.* London: Allen & Unwin, 1978, pp. 3, 4.

173. Wynyard School Diary (Nov. 1909) quoted in Humphrey Carpenter, *The Inklings: C. S. Lewis, J. R. R. Tolkien, Charles Williams, and their friends.* London: Allen & Unwin, 1978.

174. Oxford Diary quoted in Humphrey Carpenter, *The Inklings: C. S. Lewis, J. R. R. Tolkien, Charles Williams, and their friends.* London: Allen & Unwin, 1978. [13 Sept. 1923] on p. 11; [4 July 1923; 27 Nov. 1922] on p. 12; [15–25 July 1923] on p. 13; [16 Oct.; 2 Nov. 1922] on p. 14; [21 Feb. 1923] on p. 15; [19 Jan. 1927] on p. 20; [15 June 1926] on p. 21; [11 May 1926] on p. 22; [8 Feb. 1927] on p. 28; [5 Jan. 1924] on p. 39; [26 May 1926] on p. 40; [13 June 1926] on p. 40; [18 Jan. 1927] on p. 40; [9 July 1922] on p. 164; [Autumn 1923—visit to Owen Barfield] on p. 164. (Reprinted in *All My Road Before Me.*)

175. Pen portraits quoted in Humphrey Carpenter, *The Inklings: C. S. Lewis, J. R. R. Tolkien, Charles Williams, and their friends.* London: Allen & Unwin, 1978.
Of Michael Denne Parker on p. 18;
of T. D. Weldon on p. 18.
(Reprinted in the Magdalen College Appendix of *All My Road Before Me.*)

176. "Commentary on the Lay of Leithian" (for J. R. R. Tolkien) quoted in Humphrey Carpenter, *The Inklings: C. S. Lewis, J. R. R. Tolkien, Charles Williams, and their friends.* London: Allen & Unwin, 1978, pp. 30–31.

177. Oxford Diary (7 July 1923) quoted in Lionel Adey, *C. S. Lewis's "Great War" with Owen Barfield.* Victoria, B.C.: University of Victoria, 1978, p. 13. (Reprinted in *All My Road Before Me.*)

178. Boxen Manuscripts ("Boxen: or Scenes from Boxonian City Life") quoted in Chad Walsh, *The Literary Legacy of C. S. Lewis.* Harcourt Brace Jovanovich, 1979, pp. 123–25.

179. "The Quest of Bleheris," quoted in Chad Walsh, *The Literary Legacy of C. S. Lewis.* Harcourt Brace Jovanovich, 1979, pp. 126–27, 128.

180. Narnian Manuscripts in Walter Hooper, *Past Watchful Dragons: The Narnian Chronicles of C. S. Lewis.* New York: Macmillan, 1979; London: Collins, 1980. (1) "The Lefay Fragment" on pp. 48–65; (2) "Eustace's Diary" on pp. 68–71.

181. Oxford Diary quoted in C. S. Lewis, *They Stand Together: The Letters of C. S. Lewis to Arthur Greeves (1914–1963).* Edited by Walter Hooper, 1979. 4 and 5 Aug. 1922 on pp. 22–23; 9–23 Sept. 1922 on p. 292; 11 July 1923 on pp. 294–95; 18 July 1922 on p. 310.

182. Pen portraits quoted from "The Lewis Papers," in *They Stand Together,* 1979.
Of Arthur Greeves's parents on pp. 16–18;
of Arthur Greeves on pp. 24–26.

183. Martlet Society Minutes for 26 Feb. 1919 (University College, Oxford) quoted in

*They Stand Together,* p. 250, Note 6.

184. Testimonial for Norman Bradshaw (4 Dec. 1938) in the *Canadian C. S. Lewis Journal,* No. 11 (Nov. 1979), p. 2. (Reprinted in Stephen Schofield, *In Search of C. S. Lewis,* pp. 17–18.)

185. Original Spenser lecture notes used in Cambridge, quoted in Margaret Hannay, *C. S. Lewis.* New York: Frederick Ungar, 1981, pp. 158–63. (Dr. Hannay was quoting from the holograph pages in *Spenser's Images of Life.*)

186. Parts of original BBC broadcasts (1942) not included in the published versions, quoted in Walter Hooper's Introduction to C. S. Lewis, *Mere Christianity.* Anniversary Edition. Edited by Walter Hooper. New York: Macmillan, 1981, pp. xiv–xv, xvii–xviii, xx–xxi.

187. "Answers to Listeners' Questions," holograph of the typescript Lewis read over the BBC on 3 Sept. 1941, in Appendix A of *Mere Christianity,* Anniversary Edition. (Rewritten to form Chapter II ["Some Objections"] in *Broadcast Talks.*)

188. "The Anvil," BBC broadcast in which Lewis took part, 22 July 1943. Included as Appendix C in *Mere Christianity,* Anniversary Edition, pp. 207–11.

189. Wynyard School Diary (Nov. 1909) quoted in Walter Hooper, *Through Joy and Beyond: A Pictorial Biography of C. S. Lewis.* New York: Macmillan, 1982, p. 19.

190. Wynyard School Diary (Nov. 1909) quoted in Walter Hooper, "C. S. Lewis in Hertfordshire (2): Wynyard School's Tormentor," *Hertfordshire Countryside,* XXXVII (Oct. 1982), p. 35.

191. Passage from essay on "Christian Reunion" in Walter Hooper's Foreword to John Randolph Willis, *Pleasures Forevermore: The Theology of C. S. Lewis.* Chicago: Loyola University Press, 1983, p. xv.

192. "Great War" Document: *Summae Metaphysices contra Anthroposophos* quoted in Stephen Thorson, "Knowing and Being in C. S. Lewis's 'Great War' with Owen Barfield," *CSL: The Bulletin of the New York C. S. Lewis Society,* XV (Nov. 1983), pp. 1–8.

193. Oxford Diary (25 Dec. 1922) quoted in Kathryn Lindskoog, "C. S. Lewis on Christmas," *Christianity Today* (16 Dec. 1983), pp. 24–5.

194. "Great War" Document. Annotations to *Summae Metaphysices contra Anthroposophos* quoted in Lionel Adey, "A Response to Dr. Thorson," and in Stephen Thorson, "A Reply," *CSL: The Bulletin of the New York C. S. Lewis Society,* XV (March 1984), pp. 6–11.

195. Oxford Diary (4 July 1922; 12 Sept. 1923; 22 Feb. 1924; 3 June 1926) quoted in Peter J. Schakel, *Reason and Imagination in C. S. Lewis: A Study of "Till We Have Faces."* Grand Rapids: Eerdmans, 1984, p. 44.

196. "The Emancipation of Women," a portion of the essay "Modern Man and His Categories of Thought" published in full in *Present Concerns.* The essay was written for the World Council of Churches, Assembly Commission II, materials on "God's Design and Man's Witness," Oct. 1946, and this portion was published in *CSL: The Bulletin of the New York C. S. Lewis Society,* XVII, No. 4 (Feb. 1986), pp. 4–5.

197. Oxford Diary quoted in William Griffin, *Clive Staples Lewis: A Dramatic Life.* San Francisco: Harper & Row, 1986; Tring: Lion, 1988. (Nov.–Dec. 1923) on p. 15; (29 May 1923) on p. 21; (12 Sept. 1923) on p. 21; (1 May 1926) on p. 27;

[28 April 1926] on pp. 29–30; (12 May 1926) on p. 30; (24 Jan. 1927) on p. 37; [5 Feb. 1927] on p. 38; (10 Feb. 1927) on p. 38. (Reprinted in *All My Road Before Me*.)

198. "The Moral Good—Its Place Among the Values" (the fourteen lectures Lewis gave in the University of Oxford in 1924–1925). The section called the "Critique of Locke" is quoted in James Patrick, *The Magdalen Metaphysicals: Idealism and Orthodoxy at Oxford 1901–1945*. Macon, Georgia: Mercer University Press, 1987, pp. 116–17.

199. Pen portraits quoted in George Sayer, *Jack: C. S. Lewis and His Times*. London: Macmillan, 1988.
Of P. V. M. Benecke on p. 111;
of T. D. Weldon on p. 132.
(Reprinted in the "Magdalen College Appendix" of *All My Road Before Me*.)

200. "The Quest of Bleheris" (prose romance written in 1916) quoted in George Sayer, *Jack: C. S. Lewis and His Times*. London: Macmillan, 1988, pp. 59–60.

201. Diaries quoted in George Sayer, *Jack: C. S. Lewis and His Times*. London: Macmillan, 1988.
Little Lea Diary: ("My Life During the Exmas Holadys of 1907") on p. 20; (23 Feb. 1908) on p. 21;
Oxford Diary: [3 April; 25 April; 6 April; 3 June 1922] on p. 93; [14 July; 19 Aug.; 3 Aug. 1922] on p. 95; [8 Aug. 1922] on p. 96; (29 Feb. 1924) on p. 102; [13–25 July 1923] on p. 102; [19 May 1924] on p. 103; [23 May, 24 May 1924] on p. 104; (5 June 1924) on p. 105; [12 June; 21–24 June 1924] on p. 105; (6 Feb. 1925) on p. 105; (10 Feb 1925) on p. 106; (29 July 1924) on p. 106; [1–3 Aug. 1924] on p. 107; [17 Aug. 1925] on pp. 107–8; [5 Feb. 1927] on p. 118; [1 Feb. 1927] on p. 120; [24 Jan. 1927] on p. 120; (18 Jan. 1927) on p. 131.
(The entries from the Oxford Diary are reprinted in *All My Road Before Me*.)

202. Boxen Manuscripts quoted in A. N. Wilson, *C. S. Lewis: A Biography*. Collins [W. W. Norton], 1990, pp. 17, 34.

203. Essay on Richard Wagner (1911) quoted in A. N. Wilson, *C. S. Lewis: A Biography*. Collins [W. W. Norton], 1990, pp. 30, 32.

204. Diaries quoted in A. N. Wilson, *C. S. Lewis: A Biography*. Collins [W. W. Norton], 1990.
Little Lea Diary: ("My Life During the Exmas Holadys of 1907") on p. 17;
Oxford Diary: [25 May 1923] on p. 69; [24 June 1922] on p. 74; [20 June 1923] on p. 76; [1 June 1923] on p. 80 [4 Feb. 1923] on p. 81; [21 Feb., 23 Feb., 12 March 1923] on p. 82; [18 June 1923, 21 June 1922] on p. 84; [5 Jan. 1924] on p. 86; [18 June 1922], [13–25 July 1923] on p. 88; [29 Aug. 1925] on pp. 93–94; [27 May 1926] on p. 98; [24 Jan. 1927] on p. 99; [13–25 July 1923] on p. 101; [11 May 1926] on p. 105.
(All but the first two entries are reprinted in *All My Road Before Me*.)

## E. SINGLE SHORT POEMS

75. "Leaving For Ever the Home of One's Youth," *Occasional Poets: An Anthology*. Edited by Richard Adams. Harmondsworth, Middlesex: Penguin Books, 1986, p. 101.

76. "Finchley Avenue," *Occasional Poets: An Anthology*. Edited by Richard Adams. Harmondsworth, Middlesex: Penguin Books, 1986, pp. 102–4.

77. "West Germanic to Primitive Old English" (fifteen lines of a mnemonic poem) quoted in Walter Hooper's Preface to C. S. Lewis, *Selected Literary Essays*. Edited by Walter Hooper. Cambridge: Cambridge University Press, 1969, p. xv.

78. "Loki Bound" (seven lines of a poem written in 1914) quoted in Walter Hooper's Preface to C. S. Lewis, *Narrative Poems*. Edited by Walter Hooper. London: Geoffrey Bles, 1969 [Harcourt, Brace & World, 1972], p. xiii.

79. Epitaph for his Wife (a holograph) in Douglas Gilbert and Clyde S. Kilby, *C. S. Lewis: Images of His World*. Grand Rapids: Eerdmans, 1973, p. 65. (Lewis had written two versions of this epitaph, but without having his wife in mind, and one of those is found in *Poems*. Joy Davidman chose one for her own epitaph, and Lewis revised it extensively in 1963 before it was cut into the stone seen in this photograph.)

80. Verses in imitation of Ovid's *Pars estis pauci* quoted in Roger Lancelyn Green and Walter Hooper, *C. S. Lewis: A Biography*. Collins [Harcourt Brace Jovanovich], 1974, p. 38.

81. A stanza of the "Ballade of a Winter's Morning" quoted in Roger Lancelyn Green and Walter Hooper, *C. S. Lewis: A Biography*. Collins [Harcourt Brace Jovanovich], 1974, p. 44.

82. "I think, if it be truth, as some have taught," in Roger Lancelyn Green and Walter Hooper, *C. S. Lewis: A Biography*. Collins [Harcourt Brace Jovanovich], 1974, p. 49.

83. "You rest upon me all my days," with preface to the manuscript "Half Hours with Hamilton," quoted in Roger Lancelyn Green and Walter Hooper, *C. S. Lewis: A Biography*. Collins [Harcourt Brace Jovanovich], 1974, p. 112. This is an earlier version of the poem published in *The Pilgrim's Regress* (Bk. 8, ch. vi) and reprinted as "Caught" in *Poems*.

84. Narrative Verse Autobiography (the story of "Joy"; the only surviving lines), in Roger Lancelyn Green and Walter Hooper, *C. S. Lewis: A Biography*. Collins [Harcourt Brace Jovanovich], 1974, p. 127.

85. "Perelandra" (a fragment of verse that appears to be the idea for *Perelandra*) quoted in Roger Lancelyn Green and Walter Hooper, *C. S. Lewis: A Biography*. Collins [Harcourt Brace Jovanovich], 1974, p. 171, n. 1.

86. "Prayer for a Brother" (written when his brother was in World War II), in Roger Lancelyn Green and Walter Hooper, *C. S. Lewis: A Biography*. Collins [Harcourt Brace Jovanovich], 1974, p. 183.

87. "Cupid and Psyche" (lines from a fragmentary poem written in 1923 and later retold in *Till We Have Faces*), quoted in Roger Lancelyn Green and Walter Hooper, *C. S. Lewis: A Biography*. Collins [Harcourt Brace Jovanovich], 1974, pp. 250, 262.

88. "Two at the table . . ." (in the meter of *Beowulf*, about J. R. R. Tolkien and E. V. Gordon examining in the English School) quoted in Humphrey Carpenter, *The Inklings: C. S. Lewis, J. R. R. Tolkien, Charles Williams, and their friends*. London: Allen & Unwin, 1978, p. 55.

89. "Poem for Arthur Greeves" (1913) in C. S. Lewis, *They Stand Together: The Letters*

        *of* C. S. *Lewis to Arthur Greeves (1914–1963).* Edited by Walter Hooper. Collins [Macmillan], 1979, p. [5].

90. "Song" (an earlier version of the one in *Spirits in Bondage*) quoted in the letter of 23 May 1918, in C. S. Lewis, *They Stand Together: The Letters of* C. S. *Lewis to Arthur Greeves (1914–1963).* Edited by Walter Hooper. Collins [Macmillan], 1979, pp. *215–16.*

91. "Nimue" (the only surviving lines of a poem later destroyed) quoted in the letter of 18 Sept. 1919, in C. S. Lewis, *They Stand Together: The Letters of* C. S. *Lewis to Arthur Greeves (1914–1963).* Edited by Walter Hooper. Collins [Macmillan], 1979, p. 261.

92. "Lilith" (an earlier version of the poem that was first published in *The Pilgrim's Regress* [1933] and later revised for the edition of 1943) quoted in the letter of 29 April 1930; in *They Stand Together: The Letters of* C. S. *Lewis to Arthur Greeves (1914–1963).* Edited by Walter Hooper. Collins [Macmillan], 1979, pp. 353–4. (Lewis gave it no title.)

93. "Poem for Jill Flewett," written in the front of a copy of *The Screwtape Letters;* in Jill (Flewett) Freud, "Lewis teaches the Retarded," the *Canadian* C. S. *Lewis Journal,* No. 16 (April 1980), p. 5. (Reprinted in Stephen Schofield, *In Search of* C. S. *Lewis.* South Plainfield, N.J.: Bridge, 1983, p. 59.)

94. "Two Kinds of Memory." This holograph poem is found in Eugene McGovern, "C. S. Lewis," *Dictionary of Literary Biography,* XV, British Novelists 1930–59. Detroit: Gale Publishers, 1983, p. 304. There are substantial differences between this version and the one in *Poems.*

95. "Loki Bound" (nine lines, different from those in the Preface to *Narrative Poems,* written in 1914) quoted in Walter Hooper's Preface to a reprint of C. S. Lewis, *Spirits in Bondage: A Cycle of Lyrics.* Harcourt Brace Jovanovich, 1984, p. xvi.

96. "Posturing" (an early version [1929] of the poem that was first published in *The Pilgrim's Regress*), in C. S. Lewis, "Commentary on the Lay of Leithian," in J. R. R. Tolkien, *The Lays of Beleriand.* Edited by Christopher Tolkien. London: George Allen & Unwin, 1985, pp. 321–2.

97. An earlier version ("They tell me, Lord . . .") of "Prayer," not included in *Poems,* is found in C. S. Lewis, *Letters to Malcolm: Chiefly on Prayer.* A slightly different version, found in a letter to Dom Bede Griffiths of *c.* June 1931, is reproduced in William Griffin, *Clive Staples Lewis: A Dramatic Life.* San Francisco: Harper & Row, 1986, pp. 149–50. This biography is published in England by Lion, in Tring, under the title C. S. *Lewis: The Authentic Voice,* 1988, p. 152.

98. An earlier version of "Pattern" in *Poems,* entitled "Some Believe." This earlier version appears to be a revision of the poem entitled "Experiment." It is reproduced in William Griffin, *Clive Staples Lewis: A Dramatic Life.* San Francisco: Harper & Row, 1986, pp. 258–9. Published in England by Lion, in Tring, under the title C. S. *Lewis: The Authentic Voice,* 1988, pp. 248–9.

99. "Epigram ('Call *him* a Fascist?')," included in a letter to Ruth Pitter of 6 June 1947, reproduced in William Griffin, *Clive Staples Lewis: A Dramatic Life.* San Francisco: Harper & Row, 1986, p. 270. Published in England by Lion, in Tring, under the title C. S. *Lewis: The Authentic Voice,* 1988, p. 258.

100. "The Hills of Down" (1915), first of two stanzas quoted in A. N. Wilson, C. S. *Lewis: A Biography*. Collins [W. W. Norton], 1990, p. 48.
101. Fragment (describing W. T. Kirkpatrick) of Autobiographical Poem, quoted in A. N. Wilson, C. S. *Lewis: A Biography*. Collins [W. W. Norton], 1990, p. 251.

## G. PUBLISHED LETTERS

85. "Version Vernacular," *The Christian Century*, LXXV (31 Dec. 1958), p. 1515. (Reprinted in *God in the Dock*, p. 338.)
86. Letter to Roger Lancelyn Green [28 Dec. 1938] quoted in Roger Lancelyn Green, *C. S. Lewis*. London: Bodley Head, 1963, p. 26.
87. Letter to Edward Meskys (3 Oct. 1963) in *Niekas*, No. 7 (Dec. 1963), no p.n.
88. Letters quoted in *Light on C. S. Lewis*. Edited by Jocelyn Gibb. London: Geoffrey Bles, 1965 [Harcourt, Brace & World, 1966].
    To Owen Barfield ("Great War Letter" *c*. 1927, beginning "After writing lectures all morning") on p. xviii;
    to Charles A. Huttar (30 March 1962) on p. xix;
    to John Lawlor (1954) on p. 77.
89. Letter to William Borst (*c*. 1954) of Harcourt, Brace & World quoted in Walter Hooper's Preface to C. S. Lewis, *Studies in Medieval and Renaissance Literature*. Edited by Walter Hooper. Cambridge: Cambridge University Press, 1966, pp. viii–ix.
90. Letter to Dom Bede Griffiths [*c*. 1934] quoted in Walter Hooper's Preface to C. S. Lewis, *Christian Reflections*. Edited by Walter Hooper. London: Geoffrey Bles [Grand Rapids: Eerdmans], 1967, p. vii.
91. Letter to a Little Girl [Ruth Broady] (26 Oct. 1963) quoted in C. S. Lewis, *A Mind Awake*. Edited by Clyde S. Kilby. London: Geoffrey Bles, 1968 [Harcourt, Brace & World, 1969], p. 123.
92. Letter to his father, A. J. Lewis (14 Aug. 1925) quoted in Walter Hooper's Preface to C. S. Lewis, *Selected Literary Essays*. Edited by Walter Hooper. Cambridge: Cambridge University Press, 1969, p. xiii. (Reprinted in Revised *Letters of C. S. Lewis*.)
93. Letters to Arthur Greeves (2 Dec. 1918; 14 July 1919; 18 Sept. 1919) quoted in Walter Hooper's Preface to C. S. Lewis, *Narrative Poems*. Edited by Walter Hooper. London: Geoffrey Bles, 1969, pp. ix–x. (Reprinted in C. S. Lewis, *They Stand Together*.)
94. Letter to John Warwick Montgomery (29 Aug. 1963) printed in Appendix B, John Warwick Montgomery, *Where Is History Going?* Grand Rapids: Zondervan, 1969, p. 222.
95. Letters to [Arthur Greeves] (13 and 30 Aug. 1930) quoted in Glenn Sadler, "Fantastic Imagination in George MacDonald," in *Imagination and the Spirit: Essays in Literature and the Christian Faith presented to Clyde S. Kilby*. Edited by Charles Huttar. Grand Rapids: Eerdmans, 1971, pp. 218, 225, 226. (Reprinted in C. S. Lewis, *They Stand Together*.)
96. Letter to Anne and Martin Kilmer [7 Aug. 1957] quoted in Margaret Hannay, "C. S. Lewis Collection at Wheaton College," *Mythlore*, II, No. 4 (Winter 1972), p. 20.

97. Letters to Mervyn Peake (20 June 1959, 2 Oct. 1958) quoted in Maeve Gilmore and Shelagh Johnson, *Mervyn Peake: Writings and Drawings*. London: Academy Editions [St. Martin's Press], 1974, pp. 46, 83.

98. Letters to his father, A. J. Lewis, quoted in Roger Lancelyn Green and Walter Hooper, *C. S. Lewis: A Biography*. Collins [Harcourt Brace Jovanovich], 1974. [19 Sept. 1908] on pp. 27–8; (Jan. 1911) on p. 29; [? Sept. 1913] on p. 34; [28 Sept. 1913] on pp. 34–5; (18 March 1913) on p. 35; [22 June 1914] on pp. 37–8; [7 Dec. 1916] on p. 46; [28 Jan. 1917] on p. 47; [8 Feb. 1917] on p. 47; [10 June 1917] on p. 51; (27 Aug. 1917) on p. 52; [10 Sept. 1917] on p. 52; (15, 16 Nov.; 13 Dec. 1917) on p. 53; (17 April 1918) on p. 55; (14 May 1918) on p. 55; [20? June 1918] on p. 57; (8 Dec. 1918) on p. 59; (27 Jan. 1919) on p. 60; [4 Feb. 1919] on p. 61; [5 March 1919] on p. 62; (25 May 1919) on p. 64; (4 April 1920) on p. 65; (18 May 1922) on p. 68; (1 July 1923) on p. 75; [22 Nov. 1923] on p. 78; [Note to end of 1923 diary] on p. 78; [15 Oct. 1924] on pp. 80–1; [11 Feb. 1925] on p. 82; [April 1925] on p. 82; [14 Aug. 1925] on p. 83; (21 Oct. 1925) on pp. 84–5; (4 Dec. 1925) on p. 86; (25 Jan. 1926) on pp. 86–7; (5 June 1926) on p. 88; [29 July 1927] on p. 93; (10 July 1928) on p. 96; [9 July 1929] on p. 96; (10 July 1928) on p. 148; (30 March 1927) on p. 181.

99. Letters quoted in Roger Lancelyn Green and Walter Hooper, *C. S. Lewis: A Biography*. Collins [Harcourt Brace Jovanovich], 1974.

To Mrs. Edward A. Allen (26 Nov. 1955) on p. 286;

to Delmar Banner (6 June 1954) on p. 281;

to Owen Barfield (6 May 1932) on p. 127; (29 Oct. 1932) on p. 128;

to Pauline Baynes (21 Jan. 1954) on p. 246;

to Geoffrey Bles (20 March 1953) on pp. 245–6; (11 March 1953) on p. 248;

to Charles A. Brady (23 Oct. 1944) on p. 164;

to R. W. Chapman (18 Sept. 1935) on pp. 132–3;

to Claude Chavasse (25 Feb. 1934) on p. 130;

to Arthur C. Clarke (7 Dec. 1943) on p. 173; [14 Feb. 1953] on pp. 177–8;

to E. R. Eddison (16 Nov., 19 Dec., 29 Dec. 1942) on p. 213;

to T. S. Eliot (19 April 1931) on pp. 125–6; (2 June 1931) on p. 126; (18 May 1962) on p. 296;

to Vera Gebbert (15 July 1960) on pp. 276–7;

to Jocelyn Gibb (28 June 1963) on p. 233; (16, 29 Feb. 1956) on p. 261; (9 May 1960) on p. 275;

to Roger Lancelyn Green [16 Sept. 1945] on p. 70; (28 Dec. 1938) on p. 163; (17 Nov. 1957) on pp. 163–4; [25 March 1962] on p. 240; [4 April 1950] on p. 244; (6 March 1951) on p. 244; (26 Sept. 1952) on p. 245; (22 Feb. 1954) on p. 248; (1 May 1952) on p. 255; (29 March 1952) on p. 258; (5 Feb. 1957) on p. 268; (8 May 1957) on p. 268; (10 Dec. 1957) on p. 268; ([16] July 1953) on pp. 282–3; (29 Aug. 1958) on p. 294; ([6] Sept. 1961) on p. 295; ([28 Jan.] 1963) on p. 297; (11 Aug. 1963) on p. 303; (1 Nov. 1963) on p. 306;

to Joy Davidman Gresham (22 Dec. 1953) on p. 178;

to A. K. Hamilton-Jenkin (21 March 1930) on p. 106;

to Cyril Hartmann (25 July and n.d. 1919) on p. 65;

to Walter Hooper ([2] July 1962) on p. 298;

to William L. Kinter (30 July 1954; 14 Feb. 1951; 27 Nov. 1951; 28 March 1953;

30 July 1954) on p. 179;

to Richard Ladborough (28 Oct. 1963) on p. 306;

to W. H. Lewis [3 Sept. 1927] on p. 93; [12 Dec. 1927] on pp. 94, 95; ([1] April 1928) on p. 95; (25 Aug.; 29 Sept. 1929) on p. 97; [12 Jan. 1930] on p. 99; (22 Nov. 1931] on p. 124; (3 Dec. 1939) on p. 186; (21 July 1940) on p. 191; (2, 18 Sept. 1939) on p. 238;

to Sister Penelope (9 Nov. 1941) on p. 170; (11 May 1942) on p. 170; [6 Sept. 1944] on p. 177; (28 May 1945) on pp. 179–80, 224, 226; (24 Oct. 1940) on p. 198, 221–2; (4 Nov. 1940) on p. 198; (9 Oct. 1941) on p. 199; (15 May 1941) on p. 205; (30 Dec. 1950) on pp. 229–30; (5 June 1951) on p. 257; (30 July 1960) on p. 281; ([15 Feb.] 1954) on p. 297; ([17] Sept. 1963) on p. 304;

to the Marquess of Salisbury (9 March 1947) on p. 228;

to the Editor of *The Saturday Evening Post* (17 Oct. 1963) on pp. 304–5;

to Alec Vidler (23 March 1939) on p. 137;

to Chad Walsh (21 Oct. 1959) on p. 270; (23 May 1960) on pp. 275–6;

to Mrs. Watt (28 Aug. 1958) on p. 269;

to James W. Welch (10 Feb. 1941) on p. 202;

to Laurence Whistler (9 Jan. 1947) on p. 153; [April 1947] on pp. 153–4;

to Basil Willey (26 Oct. 1956) on p. 289; (22 Oct. 1963) on p. 306.

100. Letters to Arthur Greeves quoted in Roger Lancelyn Green and Walter Hooper, *C. S. Lewis: A Biography.* Collins [Harcourt Brace Jovanovich], 1974. (Reprinted in *They Stand Together.*) [26 Sept. 1914] on p. 42; [6 Oct. 1914] on p. 43; [26 Jan. 1915] on p. 44; [7 March 1916] on p. 44; [27 Sept. 1916] on p. 45; [15 Feb.; 28 Feb. 1917] on p. 48; (12 Oct. 1916) on pp. 48–9; [6 March 1917] on p. 50; [28 April 1917] on pp. 50–1; [13 May 1917] on p. 51; [10 June 1917] on pp. 51–2; [8 July 1917] on p. 52; (28 Oct. 1917) on p. 53; (29 May 1918) on p. 55; (12 Sept. 1918) on p. 58; [6? Oct. 1918] on p. 58; (2 Nov. 1918) on p. 58; (2 Dec. 1918) on p. 59; [26 Jan. 1919] on p. 61; [5 May 1919] on pp. 63–4; [June 1921] on pp. 65–6; [22 April 1923] on p. 77; ([3] Dec. 1929) on p. 88; [26 June 1927] on p. 93; [5 Nov. 1929] on p. 97; [22, 26 Dec. 1929] on p. 98; (9 Jan. 1930) on p. 104; (5, 26, Jan. 1930) on p. 105; (30 Jan. 1930) on pp. 105–6; (7 June 1930) on pp. 106–7; (30 June 1930) on pp. 107–8; (8 July 1930) on p. 108; (15 June 1930) on p. 109; (29 July 1930) on pp. 109–10; (18 Aug. 1930) on p. 110; (22 June 1930) on p. 111; (28 Aug. 1930) on p. 111; (10 Jan. 1931) on p. 113; (17 Jan. 1931) on p. 114; (1 June 1930) on p. 114; (5 Sept. 1931) on p. 115; (1 Oct. 1931) on p. 116; (11 Oct. 1931) on pp. 117–18; (1 Oct. 1931) on pp. 119–20; (6 Dec. 1931) on p. 121; (25 March 1933) on p. 128; [17 Dec. 1932] on p. 129; (4 Dec. 1932) on p. 129; (4 Feb. 1933) on p. 131; (17 Aug. 1933) on p. 131; (26 Feb. 1936) on pp. 133–4; (23 Dec. 1941) on p. 170, 203, 206.

101. Letters to Arthur Greeves (6 March 1917) and to his father (4 Dec. 1915) quoted in Roger Lancelyn Green, "C. S. Lewis and Andrew Lang," *Notes and Queries,* N.S., XXII (May 1975), pp. 208–9. (Reprinted in *CSL: The Bulletin of the New York C. S. Lewis Society,* LXIX (July 1975), p. 11.)

102. Letter to Chad Walsh (*c.* 1949) quoted in Chad Walsh's Afterword to C. S. Lewis, *A Grief Observed.* New York: Bantam, 1976, p. 110.

103. Letters to Kathryn Stillwell (Lindskoog) (24 April 1956, 29 Oct. 1957) in Kathryn Lindskoog, "C. S. Lewis: Reactions from Women," *Mythlore,* III, No. 4 (June

1976), p. 19. The same letters (24 April 1956, 29 Oct. 1957) in *Voyage to Narnia Response Book,* Lifestyle Series for Young Adults. Elgin, Illinois: David C. Cook, 1978, pp. 6–7. Holograph letter (29 Oct. 1957) in the *Canadian C. S. Lewis Journal,* No. 48 (Autumn 1984), pp. 14–15. Part of the letter of 29 Oct. 1957 appears on the back cover of Kathryn Lindskoog, *The Lion of Judah in Never-Never Land.*

104. Letters quoted in Clyde S. Kilby, *Tolkien and the Silmarillion.* Wheaton, Illinois: Harold Shaw, 1976.

To Francis Anderson (23 Sept. 1963) on p. 76;

to Charles Brady (29 Oct. 1944) on p. 48;

to Arthur Greeves [30 Jan. 1930, 4 Feb. 1933], (3 Dec. 1929, 22 Sept. 1931, 22 June 1930, 26 Feb. 1936, 11 Jan. 1944) on pp. 47, 48, 69, 70, 72, 73;

to Thomas Howard (28 Oct. 1958) on p. 48;

to W. H. Lewis (10 Sept. 1939) on p. 70;

to Sister Penelope (24 Aug. 1939) on p. 75.

105. Letters to Arthur Greeves quoted in Humphrey Carpenter, *The Inklings: C. S. Lewis, J. R. R. Tolkien, Charles Williams, and their friends.* London: Allen & Unwin, 1978. (Reprinted in *They Stand Together.*) (15 Feb. 1917) on p. 7; [4 Oct. 1916] on p. 8; (15 Feb. 1917) on p. 8; (26 Jan. 1919) on p. 10; (15 Oct. 1918) on p. 12; (3 Dec. 1929) on p. 28; (30 Jan. 1930) on p. 32; (22 Sept. 1931) on p. 33; (29 April 1930) on p. 35; [25 May 1940] on p. 38; (29 July 1930) on p. 42; (22 Sept. 1931) on pp. 43–4, 45; (18 Oct. 1931) on pp. 44, 46; (1 Oct. 1931) on p. 45; (8 Nov. 1931) on p. 47; (25 March 1933) on p. 53; (4 Feb. 1933) on p. 57; (26 Feb. 1936) on p. 99; (30 Jan. 1944) on p. 101; (27 Dec. 1940) on p. 131; (30 Jan. 1944) on pp. 179, 185; (25 Dec. 1941) on p. 189; (5 Jan. 1947) on p. 207; (11 Oct. 1952) on p. 233; (11 Sept. 1963) on p. 249.

106. Letters quoted in Humphrey Carpenter, *The Inklings: C. S. Lewis, J. R. R. Tolkien, Charles Williams, and their friends.* London: Allen & Unwin, 1978.

To Edward A. Allen (5 Dec. 1955) on p. 231;

to Mrs. Edward A. Allen (17 Jan. 1955) on p. 231;

to Leo Baker (Sept. 1920) on p. 39; (? 1921) on p. 158;

to Owen Barfield ("Great War Letter" [27 May 1928] beginning "After an unconscionable delay") on p. 18; (Letter [1928] beginning "You might like to know") on p. 42; (18 May 1945) on p. 203; (28 June 1936) on p. 219; (16 Dec. 1947) on p. 224;

to Derek Brewer (16 Nov. 1959) on p. 156;

to Arthur C. Clarke (26 Jan. 1954) on p. 158;

to Edward T. Dell (29 April 1963) on p. 175; (25 Oct. 1949) on p. 189;

to E. R. Eddison (16 Nov. 1942) on p. 190;

to George Every (4 Feb. 1941) on p. 64;

to Katharine Farrer (9 Feb. 1954) on p. 158; (4 Dec. 1953) on p. 160;

to W. O. Field (10 May 1943) on p. 35;

to Mrs. Vera Gebbert (23 Dec. 1953) on p. 237;

to Joy Davidman Gresham (22 Dec. 1953) on p. 219;

to Dom Bede Griffiths (25 May 1942) on p. 116; (10 May 1945) on p. 199; (22 April 1954) on p. 218;

to A. K. Hamilton-Jenkin (4 Nov. 1925) on p. 22; (21 March 1930) on p. 41;

to Mrs. Heck (29 Dec. 1958) on p. 223;

to Mr. Huttar (30 March 1962) on p. 186;

to William L. Kinter (29 Sept. 1951) on p. 66;

to A. J. Lewis [18 March 1914] on pp. 5, 6; [10 July 1928] on p. 17; [3 Nov. 1928] on p. 18;

to W. H. Lewis [12 Jan. 1930] on p. 14; [26 April 1927; 15 April 1928] on p. 34; (25 Dec. 1931; 24 Oct. 1931) on p. 55; (4 May 1940) on p. 115; (18 Nov. 1939; 28 Jan. 1940) on p. 118; (11 Feb. 1940) on p. 119; (18 Sept. 1939) on p. 174;

to Fr. Peter Milward (25 Dec. 1959) on p. 247;

to Sister Penelope (30 Dec. 1950) on p. 233;

to Ruth Pitter (29 Sept. 1945) on p. 47;

to Kathleen Raine (5 Dec. 1958) on p. 246;

to J. R. R. Tolkien (7 Dec. 1929) on p. 30; (21 Oct. 1949) on p. 226; (20 Nov. 1962) on p. 249;

to Basil Willey (22 Oct. 1963) on p. 246;

to Michal Williams (22 May 1945) on p. 203.

107. "Great War" Letter to Owen Barfield (beginning "I hope to return your sister's plays . . . "), quoted in Humphrey Carpenter, *The Inklings: C. S. Lewis, J. R. R. Tolkien, Charles Williams, and their friends.* London: Allen & Unwin, 1978, p. 37.

108. Letters quoted in Lionel Adey, *C. S. Lewis's "Great War" with Owen Barfield.* Victoria, B.C.: University of Victoria, 1978.

To Owen Barfield (24 Jan. 1926) on p. 14; (28 Feb. 1936) on p. 15;

to Arthur Greeves [9 Jan. 1930] on p. 11; [18 Oct. 1916] on p. 15; (21 Dec. 1929) on p. 18; ([24] Dec. 1929) on p. 18; [24 July 1915; 12 Oct. 1916; 18 Oct. 1916] on p. 126.

109. Letters to Lucy Matthews (14 Sept. 1957, 11 Sept. 1958) quoted in *Eglerio! In Praise of Tolkien.* Edited by Anne Etkin. Greencastle, Pennsylvania: Quest Communications, 1978, pp. 42–4. The second of these is G78 in this section of the Bibliography.

110. Letters quoted in C. S. Lewis, *They Stand Together: The Letters of C. S. Lewis to Arthur Greeves (1914–1963).* Edited by Walter Hooper. Collins [Macmillan], 1979.

To Leo Baker (Sept. 1920, 23 Dec. 1920) on pp. 284–5;

to his brother, W. H. Lewis, (9 June 1919) on pp. 257–8;

to his father, A. J. Lewis, (4 and 14 May 1918, 29 June 1919), 16 Feb. 1921) on pp. 213, 258, 299;

to Walter Hooper (11 Oct. 1963) on p. 31.

111. Letters to Corbin Scott Carnell (5 April 1953) and to Clyde S. Kilby (7 May 1959), in Michael Christensen, *C. S. Lewis on Scripture.* Waco, Texas: Word Books, 1979, pp. 97–9.

112. Letter to Rosamund Rieu (28 Sept. 1942) in *The Canadian C. S. Lewis Journal,* No. 4 (April 1979), p. 9. (Reprinted in *In Search of C. S. Lewis.*)

113. Letter to Patricia Mary Mackey (8 June 1960) in Walter Hooper, *Past Watchful Dragons: The Narnian Chronicles of C. S. Lewis.* New York: Macmillan, 1979; London: Collins, 1980, pp. 109–10.

114. Letter to William L. Kinter (30 July 1954) quoted in Peter J. Schakel, *Reading*

*with the Heart: The Way into Narnia.* Grand Rapids: Eerdmans, 1979, p. 9.

115. Letters quoted in Kathryn Lindskoog, *The Gift of Dreams: A Christian View.* New York: Harper & Row, 1979.
To Arthur Greeves (c. 1916; 15 Sept. 1930; 20 Dec. 1943) on pp. 136, 156–7;
to W. H. Lewis (17 April 1932) on p. 26;
to Lucy Matthews (11 Sept. 1958) on p. 76.

116. Letter to Mrs. William L. Krieg (6 May 1955) (see also G99) quoted in Martha C. Sammons, *A Guide Through Narnia.* Wheaton, Illinois: Harold Shaw, 1979, pp. 76–7.

117. Letters quoted in Leanne Payne, *Real Presence: The Holy Spirit in the Works of C. S. Lewis.* Westchester, Illinois: Cornerstone Books, 1979.
To Dom Bede Griffiths (19[13] Nov. 1950) on p. 100; (8 Jan. 1936) on p. 114;
(July 1936) on pp. 157, 161; (23 May 1936) on pp. 157–8;
to Harvey Karlsen (30 Oct. 1961) on pp. 73, 76;
to William L. Kinter (23 Dec. 1952) on p. 105;
to Sister Penelope (9 July [Aug.] 1939) on p. 154;
to Susan Salzberg (5 Feb. 1960) on p. 158.

118. Letters to Stephen Schofield (23 Aug. 1956 and 26 Feb. 1959) in the *Canadian C. S. Lewis Journal,* III (March 1979), p. 13. (Reprinted in Stephen Schofield, *In Search of C. S. Lewis.*)

119. Letter to Gracia Fay Ellwood (19 July 1960) in Gracia Fay Ellwood, "Of Creation and Love," *Mythlore,* VI, No. 4 (Fall 1979), p. 19.

120. Letter to W. H. Lewis (28 Jan. 1940) quoted in Walter Hooper's Introduction to C. S. Lewis, *The Weight of Glory and Other Addresses.* Revised and Expanded Edition. Edited by Walter Hooper. New York: Macmillan, 1980, p. xvi.

121. Letters to Mrs. Hook (29 Dec. 1958) and to Laurence Krieg and his mother, Mrs. William L. Krieg (6 May 1955, 21 April 1957, 23 Dec. 1957), quoted in Paul F. Ford, *A Companion to Narnia.* San Francisco: Harper & Row, 1980. pp. xxii–xxiii. The entire Lewis–Krieg correspondence was printed in Jeanette Anderson Bakke's "The Lion and the Lamb and the Children," an unpublished Ph.D. dissertation (Univ. of Minnesota, 1975) pp. 110–1, 342–8, along with a commentary by Laurence Krieg. Lewis's letters to Mrs. William L. Krieg (6 May 1955) and to Laurence Krieg (24 Oct. 1955, 27 April 1956, 21 April 1957, 23 Dec. 1957) are found in C. S. Lewis, *Letters to Children.* Edited by Lyle W. Dorsett and Marjorie Lamp Mead. New York: Macmillan; London: Collins, 1985, pp. 52–3, 57–8, 61–2, 68–9, 76.

122. Letters quoted in Christopher Derrick, *C. S. Lewis and the Church of Rome.* San Francisco: Ignatius, 1981.
To Spender Curtis Brown (1963) on p. 53;
to H. Lyman Stebbins (9 May 1945) on pp. 95–7.

123. Letters quoted in Walter Hooper's Introduction to C. S. Lewis, *Mere Christianity,* Anniversary Edition. New York: Macmillan, 1981.
To Rhona Bodle (11 April 1950) on p. xxxvi.
to Eric Fenn (17 May and 14 Nov. 1941; 4 Jan., 23 Feb., 28 June and 30 Nov. 1942; 16 June, 1 July, 27 and 31 Dec. 1943; 5 Jan., 10 Feb., and 25 March 1944) on pp. xiii, xvi, xvii, xxi, xxii, xxiv, xxvi–xxviii, xxx, xxxi, xxxv;
to R. S. Lee (6 and 23 Oct. 1944) on pp. xxxiii, xxxiv;

to J. W. Welch (10 Feb. 1941, 24 Nov. 1945) on pp. xi, xxxiv;

to J. R. Williams (30 Sept. 1941) on p. xvi.

124. Letters quoted in Richard L. Purtill, *C. S. Lewis's Case for the Christian Faith*. San Francisco: Harper & Row, 1981.

To Rhona Bodle (11 April 1950) on pp. 1, 10; (28 April 1955) on p. 100;

to Mr. Canfield (28 Feb. 1955) on pp. 57–8;

to Dom Bede Griffiths (8 Jan. 1936) on p. 17; (27 June 1949) on p. 81; (*c.* 1933) on p. 81; (27 Sept. 1948) on p. 84; (27? June 1937) on pp. 87–8; (20 Dec. 1946) on p. 103;

to Miss Jacob (3 July 1941) on p. 16; (13 Aug. 1941) on p. 38;

to Sister Madeleva (3 Oct. 1963) on p. 11;

to Keith Masson (6 March 1956) on pp. 97–8;

to Sister Penelope (30 Dec. 1950) on p. 34;

to Ruth Pitter (17 July 1951) on p. 11.

125. Letters quoted in Donald E. Glover, *C. S. Lewis: The Art of Enchantment*. Athens, Ohio: Ohio University Press, 1981.

To Leo Baker [April 1920; Sept. 1920] on p. 11; [July 1921] on p. 12;

to Owen Barfield (2 Sept. 1937) on p. 26;

to Harry Blamires (14 March 1954) on pp. 37, 123–4;

to Rhona Bodle (24 March 1954) on p. 35;

to Charles A. Brady (16 Nov. 1956) on p. 36;

to Arthur C. Clarke (20 Jan. 1956) on p. 38;

to E. R. Eddison (16 Nov. 1942) on pp. 31, 107, 220 [note 13]; [29? Dec. 1942] on p. 213 [note 64], 105; (29 April 1943) on pp. 78, 105;

to Allen C. Emery, Jr. (18 Aug. 1953), on pp. 36, 131;

to Katharine Farrer (4 Dec. 1953) on p. 37; (2 April 1955) on p. 187; (10 June 1952) on p. 188; (9 July 1955) on p. 188;

to Warfield M. Firor (27 June 1953) on p. 37; (15 Oct. 1949) on p. 41;

to Joy Davidman Gresham (22 Dec. 1953) on p. 38;

to Dom Bede Griffiths (8 Jan. 1936) on pp. 26–7; (20 Dec. 1946) on pp. 32–3, 124; (25 March 1948) on p. 172;

to George Rostrevor Hamilton (29 April 1943) on p. 213 [note 71];

to A. K. Hamilton-Jenkin (4 Nov. 1925) on pp. 13–4; (27 July [1928]) on pp. 15–6; (11 Jan. 1939) on p. 28; (30 May 1949) on p. 35; (27 May 1928) on p. 107;

to Carl Henry (28 Sept. 1955) on p. 131;

to Miss Jacob (13 Aug. 1941) on p. 29;

to Martin Kilmer (28 April 1958) on p. 214 [note 95];

to William L. Kinter (28 March 1953) on p. 35; (30 July 1954) on pp. 36, 108;

to Joan Lancaster (20 April 1959) on pp. 39, 189; (31 Aug. 1958) on p. 40; (15 April 1954; 7 May 1954) on p. 179;

to Keith Masson (3 June 1956) on p. 41;

to Vera Matthews (31 Oct. 1949) on p. 220 [note 15];

to Fr. Peter Milward (4 July 1955) on p. 214 [note 95]; (4 July 1955) on pp. 77, 109;

to Sister Penelope (4 Nov. 1940) on pp. 28, 92; (22 Aug. 1942) on p. 29; (25 March 1943) on pp. 30, 106; (31 Aug. 1948) on p. 35; (24 Oct. 1940) on p. 92; (9

Nov. 1941) on p. 92; (24 Sept. 1943) on p. 106;
to Ruth Pitter (4 Jan. 1947) on p. 33; (24 July 1946) on p. 34; (10 Aug. 1946) on
p. 34; (21 Dec. 1953) on p. 38; (20 Aug. 1962) on p. 41;
to Kathleen Raine (5 Oct. 1956) on p. 194;
to Susan Salzberg (5 Feb. 1960) on p. 36;
to Mrs. Sandeman (10 Dec. 1952) on p. 41;
to Martyn Skinner (31 Dec. 1959) on p. 220 [note 32].

126. Letters to Dorothy L. Sayers (23 Oct. and 14 Dec. 1945; 23 and 29 July, and 8 Aug.
1946; 11 Nov. 1949) quoted in James Barbazon, *Dorothy L. Sayers: The Life of
a Courageous Woman.* Gollancz [Scribners], 1981, pp. 235–6, 251–2.

127. Letters quoted in Margaret Patterson Hannay, *C. S. Lewis.* New York: Frederick
Ungar, 1981.
To W. H. Lewis (8 April 1932) on p. 18;
to Sister Penelope CSMV (10 Jan. 1952) on p. 180;
to Ruth Pitter (29 Dec. 1951) on p. 22;
to Mr. Welbore (18 Sept. 1936) on p. 228.

128. Letter to Cecil Roth (*c.* 1960) quoted in Irene Roth, *Cecil Roth: Historian Without
Tears. A Memoir.* New York: Sepher-Herman Press, 1982, p. 153.

129. Letters to Roger Lancelyn Green (28 Dec. 1938) and Ruth Pitter (4 Jan. 1947)
quoted in Walter Hooper's Preface to C. S. Lewis, *On Stories and Other Essays on Literature.* Collins, 1982, pp. 17, 18. [Harcourt Brace Jovanovich, 1982,
pp. xvi, xvii, as *Of This and Other Worlds.*]

130. Letter to Sarah Neylan (3 April 1949) quoted in George Sayer, "Reviews," *VII:
An Anglo-American Literary Review,* III (1982), 132.

131. Letters quoted in Walter Hooper, *Through Joy and Beyond: A Pictorial Biography of
C. S. Lewis.* New York: Macmillan, 1982.
To Owen Barfield [3? Feb. 1930] on p. 78;
to Sister Penelope (30 July 1954) on p. 129;
to Kathleen Raine (25 Oct. 1961) on p. 151;
to Dorothy L. Sayers (24 Dec. 1956) on p. 141; (25 June 1957) on pp. 143–5.

132. Letters quoted in Fred D. Crawford, *Mixing Memory and Desire.* University Park:
Pennsylvania State University, 1982.
To Theodora Bosanquet (27 Aug. 1942) on p. 99;
to E. R. Eddison (16 Nov. 1942) on p. 99;
to T. S. Eliot (22 Feb. 1943) on p. 101;
to Alastair Fowler (7 Jan. 1961) on p. 102;
to Dom Bede Griffiths (*c.* 1931) on p. 97;
to Sister Madeleva (7 June 1934) on p. 98;
to Charles Williams (20 July 1940) on p. 99.

133. Letters to his father, A. J. Lewis, ([19 Sept.] and 29 Sept. 1908) quoted in Walter
Hooper,"C. S. Lewis in Hertfordshire's 'Belsen' (1)," *Hertfordshire Countryside,* XXXVII (Sept. 1982), p. 18.

134. Letter to his father, A. J. Lewis, (1 March 1909) quoted in Walter Hooper, "C. S.
Lewis in Hertfordshire (2): Wynyard School's Tormentor," *Hertfordshire
Countryside,* XXXVII (Oct. 1982), p. 35.

135. Letters to Clyde S. Kilby (20 Nov. 1962) and to Owen Barfield (Sept. 1929 and 28
July 1927) quoted in Peter J. Schakel, "Seeing and Knowing: The Episte-

mology of C. S. Lewis's _Till We Have Faces,"VII: An Anglo-American Literary Review,_ IV (1983), pp. 85, 87, 89, 91.

136. Letters to Owen Barfield (16 Dec. 1947, and no date) quoted in John C. Ulrich Jr.'s Afterword to Owen Barfield, _Orpheus._ Edited by John C. Ulrich, Jr. West Stockbridge, Mass.: Lindisfarne, 1983, p. 118.

137. Letters quoted in Lyle W. Dorsett, _And God Came In_ (a biography of Joy Davidman). New York: Macmillan; London: Collins, 1983.
   To Vera Matthews Gebbert (23 Dec. 1953) on pp. 105–106;
   to William Lindsay Gresham (6 April 1957, two letters on same date) on pp. 134–5;
   to Dom Bede Griffiths (1 Aug. 1957) on p. 128;
   to Sister Penelope CSMV (12 Feb. 1958) on p. 137.

138. Letter to Nicholas Fridsma (15 Feb. 1946) in _CSL: The Bulletin of the New York C. S. Lewis Society,_ XV, No. 169 (Nov. 1983), p. 10.

139. Letters to W. H. Lewis (25 Dec. 1931, 24 Dec. 1939) quoted in Kathryn Lindskoog, "C. S. Lewis on Christmas," _Christianity Today_ (16 Dec. 1983), pp. 25–6.

140. Letter to Stephen Schofield (10 Oct. 1956) in Stephen Schofield, _In Search of C. S. Lewis._ New Jersey: Bridge, 1983, p. 195.

141. Letters quoted in Stephen Schofield, _In Search of C. S. Lewis._ South Plainfield, N. J.: Bridge, 1983.
   To Ruth Pitter (4 Jan. 1947) (a different portion from G95) on p. 138;
   to Stephen Schofield (23 Aug., 10 Oct. 1956, 26 Feb. 1959, 31 Jan. 1960, and c. 26 July 1960) on pp. 193–7.

142. Letters to his father, A. J. Lewis, quoted in Walter Hooper's Preface to a reprint of C. S. Lewis, _Spirits in Bondage: A Cycle of Lyrics._ Harcourt Brace Jovanovich, 1984. (14 Oct. 1914) on pp. xvii, xx; (3 Nov. 1914) on p. xxi; (8 Nov. 1914) on p. xviii; (17 May 1917) on p. xxvii; (13 Dec. 1917) on p. xxx; (3 Sept. 1918) on p. xxxiv; (9 Sept. 1918) on p. xxxiv; (18 Sept. 1918) on p. xxxv; (19 Sept. 1918) on p. xiii; (10 Nov. 1918) on pp. xxxv–vi.

143. Letter to Richard Selig (7 June 1954) in John Kirkpatrick, "A Lewis Pupil, Richard Selig 1929–57," _CSL: The Bulletin of the New York C. S. Lewis Society,_ XV, No. 180 (Oct. 1984), p. 5.

144. Letters quoted in Dabney Hart, _Through the Open Door: A New Look at C. S. Lewis._ University, Alabama: University of Alabama Press, 1984.
   To M. L. Charlesworth (9 April 1940) on p. 81;
   to Dabney (Adams) Hart (1 June 1956) and to Mr. Crow, her faculty advisor (28 May 1956), on pp. 5–6.

145. Letters to J. B. Phillips quoted in J. B. Phillips, _The Price of Success._ (Collins [Wheaton, Illinois: Harold Shaw], 1984.) (3 Aug. 1943) on pp. 100, 107; (1956) on p. 172.

146. Letter to Dom Bede Griffiths (5 Oct. 1938) quoted in Peter J. Schakel, _Reason and Imagination in C. S. Lewis: A Study of "Till We Have Faces."_ Grand Rapids: Eerdmans, 1984, p. 129.

147. "The Latin Letters, 1947–1961, of C. S. Lewis to Don Giovanni Calabria of Verona (1873–1954) and to Members of his Congregation," by Martin Moynihan in _VII: An Anglo-American Literary Review,_ VI (1985), pp. 7–22.

148. Letter to Cynthia Donnelly (14 Aug. 1954) in _CSL: The Bulletin of the New York_

*C. S. Lewis Society,* XVII, No. 185 (March 1985), p. 7.

149. Letters to W. H. Lewis [Nov. 1906 and *c.* Sept. 1906] in the Introduction to C. S. Lewis, *Letters to Children.* Edited by Lyle W. Dorsett and Marjorie Lamp Mead. New York: Macmillan; London: Collins, 1985, pp. 13–4.

150. Letters to W. H. Lewis (*c.* Sept. 1906 and *c.* June 1907 and [5 Oct. 1927]) quoted in Walter Hooper's Introduction to C. S. Lewis, *Boxen: The Imaginary World of the Young C. S. Lewis.* Edited by Walter Hooper. Collins [Harcourt Brace Jovanovich], 1985, pp. 10, 19.

151. Letter to J. R. R. Tolkien (7 Dec. 1929) quoted in J. R. R. Tolkien, *The Lays of Beleriand.* Edited by Christopher Tolkien. George Allen & Unwin [Boston: Houghton Mifflin, 1985], pp. 150–1.

152. Letter to Peter Philip (3 March 1955) quoted in the *Canadian C. S. Lewis Journal,* No. 49 (Winter 1985), p. 15.

153. Letter to John Beversluis (3 June 1963) in John Beversluis, *C. S. Lewis and the Search for Rational Religion.* Grand Rapids: Eerdmans, 1985, pp. 156–7.

154. Letter to Joyce Pearce (20 July 1943) in the *Canadian C. S. Lewis Journal,* No. 51 (Summer 1985), pp. 1, 3.

155. Letter (30 Aug. 1958) quoted in Katherine Gardiner, "C. S. Lewis as a Reader of Edmund Spenser," *CSL: The Bulletin of the New York C. S. Lewis Society,* XVI, No. 191 (Sept. 1985), p. 7.

156. Letter to Owen Barfield (28 June 1936) quoted in M. L. Mead's Afterword to Owen Barfield, *The Silver Trumpet.* Edited by Marjorie L. Mead. Longmont, Colorado: Bookmakers Guild, 1986, p. 121.

157. Letters to Arthur C. Clarke (20 Jan. 1954); to Sister Penelope (25 March 1943); and to Dom Bede Griffiths (26 May 1943) in Kath Filmer, "The Polemic Image: The Role of Metaphor and Symbol in the Fiction of C. S. Lewis" in *VII: An Anglo-American Literary Review,* VII (1986), pp. 67, 73.

158. Letters quoted in William Griffin, *Clive Staples Lewis: A Dramatic Life.* San Francisco: Harper & Row, 1986; Tring: Lion, under the title *C. S. Lewis: The Authentic Voice,* 1988. (The pagination in the English edition of this biography is different from that in the American edition. The page numbers of the English edition are not those given below.)

To Fr. Frederick J. Adelmann, S. J., (21 Sept. 1960) on p. 421;

to Edward A. Allen (10 March 1948) on p. 282; (6 Dec. 1948) on p. 292; (8 Jan. 1951) on p. 317; (10 Dec. 1962) on pp. 434–5;

to Delmar Banner (6 June 1954) on p. 354;

to Owen Barfield [March–April 1926] on p. 33; (27 May 1928) on p. 48; (9 Sept. 1929) on p. 55; (6, 12 May, 1932) on p. 85; (12 Sept. 1938) on p. 156; (23 July 1939) on p. 161; [1943] on p. 218; (19 Dec. 1945) on p. 251; (25, 28 May 1945) on p. 255; (1 Nov. 1948) on p. 290; (23 June 1949) on p. 300; (22 Aug. 1949) on p. 301; (8 Nov. 1954) on p. 357;

to Pauline Baynes (2 Oct. 1954) on p. 356; (4 May 1957) on p. 387;

to Nell Berners-Price (9 May 1952) on p. 330;

to John Betjeman (28 May 1938) on p. 151;

to Harry Blamires (12 Oct. 1945) on p. 250; (12 Dec. 1955) on pp. 372–3;

to Rhona Bodle (31 Dec. 1947) on p. 279; (10 Feb., 3 March 1948) on p. 281; (24 June 1948) on p. 284; (24 Oct. 1948) on p. 290;

to Charles A. Brady (29 Oct. 1944) on p. 238; (27 Oct. 1956) on pp. 380–1;

to Joseph M. Canfield (28 Feb. 1955) on p. 364;

to Corbin Scott Carnell (31 Oct. 1958) on p. 400; to H. C. Chang (22 June 1956) on p. 378;

to Arthur C. Clarke (14, 16 Feb. 1953) on p. 339; (20 Jan. 1954) on p. 348;

to Nevill Coghill (4 Feb. 1926) on p. 27;

to Harold Dawson (6 Feb. 1958) on pp. 392–3;

to Edward T. Dell, Jr., (25 Oct. 1949) on p. 303; (22 April 1963) on p. 536;

to Bonamy Dobrée (7 Nov. 1963) on p. 446;

to Brian D. Doud (5 June 1960) on p. 415;

to Jane Douglass (3 May 1960) on p. 414;

to E. R. Eddison (29 April 1943) on p. 218;

to T. S. Eliot (19 April 1931) on p. 76; (23 Feb. 1944) on p. 228; (14 June 1959) on p. 406;

to Allan C. Emery (18 April 1959) on p. 403;

to John S. A. Ensor (31 March 1944) on pp. 229–30;

to I. O. Evans (22 Dec. 1954) on p. 361;

to Austin and Katharine Farrer (22 July 1960) on p. 420;

to Warfield M. Firor (13 Sept., 1 Oct. 1947) on pp. 276–7; [29 March 1948] on p. 283; (10 July, 25 Sept. 1948) on p. 288; (5 Jan. 1949) on pp. 292–3; (22 March 1949) on p. 296; (15 Oct., 5 Dec. 1949) on p. 304; (12 March 1950) on p. 306; (14 April 1950) on p. 307; (26 July 1950) on pp. 310, 311; (6 Dec. 1950) on p. 314; [23 April 1951] on p. 321; (20 Dec. 1951) on p. 326; (27 June 1953) on p. 342;

to B. Ginder (18 Aug. 1960) on p. 420;

to Joy Davidman Gresham (22 Dec. 1953) on p. 347;

to William Lindsay Gresham (30 Dec. 1956) on p. 383; (6 April 1957—two letters) on p. 386, 387; (15 July 1960) on p. 418;

to Dom Bede Griffiths (26 Dec. 1934) on p. 114; (8 Jan. 1936) on p. 125; [20 Feb. 1936] on p. 128; (24 April 1936) on p. 130; (14 Sept. 1936) on p. 131; (29 April 1938) on p. 150; (5 Oct. 1938) on p. 156; (16 April 1940) on p. 171; (26 May 1943) on p. 219; (10 May 1945) on p. 245; (20 Dec. 1946) on p. 266; (13 Nov. 1950) on p. 313; (17 May 1952) on p. 331; (1 Nov. 1954) on p. 356; (1 Aug. 1957) on p. 388; (30 April 1959) on p. 403; (20 Dec. 1961) on p. 428;

to George Rostrevor Hamilton (11 March 1947) on p. 267; (14 Aug. 1949) on p. 300;

to [A. K. Hamilton-Jenkin] (4 Nov. 1925) on pp. 20–1, 22;

to Carl Henry (28 Sept. 1955) on p. 370;

to Patricia Hillis (10 March 1959) on p. 403;

to Mrs. W. W. Johnson (14 Nov. 1956) on p. 380;

to Mrs. Frank Jones (7 Dec. 1950) on p. 314; (16 Nov. 1963) on p. 447;

to Bishop Girault M. Jones (1 May 1958) on p. 394;

to Harvey Karlsen (13 Oct. 1961) on p. 427;

to William L. Kinter (28 March 1953) on p. 340;

to Richard W. Ladborough (9 Oct. 1961) on p. 427; (28 Oct. 1963) on p. 446;

to Joan Lancaster (26 Dec. 1955) on p. 373; (11 July 1963) on p. 439;

to A. J. Lewis (27 Aug. 1917) on p. 7; to [A. J. Lewis] (19 March 1921) on p. 25; (10 July 1928) on p. 51; [Nov. 1928] on pp. 51–2; (9 July, 5 Aug. 1929) on p. 54; (31 March 1928) on p. 181;

to W. H. Lewis (1 July 1921) on p. 4; (13 March 1921) on p. 11; (1 March, 10 May 1921) on p. 20; (25 Aug. 1929) on p. 54; (19 May 1929) on pp. 54–5; (29 Aug. 1929) on pp. 55, 56; (29 Sept. 1929) on pp. 55–6; (27 Sept. 1929) on p. 57; (11 Feb. 1940) on p. 176;

to Sister Madeleva (6 June 1934) on p. 109; [18 April 1951] on p. 321;

to Keith Masson (11 April 1956) on p. 375;

to Vera Matthews (Gebbert) (24 Nov. 1947) on p. 278; (10, 19 March 1948) on p. 282; (7 March 1949) on p. 294; (1 Oct. 1949) on p. 302; (9 Nov. 1949) on p. 303; (30 Nov. 1949) on p. 304; (8 Nov. 1950) on p. 312; (20 Nov. 1950) on p. 313; (27 March 1951) on pp. 320–1; (18 Oct. 1951) on p. 325; (17 Feb. 1952) on p. 327; (23 May 1952) on p. 331; (14 Oct. 1952) on p. 333; (28 Oct. 1952) on p. 334; (9 Dec. 1952, 23 March 1953) on p. 340; (20 June 1953) on p. 341; (7 Nov. 1953) on p. 345; (23 Dec. 1953) on p. 347; (18 Jan. 1954) on p. 348; (26 Oct. 1954) on p. 356; (15 June 1955) on p. 366; (19 Dec. 1955) on p. 373; (9 May 1956) on p. 376; (10 Dec. 1956) on pp. 382–3; (31 Dec. 1956) on p. 383; (12 Nov. 1957) on p. 391; (16 Dec. 1957) on p. 391; (30 May 1958) on p. 395; (17 Jan. 1960) on p. 411; (29 Jan. 1962) on pp. 428–9;

to Fr. Peter Milward (23 May 1951) on pp. 322–3; (17 Dec. 1955) on p. 373; (15 Dec. 1959) on p. 411; (7 March 1960) on p. 412;

to John Warwick Montgomery (21 Jan. 1960) on p. 412;

to Marg-Riette Montgomery (10 June 1952) on p. 332;

to the National Association of Evangelicals (3 March 1949) on p. 294;

to Sister Penelope (9 Aug. 1939) on p. 162; (24 Oct. 1940) on p. 180, 181; (4 Nov. 1940) on pp. 181–2; (22 Aug. 1942) on p. 204; (15 May 1942) on p. 206; (22 Dec. 1942) on p. 211; (10 April 1943) on p. 218; (5 Oct. 1943) on p. 224; (3 Jan. 1945) on p. 241; (28 May 1945) on p. 246; (21 Oct. 1946) on p. 261; to [Sister Penelope] (21 Nov. 1947) on p. 278; (31 Jan. 1949) on p. 293; (30 Dec. 1950) on p. 316; (15 Feb. 1954) on p. 349; (18 June 1956) on pp. 377–8; (23 June 1962) on p. 429;

to J. B. Phillips (3 Aug. 1943) on pp. 221–2;

to Joan B. Pile (5 June 1952) on p. 332;

to Ruth Pitter (17 July 1946) on p. 257; (19 July 1946) on p. 258; (24 July 1946) on pp. 258–9; (28 Aug. 1946) on p. 260; (4 Jan. 1947) on p. 266; (9 Aug. 1947) on p. 274; (31 Aug. 1948) on p. 288; [22 Sept. 1949] on p. 302; (6 Jan. 1951) on p. 316; (17 March 1951) on p. 320; (26 March 1951) on p. 321; (12 Sept. 1951) on p. 324; (29 Dec. 1951) on p. 326; (8 Jan. 1952) on p. 327; (2 Jan. 1953) on p. 337; (1 Oct. 1953) on pp. 343–4; (21 Dec. 1953) on p. 347; (19 March 1955) on p. 365; (5 Aug. 1955) on pp. 368–9; (31 Jan. 1956) on p. 374; (9 July 1956) on p. 378; (28 Jan. 1957) on p. 384; (15 April 1957) on p. 387;

to Kathleen Raine (11 April 1956) on p. 375; (21 Oct. 1961) on p. 427; (7 Nov. 1963) on p. 446;

to T. Wilkinson Riddle (16 July 1946) on p. 258;

to the Royal Society of Literature (19 March 1948) on p. 283;

to Stephen Schofield (31 Jan. 1960) on p. 412;

to Mary Willis Shelburne (17 Oct. 1963) on p. 445;

to Kathryn Stillwell (29 Oct. 1957) on pp. 390–1;

to Mrs. Stone (17 June 1960) on p. 415;

to Mrs. Roderick Watson (22 Dec. 1952) on p. 336;

to Basil Willey (26 Oct. 1956) on p. 380; (22 Oct. 1963) on p. 446;

to Michal Williams (Mrs. Charles Williams) (22 May 1945) on p. 246;

to Sir Henry Willink (3 Dec. 1959) on p. 411; (25 Oct. 1963) on p. 446.

159. Letter to Janet Wise (5 Oct. 1955) in the *Canadian C. S. Lewis Journal*, No. 53 (Winter 1986), pp. 1–2.

160. Letters quoted in George Sayer, *Jack: C. S. Lewis and His Times*. London: Macmillan, 1988.

To Dom Bede Griffiths [1932] on p. 144;

to A. J. Lewis (30 Nov. 1913) on p. 40; (29 Sept. 1913) on p. 42; [? Nov. 1914] on p. 48; (8 Feb. 1917) on p. 63; [3 May 1917] on p. 67; [10? June 1917] on p. 69; [27 Aug. 1917] on p. 70; [24 Sept. 1917] on p. 70; [13 Dec. 1917] on p. 72; (4 March 1918) on p. 73; [14 May 1918] on p. 73; [30 May 1918] on p. 74; [29 June 1918] on pp. 74–5; (18 Nov. [Oct.] 1918) on p. 77; [3 Sept. [Nov.] 1918] on p. 77; [17? Nov. 1918] on p. 78; [8 Dec. 1918] on p. 78; [4 Feb. 1919] on p. 80; [5 March 1919] on p. 85; [4 April 1920] on p. 90; [25 July 1920] on p. 90; [19 Jan. 1921] on p. 91; (9 July 1921) on p. 92; [11 May 1924] on p. 103; (15 Oct. 1924) on p. 105; (28 Aug. 1924) on p. 105; [3 Nov. 1928] on pp. 119–20;

to W. H. Lewis [8 Jan. 1917] on p. 62; [1 July 1921] on p. 92; (19 Nov. 1939) on pp. 112–13; (29 Sept. 1929) on p. 133; (2 Sept. 1939) on p. 162;

to George Sayer (15 Aug. 1951) on p. 206; (15 Aug. 1958) on p. 228; (Nov. 1959) on p. 230;

to Chad Walsh (21 Oct. 1959) on p. 230; (23 May 1960) on pp. 230–1.

161. Letter to Delmar Banner (1 Nov. 1963) quoted in George Sayer, *Jack: C. S. Lewis and His Times*. London: Macmillan, 1988, p. 250.

162. Letters quoted in Barbara Reynolds, *The Passionate Intellect: Dorothy L. Sayers' Encounter with Dante*. Kent, Ohio: Kent State University Press, 1989.

To Owen Barfield (16 Dec. 1947) on p. 242;

to Dorothy L. Sayers (30 June 1945) on pp. 47–8; (6 July 1945) on p. 48; (29 Dec. 1946) on p. 48; (18 Dec. 1945) on p. 49; (24 Dec. 1945) on p. 51; (11 Nov. 1949) on pp. 114, 115; (15 Nov. 1949) on p. 114.

163. Letters quoted in Walter Hooper, "C. S. Lewis and C. S. Lewises" in *The Riddle of Joy: G. K. Chesterton and C. S. Lewis*. Edited by Michael H. Macdonald and Andrew A. Tadie. Grand Rapids: Eerdmans, 1989.

To Jocelyn Gibb (9 May 1960) on p. 42;

to Walter Hooper (2 July 1962) on p. 43;

to Richard Ladborough (3 June 1959) on p. 36.

164. Letters quoted in A. N. Wilson, *C. S. Lewis: A Biography*. Collins [W. W. Norton], 1990.

To Rhona Bodle (25[4] March 1954) on p. 114;

to Nevill Coghill (3 Feb. 1926) on p. 101;

to Nan Dunbar [7 March 1956 and 20 April 1956] on pp. 254–5;

to Mrs. Flewett (1944 and 4 Jan. 1945) on p. 203; (5 April 1955) on p. 253;

to Mrs. Frank Jones (16 Nov. 1963) on pp. 215, 297;

to A. J. Lewis [29 June 1914] on p. 35; [10 Sept. 1917] on p. 53; [29 June 1919] on p. 67; [11 April 1920] on p. 68; [1 May 1920] on p. 68; [19 March 1921] on p. 71;

to W. H. Lewis ([18] May 1907) pp. 18–9; (9 June 1919) on p. 57; [10 July 1920] on p. 68; [10 May 1921] on p. 73; (25 March 1931) on pp. 131–2; (22 Nov. 1931) on p. 136;

to Sister Penelope [24 Oct. 1940] on p. 175;

to J. R. R. Tolkien [1962] on p. 294.

165. Letter to Sister Madeleva (19 March 1963) in Richard L. Purtill, "Did C. S. Lewis Lose His Faith?" in *A Christian for All Christians: Essays in Honour of C. S. Lewis*. Edited by Andrew Walker and James Patrick. London: Hodder & Stoughton, 1990, p. 33.

166. Letters to Delmar Banner (7 June 1944, 30 Nov. 1942) in the *Canadian C. S. Lewis Journal*, No. 72 (Autumn 1990), pp. 5–6.

167. Letters quoted in *Word and Story in C. S. Lewis*. Edited by Peter J. Schakel and Charles A. Huttar. Columbia, Missouri: University of Missouri Press, 1991. In Charles A. Huttar, "A Lifelong Love Affair with Language: C. S. Lewis's Poetry":

To Leo Baker (Sept. 1920) on p. 92;

to Rhona Bodle (24 June 1949) on p. 106;

to Katharine Farrer (9 Feb. 1954) on p. 96;

to Roger Longacre (19 June 1952) on p. 95;

to Ruth Pitter (10 Aug. 1946) on pp. 87, 92; (24 July 1946) on p. 95;

to Laurence Whistler (30 Oct. 1961) on p. 88;

in Paul Piehler, "Myth or Allegory? Archetype and Transcendence in the Fiction of C. S. Lewis":

to Paul Piehler (22 Oct. 1963) on p. 215.

168. Letter to Roger Poole (holograph) (19 Oct. 1961) in the *Canadian C. S. Lewis Journal*, No. 75 (Summer 1991), p. 1.

169. Letters quoted in the *Chesterton Review*, XVII, Nos. 3 and 4 (Aug. & Nov. 1991).

To Christian Hardie (22 and 27 March 1951, Palm Sunday [6 April] 1952) in Christian Hardie, "Three Letters from C. S. Lewis" on pp. 394–8;

to D. E. Harding (1951) on p. 486;

to Thomas Howard [1958?] in Thomas Howard, "C. S. Lewis and Purgatory: An Anecdote" on p. 390;

to Mary Neylan (21 March 1939, 26 April, 30 April, 9 May, 2 Oct. 1941) in Mary Neylan, "My Friendship with C. S. Lewis" on pp. 407–11;

to Barbara Reynolds (19 March 1959) in Barbara Reynolds, "Memories of C. S. Lewis in Cambridge" on pp. 383–4.

# REVISED ENTRIES

## D. ESSAYS, PAMPHLETS, AND MISCELLANEOUS PIECES

140. *Mark vs. Tristram: Correspondence between C. S. Lewis & Owen Barfield*. Edited by Walter Hooper. Cambridge, Massachusetts: The Lowell House Printers. A hand-printed edition limited to 126 copies, Nov. 1967, 11 pp.

Second Edition: *Mark vs. Tristram: Correspondence between C. S. Lewis &*

*Owen Barfield.* Edited by Walter Hooper. Illustrated by Pauline Baynes. Oxford: Oxford University–C. S. Lewis Society, 1990. This 18-page pamphlet was first published in 1967. The new edition, limited to 100 copies, contains illustrations specially drawn for it by Pauline Baynes.

141. Boxen Manuscripts in Walter Hooper, "Past Watchful Dragons: The Fairy Tales of C. S. Lewis," in *Imagination and the Spirit.* Edited by Charles A. Huttar. Grand Rapids: Eerdmans, 1971.

("The Locked Door") on pp. 279–80; Narnian Manuscripts: (1) "Outline of Narnian history so far as it is known," on pp. 298–301; (2) Outline of *The Voyage of the "Dawn Treader"* (holograph and printed) on pp. 302, 303; (3) Galley proofs of *The Silver Chair* on p. 304; (4) Portion of "The Lefay Fragment" (an early version of *The Magician's Nephew*) on pp. 304–7; (5) "Eustace's Diary" on p. 309; (6) Original Map of Narnia (holograph) on p. 310; Drawing of Monopods (holograph) on p. 313.

## E. SINGLE SHORT POEMS

13. "Experiment." The poem is also found in *Augury: An Oxford Miscellany of Verse and Prose.* Edited by A. M. Hardie and K. C. Douglas. Oxford: Basil Blackwell, 1940, p. 28. It is there titled "Metrical Experiment" and is a slightly different version from the ones in *Spectator* or *Poems.*

## G. PUBLISHED LETTERS

70. Letter to an American Girl [Hila Newman: 23 June 1953] quoted in Kathryn Ann Lindskoog, *The Lion of Judah in Never-Never Land.* Grand Rapids: Eerdmans, 1973, p. 16.

72. Letters quoted in Douglas Gilbert and Clyde S. Kilby, *C. S. Lewis: Images of His World.* Grand Rapids: Eerdmans, 1973.

Holograph letter to Owen Barfield (no date) on p. 45;
to Arthur Greeves [18 Oct. 1916] on p. 17; [29 May 1918] on p. 18; (10 Jan. 1932) on pp. 20–21; (13 May 1917) on p. 24; [2 June 1919] on p. 34; [24 Dec. 1930] on p. 58; (26 June 1931) on p. 70; [4 May 1915] on p. 74; [1 June 1930] on p. 75; [3 Aug. 1930] on p. 76; [30 March 1915] on p. 93; [29 April 1930] on pp. 119–36; (23 April 1935) on p. 138; [5 Jan. 1930] on p. 139; (24 July 1917) on p. 145; [29 Nov. 1916] on p. 158; (15 June 1930) on p. 162; [17 Aug. 1933] on pp. 168–71; (1 Oct. 1934) on p. 173; (19 Jan. 1931) on p. 178;
holograph inscription to his father on the endleaf of a copy of *Spirits in Bondage* (29 March 1919) on p. 188;
holograph letter to Michal Williams (22 Nov. 1947) on p. 189.

83. Letters to Sheldon Vanauken in Sheldon Vanauken, *A Severe March: C. S. Lewis and a pagan love invaded by Christ, told by one of the lovers.* London: Hodder and Stoughton; San Francisco: Harper & Row, 1977. The following letters are given in full: (14 Dec. 1950) on pp. 88–90; (23 Dec. 1950) on pp. 91–3; (17 April 1951) on pp. 101–2; (1951) on p. 104; (5 Jan. 1951) on pp. 105–6; (8 Jan. 1951) on p. 106; (24 March 1952) on p. 110; (1952) on p. 123; (22 April 1953) on pp. 134–5; (14 May 1954) on pp. 146–8; (23 Nov. 1954) on pp. 167–8; (10 Feb. 1955) on pp. 183–4; (20 Feb. 1955) on pp. 186–7; (6 April 1955) on

pp. 188–9; (27 Aug. 1956) on p. 191; (5 June 1955) on pp. 205–6; (8 May 1955) on pp. 209–10; (7 March 1957) on p. 225; (27 Nov. 1957) on pp. 227–8, 232. The following letters are excerpted: (26 April 1958) on p. 228; (15 Dec. 1958) on p. 228; (16 April 1960) on p. 228; (July–Aug. 1960) on p. 229; (23 Sept. 1960) on p. 229; (30 June 1962) on p. 229.

H. BOOKS CONTAINING NUMEROUS SMALL EXTRACTS FROM LEWIS'S UNPUBLISHED WRITINGS (All the books listed in Section H of the original bibliography have been broken down in the supplement. The exception is no. 2 below.)

2. Lionel Adey, *C. S. Lewis's "Great War" with Owen Barfield.* English Literary Studies Monograph Series, No. 14. Victoria, B.C.: University of Victoria, 1978.

# An Alphabetical Index of the Writings of C. S. Lewis

*All items following an asterisk (\*) are entered in the Supplement.*

BOOKS REVIEWED (Short Titles):

*Allegory of the "Faerie Queen," The*, F31
*Art of Courtly Love, The*, F18
*Arthurian Literature in the Middle Ages*, F30
*Boethius*, F15
*Bride of Christ, The*, F13
*Collins*, F4
*Death of Tragedy, The*, F34
*English Literary Criticism: The Medieval Phase*, F19
*Erotic in Literature, The*, F35
*Fellowship of the Ring, The*, F27
*Form and Style in Poetry*, F3
*Hobbit, The* (in *The Times*), F10
*Hobbit, The* (in *The Times Literary Supplement*), F9, *A59
*Lectionary of Christian Prose, A*, F12
*Life of Samuel Johnson, The*, F36
*Longinus and English Criticism*, F7
*Matthew Arnold*, F2
*Milton and His Modern Critics*, F16
*Mind of the Maker, The*, F17
*Mirror of Love, The*, F26
*Neoplatonism in the Poetry of Spenser*, F33, A44
*Odyssey, The*, F37
*On Aristotle and Greek Tragedy*, F38
*Other World, According to Descriptions in Medieval Literature, The*, F25
*Oxford Book of Christian Verse, The*, F14
*"Paradise Lost" in Our Time*, F22
*Passion and Society*, F13
*Poetry of Search and the Poetry of Statement, The*, F40
*Principles and Problems of Biblical Translation*, F29
*Return of the King, The*, F28
*Romanticism Comes of Age*, F20
*Rossetti*, F1
*Shakespeare and the Rose of Love*, F32
*Sir Thomas Wyatt*, F6
*Taliessin Through Logres* (in *The Oxford Magazine*), F21
*Taliessin Through Logres* (in *Theology*), F11
*This Ever Diverse Pair*, F24
*Three Estates in Medieval and Renaissance Literature, The*, F5
*Two Towers, The*, F28
*Visionary Company, The*, F39
*Works of Morris and of Yeats in Relation to Early Saga Literature, The*, F8
*Works of Sir Thomas Malory, The*, F23, A44

*Boxen and Narnian Manuscripts*, D141, D156, *D202, H6
*Boxen: or Scenes from Boxonian City Life*, *D178

# Index